JOURNEY THROUGH MY YEARS

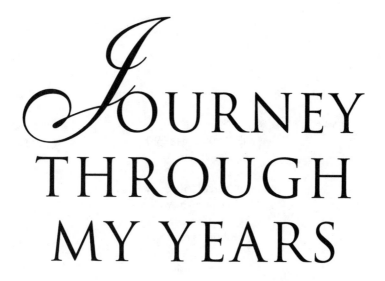

JOURNEY THROUGH MY YEARS

JAMES M. COX

MERCER

MERCER UNIVERSITY PRESS
MACON, GEORGIA

ISBN 0-86554-959-1
MUP/H684

© 2004 Mercer University Press
1400 Coleman Avenue
Macon, Georgia 31207

First printing.

The main text of this book
was originally published in 1946
by Simon and Shuster, Inc.

Jacket design by Burtch Hunter Design LLC
Cover portrait of Governor Cox by Douglas Chandor, 1949

TO MY MOTHER

PREFACE

MORE THAN a century has passed since my grandfather bought the *Dayton Daily News* and began a mass media career that ultimately led to the creation of Cox Enterprises, Inc. Not surprisingly, many things have changed during that time: newspapers are now available online as well as on paper; radio and television have evolved from cutting-edge novelties to mass media status; cable television has nurtured the most diverse programming imaginable and technology has improved so that it delivers not only entertainment, but high-speed data and telephony as well; telephones have become wireless; and the automobile has revolutionized personal mobility and our society.

But despite the fantastic changes that have occurred in the past one hundred-plus years, the principles that my grandfather, James M. Cox, believed in and exercised in his business and personal life remain fresh and valid. His belief in a free press that supports and fosters community, in fair play and hard work and in the democratic process remain part of the foundation on which our company has built its success.

For that reason, I am pleased to see my grandfather's autobiography, *Journey Through My Years*, republished and once again available to the people my grandfather valued so much, our employees. His perspective of the first half of the 20th Century is unique, and his insight is valuable to us all as we confront the challenges of the 21st Century. I recommend it to you with pride.

James C. Kennedy
Chairman and CEO
Cox Enterprises, Inc.

FOREWORD

—◆—

JOURNEY THROUGH MY YEARS *means just what it says; yet what I saw, not what I did, is the important thing. In more than fifty years of contact, as newspaperman and official, with public affairs, I have been privileged to observe at close range a procession of events and personalities which even yet I look back upon in awe. It seems not possible that all of it could have occurred in one lifetime. Regarding myself, and in no mock modesty, as a very unimportant factor in these events, I have thought primarily to report here on what I saw and upon the men I knew in the course of the pilgrimage. It has been a very happy journey through the swiftly moving times—times which have laid the background and foundation of the world of today. Words cannot express my gratitude for the good health which sustained me, or for the many wonderful persons whom I have met along the road.*

I have tried to make this a simple story, told in full awareness that it must be a very indulgent public which gives attention in these momentous times to the backward look of any man. The hope that in such a review of the past may be found some clue to the enigma of the future is my chief excuse for this book.

JAMES M. COX.

CONTENTS

◆

CONTENTS

PART NINE

PART ONE

Ancestors

Glimpses of Pioneer Life

The Struggles of Boyhood

Churches and Schools

From Country Schoolteacher
to Newspaper Reporter

IN THE LAND OF MAD ANTHONY WAYNE

◆

WHEN Mad Anthony Wayne was perfecting his campaign against the Indians in western and northern Ohio, his first task was to establish communications between Fort Washington, now Cincinnati, on the Ohio River and strategic points to the north. There were several of these points and Wayne determined to link them by road. Fort Hamilton on the Miami River in what is now Butler County had been maintained for some time. Fort St. Clair, now Eaton, Ohio, was built by General St. Clair. Still farther to the north was Greenville where a treaty was made in 1795 with the Indians. Wayne insisted that the road should be cut sixty feet wide through the forest. He was more constructive in this project than he knew. He opened a potentially rich country for the rugged settlers who were later to come.

As this work proceeded north of Fort Hamilton, the line crossed Four Mile creek and then on through what is now known as the Village of Seven Mile. This is still called the Old Trace Road. As the engineers left the Four Mile valley, they came to higher ground two or three miles north of Seven Mile. Due east of this point, as the crow flies, was a beautiful forest which ran to the banks of the Great Miami River—a forest of sloping hills, gentle brooks and creeks, level, rich land where giant oaks, hickory, ash, maple, beech and other hardwoods grew.

It was on these lands that I was born. The settlement, which had grown into a stagecoach station, was named Jacksonburg. That means there must have been some Democrats in the vicinity. In due time the settlement assumed the dignity of a municipality, but although its maximum population was 302, it is not more than half that now. On the west end of the village, my grandfather, Gilbert Cox, purchased land upon which he settled. Its title had come by patent dated April 24, 1809.

3

Gilbert Cox came of a family which settled in Virginia and then in New York before making their home in New Jersey. These and other data have been preserved by the historian of the Cox family, the Reverend Henry Miller Cox, Harrington Park, New Jersey, who published his book in 1912. With painstaking care he produced a comprehensive record entitled *The Cox Family in America*. Families of this name came from England to the New England states, New York, New Jersey, Maryland and Virginia, in the seventeenth century. The ancestor from whom direct descent is traced was Thomas Cox. He was born in England and the records there show that he went first to Virginia, afterwards for a brief time to Newtown in New York. Historian Cox says, "Nothing is positively known of his ancestry. An old plate now in the possession of one of his descendants and bearing the date of 1661, is said to have been brought by one of the family from Virginia."

The author later notes, "The first authentic record that we have concerning Thomas Cox is found in a license, dated April 17, 1665, signed by Richard Nicolls, the first English governor of New York, authorizing his marriage to Elizabeth Blashford, also of Newtown. This is believed to be the oldest marriage license of record in the State of New York and it is our first introduction to a man who afterwards figured somewhat prominently in the early history of Monmouth County, New Jersey."

The wife of Thomas Cox was a Quaker, he a Baptist. On documents signed by him appears his mark, which indicated that he could neither read nor write; but his participation in affairs indicates clearly that he was a man of some force and character. Historian Cox further says, "It would have been more gratifying to family pride if this suggestion of illiteracy had not been discovered. But in his day, the schoolmaster was not largely in evidence and comparatively few of the early pioneers had opportunity for acquiring even the rudiments of an ordinary education. In spite of this handicap, many of them through sheer force of character, industry, and native ability, were able not only to accumulate wealth, but also to exercise large influence in the social and political life of the communities in which they lived. Thomas Cox appears to have been of that number.

"Within a few years he had become an extensive land owner and a recognized man of affairs in Monmouth County. In 1676, he was chosen a deputy, to meet the Governor and his Council at Woodbridge, a circumstance which seems to indicate that he was a man of some consequence and a representative citizen.

"The occasion of his errand to Woodbridge is not a matter of record, but in the light of contemporary history, it is fair to assume that he appeared in support of the popular, as opposed to the proprietary interests."

He died at Middletown, New York, in 1681. His descendants are very clearly traced to the present generation. In the fourth generation is found General James Cox, who enlisted in the Revolutionary War and rose to the rank of brigadier general. He was the grandfather of Honorable Samuel S. Cox, known as "Sunset" Cox.

"Sunset" Cox was a well-known name in Ohio. He served the Zanesville district in the national House of Representatives for eight years, and for twenty years, a district in New York City. He seemed to have landed upon his political feet in his new habitat rather quickly because four years after he was an Ohio congressman he enjoyed the same distinction in New York.

In my first campaign for the governorship in 1912, I was introduced by the chairman of the meeting as "another Sunset Cox." Measured by the local tradition, that was the highest compliment to be paid. An Irishman arose, however, and dissented, "No, begorra, this is *Sunrise* Cox."

General James Cox was listed as of the fourth generation; my grandfather, Gilbert Cox and his sister Maryan Cox, children of Benjamin Cox, of the sixth generation. Gilbert Cox was orphaned when he was fourteen and placed under the guardianship of an uncle, Abel Cox. It is recorded that during the Revolutionary War the silverware of his family had been buried and thus kept in safety until hostilities were over. That he was a constructive pioneer was learned from the minutes which are still in existence of a historic local meeting. It was he who called the pioneers together in his log cabin for the purpose of establishing a public school. Some of the settlers gave cords of firewood, others so many weeks of board for the teacher, while a few contributed money.

Gilbert Cox had come west for what was intended as a brief visit in Franklin, Ohio. There he fell in love, and this changed the whole course of his life. His wife was Anne Craig. Her family, which was Scotch, made their first stopping point on the way west at Franklin on the Great Miami River in what is now Warren County.

5

In changing their habitat to higher land which was to be found south of Franklin and then westward to what is now the Jacksonburg settlement, the party of which she was a member crossed the Miami River on log rafts at a point near by the village of Trenton. The waters were high from the spring freshet; one craft capsized and five members of the little colony were drowned.

In the log cabin home were born to Gilbert and Anne Cox some of their eleven children. In due time a more pretentious residence was staked out across the creek. Here, Gilbert Cox burned the brick, quarried the stone, cut the walnut and erected an abiding place for his family. Without knowing it, he must have inherited some artistic qualities, for even to exacting modern taste some features of this house are most unusual and it is still a very attractive residence. Wooden pegs are to be found in the flooring, doors and cupboards, and a New York architect once said that the bricks could be sold in the east for "almost their weight in gold." For some reason the modern production from yellow clay soil is not comparable either in quality or appearance to the handiwork of the pioneers.

The countryside about Jacksonburg could be very properly compared to many scenes which one encounters from Southampton to London in England. The land is undulating and affords easy, ample drainage. The soil, a chocolate-colored clay, is very fertile. I well remember as a boy that when we were constructing a tile ditch we came across the old-time drainage system—the material in chief part consisting of hickory bark. It was amazingly well preserved and there was still water trickling through the underground passage.

It required three years for the builder to complete the house, which must have been the great pride of his life. He moved into it in 1820. That was six years before the death of Jefferson and Adams. There was a fireplace in every room and in the combination dining and sitting room a huge one about five feet high and between eight and ten feet wide whose fire-walls are still well preserved. There were no stoves either for heating or cooking. This house I still preserve as a supplementary residence 25 miles from Trailsend, near Dayton. The lands attached to it now aggregate close to one thousand acres and have been a blessing for the health-giving and stimulating diversions they provide.

All the Cox children lived to a good old age save one, who died as an infant. The rest reached ages which ranged from 80 years to

6

101. Gilbert Cox, my father, was the youngest of eleven children and at the death of his mother the farm was acquired by him. My mother was Eliza Andrew. Her ancestors, as she heard her parents' discuss them, were all hardy seagoing people. The drift westward started from Philadelphia. She was born about a mile from the Cox homestead in a log cabin, sheltered by oak and beech and ash and maple, on a little stream called Dry Fork. As a girl going to school she often encountered deer and bear in the woodlands. I have known no one possessed of calmer, more persevering industry than she. When the laborious part of her life was over and she had more time for ease, I was surprised to find she was a steady reader, even though she was as unlettered as the average pioneer woman. Speaking once of her service to the community as a volunteer nurse, she said that all the babies which she had helped bring into the world—because doctors could not be procured at the moment—could not be laid out one deep in a large room. Mother and my sister Anne Baker rendered great assistance to me when I was getting away from the farm and becoming established as a teacher. Surveying my whole life, I cannot but feel that this was my major debt.

I was the youngest of a family of seven. They all attained the age of maturity. A sister now living is 91, a brother 89, a sister 87, a brother 85. The eldest brother died at 91, another in middle life. Well do I remember the first life insurance policy I ever took out. The companies apparently were more painstaking with details then. The ages of the four grandparents were stated as something over 85 years at the time of death. The cause of death was asked and my response was that as far as I knew they had all died of croup.

Life for me began on March 31, 1870. As I run back over the chronological tables, it doesn't seem possible that events so long ago were contemporaneous with my youth. A writer in describing certain phases of American life as of that time said: "The buffalo herds still roamed the Western plains; there was still the overland stage coach with its four- and six-horse teams carrying only the mails, passengers and light baggage, while ten and twelve ox-and-mule teams pulled the burdens of heavy freight. The Arapahoes, Cheyennes and Sioux were on the warpath; the Younger brothers, Dalton boys and Jesse James gang were engaged in their nefarious raids; and last but not least among these primitive methods and hardships, to be endured, was the devastating pest, the grasshopper, devouring every-

7

thing. The Black Hills gold excitement and the Custer Massacre were boyhood recollections."

I started to school when I was five. When one reflects on the great care with which children are now brought up and how changed sanitary practices now are, he wonders how anyone survived in those days. It seemed to me that every child in school was not without a common cold all winter long. In some parts of the countryside there were still open wells, catch-alls for much contamination. There was some typhoid fever and a good deal of tuberculosis. Doubtless these hardy pioneers and their offspring became partially immunized against the infections which now bedevil mankind, for I have no recollection of ever seeing a doctor in our household. Herbs and liniments were our only medical aids. We have a false impression about the longevity of our pioneers. Those who had overcome, in their early life, the obstacles to health, attained old age, but we seem not to have taken into account the large numbers of young people who died in their twenties. This came vividly to my mind not long ago when I visited the oldest burial ground near the village of Jacksonburg. Gravestones marking the demise of young men and women vastly outnumbered those erected over the burial spaces of men and women who lived a long time. The dates showed, however, that this was in days that go back beyond my memory. It is fair to assume therefore that the turning point in better sanitation and long-living must have come about the time of the War Between the States.

Compared with life on the farm now, existence in the old days was a good deal of drudgery. It was hard work in season and out. In summertime we were in the fields at sunrise; we came in for dinner at eleven o'clock, had supper at four o'clock and then followed the plow or the sickle until sundown. On some occasions in the corn-husking season we went to the fields by morning moonlight. When the moon went down, there was not enough light to work by and we ran up and down the fence corners to keep warm till the labor of the field could start.

Grain was cut by the scythe and the cradle. The cradle had wooden hands three or four feet long parallel to the blade. When the implement was properly handled the grain was caught by these "hands" and laid in even swathes to be bound into sheaves. Someone burned the first self-binding harvester, a product of the Walter

Wood Company. Coal oil was poured over it and the match applied to remove this menace to labor. Every task was laborious yet these were happy days withal.

In the winter evenings corn was popped and apples were brought from the cellar. The diversion was usually history and geography tests. There was not a playing card in the house and definitely no liquor. The saloon in the village I never looked into. We were taught to believe that it was a den of the devil and it remained so abhorrent in my consciousness that when I became governor I had it condemned as a fire menace and torn down by the state marshal.

With the first thaw of spring when the sap was running in the maple trees came a joyful season. The gathering of buckets filled with sugar water, the boiling process running through the night as well as day, and then the taffy pulls—those were the times!

And who can forget the butchering season? The wood fires were set under the kettles before daylight to heat water for scalding the hair off the animals—the same vessels to be used later for the making of lard. It was our practice to slaughter a lamb or two in the early autumn and then a beef. We had no way of keeping it, so parts of it were distributed among the neighbors who made return later. Seven hogs were regularly put in prime condition for the winter kill. That the butchering season still lives in the public imagination is shown in the fact that recently an editorial describing the romance of this yearly event appeared in the New York *Times* and was copied generally over the country.

April Election Day was the beginning of the barefoot season and "stone bruises." On the Sabbath, for Sunday school and church, shoes that pinched painfully were worn. We went barefooted until frost time and sometimes later than that. This reminds me of a story that is told of President McKinley. He was making a trip through the Northwest; one morning soon after dawn the train stopped at a remote water tank. McKinley, an early riser, came back to the observation car and saw a young farm lad warming his feet in the nest of an old cow. McKinley summoned the members of the cabinet who were with him and all but one had gone through the same thing. No lad on any farm had missed the thrill of that experience.

Then there were other customs—the ice-cream social at the church in the summer, the county fair in the autumn, the oyster supper in the winter and the Christmas celebration. Those events

9

we always looked forward to. There was family worship every morning, a chapter from the Bible and a prayer no matter whether it was harvesting season in the summer or corn-shucking time in the autumn. Nothing interfered with the regular religious routine. The revival meeting always lasted one month in the winter. In this way the church membership was recruited. In the consciousness of the attending families was ingrained a thorough recognition of the arbitrary customs—the mourners' bench for youngsters and some oldsters as well, the joining of church the last Sunday of the revival and, in the summertime, a trip to Elk Creek for the baptism. I went through all of this and it certainly did me no harm.

The budget on the farm was rather simply conducted. The sale of lambs and wool usually took care of the June taxes. The December assessments were met by the sale of hogs. These taxes were the major expenses. Groceries, in the main, were purchased by the marketing of butter, eggs and chickens. The early part of the winter was the clothing era. It was usually the sale of surplus wheat or corn that met this requirement. We were all bundled into the old three-seated spring wagon and ordinarily taken to Hamilton, the seat of Butler County. A suit of clothes and an overcoat, a pair of boots, a pair of shoes, a hat and ties filled out the wardrobe. Underclothing was homemade from Canton flannel. There were no "store" shirts, and socks, of course, were knit from yarn. In the old house which my grandfather, Gilbert Cox, built and where we go frequently for week ends, is a coverlet made by Grandmother Cox. She raised the sheep, washed the wool, spun the yarn and made the beautiful spread. The colors are blue and white. Singularly, they are not yellowed by age and seem as fresh as they ever were.

I cannot remember ever being without a little money after I attained the age of about ten. I was janitor of the school building and sexton of the United Brethren Church. I attended to these tasks in addition to the chores which were parceled out to all of us on the farm. Forty cents a week was the compensation for building the fires in the morning, sweeping out and dusting the schoolrooms, two in number. A dollar a month was paid for taking care of the church. This income was always carefully treasured. The old church, which was large, had a stove on either side of it. Small pipes ran from the stoves towards the ceiling and converged at a central point for contact with the flue. This old-fashioned arrangement enabled us to gain a great deal of heat from the unusual length of the pipes. Wood was supplied in turn by the three trustees: my father, Gilbert Cox; Henry Kumler and Joseph Kumler. One year when it was the turn of Joseph Kumler to supply the wood, he hauled several loads of peach trees which had been taken out of the ground, still with a good deal of sap in the wood. That winter it required much coal oil to keep the fires going. One night when the revival meeting was over, an old soldier, Charlie Russell, asked a neighbor how he liked the sermon. He replied that there was a little too much hell and damnation in it. With a chuckle old Charlie said, "This church is so d——d cold that it was comforting to hear the preacher talk about a place as hot as hell is."

The Christmas season always was a gala event. There was no distribution of gifts at the family circle. Everyone assembled, usually on Christmas Eve, at the church. A tremendous tree was brought in from the woods and all the gifts in the community were hung on it. Usually there were rehearsals of Christmas music covering a period of about three weeks. The presents were taken from the tree, some witty fellow usually called the names of the recipients and the youngsters who were always selected the preceding Sunday were delegated to distribute them. No recipient was ever absent. Some may say Christmas meant a great deal more in those days.

At election times there was great political excitement in our boyhood days. Even in this community made up of a small village and farms, partisanship ran strong. I was first conscious of it in 1880, during the Garfield-Hancock campaign. A boys' club was organized. Its members went on parade a number of times. They wore cloaks of gaily colored oilcloth and caps with torches attached. Then in the corn-harvesting period of 1884 we were much distracted by the uncertainty over the presidential election. In the fields we would hear the Republican cannon of two shots to be followed soon afterwards by the Democratic explosion of a single shot. Feeling ran high. The Democrats, stirred by their belief that the presidency had been stolen from them in 1876, became very militant. At the county seat a Democratic organization known as The Miami Club paraded at midday with white plug hats and gray coats, singing as they went down the street:

Hurrah for Maria, hurrah for the kid,
We voted for Grover and we're d——d glad we did.

In defiant song they were scorning the Republicans who had circulated against Cleveland so many versions of the Maria Halpin scandal.

Like most other Ohio children of the period, I owed much to the readers of William Holmes McGuffey. I went through these in order, from the first to the fifth, and they not only made me master of many classic selections of English and American literature, but aroused in me a thirst for more reading in the masterpieces of our tongue. Here it was that I became familiar with lesser-known lyrics like *The Burial of Sir John Moore.* Once our school gave some amateur theatricals and used the proceeds to buy a small school library of good books, which circulated among the pupils' homes. It had some of the best novels of Scott, a good deal of Dickens, and lives of Washington, Jefferson and Jackson. But the community did have a taste for the moralistic, and books with a message—T. S. Arthur's *Ten Nights in a Bar-Room* and Mrs. Stowe's *Uncle Tom's Cabin*—were much esteemed. *Tom Sawyer*, which came as a Christmas gift, was read and reread, always with increasing interest.

We hear much said about the inadequate teaching of history in the schools. The New York *Times* during the Second World War conducted a highly commendable crusade to improve it, showing how ignorant many children were of great American forces, heroes and events; and the subject will demand continued attention. My impression is that in the days of my youth such ignorance of fundamental studies did not exist, because we were thoroughly drilled in them. We used W. H. Venable's *History of the United States*, a thoroughly good work by the historian of culture in the Ohio Valley. I knew it from cover to cover. Supplementing it, we used an excellent historical chart. I received a similar discipline in Ray's *Third Part Arithmetic* and *Higher Arithmetic*, and in Green's textbook on grammar. It was rarely that a bad speller was found in those days, or a boy or girl who was not rapid and precise in arithmetic. To be proficient in "mental arithmetic" was a special boast of bright youths. Then, in addition to spelling matches, we had hot contests in history and geography. In the back of our text in physical geography was an index of every geographical name contained in the book—cities, countries, isthmuses, capes, lakes and what not.

There were two boys in that school who knew every one of them.

I suppose everyone looks back upon some event of his youth as more or less epoch-making. Occasionally I went to Middletown, about five and a half miles away, to spend the week end. One Saturday afternoon I was on my way in my Sunday-best clothes. There had been a heavy rain the night before and the graveled roads were soft and good going for bare feet. A formation of clouds in the western sky warned of a coming storm, so I pulled off my shoes, fell into a dog trot and maintained it the whole distance. I did this many times afterwards. It made me realize then that life and hard work in the open had given me health, agility and endurance.

Miami University was fourteen miles away, at Oxford, in one of the most delightful spots to be seen in America or abroad. It was opened in 1824 and became known as the "Yale of the West." Two of its graduates, Benjamin Harrison and Whitelaw Reid, were candidates together for president and vice-president on the Republican ticket in 1892. Harrison was in the class of 1856 and Reid, 1852. This is a distinction which old Miami treasures, for at no other time in the history of our country have both the candidates for president and vice-president been graduates of the same institution. The McGuffey eclectic readers were conceived and partly written while William McGuffey was a professor at Miami. William H. Venable, the historian, trod its famous halls and there is a tradition that he taught in what was known as the adjoining Kumler School District. It can be understood how this school derived its name, for Henry P. Kumler, a farmer, garnered enough profit from his place to send seven sons to college. Three of these were judges of courts.

Three Kumlers were at times my Sunday-school teachers. The Kumlers and the Landises, who were closely related, supplied outstanding ecclesiastics in the United Brethren Church. Their blood was in the veins of Judge Kenesaw Mountain Landis and the other Indiana Landis boys. Also related are Fred H. Rike of Dayton, a nationally known businessman and civic leader, and Robert K. Landis, one of the ablest lawyers in Ohio.

The pioneer Kumlers were devout church people. One of them whom we called Uncle Joe was famous for his long prayers. Many times while he was in articulate communication with Providence in the church, parts of the congregation would give evidence of impatience. There were no open-faced watches then and those old

13

double-case timekeepers could be heard snapping all through the congregation long before Uncle Joe became conscious of passing time. It was said of him that at prayer-meeting services one evening he led in prayer and when he finished the doxology was sung.

A number of men widely acclaimed afterwards as journalists had their source in this section. Murat Halstead was born in our county at what was called Paddy's Run. After Halstead moved to Cincinnati and became famous, it was proposed to change the name of both the place and the post office; Paddy's Run was not tuneful to the modern generation. The controversy brought on a near approach to a community civil war. The name was first changed to Glendower. The old timers upset this arrangement and restored the name to Paddy's Run, but five years later a compromise was effected by calling the place Shandon.

John A. Cockerill, who rose to distinction as an associate of Joseph Pulitzer of the New York *World* and St. Louis *Post-Dispatch*, came from our county seat. William Dean Howells labored there in a print shop and on a small paper. Twenty miles to the north of us, at Dayton, C. L. Vallandigham edited the *Empire* and in Greene County, almost in the suburbs of what is now Dayton, Whitelaw Reid was born. His birthplace is still preserved.

I attended the local school until my sixteenth year, meanwhile reading as voraciously as my time would permit. I had formed a passionate interest in newspapers. When we came in from the fields after our long hours of work, I was always ready to go to the post office for our copy of Murat Halstead's paper, the Cincinnati *Commercial Gazette*. It became plain that there was no real future for me in farming. In the middle of the forenoon, while I was following the plow, I would often see one of the neighborhood schoolteachers starting to work, and about four in the afternoon, while I still had long hours of toil ahead of me, I would see the teacher coming home. This spectacle might have given spur to my ambition to make a brief pedagogic career a steppingstone to something better.

Living in Middletown, I attended the high school in Amanda, a suburb two miles away. Off hours, I was employed as printer's devil in the newspaper office, which also did quite a lot of job work. The school was known, and deservedly; it was a country academy presided over by John Q. Baker, who married my sister, Anne, a remarkable woman, widely beloved. He was the most natural teacher

I ever knew and he made the tasks of the schoolroom pleasant and stimulating. In the lesson period the class completely exhausted the subject of the moment. He would often select a pupil to arise and be questioned by members of the class. We were also permitted to widen our questions to information gained outside our textbooks. The average pupil has trouble with mathematics and when he arrives at the algebraic period he is pretty well stumped. Professor Baker taught his pupils the art of reasoning and thus algebra became easy and understandable. Later in life he became a newspaper publisher and editor. He was a ripe scholar and wielded an eloquent and forceful pen. He was born in Jacksonburg just across the pasture from the old Cox homestead.

Chancing to be in Hamilton, the county seat, one Saturday, I took the teachers' examination and to my surprise received a two years' certificate to teach. Soon thereafter there was a vacancy at West Middletown, once Madison, then known by the post-office name of Heno. I applied and received the appointment in my seventeenth year. Then I taught at Rockdale, a paper-mill village south of Middletown, located on the C. & D. Railroad, and graduated from there to what was known as the best country school in the county, the Titus District School, two miles north of Middletown. The pupils ranged in their studies from alphabet to geometry. At nighttime, during the winter months, I was superintendent of the night school in Middletown, conducted by the board of education before the days of compulsory education. A regular attendant was an old ex-slave, Sarah Mitchell.

On Saturdays I delivered the entire local circulation of the Middletown *Weekly Signal* that was owned by my brother-in-law, Mr. Baker. This was an all-day job. My teaching experience was never more than an incidental pastime because, to use an old expression, printer's ink had moved into my blood.

CHAPTER II

A LARGER FIELD

◆

WITHOUT an exception known to me, men who have achieved success in their mature years are proud of having been newsboys. There is no better training even now. The lad is no longer paid a weekly amount to cover his route, for now he is a merchant. He buys papers and sells to his customers. Thus, early in life, he sees the advantage of courtesy and efficiency. He gets his first lesson in keeping books. He knows what it means to be on time and to appeal to the convenience and favor of his patrons. In short, he soon learns how to attain success in life.

Mr. Baker's paper, the *Signal*, finally blossomed into a daily publication and then it was that I ceased to be a pedagog. I was the only reporter on the paper. This was a very valuable experience. It enabled me to know the leading men of the town. I wonder whether we all realize what it means to youngsters to be taken seriously by their seniors. In my early years many of my closest friends were men much older than I. They gave a cooperation which was helpful and will never be forgotten. In my later years a great many of my most intimate friends have been of the younger generation. There was a real compensation in both of these circumstances.

The year 1892 brought two major events that gripped public interest. One was the Sullivan-Corbett fight in New Orleans and the other the political tidal wave which returned Grover Cleveland to the presidency. But it brought something which meant more to me. I was offered a position, in April of that year, on the Cincinnati *Enquirer*. I had done some suburban work at Middletown and in this way became known in more or less remote degree to John T. McCarthy, the managing editor at Cincinnati.

It was an epochal day when I reported there for work—much overawed but having a "nose for news" and able to write my story. Irving Stone, in his friendly book, *They Also Ran*, records that I was a star reporter but that most of my stories were written for me. That never happened once.

The *Enquirer* and the St. Louis *Globe-Democrat* stood first in the country in the amount of telegraph news which they printed. George Alfred Townsend, who signed his *Enquirer* articles "Gath," was one of the best-known writers of his day. I handled all of his copy and wrote heads for it. Among my other tasks was "heading up" the Rev. DeWitt Talmadge sermon which was run in full on Monday morning. Once when Townsend was about to start on a European trip, we in the telegraph editor's room calculated with relief that we would have none of his letters for at least two weeks. Within a day or two came a package containing more than a dozen of his daily contributions.

There were unusual men on the *Enquirer*. Charles L. Doren, the chief telegraph editor, had a reputation all over the country. The paper carried heavy and unusual headlines and when a famous criminal was executed, the Doren head for the story was, "Jerked to Jesus." Doren was soon discussed in most newsrooms in the country. For a fortnight preceding the election in 1892, he carried on an imaginary dialogue between Ruth Cleveland, whose father was endeavoring to return her to the White House, and Baby McKee, grandchild of President Harrison, who would be removed by a Democratic victory. This gave Doren further acclaim. Then there was Harry Weldon, who stood first in the country as a sports editor. Jim Corbett once said that he could describe a round better than any man in the profession. Weldon had come from Circleville, Pickaway County. One evening I was going through his office and he must have observed evidences of homesickness. He said to me: "Young man, I came on this paper years ago just like you, from a country town. It was pretty hard going for a time. It may be for you. Whenever you get lonesome, just come up and sit down with me for a while." These words and the fine impulse which prompted them have never been forgotten. Of course, James W. Faulkner was also there, one of the newspaper greats of his time. No two men took hold of my imagination as did he and Frank Cobb of the New York *World*.

I covered the railroad route, beginning at two o'clock in the afternoon, and at eight o'clock in the evening joined the telegraph editors. This was a magnificent training. Young newspaper men should try

17

to get this touch of the world which comes from the news wires.

One morning, to my surprise and infinite pride, one of my stories, an exclusive one, was the leader on the first page. My future seemed assured. John T. McCarthy, the managing editor, was one of the ablest judges of news and developers of men I ever knew. The reporter who turned in a story that had been printed before was on the suspended list. If it happened the second time, his name was off the pay roll. I do not know what the experience of other newspaper publishers has been, but it has always seemed to me the hardest of tasks to get your own staff to read carefully the daily product of the plant to which they give life.

Samuel M. Felton, president of the Queen and Crescent Railroad system, was a very rugged character, but inept in public relations. He was not much interested in reporters and when they went to him, even for the purpose of confirming news events, he was gruff and undiplomatic. It was necessary at one time to follow up a story which concerned his company. The reception given the reporter enraged McCarthy and he directed me to write an account along the specific lines which he outlined. This was done. Felton was in a fury. In his rage he asked John R. McLean, owner of the *Enquirer*, then living in Washington, to have Cox, the railroad editor, discharged. McLean was under some obligations to Felton. He had often used the railroad executive's private car and subsequently Felton designed one for McLean's private use. There was a private wire from McLean's Washington office into the *Enquirer* at Cincinnati, and the order came that I was to be let out. There was a remonstrance from the *Enquirer* newsrooms, but it was finally arranged that I was to be relieved from my railroad assignment and put on other work. Out of this incident came a turn in my whole career. I could not help being impressed by the thoughtless injustice imposed upon me and when an offer to go to Washington came, I accepted. I doubt whether I would have left the *Enquirer* except for that order from McLean.

In after years when I was elected to Congress, McLean apparently had forgotten about the event which so vitally concerned me. It is doubtful whether he identified the young reporter, whom he had never seen, as the young congressman. McLean proclaimed me as one of his boys. In due time, too, Felton and I were thrown together through Chicago acquaintances. Some time after the campaign of 1920, Felton, then president of the Chicago and Eastern Railroad, came to Dayton with Edwin N. Hurley, who had been head of the Shipping Board in the First World War, Charles Markham, president of the Illinois Central Railroad system, and Gilbert E. Porter, head of the legal firm of Lincoln, Isham & Beale. The Lincoln mentioned was Robert T. Lincoln, son of the martyred president. On their way back to Chicago, Felton remarked how pleasant the visit had been. With a chuckle Hurley said, "Well, Cox ought to treat you well. You came very near kicking him into the presidency of the United States." Felton and I never referred to the unpleasant affair but he must have known that his host was the reporter that he had asked to be fired. In fact, Sam Blythe, who was writing page features in the *Saturday Evening Post,* made quite a yarn out of it after I was in Congress.

PART TWO

First Touch with Politics

Entrance to Washington as
Congressman's Secretary

A Study of Cleveland's Cabinet

Striking Figures in House and Senate

McKinley Warned to Take Over Philippines

A Young Newspaper Publisher

Notable Libel Suits

CHAPTER III

FIRST GLIMPSE OF WASHINGTON

◆

ON AN April day in 1894, the news flashed from Washington to the Miami Valley that the representative in Congress, George W. Houk, had died suddenly. The governor ordered a special election to fill the vacancy. At this time the political tides were running very strongly against the Democratic cause and the Republicans were anxious to have a test at the polls. The Democrats met the challenge by nominating their strongest candidate, Paul J. Sorg, a multi-millionaire tobacco manufacturer in Middletown. He was born at Parkersburg, West Virginia, but came early to Cincinnati and most of his education was procured there in the night schools. One Sunday afternoon John Auer, a foreman in a tobacco factory in Cincinnati, remarked to Sorg that he would like to go into business himself, but that he had no education and could not keep books. Young Sorg said that he had picked up the rudiments of bookkeeping and would like to join him. He inquired how much capital would be required and Auer thought that a thousand dollars would do for the half interest. Sorg had $100 saved and borrowed $900 from a cousin; with this sum the two men started business in an attic on Pearl Street in Cincinnati. The enterprise prospered and they moved to Middletown, where one of the largest factories in the country was established.

Although a younger man, George W. Houk had been a close friend of Vallandigham, and William Jennings Bryan was a member of the congressional party which came to Dayton at the time of Houk's funeral. Bryan was very fond of Houk and delivered a eulogy at the grave. A daughter of Houk's, and a neighbor of ours in Dayton, Katharine Houk Talbott, grew into one of the best-known women in the country—a patron of music and a leader in many public movements. She established and put on a firm footing as an institution the Westminster Choir, now nationally famous. From it grew,

23

under the leadership of Mrs. Talbott, the Westminster Choir College at Princeton, New Jersey. It trains promising musicians as leaders of church choirs. Obviously this is an important contribution to church services. What would they be without music? What would life itself be without music? At present the college has 250 students. These include nationals from Argentina, Uruguay, Chile, Mexico, Korea, China, Japan, India, Hungary and the Philippines. At her death, Mrs. Talbott counted with pride twenty-three grandchildren. Eleven of them, all college men, joined the armed services of the' country in the Second World War. One of them, George Mead, a Yale athlete, died a hero's death at Guadalcanal. He had gone forward to recover the body of a stricken comrade when wounded mortally. He rose to his knees and killed his assailant before yielding up his life. I knew him from his babyhood. Posthumously he was highly honored by the government. His father, George H. Mead, was a member of the National War Labor Board. Previously he was on the National Defense Mediation Board. He was the only member of the industries group that continued in this labor from the beginning. He has recently been assigned to reconversion tasks.

The political eyes of the whole country were upon this special election in 1894. The feud between President Cleveland and the reactionary Senate cabal headed by Arthur Pue Gorman, David Bennett Hill and Calvin S. Brice had demoralized the Democratic party. The hostility of western silverite Democrats to Cleveland had added to that demoralization. Business was in the grip of a terrible depression, and Cleveland had been forced to begin the sale of government bond issues to maintain the gold reserve. Republicans criticized him harshly for this, although his predecessor Harrison had prepared the plates for a bond issue—and although the Sherman Silver-Purchase Act, the McKinley tariff and the expenditures of the "billion dollar Congress," all belonging to Harrison's administration, were chiefly responsible for the financial plight of the nation. It was a spirited campaign in the famous district, long known as a hot political battleground. To the jubilation of Democrats, Sorg was elected. In the circumstances of the time, his victory made him a national figure, and he went to Washington with more prestige than most congressmen initially possess.

Soon after his election he lunched one day at the St. Nicholas Hotel in Cincinnati, a famous hostelry, with Judge John F. Neilan

24

of the Common Pleas Court of Hamilton, Butler County. Prophecies were being indulged in as to Sorg's future and the governorship was discussed as a probability. The matter of selecting a private secretary came up and Sorg, doubtless mindful of the political portents that were running in his favor, said he would like to have a newspaperman. What followed shows how a small event can have a vast cumulative influence on one's later life. "I have the man for you," said Neilan. "He comes from your town and you must know him. He is young Cox, now working on the Cincinnati *Enquirer*."

I left the Cincinnati *Enquirer* with reluctance because I loved the newspaper business. Yet the thrill that came to me when I first saw the Capitol and the White House at Washington must have been the same which comes to every youngster when he first steps on what to him has been sacred soil. Washington was infinitely more attractive then than now. Those were the horse-and-buggy days and in the White House stables were beautiful steeds and handsome equipages. Each member of the cabinet was allotted a fine team and a Victorian carriage. The President and his wife, the former, beautiful Frances Folsom of Buffalo, always attracted great attention on their more or less regular drives through the city and suburbs. The President's wife, a queenly person, was ranked with Dolly Madison among the outstanding mistresses of the White House.

Distances were great then. The Cleveland family maintained a summer residence at Woodley, then regarded as a faraway suburb—though the city was growing so fast that Cleveland soon sold it and the surrounding land at a very handsome profit. Now "Woodley," which in much-remodelled form became the home of Henry L. Stimson, successively Secretary of State and of War, is in the heart of the northwestern part of the city.

Cleveland took hold of my imagination. His common sense, his rugged integrity, his courage and his intellectual honesty inspired the reverence of men who were closely associated with him. He was roundly abused in the country. Pot shots of gossip were as much a form of American recreation then as now. When Cleveland called out federal troops to move the mails, he served notice that he was not one to be fooled with.

The office buildings for senators and members of the House had not been built. Constituents of members of both houses ordinarily called on their representatives at the Capitol. The clerical work was done at home. Mr. Sorg maintained our headquarters in the Arlington Hotel, a famous hostelry for more than a generation.

Visiting foreign dignitaries were usually put up at the Arlington. In the lobby were assembled of evenings the official and social elite of the nation's center. Many senators and members of the House maintained quarters for their families there. I well remember the visit of Li Hung Chang. He was the outstanding Chinese of his day and came to know all that it was possible to know about this country. He seemed to be curious about the wealth of individuals. When he was presented to Mark Hanna, his first words were, "Tell me how much money you have." An amusing incident was attached to Li Hung Chang's visit. An institution of the hotel for many years was the old Irish housekeeper. One morning she saw smoke in abnormal volume blown like a cloud past her window. She immediately gave the fire alarm. When an investigation was made, a Chinese head was found protruding from every window in this wing of the building, in some instances more than one head. Every one was smoking a cigarette. Apparently it was the morning routine of the Orientals.

Senator Calvin S. Brice lived one square away in the old Corcoran home, a palatial mansion. His operations as a railroad entrepreneur and other business ventures had made him very rich, and he and his family entertained lavishly. He was one of the most picturesque figures in Washington; he had a tremendous shock of red hair, with a close-cropped but full red beard, and he usually wore a bright red flower in his lapel, so that he could well be termed colorful. His features, the most prominent of which was a tremendous nose, were almost grotesquely homely. Brice had little interest in public affairs, except as his seat in the Senate gave protection to his railroad and other business affairs, and prestige to his Wall Street operations. In fact, he was frankly and cynically in politics for the good of his pocket— a type of cynicism I have always especially detested. One of his first great business coups had been the sale of the Nickel Plate Railroad after cleverly establishing a bidding competition between the Gould and Vanderbilt interests. He maintained a voting residence at Lima, Ohio, but when not in Washington lived in New York, where he had another splendid house. His election to the Senate cast discredit upon the State of Ohio. In 1889 he had furnished lavish funds for the support of Democratic candidates for the legislature; and though public sentiment after the election was preponderantly in favor of John A. McMahon of Dayton, who would have cast luster on the Senate, Brice had the votes of the grateful legislators in his vest pocket.

But my first impression of the high ability of Cleveland's cabinets has not been altered. Time has not diminished the stature of Richard Olney of Massachusetts, first Attorney General and later Secretary of State, a conservative, to be sure, but one of the leaders of the American bar, of keenly incisive mind, ruggedly honest according to his own lights, and possessed of a blunt determination that seemed revealed in his bulldog face and figure. Nor could anyone doubt the capacity of the brilliantly attractive William C. Whitney, always dapper, well dressed and socially at ease, but the most briskly efficient of executives. He, more than anyone else, founded the modern American Navy. John G. Carlisle, the oaken-hearted Kentuckian who became head of the Treasury Department, had Gladstone's gift for making the exposition of financial problems so lucid that it was fascinating. Hoke Smith, Secretary of the Interior, was a young man, not yet forty. One got the impression that he was always in complete command of himself. He grew later, as Governor of Georgia and as United States Senator, but in the advisory group which surrounded Cleveland the younger Hoke Smith was recognized as a man of high ability.

I saw Hoke Smith frequently and little could he know, nor could I, that the Atlanta *Journal*, owned by him and even then a powerful newspaper with a marked liberal tradition which appealed to the most progressive elements in the new South, would some day become the property of the impecunious young congressional secretary in front of him. The forward-looking ideas which animated some of the best members of Congress completely gripped my youthful imagination. While I did not sympathize with the rising demand for the free and unlimited coinage of silver, I did sympathize with the demand for a greater measure of social justice that was coming from the suffering masses of the West and South. Members of the Senate and House were then beginning to lay the foundations of many great achievements which have changed the face of the social landscape.

Daniel S. Lamont, quiet, unobtrusive and tranquil as Secretary of War, was regarded highly both in the cabinet and in his years use-

27

fully spent afterwards. In Cleveland's first cabinet was William C. Endicott, whose daughter married Joseph Chamberlain, the English statesman. Austin Chamberlain, a half-brother of Neville, was his grandson. William L. Wilson of West Virginia, student and states- man, afterwards Postmaster General, was accompanied by Newton D. Baker as private secretary. A mental giant was Lucius Quintus Cincinnatus Lamar. If you draw a line below Virginia I would say that Lamar was the ablest man the South ever produced. I do not except Calhoun. Webster once said that Calhoun's was the best mind he ever encountered, but of course Webster never knew Lamar. The longer the perspective of time, the more evident it becomes that, while Calhoun did much to destroy the Union of states and ruin the South, Lamar contributed more than any man in the South (and probably than any in the North) to bind the two sections to- gether again and reconstruct Southern energies.

With his beard, his flowing hair, his keen eye and benign features, his gigantic frame and ponderous movements, he was an impressive man to behold. His greatness was both intellectual and spiritual. As orator, statesman and justice of the Supreme Court, he showed the highest ability. But he also revealed great magnanimity and rare foresight. It was an act of courage for Lamar, a Southerner who once served with the Confederate Army, to stand by the bier of Charles A. Sumner, the New England abolitionist, and deliver a eulogy extolling virtues which Lamar felt could not be denied. If Lamar had not exerted his great influence in behalf of peace after the presidential campaign of 1876, we could have had another civil war. He frankly said that the South could not go through another such ordeal.

There is no doubt that while the issue was in question he met Rutherford B. Hayes or some accredited agent of Hayes, such as Stanley Matthews, and drew from him promises which resulted in the final withdrawal of Federal troops from the three Southern states in which they had remained, and full restoration of govern- ment by the whites. Lamar defied the public opinion of his own state on two major questions, the granting of a pension to Grant, and the Bland-Allison Silver-Purchase Act, which he opposed. He triumphed in both instances.

Mr. Sorg did not pay much attention to departmental affairs and this enabled me to meet the cabinet members in his stead. I remember calling on John G. Carlisle concerning the appointment of a cabinetmaker from our district. He said a complication had arisen and that he had been advised that a civil service examination would have to be held. It was taken by a number of men. One of the questions was, "How many Hessians did the British send to America during the Revolution?" An Irishman's response was, "A damn sight more than they sent back."

Serving under Fourth Assistant Postmaster General Maxwell was George B. Cortelyou. We had many fourth-class post offices in our district and this brought me many times in contact with Mr. Cortelyou, a very serious-minded, competent, agreeable young man. He became confidential stenographer to President Cleveland, then secretary to President McKinley and later Postmaster General in Theodore Roosevelt's cabinet, finally coming to rank as one of the most astute business leaders of the country.

Senator John T. Morgan, of Alabama, a man of commanding personality and one of the last of the old plantation aristocrats, with all the graces and dignity of that vanished type, will always be regarded as the father of the Isthmian Canal. It is well known that he favored the Nicaraguan route and that it was only a dramatic final sequence of events, including an influential speech by Mark Hanna to a much-impressed Senate, which resulted in the final choice of the Panama line. Ultimately we are likely to have a Nicaraguan Canal as well. In the House from that state was John G. Bankhead, whose two distinguished sons (and distinguished granddaughter Tallulah) were later to be much in the public eye. Senator George Gray of Delaware, later a Federal Circuit Judge, had a judicial ability that was internationally recognized. In 1920 he introduced me to a great Wilmington crowd. Edward Oliver Wolcott, the Colorado senator, was one of the most brilliant silverites. I recall an instance of his ready wit. Once when he was addressing a Colorado audience in defense of his course, some man in the audience interrupted by shouting, "Rats!" "Will someone please take the China-man's order?" asked Wolcott.

Orville H. Platt, of Connecticut, a very tall, slender man, quiet in demeanor, was to remain in the Senate until his death in 1905. Though conservative, he was one of its hardest-working and most conscientious members; and along with Hanna, Spooner of Wisconsin, Allison of Iowa and Aldrich of Rhode Island, he gave the chamber its leadership until the day of the insurgents dawned. My political feeling, needless to say, was always hostile to these conservatives. Joseph G. Cannon, of Illinois, a veteran member, represented standpattism in the House. Among the other interesting senators were: Hoar and Lodge of Massachusetts, the former of whom I esteemed; Joseph C. S. Blackburn of Kentucky, then in the prime of life, and Edward D. White of Louisiana, at that time rated a special representative of sugar, but a man of integrity, later to be Chief Justice of the United States. In the House, Joseph P. Dolliver was attracting attention by his oratorical powers; Samuel W. McCall of Massachusetts was notable for his evident cultivation and his elevated view of politics and John Sharp Williams of Mississippi was marked by qualities of scholarship and wit of which I shall speak later. The Speaker of the House, Charles R. Crisp, was a man of dignity who usually wore a Prince Albert coat and who in spite of his free silver convictions acted with great impartiality.

Nobody interested me more than W. C. P. Breckinridge, whose congressional career was coming to an end, for he was defeated in the 1896 elections. Known as a silver-tongued orator, he had become a national figure. I once asked his son, Desha Breckinridge, whom he would regard as the ablest member of the Breckinridge family, which in our political life dated back to Jefferson's administration. His reply was, "Naturally, I would say my father." I have always felt that Desha Breckinridge would have made an admirable minister to the Court of St. James. Coming from the Bluegrass country, and a devotee of the sport of kings, he would have had a quick introduction to the English people. He was an able writer and editor and was prominent in political affairs.

There is much of interest to be found in the Breckinridge family. The branch that we knew most about descended from John Breckinridge, who was Attorney General in Jefferson's cabinet. His span of years was brief—forty-six. He had three sons, two of them ministers of the gospel. The eldest, John, who died at forty-four, was not known outside affairs of the church. The second son, Joseph C., died at thirty-four. His son, John Cabell, I think would have to be listed as the ablest of the clan. He was Vice-President during the Buchanan administration, was nominated for the presidency by the revolting Democrats in 1860, and was Secretary of War under the Confederate regime of Jefferson Davis. The third son of John Breckinridge was Robert Jefferson, the father of W. C. P. In his ecclesiastical activities, he led a movement which split the Presbyterian Church wide open. He then took to politics and was Lincoln's adviser all during the War Between the States. He was a delegate to the Republican convention at Baltimore in 1864 and temporary chairman. In 1849 he had introduced a proposal in the Kentucky Constitutional Convention for the gradual emancipation of slaves. We find here an instance of family ties completely severed by the conflicting opinions prevalent in the border states in the sixties. While Robert Jefferson Breckinridge was a strong supporter of Lincoln, his son, W. C. P. Breckinridge, served in the Confederate Army and rose to the rank of colonel. He was in command of the Kentucky cavalry designated to act as bodyguard for President Jefferson Davis and members of his cabinet at the close of the war.

Missouri had two strong senators in George G. Vest, remembered for his famous *Tribute to a Dog*, and Francis M. Cockrell, a picturesque figure of cyclonic quickness, who always seemed to be moving so rapidly that his long hair and coattails streamed behind. I found David Bennett Hill of New York a curious study. This typical machine politician, rather short, partially bald, with small eyes, was rescued from insignificance by his penetrating glance and shrewd look. It was well known that he would do anything for the profit of the Democratic organization, thought Cleveland much too indifferent to party interests, and was ambitious to advance his own political fortunes. Another remarkable New Yorker was Dan Sickles. He lived in the Arlington Hotel, overlooking the very spot where in Buchanan's presidency he had killed Philip Barton Key, and had with him his beautiful daughter. He walked with something of a strut, and used to act as if proud of his wooden leg, a souvenir of Gettysburg. With his swaggering air and his reputation for lifelong recklessness he always commanded attention. On the floor of the House his one great interest was pension legislation. At least brief mention should be given to Senator John B. Gordon of Georgia, one of Lee's best staff officers. From Nebraska came Representative William Jennings Bryan, then in his second term. We all knew of his oratorical powers and of his fierce fanaticism in the silver cause, but we did not know that he had a strong personal organization in the making.

As I look back upon the Fifty-third Congress, I feel that the interest which I took in live public questions and in the Senate and House debates upon them was the equivalent of a university course. The time I took from my office duties for attending the sessions at the Capitol was made up by night work.

While Mr. Sorg had gained a safe plurality of 1800 votes in the special election, it was evident that the contest in the fall of 1894 would be spirited and the result doubtful. The tide which had carried Cleveland into office two years before had ebbed. The Wilson tariff was unsatisfactory to much of the Democratic party, and the economic outlook was growing darker and darker. The Republicans nominated Andrew L. Harris against Mr. Sorg. Harris had a good war record and although a very quiet, non-assertive person, had few enemies as lieutenant governor. In later years he became governor at the death of John M. Pattison, the incumbent. Third party movements were assuming increased proportions and this introduced an element of uncertainty. In the district was—and still is—the National Soldiers' Home. Its vote had been cast almost solidly for the Republican party and it was important to increase the Democratic vote in this institution. I organized an office force which dealt exclusively with the handling of pension matters and personally examined individual cases at the pension bureau. This effort bore fruit for Mr. Sorg's vote was increased there and evidently this was a factor in his election by a plurality in the district of only 202 votes. Democratic tickets all over the country suffered severe defeat. In Ohio only two Democratic congressmen were elected, Sorg in the Third District, Layton in the Fourth District.

When the Fifty-fourth Congress assembled, Thomas B. Reed of Maine was Speaker of the House. But for a sarcastic turn of mind and a sharpness of tongue, he might have been President instead of McKinley. The routine of politics did not appeal to him, and the nomination of McKinley, who was vastly his inferior in mind, developed a cynicism in him which he never outlived. As Czar Reed, he was the first autocrat of the speaker's chair. The rules of the House adopted in his regime culminated in a revolution under Cannon, a factor in bringing Democratic control in the congressional election of 1910. If Reed had possessed the amiable qualities of McKinley and had not been inclined to the inflexible reaction which was the very fiber of the political life of Maine, his place in history would be more outstanding.

George Gilliland, veteran newspaperman and secretary to Senator Calvin S. Brice, once told me of an interesting incident connected with Reed. Gilliland was originally a telegraph operator, and had heard the flash come over the wires that Dewey had destroyed the Spanish fleet in the Philippine Islands. He lost no time in telling Speaker Tom Reed, who was in the chair. Reed called a member to preside and strolled off into the corridor to get all details from Gilliland. He dismissed the matter with these words: "I hope the Almighty keeps him from setting foot on Philippine soil." That wish fulfilled would have changed the course of history. Just why we took over the Philippines may be explained by what was once told to me by Talcott Williams, a close friend of McKinley. Salisbury, then the Prime Minister of Great Britain, dispatched a trusted lieutenant to Washington to bear a message to President McKinley. Its nature was so confidential that neither the mails nor the cables could be trusted. Salisbury's message stated that Germany was ready to take the Philippines, if we failed to do so. The German fleet was in the Far East at that time.

In the Fifty-fourth Congress appeared Oscar W. Underwood, thirty-three years of age. Here, for the first time, we find William Lorimer of Chicago, whose tempestuous congressional career ended with his rejection by the Senate for alleged corrupt methods employed in his election to that body. Here we find James E. Watson, a newcomer from Indiana. A promising career in the House for Charles A. Towne, from Minnesota, was budding. He served as a Republican in the House, but went over the party wall when the silver issue came up and was defeated on the Democratic ticket while running for the Fifty-fifth and Fifty-sixth Congresses. He declined the nomination for vice-president by the national convention of Populist and silver Republican parties, ran unsuccessfully for the Senate as a Democrat in 1900, but served in the upper branch for one year by appointment after the death of Cushman K. Davis. Moving to New York, he was elected as a Democrat to the Fifty-ninth Congress. He was one of the most attractive public speakers of his time. It always seemed to me that his talents deserved a better reward.

Our Ohio delegation in the House was adorned by Theodore E. Burton, who had been absent since 1891. A close friend of Senator John Sherman, whose biographer he became, he was a man of schol-

arly tastes and great breadth of view. In person he was an unforgettable figure; very tall, with exceedingly large hands and feet, and a
general ruggedness of aspect which faintly recalled Lincoln. He was
one of our leading authorities on the improvement of rivers and
harbors, and constantly inveighed against logrolling and waste. Another interesting figure in the House was George B. McClellan, son
of the Civil War commander, and later mayor of New York and
professor at Princeton.

It was interesting to see a Republican senator appear from North
Carolina—Jeter C. Pritchard, who had been elected by a legislative
fusion of Republicans and Populists. He made no mark. But another
product of the Populist movement, this time nominally a Democrat,
Benjamin R. Tillman, did. A political overturn in South Carolina
had put him into one of the seats usually occupied by men of aristocratic position. With his one eye, often lighted up by ferocious joy
of combat, his vigorous gestures and his stream of incisive denunci-
ation of Cleveland and the gold interests, he was much derided by
the conservative press; but I never felt any doubt as to his sincerity
and honesty. In sharp contrast was Stephen B. Elkins of West Virginia, a man of wealth who represented great corporate interests. It
was the healthy revulsion from senators like Elkins and the selfish
greed behind them which resulted in the long-overdue amendment
for the direct election of senators.

Mr. Sorg did not attempt to run for re-election in 1896. Following
Cleveland and the so-called sound money forces, he was not in sympathy with the Bryanite element which captured the Democratic
party at the Chicago convention that year. On March 4, 1897, our
time was up in Washington and we turned back to the Miami Valley. The nearly three years spent at the capital had been a tremendously useful experience to me. I departed from the city with some
regret, though I retained my passion for the newspaper business.

I had in fact learned even more from my Washington years than
I supposed. Not merely had I seen President Cleveland and his cabinet struggling with all the economic troubles and political confusion
of the time; not merely had I learned how Congress works and become acquainted with the practical side of politics—the logrolling
and maneuvering on tariff, rivers and harbors improvement, and
other questions. I had also begun to appraise some of the forces underneath the politics of the day. Young as I was, I could see that

34

the country was full of discontent, that a demand for correction of social and economic abuses was rising, and that great changes would have to be made. My sympathy was with these impulses. I had a young man's interest in new ideas and new movements, and I could see that there was a great deal in the Populist movement and the radical philosophy of the West that deserved support. Ohio in 1896 and for long afterwards was ranked among the conservative Republican states. I was a dissenter in that environment. I was a Democrat and something more; my experience as a farm boy and my work with Mr. Sorg in Washington had made me a Democrat aligned with the progressive tendencies of the time.

CHAPTER IV

A PUBLISHER AT TWENTY-EIGHT

◆

AFTER LEAVING Washington, I resided for a time in Middletown. Mr. Sorg was a man of large means and diversified interests, and suggested that I become identified with these interests. This had no appeal. I could not get out of my mind the idea of owning a newspaper. Dayton and Toledo seemed attractive fields—Dayton perhaps more so because it was not so far away and I was more familiar with the elements in it that seemed to presage a growing city. It was the very heart of the Miami Valley which Mark Twain is alleged to have described as "the garden spot of America." I suppose there are many such spots and all have been described in much the same enthusiastic phrase.

I was impressed by two things. There was no richer farming country on earth and the whole area from Lima and Springfield on south to Cincinnati was thickly populated. It was alive with industry too. The Ohio and Erie Canal had attracted manufacturing plants to this section early in its history. Eight electric interurban lines, then a novelty, had either been built into Dayton or were projected. With these feeders it was easy to foresee an important trading center.

The population was homogeneous. A tide of immigration had come over the mountains from Pennsylvania, from the Western Reserve and from Virginia and Kentucky. The resistance to military service in Germany had brought here a good rugged stock which included many fine mechanics. New Englanders had crossed New York and Pennsylvania, embarked on the Ohio River at Pittsburgh and come via Cincinnati to Dayton. In the very early days it had not been uncommon to load flatboats on the Miami, Little Miami, Muskingum and Hocking Rivers, to be carried in the early spring freshets to the Ohio and Mississippi and on to New Orleans where cargoes were sold.

The so-called old families of Dayton were of fine blood and tradition, and helped maintain an attractive community. The McMahons, Pattersons, Barneys, Platts, Smiths, Harrieses, Huffmans, Schencks, Reynoldses, Houks, Meads, Spriggs, Rikes, Dickeys, Stoddards, Parrotts, Shoups and others made up a body keenly interested in education, the churches and general culture. Dayton was a city of such wide streets that when the era of street-paving came the expense was burdensome. Dayton would not have the distinctive beauty of broad streets now except for William P. Huffman, a dominating figure in the local government. A group of timid souls inaugurated a movement to make narrower thoroughfares. Happily, Huffman's robust opposition to that prevailed.

Socially Dayton was attractive. A noteworthy percentage of the families were sending their sons and daughters to colleges and there were many alumni of Yale, Harvard and Princeton as well as of Ohio State University at Columbus, Ohio University at Athens and Miami University at Oxford. Church schools, notably Wittenberg at Springfield, Ohio Wesleyan at Delaware, Otterbein at Westerville, Muskingum College in Guernsey county, Denison at Granville and Oberlin in the Western Reserve claimed many students. Dayton had a very distinguished bench and bar. It was rich in its political traditions and its sons were listed among statesmen and notable generals and admirals of the Army and Navy. Vallandigham, Major Bickham and John G. Doren had attracted national attention as newspaper editors. I was wiser in my selection than I knew.

There were three afternoon newspapers and one morning publication in Dayton. The Cincinnati *Post* had more circulation in our city than all the Dayton papers combined. I decided to purchase the *Evening News* because it had an Associated Press franchise. The paper was bought for $26,000, mostly in cash. Mr. Sorg loaned me $6,000, I had a little money myself, borrowed some more and then proceeded upon the task of procuring subscriptions for stock. I argued with Mr. Sorg that this was not a good policy. It was the day of railroad and theater passes. I contended, against the judgment of an older man, that the favors to be exacted by stockholders would be very embarrassing. He thought differently and his opinion controlled. It became apparent in time, however, that he was wrong.

37

The project was favored somewhat by the prestige of his name as backer. Stock was sold in amounts as low as fifty dollars a share and on August 15, 1898, we made our bow to the community. I was twenty-eight years old—too young to be running a newspaper.

Looking back upon those days, I cannot but feel that the gods were kind. When it became apparent that we would soon be "turning the corner" financially, I bought in all the stock, giving my personal notes in payment. The purchases were at par and thus every dollar invested was returned. These certificates of indebtedness were discounted at the local bank and for what seemed to be a long time as many as two or three of them fell due every week. Mr. Sorg, himself a banker, had once said that a man will always maintain good credit if he pays something, no matter how little, on a note the day it is due. This was done. It was sound advice.

We bought supposedly 7500 circulation, but we could only find 2600 subscribers. The building was a narrow, four-story affair and although a newspaper had been housed in it for years, it was very ill-fitted for this purpose. An eight-page perfecting Bullock press which twenty years before had been the pride of the city, although pronounced by old Major Bickham, the *Morning Journal* editor, to be one hundred years ahead of the times, was our chief vehicle of production. The first time a supplement had to be printed it was a gala occasion. That edition was a triumph and stimulated our early hopes.

Our staff was necessarily small. When I took charge we had a staff of four reporters, to which I added a woman society editor. We all worked like beavers and with fraternal cooperation. I read all the copy, looked after make-up, answered the business correspondence and kept an eye on details, writing my editorials after dinner at night. Competition was keen and we were kept hustling. But we all loved the work, and I in particular found it fascinating.

The large retail stores each ran a half-column advertisement three times a week. Many trade announcements were printed without change from one season into another. I found watermelons advertised in the Christmas holidays and ice skates on the Fourth of July. Someone brought this to the attention of *Printers' Ink*, the leading trade publication of the day, and the editor said, "Well, this might not be so bad after all because the chances are the editor got a skate on anyhow on the Fourth of July."

The bookkeeper was once asked how much business we would have to carry to break even. His figures seemed to confuse him, but he finally said that if we had no news and every column was filled with advertising we would lose $500 a week. There might have been some value in unbridled youth after all. A wise man might well have quit then. We adopted the rule that no advertisement would be run without change. A competitor protested, saying that this would bankrupt every paper in the city. He was told that in the present way of doing things we would all fail anyhow, so it seemed desirable to try something new.

A brief telegraphic report was received over the wires and a goodly part of the paper was filled up with what was called "boiler plate," shipped in daily from the American Press Association and the Kellogg Company in Cincinnati. Occasionally a thrilling love story would be a part of the artificially created portion of the paper. Finally the order was given that no more boiler plate was to be used. The foreman said it would be impossible to get out the paper. In order to emphasize the meaning of the new order, the boxes of plate arriving about noon were thrown out of the back window. We had only three typesetting machines and from that day on the paper was set every day. We paid bonuses for high production from our linotype operators and within the course of two years we broke the world's record in line production three times.

There were signs of progress. The community from the outset seemed responsive. Competing papers spread the streets with rumors that our paper bills were unpaid (even though one car of white print lasted us for four months), that the pay rolls had not been met, and so forth. The day came when a merchant, Mr. M. L. Adler, met this propaganda in substantially these words: "I haven't paid much attention to the paper, but if this fellow can continue to print without paying his paper bills and his printers and reporters, then if he hasn't already made trouble for you fellows, he will." He increased his copy at once.

Another factor in the success of our paper was the high character of our merchants. Mr. Adler has already been mentioned. Then there were Fred H. Rike and Thomas E. Elder, two men who would have stood out in any field. Rike came from the famous Kumler family, was a born merchant and possessed in rare degree a sense of civic responsibility. When the Dayton flood devastated the business section of our city, a man of less courage would have quit. Mr. Rike asked no quarter from the wholesalers who had to replenish his lost stock. This gave him a very solid reputation in the whole sphere of business. His establishment now ranks with the best.

There is an interesting story connected with Mr. Rike's breaking the fetters of the old and becoming a modern merchant. His was one of the stores that inserted small advertisements three times a week. I proposed to the establishment that it run a half page every weekday for ninety days. If results accrued, we would be paid card rates. Otherwise, nothing. I imposed a condition, however, that the copy must be prepared by someone who devoted all his time to it. A cousin, I. G. Kumler, was just out of college. There seemed nothing for him to do so he was assigned to the experimental task. He gathered in his items daily from the departments and was not long in becoming very enthusiastic over his job. From that day until this, covering a period of almost fifty years, this store has been one of the largest advertisers in the country. When its beautiful new plant was completed, I reminded Mr. Rike of this circumstance and facetiously took credit for the great transformation. "Yes," he replied, "and I helped build the imposing *Daily News* plant." Both statements were correct.

Thomas E. Elder was born in Scotland, a very deeply religious man who pulled the curtains down over his show windows so that nothing would be exhibited on the Sabbath day. Under his reserve was great kindness. He watched our growth with an interest which, in his characteristic conservatism, he concealed. He lived to a very ripe old age, and his memory is still revered in our community. It would be ungracious in any review of our early struggles not to avow our debt to as fine a group of merchants as was to be found anywhere.

Our competitors were very helpful although their efforts were not so intended. When we threw out the pony Associated Press report and put in a double-wire service, it was another sure symptom of the approaching end. Then we started getting pictures in our paper, even though it was by the crude process of chalk plates. Photoengraving was not available. It wasn't long before we added a market page, not only giving attention to livestock and grains, but carrying the stock table as well. All of this indicated to some that we had over-guessed the importance of the field and that our venture would end in disaster. From this experience I learned the importance of saying nothing about competing newspapers. Our advertising and circulation departments were told, and they still are so advised, not to discuss competitors. We were not long, either, in finding the great advantage of another practice—that of treating all our advertisers alike, of making no side deals. The card rates, as announced, were to be maintained. The advertisers were not long in discovering that we were dealing in good faith with all alike.

It was about this time that we began printing a New York letter by O. O. McIntyre. These letters were interesting from the very outset. McIntyre would artfully work in the names of business concerns in the East and from them he derived meager compensation. He made no charge against us at first, but finally, in very evident trepidation, he asked whether we did not think the service was worth one dollar a week. It was here that his career, a very notable one, began. I told him a New York letter would always be a valuable addition to newspapers and that he had the genius to put together items of great human interest. At my suggestion he was turned over to Charles McAdam, a very active, ambitious young fellow, who was with the McNaught Syndicate. McIntyre, as might well be expected, was a temperamental fellow, but McAdam handled him well. McIntyre's death was a loss to newspaper readers. It is doubtful whether anyone of his time enjoyed such a large reading constituency. He came from Gallipolis, Ohio, on a rocky point overlooking the Ohio River. He is buried there on the spot where his daydreams began.

Our efforts, energetic but probably quite amateurish, came to the attention of other newspaper offices and outside talent started to flow in. Charles W. Wilson, a tramp newspaperman, so called because he was constantly on the move, joined our force. He was a Scotchman and claimed that his father had been prominent in the early history of the Y.M.C.A., which was founded in Britain. He was a man of wide information and well read in all the classics. He could write a fine newspaper story on any kind of assignment. His editorials were of high quality and he could clear a copy desk as fast and efficiently as any man I ever saw, but he had the weakness for drink. Once when we were attempting to get out our first industrial edition, I took the precaution of locking him in his room at the office. He took the imprisonment good-naturedly, but after a week he went down the fire escape and was on his way to other parts of the country. He once told me that after he had been on a spree, which usually lasted about ten days or two weeks, his mind was so muddled that it would not function. Then he would take to the road, sleeping in haystacks and other places of shelter, but always making it a point to be up and on his way at dawn. The crow of the rooster in the early morning and the inimitable music which nature provides at this hour straightened him out mentally, and lines which had passed entirely from him came back. When he found that he could quote the Bible and Shakespeare, he knew that he was ready for work again. He came back to us recurrently over several years. He was a man of gentle sensibilities, easy to get on with, and everyone around the plant developed an affection for him. When news came of his death, every heart was saddened and everyone was reciting the man's virtues.

We imported a good ad-writer. He would go into a store, make note of merchandise on display and in stock, and then prepare an attractive trade announcement. Some merchants looked with doubt upon the new idea but customers increased and the idea was accepted as a better way of doing business. All of this was inspiring, but we were conscious of our duties which ran beyond the business office and the paper gave editorial attention to affairs long neglected in the community.

A financial adventurer named Appleyard, of Boston, purchased the D. & L. Railroad running from Dayton to Lebanon. His Dayton terminal was poor and to correct this he proceeded to lay out a right of way through sections that had not yet been defaced by grade crossings. We opposed the construction at grade and led the fight against it. The culmination of this was a suit for large damages against the *News*. Under Ohio law, if criminal libel was alleged against a newspaper, the plaintiff by giving bond to the court could have the property taken over by the sheriff. This the plaintiff did and the sheriff with his deputies took charge about noon. The front door was locked and apparently the jig was up. Under the law, however, we had the right to give a redelivery bond which made the surety answerable for a deficiency judgment, if one were awarded.

Mechanical operations in the building went on, apparently without the sheriff's knowledge. Quick action was necessary. There was no time to make contact with a bonding company. I telephoned

Frank J. McCormick, Sr., who was a wholesale dealer in plumbing supplies and a Democratic leader in the community who had taken a kindly interest both in me and my newspaper. His business standing was high and he had great influence in the community. He rushed from his place of business and gave the bond. The two other afternoon papers came on the streets with extra editions stating that the *News* had been closed. The county fair was on and the papers were grabbed up in excitement. Within a half hour the *News* was on sale all over the city and at the fairgrounds with the front page emblazoned with the story of the closing that had not closed.

Mr. McCormick, who came to our rescue, was a very unusual man and his name will always remain in my grateful memory. It might be stated that his wife was a full cousin of Cardinal Gibbons of Baltimore. His daughter-in-law, Anne O'Hare McCormick, is now a member of the editorial board of the New York *Times*.

Well, the suit was finally dismissed. Appleyard lost his railroad and passed out of the picture. This experience naturally did the paper a great deal of good. We installed a three-deck press and typesetting machines, and red ink disappeared from our ledger.

It was an epoch when the three-deck press came into our plant. The building was less than thirty feet wide and the problem of building a substitute for a brick or cement foundation and pit was solved by setting up cast-iron sewer pipes set in concrete bases. We made an advertising deal for a gas engine and the belt had to run under part of the press to the driving shaft. Later we looked upon this as a very crude arrangement, but no one will ever know the pride and enthusiasm of our outfit when the new press—secondhand and quite old—a Scott, but purchased from the Goss Company, was turned over for the first edition.

The thriller was to come later. I would pronounce it the most unusual libel incident in the history of American journalism. This involved John H. Patterson, the genius who created the National Cash Register Company, one of the first American concerns to be known all over the world. He had many of the eccentricities of genius, and was a distinct pioneer in many features of industry. He had few, if any, peers in the conduct of his sales department and he was among the first, if not the first, to recognize that humanitarian measures with employees promoted ledger results. With this in mind, he brought in Olmsted Brothers, landscape architects. The grounds

43

of the Cash Register Company were landscaped and beautifully planted. He offered prizes to his employees and finally to others in the community who planted and cultivated flowers and perennial shrubs most skillfully. He was distinctly the community's most valuable asset. A man of great nervous energy, he grew health-conscious and at one time fasted for sixty days, dwindling to a shadow. A subsequent fad of his was the Fletcher system of extended and monotonous mastication of food.

On a European trip he ran into Sandow, the strong man, and was greatly impressed with his system of physical rehabilitation. One of Sandow's men, Charles Palmer, an Englishman, was brought back to America as his constant companion and attendant. Under his care Mr. Patterson improved so much in health that he bestowed complete confidence, if not dependence, upon the imported expert. Palmer was a man of insignificant personality and poor education who excited general distrust, but he had established an ascendancy over Mr. Patterson that amounted to hypnotism. He made no friends in Dayton, and was regarded with dislike. Naturally he did not like the city, and it was not long before Mr. Patterson announced that he was going to move his factory elsewhere. He said that the climate was bad, railroad facilities were inadequate and in fact there was nothing in the local scene where he had spent most of his life that suited him. He even asserted as a reflection on our citizenship that the local county of Montgomery had more men in the death house at Columbus than any other community in the state. He went through the motions of looking over Rochester, N. Y., and Bridgeport, Conn., for his new scene of operations.

Palmer's control over Mr. Patterson opened the way for his own advancement in the affairs of the corporation. He ran at once into opposition from valued officers, some of whom had spent long years in the service. Hugh Chalmers, the general manager, at that time regarded as the most efficient sales manager in the country, resigned. He had started as a boy on the janitor force. Later he was to become associated with the Thomas automobile enterprise centered in Buffalo. Chalmers became the head of the Thomas Detroit company, and made a high place for himself in the automotive industry.

Palmer was gradually moved into the front of the organization. Other men, important in the company, either resigned or were let out. A mandate was issued that in the officers' dining room butter,

44

eggs, salt and pepper should not be served. Palmer organized a company of horsemen. Men who had never been in the saddle were compelled to go through all sorts of maneuvers. One of them was thrown and killed. The public was shocked, but only one newspaper, the *News*, raised its voice in protest.

Patterson brought a series of libel suits against our paper. Palmer convinced him that his life was in danger and in trips to and from the factory Patterson and Palmer were hedged in with four mounted riflemen. Libel suits fell like raindrops upon us, first in the local and then the federal courts. One day it would be the Dayton paper that was sued and the next the *News* in Springfield, which we owned and operated.

J. K. McIntire, a fine old gentleman, was president of the bank with which we dealt. I asked him one day if he considered John H. Patterson an astute businessman. He replied affirmatively. "Then," I said, "he has sued me for something over a million dollars and you only give me a line of credit for ten thousand dollars. Why is that?" With a smile he responded: "Well, John might not make a good banker, and besides, Jimmy, you know you can always get what you need at our bank."

After all the Patterson libel actions had been filed, Palmer, in the courts, started asking for damages. Little else was discussed in the city. Patterson, resenting the flow of public feeling against him, assembled all his employees in the dining hall and later held a public meeting in the opera house where he indulged in intemperate and vituperative language against prominent citizens, and where pioneers, long since dead, were attacked and held up to ridicule. All of this began in the summer of 1907. In the midst of the excitement, Patterson and Palmer went abroad. Palmer's salary was increased from $40 to $1000 per month. Patterson's brother-in-law, Joseph H. Crane, a highly respected citizen who was the local sales manager, refused to be discharged, but Patterson removed Crane's downtown office to the National Cash Register plant and Crane passed off the pay roll.

Patterson at first denied the resignation of Mr. Chalmers, but when everyone knew that it had taken place, he announced that his general manager had been discharged for incompetency.

An editorial which appeared in the *News* at that time pictures a dramatic story of what still might be regarded as a complete case of hypnotic control: "Behind the resignation of Hugh Chalmers rests

45

a story which partakes of so many unusual features as to depict a situation absolutely anomalous in the commercial world. It is a story of an English lackey, a butler, a valet, who has completely practiced the art of hypnotism and so dominated the mind of his master as to sunder all friendship—his family, business and social. The valet, Palmer, was procured in England some two or three years ago. He was said to be a smart physical instructor; a diminutive chap not much over five feet tall, a countenance suggestive of the English lower classes, an attaché of Sandow, the strong man. He has been with his master every month, week, day and minute and has succeeded in converting a confirmed invalid into a specimen of good physical vigor, age considered. Seemingly, he has dominated the mind as completely as the body. It is this story which enters into the operation of this vast commercial plant."

This pretty completely phrased the feeling of the whole community, yet Patterson, at a meeting of the board of directors, stated that Palmer was more useful to him than any man in his employ and that he had never been able to judge men well until he had become associated with the English servant. Before going abroad Patterson and Palmer were presented with gifts. Palmer got a letter of appreciation and the bronze figure of a man on horseback.

In Patterson's absence libel suits against our papers continued to pile up. Apparently these were intended to impose silence upon the *News*. Telegrams came back from abroad to the sales department, one in particular reading, "Mr. Palmer and I congratulate you." When they returned, Patterson found himself quite alone in the community's affairs. The *News* announced that every suit in the courts would be met and vigorously contested and an editorial which must have convinced Mr. Patterson that our paper was not to be intimidated appeared in these words:

"John H. Patterson, 64 years of age, the sunset of life already casting its glow upon him, sits alone at Far Hills—with Palmer.

"The associates of his boyhood are gone; in their place—Palmer. His own family separated by differences which cast away from him his own flesh and blood; and in their place—Palmer. . . .

"Patterson scorns the place of his birth and says it is a disgrace to have been born in Dayton and sits in silence and alone, communing with Palmer.

"But this is not all. The four distinctive features of trade which

46

the mastermind of John H. Patterson evolved and applied to the operation of the NCR were: first, welfare work; second, carefully schooled and educated salesmen; third, the most wonderfully organized publicity department in America and fourth, the suggestion system.

"These four departments have been wiped out as if by magic, men of 20 years' training and association with the business go as by the passing of night. Beside the man who has made these fantastic changes in his declining years, in his wretched and restless state of mind—sits Palmer."

The club was to be used on other newspapers. About all they had done was to print the resignation of Chalmers and the "voluntary" retirement of officers. However, Palmer sought damages. Then came a most disgraceful episode. The *Herald*, an afternoon publication, made humble apology. This seemed to indicate to the public that the process of intimidation was working. The incident, however, brought the *News* back to the subject. It said:

"The most despicable thing in the world is cowardice. Whether it is displayed in a dog or a man, it invariably calls forth contempt upon the part of those observing it. In business affairs, it is equally despicable and there is not on record a single instance of where the coward in business has succeeded."

Of the *Herald* the *News* said directly, "Then rather than face the music and fight it out, the paper, like a wanton coward at the first sign of bristling, tremblingly recants and licks the boots of Patterson and his valet." The morning paper, the *Journal*, came forward with apologies to Patterson and Palmer. It would be ungracious to the memory of Major Bickham, the distinguished journalist, not to state that the *Journal* had passed from the control of members of his family at this time. Both papers not many years afterwards passed into self-respecting ownership.

These two evidences of journalistic surrender apparently emboldened Patterson and while in New York he was responsible for an interview which appeared as a dispatch to the Cincinnati *Times-Star*, quoting a friend of Mr. Patterson's as follows:

"Mr. Patterson proposes to leave Dayton because of the smallness, the littleness, the inexpressible meanness of its people. He is going to get away from them—that is all; to get where he won't be interfered with. I don't know where he will make his home.

47

"Dayton's name must have been Day-town originally. A one-day town. No one should stay there any longer. Mr. Patterson won't stay there long in the future. Dayton's one output besides cash registers is meanness and pettiness. To all of which Mr. Patterson subscribes."

This put the Chamber of Commerce up in arms and it made public a resolution stating that Mr. Patterson had never been annoyed nor opposed and that everything he had asked for from the city government had been granted.

We decided that Mr. Patterson would either have to dismiss his suits or try them, and our attorneys started taking depositions. Whereupon Mr. Patterson announced that he could not put in his time in the courts and conduct the affairs of the National Cash Register Company. His employees were brought together in the general assembly room and an announcement was made that the factory would close because he had to spend his time in the courts. Of course, the suits had all been brought by him and the workmen of the NCR and the whole community knew full well that whatever trouble Mr. Patterson was in he had made himself. The depositions were taken in the law offices of attorney Oscar Gottschall. Mr. Patterson appeared with an armed guard.

The proceedings ran for a week or ten days. It was arranged that two questions were to be propounded on a given day, about a half hour before the noonday recess. One related to a campaign contribution made by Patterson to a judge in the Franklin County courts who had rendered a decision against the Hallwood Cash Register Company and in favor of the National company. There was a long exchange between the two groups of lawyers as to the admissibility of the evidence. Then there was another inquiry which involved the payment of money to international labor officers during the pendency of a strike.

At this juncture Patterson's lawyers asked for an adjournment. Patterson did not show up that afternoon. He and Palmer had taken the train for New York and the next day they sailed for England. In the middle of the ocean, he instructed his attorneys to dismiss all suits and assume all legal expenses that had fallen upon us. This was a surprise to Patterson's lawyers, our attorneys and myself. What Mr. Patterson did was without reservation or condition imposed. He was gone for quite a while. When he returned, Palmer was not

48

with him. He never appeared again. I was making my first campaign for Congress and Patterson on his own motion supported me.

So far as I know, nothing quite like this ever happened in any newspaper field in the country. One cannot but think that it all grew out of Mr. Patterson's state of health. After this experience he soon returned to a normal life. He purchased large tracts of land in meadows and woodlands and gave them to the city for public parks. He instituted many projects in furtherance of community development. He was more responsible than anyone else in bringing about the city manager form of government in Dayton, a system that was to be followed in many other places. He was a good deal of a hero in the great flood that came later and he and I were friendly until he died. He had elements of greatness in him, but he was an odd combination. The episode was doubtless a factor in my election to Congress.

The whole experience was a vindication of the courage of youth because I was in my thirties when I went to grips with Mr. Patterson. A great many of my friends, with perfectly good intent, begged me to keep out of the fight. They regarded it as foolhardy. Patterson conducted by far the largest organization in the city at that time. He made large contributions to all our public institutions and the fame which he had brought to the place as a city of homes having a great industrial future made him the leading citizen. At times he seemed possessed of a spirit of grandeur and felt that he should boss the community, socially, politically, industrially and otherwise. Naturally he had tremendous influence and if his attack on the city had not been so ruthless things might have turned out badly for us. I had a great liking for Dayton and was outraged by the unwarranted attack upon it and its citizens. I could not dismiss the conviction that it was the duty of our newspaper to stand by the community regardless of consequences. And, incidentally, any newspaper in time of stress which does not recognize its duty to a community is not deserving of the name. There is nothing worse than an invertebrate publisher. He does neither the public nor his profession any good. When the libel suits started falling upon us we were strengthened by the flow of public opinion in our favor. There was no mistaking that. The end was in sight.

The name of John H. Patterson should not be passed without a reference to what he contributed to the distinguished industrial personnel of the country. From the National Cash Register Company went: Hugh Chalmers, prominently identified with the Thomas Detroit Motor Company and the Chalmers Motor Company of Detroit; William A. Chryst, consulting engineer, General Motors Corporation; Frank O. Clements, research department, General Motors; Colonel E. A. Deeds, prominent in the direction of airplane production in World War I, now chairman of the board of the National Cash Register Company and director of the National City Bank of New York; Frank Parker Davis, patent lawyer, Chicago; Frank L. Ditzler, Pacific coast manager, Toledo Scale Company; Joseph E. Fields, vice-president, Chrysler Corporation, Detroit; O. P. Gothlin, former chairman of the Railroad Commission of Ohio; R. H. Grant, vice-president, General Motors Corporation; C. F. Kettering, vice-president, General Motors Corporation; Alvan Macauley, chairman, Packard Motor Car Company; E. C. Morse, president, Export Division, Chrysler Motor Corporation; Joseph E. Rogers, president, Addressograph-Multigraph Corporation; J. M. Switzer, of the Joyce-Cridland Company; Thomas J. Watson, president, International Business Machines Corporation; Wendel E. Whipp, president, Monarch Machine Tool Company, Sidney, Ohio; Henry Theobald, president, Toledo Scale Company, and Thomas Midgley, Jr., acknowledged to be one of the greatest chemical engineers of all time. Happily for Dayton, both Deeds and Kettering remained here, as did Grant.

Deeds came from the hills of Licking County; Kettering from Ashland County. They were the joint inventors of the electric self-starting and lighting device which, in a sense, revolutionized the operation of automobiles. Subsequently, their Delco company made widely used small lighting plants. When their holdings were sold to General Motors, plants which these two men had developed had grown to large proportions. Their operation has been tremendously multiplied under the consolidation and at the beginning of the Second World War they were employing almost 30,000 people. In large degree, Deeds was responsible for the flood control project in the Miami Valley.

Kettering is a rare genius and recognized as one of the ablest research men living. He once said to me that there was no such thing as an invention. The inventor, so-called, as he put it, simply makes a discovery. The mysteries of Mother Nature have not been penetrated. Responsive to research she gives them up now and then, but there is much yet to be learned. Kettering is a humanitarian in the broadest sense and never loses interest in the promotion of hospitals and the science of medicine and education.

During World War II, Mr. Kettering was chairman of the National Inventors Council. To this distinguished group must go much of the credit for initiating our secret weapons. We have heard very much about the new devices of enemy nations, but for military reasons the country has known very little of the organization with which Kettering was associated.

In a recent conversation with Mr. Kettering he said that this was the reason that the work of the Council was so little known to the public. He dwelt upon the fact that civilians had responded to the wide appeal for ideas and said: "Up until the autumn of 1944, 200,000 suggestions had come in and many devices proposed were so simple that we all wonder why someone had not thought about them before.

"Basic ideas invented or discovered by civilians have been developed into some of our most useful items of military equipment. A few famous examples are the screw propeller, invented by Stevens in 1804; the revolver pistol, invented by Colt in 1835; the revolving turret warship *Monitor*, invented by Ericsson in 1861; the motor-driven airplane, invented by Orville and Wilbur Wright in 1903; the torpedo, invented by Whitehead in 1866; smokeless powder, invented by Vielle in 1886; the submarine, invented by Simon Lake; and the internal-combustion engine, invented by Dr. Otto and developed by others. The list might be extended to include many other inventions which have had far-reaching effects on modern warfare and military tactics."

The growth of our newspaper was rapid and we looked for a new location. When a loan was sought at a local bank, the fine, kindly, conservative banker said, "Why, I didn't think you were making your salt. Newspapers have never been known to earn money. Of course we can't accommodate you." If the banker was shocked by the mere request for the loan, then his reaction must have been more than a shock because I said to him, "Mr. Winters, I do not want to be disagreeable, but I have such faith in the future of our business that I wouldn't trade it for your bank." He smiled at the indiscreetly expressed enthusiasm of the youngster and that ended the interview.

The impression of this banker was the common impression in those days. There were too many newspapers everywhere. It was a common practice for opposing political factions to have an organ. Sometimes corporations with selfish aims maintained a newspaper organ as a side issue. Pay rolls and paper bills in too many instances were supplied by individuals or concerns interested primarily in promoting some project outside the newspaper. The Fourth Estate was not regarded as a good base of credit at the banks. It was that very thing which prompted us to erect a very attractive building, classic in its features, looking more like a bank than a newspaper plant. It was to symbolize the solid institution, which the public was late to recognize.

The year in which we erected our new building was 1910. I could then look back over a dozen years of strenuous but profitable news-paper activity. It was in 1898 that I had paid $26,000 for the prop-erty; it was in 1903 that it turned the corner and became an un-questioned business success; it was in 1905 that this success enabled us to begin accumulating funds for expansion, profits amounting each year to about my purchase price. The country and city were prosperous, and we had shown an enterprise which more than en-abled us to share in their growth. The new building marked the centenary of the paper, for it was projected just a hundred years after the first press was brought over in 1808 from Lebanon by oxen. Our staff had been steadily increased. When we entered our new quarters we had a double-wire Associated Press service; our news department employed ten or twelve people; our advertising, circulation, bookkeeping and other departments were well manned; and we had two presses of the latest design. We held a gala opening, and ten thousand people visited our quarters in a single afternoon and evening. Our circulation, which I have said was initially only 2600, was approaching 20,000; I well recall my thrill of pride when it passed the 16,000 mark.

There is not a sign on the Dayton *News* Building and people still come into it thinking it is the post office or a bank. Internally, how-ever, our plans involved careful engineering to insure fine continuity of operations as between our several departments, particularly the news, composing, stereotype, press and circulation departments. The fine old banker probably gave me the cue to this. In other cities

52

where we are operating, we try to see that our newspaper structures have a like meaning.

One of the afternoon papers, the *Press*, which at one time had the largest local circulation, fell into financial difficulties and was ordered sold at receiver's sale after publication had ceased. It was understood between H. H. Weekly, proprietor of the *Herald*, and me that I was to purchase the property of the *Press* and we would divide the expense and the assets. He forgot the agreement, or said he did, and then in looking about for a field where the purchased equipment might be used, our eye fell upon Springfield, a thriving city, twenty-five miles northeast of Dayton. There were two afternoon and two morning papers there. We purchased one of the latter, the *Press-Republic*, on June 1, 1905, changed its name to the *News*, and changed its politics. We took it from the morning into the afternoon field. A great many newspapermen looked askance at this project, but the afternoon field, even though there were two publications in it, had been greatly neglected. Within a few years both of these papers, the *Democrat* and the *Gazette*, ceased publication.

Besides the *News*, an afternoon paper, there was the *Sun* in the morning field. The *Sun* had been established by a group of striking printers and had been quite successful. It was subsequently sold to Charles S. Knight, who had made a fine property out of the *Beacon-Journal* in Akron. In time it became apparent that Springfield could support two newspapers, but only one operating plant. Mr. Knight offered the *Sun* for sale. I questioned whether the consolidation would not be regarded with disfavor by the merchants, but a committee of them called on me and urged that the deal be made. They feared that if the *Sun* passed out of the field, Dayton and Columbus morning papers with trade announcements would enter and that injury would accrue to their business. The deal was concluded and the *News* in the afternoon and the *Sun* in the morning are still printed in the same plant.

PART THREE

CHAPTER V

CONGRESS IN TAFT'S DAY

◆

THE YEAR 1908 brought Bryan's last attempt for the presidency—at least as the nominee of his party—and my entrance as a candidate into public life. Bryan's return to leadership was very inspiriting to the Democrats. It was a factor in our carrying Ohio for the state ticket and for the election of Judson Harmon as governor.

I was deeply absorbed in the newspaper business. Our enterprise, ten years old, was doing well and we were making plans for the erection of what we thought was a beautiful building to house it. The leaders in our county suggested that I become a congressional candidate. I was not easily persuaded. Doubtless the one person more responsible for the idea than any other was Edward W. Hanley, chairman of the county committee and afterwards of the state committee, a self-made businessman and an astute politician. Amid portents of the division in the Republican party which was to come to its climax in 1912, there were two opposing candidates for Congress, the regular Republican nominee and an Independent.

I am not sure that I ever enjoyed a campaign more than this one. Early in the autumn I began the canvass in my native county, Butler. We would cover a township by automobile during the day and then wind up with a meeting in the evening. To meet the farmers I walked across plowed fields which were being seeded for wheat and barley, and made an exhaustive visitation in every community.

There was doubt then of the expediency of campaigning by automobile. A candidate for the state legislature a year or two before had been defeated because his automobile scared horses on the highway. In Morgan Township one day, an approaching horse hitched to a buggy did everything but climb a rail fence to get away from our own moving machine. The chairman of our county committee, who had always opposed the automobile in politics, viewed the scene with alarm. He was certain that the driver of the horse was a circuit-riding minister who doubtless would control many votes. The man got out of his buggy, holding the animal by the bit. As we approached him he certainly did have an ecclesiastical look, but his face broadened into a smile as he said, "Don't mind this horse, fellows, he always was a damn fool." We went on convinced by his language that we had there no minister of the gospel to fear.

The congressional district consisted of Butler, Montgomery and Preble Counties, all forming one of the most attractive stretches of country in the nation—rich in agriculture, teeming with manufacturing industry and graced by fine villages and cities. Indian summer in the Miami Valley is something to stir the soul of the poet and I enjoyed driving through it, but speaking was a good deal of a struggle at the outset. A year or two before I had presided at a congressional convention. I had memorized the speech and I will never forget the physical and mental torment that possessed me while I delivered it. Inwardly I said to myself that if I ever got through I would never make another. But it all turned out well enough. At first I made notes and within a couple of weeks, to use a turf expression, "I was going along easy." This campaign was an interesting and stimulating experience. The day of political processions had not passed and there were groups of horsemen parading before some of the important meetings. There were brass bands galore and great enthusiasm. The vote was as follows: James M. Cox (D) 32,324; W. G. Frizell (R) 12,593; John Eugene Harding (Ind.) 19,306.

Judson Harmon was elected governor after a most skillfully conducted campaign. Taft, personally popular, became occupant of the White House. Uncle Joe Cannon was Speaker of the House, Champ Clark was leader of the Democratic minority in the lower branch. Taft got on well with individual members of the Congress. On my first official visit to him, my son, Jim, then six years old, later a lieutenant commander in the U. S. naval air arm, World War II, went along. Taft made quite a fuss over the youngster and the next morning the lad broke out with measles. The question was widely discussed in the press of whether the President was immune. Some editors facetiously asked whether the President had been deliberately exposed to a Democratic infection.

Only those who knew Champ Clark appreciated the sweetness of

58

his nature. What seemed to some a brusque exterior was doubtless occasioned by modesty and diffidence. He suggested that I go on the District of Columbia Committee because it occupied a full day each week in the deliberations of the House. This enabled me to take the floor quite often. I shall never cease being grateful for a circumstance which tied me in affection all through life to James R. Mann of Illinois. He was not the titular leader of the majority, but he was the actual leader. A day came when he asked me many questions relative to some measure which I was handling on the floor. He must have recognized my embarrassment and when the House adjourned he came to me with these kindly words, "My boy, I was simply doing that to help you get your legislative legs." I have always felt that Mr. Mann was the most useful member of Congress, House or Senate, during his entire service. No man labored so hard and none more conscientiously. As the session opened at noon, he knew what was on the calendar and was well grounded in the facts of every measure that was to come up. He had not only absorbed the reports of the committees, but in many instances had taken home with him copies of the hearings before the committees. He was a powerful advocate of the right and a devastating antagonist to anything that was off-color. Hesitant congressmen would often go to Mann on some pending question, and ask, "Mr. Mann, how are you going to vote on this matter?"—with the intention of following his lead.

By all the claims of service, he should have been elected Speaker of the House when Nicholas Longworth of Ohio was selected. This is no reflection on Mr. Longworth. Nick, as he was popularly known, made a fine presiding officer. He was a diplomat in the best sense and got on well with the minority. Mann probably would have been chosen except that he was regarded by the regulars in the Republican organization as being too independent in thought and action. This disappointment to him was the turning point in his career and after the untimely death of his only son and child, he did not live long. There was a tender poetic side to his nature, and in his garden at Evanston, Illinois, he grew what were said to be the most beautiful peonies in the country. Students of congressional action during his time will always give him high rank as a statesman and a patriot.

Champ Clark, too, was helpful to new members. In the early days of the session he accosted me in the cloakroom and said, "Cox, I have observed that you have no difficulty in expressing yourself on the floor. Go right along now because you have every reason to have confidence in yourself."

My predecessors from our district for several years had been Republicans. I was not blind to the fact that my election was due in part to a division in the ranks of the opposition party, although I polled more votes than the two contesting candidates combined. Unquestionably there was a hard battle ahead in the next election. A seemingly unsurmountable barrier was the Republican strength in the Soldiers' Home near Dayton. There were about seven thousand inmates of the institution and they had not forgotten Cleveland's vetoes of private pension bills. They were led to believe that the policy of the Pension Bureau was dictated by Hoke Smith, a Southerner, Cleveland's Secretary of the Interior. Their slogan was, "Vote as you shot." The Democratic party had not been able to poll more than about two hundred votes at the Home and there seemed to be no way of breaking down this adverse front.

When the Sundry Civil bill was before the House during the summer months of the long session, I noticed that the appropriation for the Zoological Garden near the city of Washington had been increased. I very innocently asked the chairman of the Appropriations Committee, James A. Tawney, why this was. Facetiously, but good-naturedly, he replied, "It is the high cost of living. We have monkeys in the zoo to feed." Again innocently, I asked whether the ape tribe had multiplied much in the last year and he thought it was about the same. The Sundry Civil bill usually took from two to four weeks in the House. In due time that part of the bill which carried an appropriation for the national military homes was reached. I had observed in the meantime that the subsistence item had been cut. I inquired quite innocently again what the membership of the homes was and what it had been the year before. As Tawney was told after turning aside and asking Courts, the clerk of the committee, who, by the way, had served through all administrations for a generation, it had increased. I then proposed an amendment carrying an increase of $250,000 in the subsistence item and upon that, under the rules of the House, I was entitled to be heard. I contrasted the menus for a given week in the Dayton jail and the Dayton Soldiers' Home, also in the federal prison at Leavenworth, Kansas, and at the Soldiers' Home at Leavenworth. Prisoners were being better fed than the soldiers. That was apparent. The picture was drawn of the Republican party, the widely-heralded friend of the soldier, adding to the food supply of the monkeys in the zoo and neglecting the men who had saved the Union. There wasn't a vote cast against the amendment. The bill, as changed, went through the Senate. I carried every precinct in the Soldiers' Home.

Our congressional district was made up of people very proud of its traditions. It had been represented by some of the ablest men in the nation. In those days it was considered a breach of legislative ethics for a newcomer to make a speech before "his seat was warm." Early in the Taft administration the Payne-Aldrich tariff bill was up for consideration and the debate on it ran for weeks. Time was allotted to speakers by the chairman of the Committee of the Whole, Marlin E. Olmstead of Pennsylvania. The senior members were naturally first on his list. For some reason Mr. Olmstead, although on the other side of the aisle, was very kind to me. I told him I was anxious to say something on the tariff. One afternoon he told me that he had assigned time to a member who, as he put it, was not overly regular in attendance and might not be present the next morning. If he did not appear I could have his time. True to prediction, he was not there and Olmstead recognized me. It was the thirtieth of March, 1909. It was not the quality of the speech, but the mere circumstance of my making it so soon which made a fine impression in my district. The time allotted was thirty minutes. When this had expired Champ Clark moved for an extension which was granted by the chair. The Mark Hanna slogan at that time was that the country should "Stand Pat." I referred to this by saying that out in our country it was usually the fellow who held four aces who stood pat. Ollie James, the Kentucky giant, bawled out, "Not always, sah."

I called attention to the industrial strength of the Third Ohio District and the claim that it produced and exported more manufactured goods than any congressional district in America. The tariff lobby was the best organized and most active of all time. The platform on which Taft was elected provided for schedules sufficient only to meet the difference in the cost of production at home and abroad. The lobby busied itself in showing what it falsely contended was a vast differential in the general costs of labor and manufactur-

61

ing. They piled it on so heavy that although the Payne-Aldrich bill passed, it met a heavy weight of public condemnation and was widely recognized by thoughtful people as an economic outrage.

My own conviction was strong that the bill was both foolish and iniquitous. I argued that the greater part of American industry was no longer in the "infant" class, but well able to take care of itself without tariff barriers that merely meant heavily increased burdens on the consumer and strangulation of our export trade. One of my paragraphs may be quoted from the *Congressional Record*. "It is worthy of remark," I said, "that our district, a great industrial center, has not been a part of the attempted misrepresentations in tariff hearings before the Ways and Means Committee. I am sure I speak entirely within the truth when I assert that not one manufacturer from this very important industrial scene has asked for a schedule in his own behalf at the expense of the great American consumer . . . Our industrial concerns not only feel secure against foreign invasion, but, gentlemen, they stand ready to beat any foreign competitor on his own soil if this government will give them half a chance."

I had letters supporting this statement read into the *Record*. They protested against high schedules and suggested reductions to enable domestic enterprises to compete with Germany, which was expanding industrially under reciprocal arrangements. A plea was made for reciprocal treaties. The tariff bill under discussion allegedly permitted trade arrangements, but the high protectionists saw to it that if a reciprocity treaty disturbed a single tariff schedule, it had to come before Congress to be confirmed.

My liberal instincts were deeply aroused by this battle over the Payne-Aldrich tariff. The fact that I represented an exporting district, which shipped cash registers and other goods all over the world, was only incidental in forming my convictions. From my early years I had read much on the tariff and had become persuaded that the excessively high duties of the McKinley and Dingley tariffs fostered monopoly, gave many corporations outrageous profits and worked hardship on farmers, workingmen and consumers generally. Pulitzer's New York *World*, Cleveland's attacks on high protection, and the fine low-tariff fight of Frank Hurd, congressman in the 1880's from the Toledo district, had all helped shape my opinions. During the battle in the House I watched Sereno E. Payne, who had the bill in charge, closely. He was a forceful man, of big head, big limbs and big paunch, who had well earned his leadership, but was now beginning to fail. When on the floor he fought hard, but in his seat he often relapsed into inertia and was caught napping. It struck me that like other high tariff men he was arrogant and too disdainful of opposition. The bill became much worse when Aldrich reported it in the Senate, and the struggle of La Follette, Dolliver, Bristow, Clapp and other insurgent senators against it shook all Washington. I used to go over to the Senate to listen to the debates. La Follette was the opposition leader, but it seemed to me that the fiery Dolliver contributed more to the attack than any other man.

There was a good deal of talk those days about the national debt. It amounted in 1910 to $1,176,939,969. Mr. Boutell of Maine, an old-time conservative, argued for a large indebtedness. He went so far as to say that "in computing federal expenses it is necessary to have a large interest bearing debt to take care of the banking interests." In my speech I said, "I have no doubt the bankers will be both interested and surprised to know that they can only keep going forward by the government's going backward, that their growth and development are contingent upon the government's spending more than it receives. . . . If the government were a private enterprise and conducted its affairs with such ridiculous disregard for the rules of common business sense, it would have been in the hands of a receiver long ago." The testimony given by many manufacturers before the Ways and Means Committee, in an attempt to show the need of higher schedules to meet the difference in cost of production at home and overseas, was nothing less than disgraceful. Adverting to this I said, "Many men have come here to promote their selfish interests. Some of them have actually sworn their souls down to the gates of hell in order to gain a governmental license to rob the American people." It might be worthy of note that through our whole argument ran the vein of economic freedom, something for which our former Secretary of State, Cordell Hull, has contended always.

The act of Congress creating the parcel post was passed at this time. The most active lobby in opposition to it was that of the National Wholesale Hardware Dealers' Association. The claim was made that if merchandise were delivered on rural routes, the farmer would stay at home and the village merchant would be wiped out.

It was not long until automobiles and the movies stimulated a volume of travel to the villages, which alarmed our economists. I was a strong believer in the parcel post and in that behalf was closely associated with David J. Lewis of Maryland, I. L. Lenroot of Wisconsin and Victor Murdock of Kansas. To Lewis of Maryland belongs the major credit for the establishment of parcel delivery by mail.

I was also active in supporting an appropriation to build two battleships. There was a great deal of opposition to this measure, but President Taft was very much in favor of the increased expense and through Nicholas Longworth, a colleague from our own state, he sought my assistance. Longworth afterwards told me that I delivered to him twelve votes from our side which was sufficient to carry out President Taft's desires.

My efforts during my first term had naturally my re-election in view. Our manufacturing concerns had many contacts with the departments in Washington. The rich Miami Valley had become conscious of the advances in scientific farming and was interested in the research and experiments carried on by the Agriculture Department. This made the office of the congressman a clearinghouse and gave an opportunity to serve and know well influential persons and concerns in the constituency. No request made either for service or information was denied if it was humanly possible to meet it.

It need not be said that I took a keen interest in the great contest to limit the powers of the speaker which marked this Congress of 1909–11. My sympathies were all with the Democratic majority and the Republican insurgents who revolted against the czaristic rules. Like nearly everybody else, I felt a warm personal liking for Uncle Joe Cannon, but I hated the autocratic House management, exercised for the benefit of selfish special interests. I became a warm friend of Lenroot of Wisconsin, a serious-minded, hardworking and extremely useful member; of Victor Murdock of Kansas, a fiery, redheaded, implacable and erratic hater of the standpat reactionaries; and of the reserved, soft-spoken, but indomitable George Norris, who always paid me the compliment of listening attentively to my speeches. Of course I voted with the coalition against Cannon. For a time we were hopeful of victory, and it was a great shock to me as to others when a little group of conservative Democrats, led by Fitzgerald of New York, and "Bill" Howard, broke away from our ranks and enabled Cannonism to win a short-lived victory. Cannon's defeat and a much-needed revision of the rules were merely postponed for one year.

This contest generated great excitement but no lasting hatreds. All the men I have named took me into their confidence. George Norris, for whom I had the greatest admiration, showed me many kindnesses. Lenroot often spoke to me of his devotion to La Follette. Early in 1912 I sat beside Lenroot at the famous Philadelphia dinner where the overworked and overwrought La Follette temporarily broke down and thus ruined his presidential chances; that evening Lenroot was the most brokenhearted man I ever saw. Victor Murdock once told me a good joke at his own expense. In his belligerent, excitable way he was defending his record before a Kansas audience. He attacked his unscrupulous opponents. "Why," he said, "they even say I'm crazy. How many of you think I'm crazy? All of you who do stand up!" "And by Gad," he said to me, "you know they all stood up!" Fitzgerald and Howard were expelled from the Democratic caucus, and later asked for reinstatement. They came to me to talk it over. "I think," I said, "there should be a silent ballot in the caucus on the question." "Oh," said Fitzgerald, "I don't like that idea. Give those fellows a secret ballot, and they may murder us." "You don't understand the situation," I explained. "These men are really for you. They want to vote for reinstating you, but they won't want their constituents to find it out." Both men beamed at me with delight. "Well, Fitz," said Howard, "I want to appoint Cox to be my political manager from now on!"

An episode in the House during the long session beginning in March is a reminder that a great deal has always been accomplished by parliamentary strategy. My immediate predecessor had been able to include in the Public Buildings Act an appropriation for the enlargement of the post-office building in Dayton. The city was in the midst of a healthy growth and it became apparent that the rebuilding plan would be wholly inadequate and very unsatisfactory. I had the ambition to acquire an expansive site for a combination post-office and federal court building and to have something erected which would not only take care of the needs of the public service, but would be an architectural ornament to the city. It was one task to procure the necessary appropriations, but a more difficult one to repeal the old provision. The rules of the House plainly bar new legislation in an appropriation bill. However, I had inserted in the Sundry Civil bill not only a repealing clause, but an appropriation for an entire new site and structure. A single member of the House could have defeated this by making a point of order against it. I canvassed our membership and found two members who were hostile—Macon of Arkansas and Stafford of Wisconsin. We came to this part of the Sundry Civil bill about lunchtime. Ollie James very accommodatingly invited Macon to the House restaurant for lunch. James R. Mann, who was presiding over the Committee of the Whole, honored Mr. Stafford by calling him to the chair while Mr. Mann went down to lunch. Thus it was that a project which meant so much to our community and a great deal to my political interests went through the House. Macon was enjoying his meal and Stafford, in the chair, was unable to make the point of order. Attention would not be drawn to this if the public interests had not been promoted by the episode. No objection was made to it in the Senate.

Someone whose mind runs to such things could write a very interesting book on the important things that have been accomplished in the Congress through the ingenuity of members who knew parliamentary procedure and rules. Under the speakership of James G. Blaine, L. Q. C. Lamar was able by a parliamentary device to defeat the Force bill, a proposed iniquity forming a part of the carpetbag regime in the South.

The story of this action is an interesting one. In the elections of 1874 the Democrats had won a majority of the House of Representatives and in the ensuing Lame Duck Session the Republican majority of the old Congress prepared to push through an act, known as the Force bill, which would have given the President control of the elections in Mississippi, Louisiana, Arkansas and Alabama, a measure deemed necessary to assure Republican supremacy in the elections of 1876.

The Lame Duck Session would expire by limitation on March 4. The bill was taken up, with Ben Butler pressing it, on February 24. It was the hope of the Democrats to delay its passage until too late for the Senate to pass upon it as it came from the House. With these few days to go the minority had exhausted its known means of delay. At this point Lamar called upon Blaine, then speaker, and convinced him that the passage of the act would be a national disaster. Blaine thereupon suggested to Lamar that the minority could require the clerk of the House, in reading the Journal of the previous day, to read in full the affirmative and negative votes taken. The Democrats, in their effort to delay action, had forced some forty votes on the previous day. To read them in full would take the whole day. The Democrats adopted the suggestion of Blaine and the ensuing delay prevented the passage of the act until midnight, February 27, when it was too late for the Senate, under its rules, to complete the passage of the measure before the session expired. Thus the Force bill died, and to seat their candidate for President in the 1876 elections the Republicans were driven to the impromptu measures which marked this, in history, as the stolen presidency.

Senator Norris saved Muscle Shoals through a point of order. A bill had passed both the Senate and the House for the sale of that great power site to Henry Ford. There were slight differences in the Senate and House bills, requiring a conference. Conferees, in submitting their report, had introduced a provision not in either the House or Senate bill. Norris made the point of order—a conference committee had no right to introduce new legislation—and the point was sustained by the presiding officer, Vice-President Charles G. Dawes. This happened in the closing hours of the session, too late for the defect to be remedied. Except for this, Muscle Shoals might not now be government property.

CHAPTER VI

THE FAMOUS THIRD DISTRICT

◆

I WAS overwhelmed, if not bewildered, at the outset of my career as I reflected upon the historic importance of the Third Ohio District. It was famous because it had been represented by famous men. I doubt whether any district in the whole country could match, in point of ability, achievements and fame, such men as Tom Corwin, R. C. Schenck, C. L. Vallandigham, Lewis D. Campbell, John A. McMahon and James E. Campbell. They were all national figures, as well known in far sections as at home. It used to be told in my boyhood days that a distinguished Englishman who came into the gallery of the House asked to be shown the member from the Third Ohio District. I speak of it as the Third Ohio District in its broadest sense because the congressional subdivisions in the old days often changed and their limits were determined largely by partisan politics. I am referring specifically to the Miami Valley area centering through changing years in Butler, Montgomery, Preble and Warren Counties.

Tom Corwin came from Warren, the two Campbells, Lewis D. and James E., from Butler, and Schenck, Vallandigham and McMahon from Montgomery. As far back as 1842, Montgomery and Warren were in the Third District. In 1852 it consisted of Butler, Montgomery and Preble, which it now is and was in 1908. In 1862 it was made up of Butler, Montgomery, Preble and Warren. Of the counties mentioned, only Butler and Warren were in it in the redistricting arrangement of 1872. Usually after each census, the controlling political party carved out the state in such a way as to obtain political advantage. I have always had some pride in the fact that the redistricting bill passed in 1913 under my administration as governor has stood for over thirty years. It was framed with a great deal of care and with proper regard for the spirit of representative government rather than for any political advantage. When the Willis administration came in, in 1915, it passed a gerrymandering measure, but it was submitted to referendum and rejected. This has discouraged political meddling throughout later years.

The remark of the visiting Englishman might have been influenced by one of our distinguished representatives, General Robert C. Schenck having served very popularly at the Court of St. James. We often heard it said that his chances for the presidency were ruined by a trifling circumstance. He was a skillful poker player, and his English friends were impressed by the ease with which he took their money from them. At their request, he wrote a booklet dealing with the fundamentals of the game. This enabled his political opponents to describe him as a gambler, and his political career was injured. It ought also to be added that, being under heavy pressure to meet living expenses for which his salary as Minister to Great Britain was inadequate, he allowed his name to be used in promoting a dubious business enterprise in England, the Emma Mine, and suffered severely in reputation from the resulting scandal. But he had given distinguished service in the War Between the States. A younger brother was Admiral Frank Schenck of the United States Navy. A grandson of Admiral Schenck once told me the story of his naval beginning, which I think has never been printed.

The young man had tried unsuccessfully to be appointed a cadet in the Navy. In desperation he took a train to Washington to press his case. On arriving at the capital he went down to the Potomac River for a swim and bath. While dressing on the shore, he was accosted by a fellow bather, an elderly gentleman who had shown himself a very expert swimmer. The older man questioned the youngster as to his name, where he was from and what he was doing in Washington. His reply was that he had failed in every effort to get into the Navy and he had come to Washington to see whether he might gain an appointment at the hands of the President. When they were about to part, the older gentleman gave him a notation on the back of an envelope and told him if he presented it at the White House it might help him. He lost little time getting to the seat of power and when ushered into an imposing room his companion in the waters, John Quincy Adams, was sitting in the presidential chair. It goes without saying that he soon became a naval cadet.

Tom Corwin was one of the brilliant men of his time. We recall a tradition which is pretty generally conceded that, except for Corwin's unfortunate speech on the Mexican question, he would, in all probability, have become President or at least a presidential nominee. His home was at Lebanon, Ohio, and he was a close friend of Henry Clay. The Kentucky statesman on his trips from Washington to Lexington always came by way of Lebanon and thence to Dayton, Cincinnati and the Bluegrass country. On one of these visits an infant child of Clay's died in Lebanon and was buried there. The body was subsequently removed to Kentucky.

Corwin was born in Bourbon County, in Clay's state. His father did not possess means to educate two sons so the older one was favored. Tom, however, made the best of his brother's books. He served for a decade in Congress, was elected governor in 1840 and subsequently went to the United States Senate. He besought Webster to stand with him against appropriations for the continuance of the Mexican War, contending that acquisition of the Mexican territory would surely lead to a sectional conflict in this country. Fillmore appointed him Secretary of the Treasury and later Minister to Mexico. It is related of Corwin that in one of his congressional campaigns, the opposition candidate made his campaign largely by horseback, putting up at night wherever he chanced to be. He was making headway and Corwin was worried. In some way it leaked out that he wore a nightgown when he retired. Corwin held him up to scorn as an effeminate character who even wore women's clothing, and he was beaten by ridicule. Corwin's nephew, Franklin Corwin, was a member of Congress from Illinois, and his brother, Moses Bledsoe Corwin, represented the Urbana, Ohio, district. Here it was that Simon Kenton, the rugged pioneer, was imprisoned in the county jail for a long time as a prisoner for debt. Kenton was being taken as a prisoner by the Indians to the Lake Erie region, there to be burned at the stake. He was highly prized as a captive because he had made a great deal of trouble for the red man. The party camped for the night on this planned pilgrimage of death at a point north of Springfield which was then known as the Indian village of Wapakoneta. This is not to be confused with the present city of that name, located farther to the north in Auglaize County. Kenton, in the morning, was struck by the beauty of the vast prairie which lay on either side of what is now Mad River and he remarked to himself that when he got out of his trouble he intended to come back and locate there. This he did and lived out his life at Urbana. Here, too, Brand Whitlock, the writer and diplomat, was born. As our ambassador to Belgium he rendered conspicuously able service. He was private secretary to Governor John P. Altgeld of Illinois who lived in Richland County, Ohio, before going to his adopted state. It ought to be said too that Altgeld, who was very much misunderstood by his contemporaries, is receiving credit now by students and writers for qualities of courage not recognized when he was thrust into the public eye at the time of the Chicago riots.

Lewis D. Campbell was known as the Butler Pony. He was an uncle of James E. Campbell, afterwards governor of our state. His political contests were thrilling, if not dramatic. He was a follower of Clay and published a Clay newspaper in Hamilton in the 1830's. In 1840, 1842 and 1844 he had been defeated as a candidate for Congress. As a Whig he was elected to the Thirty-first, Thirty-second, Thirty-third and Thirty-fourth Congresses. He presented his credentials as a member-elect of the Thirty-fifth and served from March 4, 1857, to May 25, 1858, when he was succeeded by Clement L. Vallandigham, who contested the election. He tried again in 1858, but was defeated. He served in the Union Army during the War Between the States and was Colonel of the Sixty-ninth Ohio Regiment. He gave up military service because of health and was appointed by President Johnson as Minister to Mexico. He went into the state senate in 1869 and then again was elected to the Forty-second Congress, serving from March 4, 1871, to March 3, 1873. He was not a candidate for re-election, but was a member of the state constitutional convention in 1873. The members of that body were privileged to take home with them the two individual chairs which they used. Mr. Campbell's nephew, James E. Campbell, presented one to me and it is now a treasured possession at the Old Home Farm, the place of my birth.

It was during his congressional career that Mr. Campbell met and became an intimate friend and companion of Andrew Johnson. For several summers, Johnson spent a part of his vacation in Hamilton, Ohio, the guest of Mr. Campbell. There Johnson met Peter Schwab, who was to be a picturesque political figure for a generation. Mr. Schwab once told me that during the Johnson impeachment proceedings he went to the White House at two o'clock in the morning to give the President the authentic forecast that the charge would fail. It was generally known that Mr. Schwab played an important part in this famous controversy. However, he would never go beyond saying that he had carried the message to the White House. In after years, George Alfred Townsend, nationally famous journalist, whose nom de plume was "Gath," tried with all his ingenuity to get the details from Mr. Schwab. He arranged a meeting at the St. Nicholas Hotel in Cincinnati, one of the most famous hostelries in the Middle West. He provided an abundant feast and at what he considered the psychological moment, he said to his guest, "Now, Mr. Schwab, I would like for you to tell me all you know about the Andrew Johnson affair." All Mr. Schwab would say was, "Now, Mr. Gath, I tell you what you do. If anybody asks you about that, you just tell them you don't know." Incidentally, Mr. Schwab was the grandfather of Gordon S. Rentschler, now chairman of the board of the National City Bank of New York.

In one of my campaigns, either in 1908 or 1910, I spoke from a stand erected on a prominent corner of West Alexandria, Preble County. Old timers recalled that it was upon this very spot many, many years before that Lewis D. Campbell and Vallandigham, opposing candidates for Congress, met in a joint debate which wound up in a fist fight between the two.

Clement L. Vallandigham was a hero of the Democratic party in the years immediately preceding and after the War Between the States. He was born in New Lisbon, Columbiana County, Ohio, on the same street where John H. Clarke, afterwards Justice of the United States Supreme Court, and Marcus A. Hanna, so long the leader of the Republican party, saw the light of day. He married the sister of J. V. L. McMahon of Cumberland, Maryland, and entered the practice of law in Dayton, Ohio. His whole mature career was a part of the tempestuous period accompanying the secessionist movement. He took high rank at the bar, edited the *Western Empire*, a vigorous Democratic organ, and offered himself for Congress in the election of 1854. He won a seat two years later, was re-elected to the Thirty-sixth and Thirty-seventh Congresses and served until March 3, 1863. He was overwhelmed in the election of 1862 by the war feeling, and that ended his congressional service.

In mind and facility of speech Vallandigham is to be compared with Woodrow Wilson. He served in Congress at a time when most members came to the chamber with pistols in their pockets. If a

72

conflict had to come between the North and the South over the question of states' rights, there was enough inflammatory leadership in both sections in the late fifties to bring it to a head. It is difficult in this day to understand the real depth of bitterness that was engendered. Vallandigham bravely stood up in Congress to contend for his convictions, even though he was condemned as a traitor for doing so. There was something peculiar in the man in that men could utterly abhor his beliefs, and yet his eloquence, courage and sincerity compelled respect. He was radically opposed to disunion, yet the historian in turning back to that period may say, and with full propriety, that while Vallandigham was opposed to war and to disunion, he did not come forward with a preventative formula.

When war is on, any public figure who sincerely opposes it—as history has shown—becomes a martyr to his own convictions and bravery. There was never any question about Vallandigham's sincerity. There was great excitement in his home city, Dayton, Ohio, when he was arrested and turned over to General Rosecrans of the Union Army to be conducted through the Confederate lines in Tennessee. In the day or two spent at Rosecrans' headquarters in the South he completely captivated the military leader, who said at the time that he did not look like a traitor to him. He went to Bermuda and then to Canada. During his exile, his party nominated him for governor of Ohio. In the trying days when he, as he believed, was totally misunderstood, he remained the leader of his party in his state, if not in the nation. He was a delegate to the Democratic National Convention at Chicago in 1864 and four years later in New York City. That same year he was the nominee of his party for the United States Senate, but was defeated. We have had distinguished men, notably Senator Norris of Nebraska, who opposed the First World War and yet lived through trying condemnation to become trusted leaders in our national councils. No one ever questioned Senator Norris' sincerity. It was this full confidence in the pure gold of his character which carried him through. Once it became apparent to him at the approach of World War II that our whole civilization was menaced by Nazi fascists and Japanese militarism, he gave the whole weight of his power and influence to the support of a war in his country's behalf.

There can be no doubt that Vallandigham, in the late sixties and the two years of his life following, regained for himself the respectful attention of many who had previously condemned him. He created a following as loyal as that which made William J. Bryan a hero in his day. There was a distinction, however, between the two men. In a considerable sense Bryan's appeal was a class argument. Vallandigham's was not. This was in part due to the vast difference in the issues of the two periods. Vallandigham, prior to the National Democratic Convention in 1868, was devoting himself to his creed of "the New Departure." It took concrete form as a movement and issue on the 18th of May, 1871, when it was given to the country in the form of a document adopted at a Democratic convention in the city of Dayton. With its wider acceptance, Vallandigham became the leader.

Salmon P. Chase, by letter, heartily congratulated Vallandigham upon his conception of national duty. The New York *Sun*, an independent Republican paper, said, "The hour has struck, and the man has arrived. Mr. Clement L. Vallandigham has sounded a trumpet that will reverberate through the land." The New York *Herald* declared, "Vallandigham is the Phil Sheridan of his party, and has sent the old Democratic leaders whirling in every direction. His platform, enunciated at the Dayton Convention, meets with general favor, despite the opposition of the timid, badly scared Bourbons." The New Departure was adopted by Democratic conventions in so many states and with such promptness that no one could doubt the advent of a new day in our political affairs. It doubtless greatly influenced the election of Tilden in 1876, but the Fates remained unkind to Vallandigham. As the tide of public favor was running towards him, he died an untimely death. Pursued by the same nemesis of ill fortune, he lost his life under dramatic circumstances. In 1871 he was a defense counsel in a famous murder case which, on change of venue, had been transferred from Hamilton, Butler County, to Lebanon, Warren County. It was his contention that the man who lost his life did so by the accidental discharge of his own pistol when he nervously attempted to defend himself from assault. Vallandigham had two revolvers for the purpose of demonstrating his theory. One unfortunately had remained partially loaded and when he picked it up to show what might have happened—and as he insisted did happen—there was an explosion and he received a mortal wound.

It is fitting that we go from Vallandigham to his nephew, John A.

74

McMahon, a man for whom I had always felt great love and affection. He was my trusted friend and the godfather of my son, James McMahon Cox. His father, J. V. L. McMahon, is still referred to, after more than a century, by eminent authorities in railroad law. It was he who drafted the charter for the Baltimore and Ohio Railroad which became and still is a model instrument. In the directors' room of the Baltimore and Ohio Building in the Maryland metropolis is a large painting of a group of men seated in a boat. McMahon is standing bareheaded and pointing the way to the future. He was a close friend of Andrew Jackson and declined three great honors —membership in Jackson's cabinet, the senatorship from Maryland and an appointment to the Supreme Court of the United States. He gave to his son a beautiful cane presented to him by Jackson and a brace of the pistols used in the famous Clay-Randolph duel. There has been a great deal of controversy about the authenticity of the weapons reputed to have played a part in that affair of honor. There can be no doubt about those owned by Mr. McMahon.

Following the heat of Vallandigham's bitter political campaigns and not long after his death, McMahon was elected to Congress from the Dayton district in 1874. He served until March 3, 1881. He was defeated in 1880, his last campaign, and returned to the practice of law, in which he continued until his death, March 8, 1923, in his 91st year. Speaker Cannon, whose long service in Congress made him an authority, once said to me as I sat beside him on the Appropriations Committee, "I have seen all the great lawyers of my time in Congress. McMahon was the king of them all." He was selected as one of the managers appointed by the House of Representatives in 1876 to conduct the impeachment proceedings against William W. Belknap, Secretary of War in the Grant administration. He served in the Louisiana inquiry at the time of the Hayes-Tilden contest. One of his most signal triumphs in Congress was the presentation of the minority committee report on the form of accepting the terms of the Geneva award growing out of the Alabama claims. John G. Carlisle, then a colleague, had signed the majority report. He sat only a few feet from McMahon and when the latter had concluded his argument, he grasped his hand and said, "Mac, you are right, I must do the unusual thing and vote against the report of the majority which I myself signed." The views of Mr. McMahon prevailed and were adopted by the House.

J. A. Garfield had reason for saying that McMahon, with his clear legal mind and his command of simple language, was a dangerous man to contend with on the floor. McMahon was a close friend of Samuel J. Tilden and, while admiring him as a great lawyer, felt that his timidity was largely responsible for the seating of Hayes. Mr. McMahon once told me of visiting Tilden at his home in New York City while the controversy over the presidency was still on. As Mr. McMahon put it, "Tilden took me into a corner and said in almost whispered words, 'We must not do anything to disturb business.'" It was often Mr. McMahon's contention that if Tilden had exhibited the same qualities possessed by Grover Cleveland, he would have been proclaimed President. When some doubt was expressed about the result in New York State in the election of 1884, Cleveland summoned newspaper correspondents and said, with resounding fist on his desk, "I have been elected and I will be inaugurated in March."

Mr. McMahon was also the source of another interesting story about presidential candidates. This story was told many times by C. L. Vallandigham to Mr. McMahon, his nephew, who related it to me. The Democratic convention of 1868 was held in Tammany Hall in New York. Horatio Seymour, who had been wartime Governor of New York, was chairman. Most leaders of the party were convinced that their one hope of defeating Grant, as head of the Republican ticket, would be to nominate Salmon P. Chase, then Chief Justice. It was agreed by these leaders that as a compliment to the Democracy of New York, Seymour should be given a high vote, with the understanding that he would in any event decline a nomination. Vallandigham was to present the name of Chase, and at the proper moment the majority would unite upon him. Word was sent quietly through the state delegations. Intently they awaited the consummation of the plan. At one point Thomas A. Hendricks of Indiana seemed about to carry off the prize. He would be a weak candidate, and his opponents united on Seymour, giving the latter the nomination. He had left the hall, but was brought back. When he entered the delegates gave him a tremendous ovation, half of them doing this in compliment to his fine sportsmanship in the declination they expected to follow. But Seymour misinterpreted the applause as a mark of enthusiasm for his candidacy and accepted. Chase, who had been Governor and United States Senator from

Ohio, a member of Lincoln's cabinet and at the time Chief Justice of the United States, and was regarded as a war Democrat by the country at large, was probably the strongest man that could have been placed against Grant. This failure of his plan was one of the great disappointments of Vallandigham's life.

The record of the convention gives confirmation to the story. In the first five ballots, Senator George H. Pendleton of Ohio led with 156½ votes. He soon passed out of the picture and a contest developed between Winfield S. Hancock and Thomas A. Hendricks. On the twenty-first ballot, the former received 135½ votes, the latter 132 votes. On this twenty-first ballot Chase received half a vote. This obviously was intended as the signal for what was to follow on the next ballot, which was now never to be concluded. Prior to this Seymour had not received a vote. It seems fair to assume that the unanimous change to him was the result of a general agreement among the leaders of the party. All of this bears out the Vallandigham-McMahon story.

Mr. McMahon many times recounted a story told to him by Abram S. Hewitt, who was chairman of the National Democratic Committee in 1876. Hewitt insisted that it was a prayer delivered in the home of Frederick Theodore Frelinghuysen that brought about the final decision for Hayes over Tilden. Five members of the Senate and an equal number from the House of Representatives and the Supreme Court formed the electoral commission. Before this body took final action one of its members, Justice Davis, was appointed to the Senate by the governor of Illinois. He was succeeded by Joseph P. Bradley on the commission. Davis was supposed to be favorable to Tilden and this belief was borne out by his subsequent votes in the Senate. Bradley was a week-end guest at the home of Frelinghuysen. After dinner was served Saturday evening, those present fell to discussing the all-absorbing question of the presidency. The talk ran on and on with everyone oblivious to the passing hours. Someone observed that the dawn of the Sabbath had come, whereupon Frelinghuysen, in a very impressive manner, said, "Let us pray." He was filled with emotion and earnestly besought the Almighty to preserve the Union, save the government and keep it from falling into the hands of its enemies. Bradley went back to Washington and cast the deciding vote for Hayes. Abram S. Hewitt was a man of most dependable character and the story coming from him—a story which I think has never been printed—is one the truth of which he believed. It was told to him by one of the guests at Frelinghuysen's home. Frelinghuysen subsequently served as a member in the cabinet of President Arthur.

Soon after Mr. McMahon had resumed the practice of law, he met with the board of managers of National Military Homes to present the application of a local railroad to build a spur into the Soldiers' Home at Dayton. The president of the board was an old friend, Martin McMahon of New York. After the meeting had adjourned, the president of the board suggested to the Dayton lawyer that they go over to the Senate and meet Vice-President Chester A. Arthur. As he put it, "I have known Chester for a long time. He is a fine fellow and I think you would enjoy an introduction to him." Arthur was a handsome man, faultlessly dressed. He reminded Martin McMahon that their ancestors had both come from the same county in Ireland. The three stood talking together and the New York McMahon remarked upon the good fortune which had always accompanied Arthur in his political life. "Chester," he said, "with all of your luck, I wouldn't be in Garfield's shoes for one thousand acres of the finest land in New York State." These soon seemed to be prophetic words. Garfield died in September and Arthur became his successor. McMahon wrote the famous flood conservancy act which was passed by the Ohio legislature during my first term as governor. It met every test before the courts. The brief which he presented to the Supreme Court of Ohio was written in his own hand after he was eighty years old. For its legal and literary qualities, it was considered a document of historic interest and James G. Johnson, a member of the court, took steps to guarantee its preservation.

As measured by present standards, Mr. McMahon would be considered a conservative, and yet I remember well an observation of his when Brandeis was appointed to the Supreme Court by Woodrow Wilson. There was very bitter opposition to it, but Mr. McMahon observed, "I think there should always be one Brandeis on the court." I was first elected governor in a liberal and progressive movement; my position was well understood, but Mr. McMahon never argued about it with me. As he once put it, "We are in the midst of change and perhaps it is badly needed. I have confidence

that in it you will play your part with good sense." Whenever he
and I were in Dayton, I lunched with him at his home on Thursdays
and remained during the whole of the afternoon. In his reminiscences and his discourses on life there was never a tiring moment.

There is an interesting sidelight which bears on Mr. McMahon's
prestige as a lawyer. John H. Patterson, the head of the National
Cash Register Company, was leaving on a trip around the world,
and Hugh Chalmers, the General Manager, saw him off at shipboard. Mr. Patterson's parting words of advice were these: "I think
we have taken up everything except any legal questions that might
arise. If they do, go to John A. McMahon and do what he tells you
to. If he should be out of the city and you are unable to reach him,
then go to some other lawyer and do just what he tells you not
to do."

As Vallandigham was succeeded by his nephew, McMahon, Lewis
D. Campbell's nephew, James E. Campbell, came to Congress from
the same district as his uncle. Here was one of the most attractive
personalities in all the political history of our state. He came of
fighting stock. His Grandfather Campbell came home one blustering
day and was told that Hull had surrendered at Detroit in the War
of 1812. His wife was in the neighborhood somewhere and when
she returned home, young Campbell, who had oiled up saddle and
molded bullets for his rifle, said to Mrs. Campbell, "I am off to the
war." Mounting his horse, he made his way over mud roads and
through forests to join the American Army which was put together
after the disgraceful affair at Detroit.

James E. Campbell was a matchless campaigner and was very
quickly recognized by opposing political forces as a dangerous competitor. In order to get him out of the way, the Republican legislature changed the Third District, making it supposedly safely Republican. Campbell carried it by two votes and thus caught the eye
of his party in the state. He was nominated for governor against
Foraker in 1889. Foraker was then seeking his third term. The campaign was historic. Both candidates were handsome men, aggressive,
skilled campaigners with equal capacity to take advantage of any
weakness in the opposition line. *The Campbells Are Coming* was
the martial song which was heard in every city, village and county
seat. This helped bring a real swing to the campaign of the son of

Scotch ancestors. Campbell's speeches were reported by Claude Meeker of the Cincinnati *Enquirer*, a graphic writer whose stories daily held newspaper readers everywhere.

One of the biggest meetings of the autumn was held in front of the house in which Campbell was born in Middletown. It so happened that Cordell Hull and I were both a part of that gathering but neither of us knew it until we were exchanging reminiscences at the World Economic Conference in London in 1933. Hull was a student in the normal college at Lebanon, I was a country schoolteacher. The campaign took on such excitement that the Democratic blood in Hull's Tennessee veins was deeply stirred. It was in the horse-and-buggy days and for the occasion he was compelled to make the trip from Lebanon in an outfit hired at a livery stable. Campbell won the contest. It was a bitter blow to Foraker, whose political star was in the ascendancy at that time.

Campbell made an exceptionally fine record in the governor's chair. He introduced reforms needful to the hour and when it became apparent that the city government in Cincinnati, dominated by members of his own party, had grown corrupt, legislation was passed uprooting the whole local structure. Except for this, Campbell would unquestionably have been re-elected in 1891. The entire Democratic organization, dominated by John R. McLean, opposed him in Hamilton County. There were precincts in which no Democratic ballots were reported for the use of the voters. Another factor in his defeat by William McKinley was the high price of wheat. It was an old saying that dollar wheat would elect any party in power; wheat in 1891 touched a high point in Chicago of $1.14 and the Republicans in Washington were given the credit. The campaign attracted national attention because McKinley was prominently mentioned for the presidency. Had Campbell defeated him, he might possibly have been the Democratic nominee in 1892. As it was, there was a strong movement in his favor at the national convention held in Chicago, but Campbell refused to be tempted. He stood solidly for Cleveland, was one of his strongest supporters during his presidential tenure and was offered a place in the cabinet.

One of Campbell's speeches, on *The Navy*, made at a meeting of the Ohio Society in New York, was widely circulated, but not more so than a reply he made to Theodore Roosevelt at a Jackson Day banquet. Roosevelt had denounced Jackson as a barbarian. In eloquent words Campbell presented the real Old Hickory. He pointed out that the English Minister to Washington had seen Clay, John Quincy Adams and Jackson in one company and held that of the three men Jackson possessed more of the presidential presence. Governor Campbell spent his later years at Columbus, Ohio, where he was universally beloved. I remember his coming into the governor's office during my incumbency with a document which pleased him very highly. He was honorably discharged from the Federal Navy during the War Between the States for physical disability. Soon thereafter, eight of his friends and he had been examined for life insurance and he was the only one rejected. Now he showed me a newspaper clipping which recited the death of the last of the eight men. Campbell, the one regarded as a poor risk, was still alive and enjoying his eightieth year. Like John A. McMahon, he was my trusted friend. Both were much older, Campbell my senior by 27 years, McMahon by 37 years.

In the campaign of 1920 I was introduced to a magnificent audience in Portland, Oregon, by Benjamin Franklin Irvine, editor of the Portland *Journal*. He was a blind man with the face of a poet and a saint. He told me that he sat all through the San Francisco convention and whenever Ohio was called in the roll of states, Governor Campbell arose and said, "Ohio casts 48 votes for Governor Cox." Irvine said, "I fell completely in love with Campbell. There was something in his voice besides confidence in his candidate. His words and his intonations suggested an affection as well. That is why I was in favor of your nomination." I had a two-hour visit with this distinguished editor in the course of which he told me how he came to be blind. "If the Almighty were to tell me that I was to have my sight restored," he said, "of course, I would be very happy about it, but I would leave my life of darkness with many a tug at the heartstrings because as I have lived through it, I have seen so much of kindness, unselfishness and helpfulness. These qualities of human character told me how much good after all there is in human nature."

CHAPTER VII

THE WRIGHT BROTHERS

◆

THE WRIGHT BROTHERS had caught the imagination of mankind and there was discussion in the Congress about their triumphs and just what the government should be doing in the matter of making use of the great discovery. In 1909 the two brothers were in Washington preparing for a test flight under official observation. The newspapers would announce that the flight would be made on a given day, but there were many postponements. Wilbur and Orville knew what they were about and they were more interested in the weather than they were in the convenience of lawmakers on Capitol Hill. As the House, in its usual routine, assembled at noon I was asked many times, somewhat sarcastically, whether we ought to adjourn to go out to Fort Myers.

The day finally came for the great event, July 30, 1909. The spectacle will probably never have its parallel in the history of our country. President Taft, Vice-President Sherman and every member of the cabinet, of the Senate, the House and the Supreme Court that was in Washington and able to be present, was there. Of course the public had made its contribution in numbers running into the tens of thousands. The ship in flight was noisy and Orville Wright sat out in front without any kind of protection against the elements. The course was to be from Fort Myers to Alexandria and return. A balloon had been raised at the first terminal for the turn. There was great excitement when the word was given and the propellers were turned over by hand and the machine catapulted over a track through the operation of a series of weights. The ship seemed to have the wings of a bird and rose proudly to a height of about three hundred feet. Soon we could see it circle the balloon. At that point Orville was compelled to lower his altitude in order to pass by the cable attached to the balloon. The ship passed from sight behind the hills on the horizon. Seconds grew into minutes and minutes seemed to be hours. The audience was in great suspense. Beads of sweat broke out over the forehead of Wilbur Wright. In our imaginations, anything could have happened. Finally, the ship broke into the skyline and came rushing to the finish with a speed that seemed tremendous. The distance of ten miles was covered in fourteen minutes.

The Wrights received a bonus of $5000 more than the basic price agreed upon. The machine became the property of the government on payment of $30,000.

I had been living in Dayton almost ten years when we began to hear rumors about the exploits of these two young men; I had never seen either of them until after they came back from Europe about 1908. It is difficult nowadays to understand the incredulity that possessed the public mind. Reports would come to our office that the ship had been in the air over the Huffman prairie just east of the city, but our news staff would not believe the stories. Nor did they ever take the pains to go out to see. In after years Daniel E. Kumler, our very efficient managing editor, admitted that the staff was just stupid in not establishing the fact of the flights. I frankly confess my own share of culpability in missing the greatest news that ever came out of Dayton. It is not much comfort to think that other newspapers were equally negligent and that the general public refused to credit the flights even when evidence had become overwhelming. We began to wake up when we heard of correspondents arriving in Dayton from abroad, chiefly France and England, to investigate.

None of us knew anything of the years of toil, trial and trouble through which the Wright boys had lived. They found that the figures that had been published about air pressure on surfaces could not be depended upon. They built a wind tunnel out of an old box with an internal clearance of less than two feet. Finally this was enlarged to about six feet. At Wright Field, near Dayton, there is now a wind tunnel in which the air is driven 400 miles an hour by a 40,000 horsepower electric motor. It creates a man-made hurricane for testing airplanes. Pigeons were caught by the Wrights and their tails tied up in all sorts of shapes and forms in order to learn something about the rudder. There were disappointments, but no defeats. These boys were made of stern stuff. Their ancestors had been good to them and their dream of flying was never abandoned.

Wilbur Wright was born in Indiana; Orville in Dayton. Their forebears were part of the very early history of Dayton. An interesting ancestor was Catherine (Benham) Van Cleve. She was the first white woman to set foot on the soil of what is now the city of Dayton. Her husband, John Van Cleve, whom she had married in New Jersey, was killed by the Indians about fifty miles south of Dayton. Tecumseh, the Indian Chief, lived at a point on the Ohio River north of Dayton in the vicinity of what is now Troy. He often came to the outpost by canoe and it is probable that Catherine Van Cleve, who by second marriage became Catherine Thompson, was the first white woman Tecumseh ever saw. Her son, Benjamin, was the first postmaster of Dayton, the first schoolteacher, the first county clerk. His marriage in 1800 was the first recorded in Montgomery County. A niece, Catherine Van Cleve, became the wife of Dan Wright. His son, Milton Wright, was the father of Wilbur and Orville. Milton attended a small college in Indiana and at twenty-two years of age was a licensed minister in the United Brethren Church. The church publication of the United Brethren creed was called the *Religious Telescope*. He became its editor in 1869. This brought him to Dayton. Orville was named after a Unitarian minister, Orville Dewey; Wilbur after Wilbur Fiske, a prominent churchman and a close friend of Father Wright. In after years there developed a serious division in the United Brethren Church between the progressive and conservative groups. It was carried all the way to high courts because the title to church property was in question. The father of the Wright boys was a militant participant in this controversy. He was a man of strong convictions, as were both of his sons. They were never obtrusive with their opinions, but there was never any doubt about where they stood. In after years Orville was a prohibitionist, even though most of his friends were opposed to it. Inheritance could have played its part in this, for Dan Wright, the grandfather, had refused to sell corn grown on his farm to a distillery. Orville expressed his feelings in a quiet, dignified way, and there are probably very few people in his circle who ever knew how deeply he felt on the subject.

A great many of our American heroes have not stood the test of the halo. The Wrights did, and in a most impressive way. When they were abroad in the hour of their triumph and kings and queens were at their feet, they never lost their balance. Lord Northcliffe

84

said of them at that time, "I never knew more simple, unaffected people than Wilbur, Orville and sister Katharine. After the Wrights had been in Europe a few weeks they became world heroes, and when they went to Pau their demonstrations were visited by thousands of people from all parts of Europe—by kings and lesser men— but I don't think the excitement and interest produced by their extraordinary feat had any effect on them at all."

Neither of the Wright brothers was given to speechmaking, although a very clever and witty remark was made by Wilbur at a banquet given in his honor after his flights in France. He said, "I know of only one bird—the parrot—that talks and it can't fly very high." Orville once told me that it was impossible for him to speak in public. When we dedicated our Radio Station WHIO in Dayton, a very large company was assembled and the program was broadcast nationally. I said to Orville that the American public had never heard his voice and comparatively few people had ever seen him. He would not only give honor and distinction to the occasion in question, but he would tremendously please the whole country if he spoke only a few words. He said the request was embarrassing because I had been a loyal friend. He explained that when he attempted to put thought to words, he had complete paralysis of the vocal organs. He is an extremely modest man, but modesty alone does not account for his never having been heard in public. Occasionally he attends dinner parties, where he is always interesting, in fact charming. Both boys were blessed with fine minds and the sensibilities of gentlemen.

Their sister, Katharine, was a remarkable woman, well educated and highly respected for fine qualities of mind and character. There was an impression in Dayton that in the struggling days she gave financial support to the brothers out of her wages as a teacher in Steele High School in Dayton. Orville Wright said there was no truth in the rumor.

If anything were needed to discourage the Wright brothers completely, it was the conduct of our own government in Washington. Fifty thousand dollars had been voted to Dr. S. P. Langley of the Smithsonian Institution for the purpose of continuing his flying experiments. That institution was to disgrace itself later by claiming for Dr. Langley, its head, primacy in invention and demonstration of the flying machine. Orville Wright has said to me many times that if Dr. Langley were alive at the time he would have been greatly embarrassed by the unaccountable actions of his successor, Dr. Walcott. At one time in the course of the Wrights' experiments, a man who had been around the field where the Wrights were making their experiments had gone to Washington and sought to reveal what he had seen to Dr. Langley. That high-minded gentleman spurned the suggestion and would have nothing to do with it.

The government not only treated the Wrights slightingly, but ignored their patent rights. During the pendency of the suits brought against infringing companies, the government purchased rival machines built on the precise lines of the Wright invention. Wilbur Wright died May 30, 1912, of typhoid fever at the age of forty-five. I was one of the honorary pallbearers at his funeral and that day I could not resist the feeling that his strength had been spent in seeking to preserve their rights in the courts. His physical resistance was brought so low that he could not survive. I asked Orville about this directly one day and he said he was positive that this experience had contributed to his brother's death. The Wright biography touches upon this in these words, which cannot be misunderstood, "Worn out from worries over protecting patent litigation, the rights he knew were his and his brother's, Wilbur was not in condition to combat the disease."

It will be remembered that the famous test of the Langley machine, after it had been partially reconstructed, took place in the spring of 1915. Immediately afterwards I received from Katharine Wright, the devoted sister of Orville and Wilbur, a letter which is of genuine historical significance. It has never been printed; in fact, Orville says that if he had ever known of the existence of the document, he had forgotten it. Writing from Dayton under date of June 9, 1915, she set down the following vivid record:

My dear Mr. Cox:
I was too worried Saturday morning to be coherent. I had just come from the doctor's and my talk with him had worn me out. Therefore, I am putting into writing the information which I was trying to give you.
The Langley machine—so-called—was tried Saturday morning and the two rear wings collapsed. We had a man there who saw the trial and who took five pictures of the wreck. He was compelled to give up the films, the Curtiss people explaining

that because of "legal complications" they could allow no pictures to be taken. Orville wishes nothing said about it now, for important reasons. Curtiss does not know that Orville knows anything about this.

It is rather interesting to follow up the reasons why the Smithsonian is allowing one of its historical exhibits to be kept at the Curtiss factory for more than a year, to help Curtiss out of his "legal complications." The machine at Hammondsport has never been a restoration or reproduction of the original Langley machine which Langley tried to fly in 1903, nine days before Wilbur and Orville made their first flights. But the amusing thing is that the machine is changed every few months. Still they talk of it as *Langley's* machine.

It is hard to make most people believe that the Smithsonian would let itself be used except for the furtherance of "scientific" ends. I am hopeful that you will understand.

Secretary Walcott *may* have been perfectly honest in letting the Langley machine go out of the Museum, hoping that it could be shown that Langley had produced a machine that would fly, but had been cheated out of the deserved honor because of a defect in the launching gear. It was natural that he should have great interest in honoring Langley's memory. Langley was a warm personal friend of his and his own position as Langley's successor would be more honorable and conspicuous. He *may* have been actuated by the desire to secure just recognition for Langley.

If that was his motive, it seems strange that he took no precaution to see that the historical relic, left by Langley, was preserved, to be shown to future generations. An exact copy could have been made for experimental purposes. But instead, the original machine was allowed to be taken out and changes made in it so that no one can *ever* know what the machine was that Langley built and tried to fly on December 8, 1903, the date of his last experiments. It may be that Walcott does not know what the original machine was and perhaps he does not know that changes have been made. At the very least, he has been careless.

The head of the Aerodynamic Laboratory of the Smithsonian is a man by the name of Zahm, a so-called scientist whose scientific computations, as an expert witness for Curtiss, were proved to be in error, anywhere from twenty per cent to *one thousand* per cent. After Wilbur got through with him, the Curtiss lawyer was so flabbergasted that he said "Experts? D—— the experts. I don't want to see any more experts." This man Zahm is financially interested in the outcome of the litigation. It is to him and Curtiss, who had already been decided, by the court, to be infringing inventors' patents, that the Secretary of the Smithsonian entrusts the historical Langley machine, for the purpose of vindicating a dead inventor. Wasn't that "quaint"?

In the next place, the Smithsonian was trying to get an appropriation from Congress, for this Aerodynamic Laboratory of Zahm's. It is said now by the Curtiss people that these efforts in Langley's behalf were for the purpose of convincing Congress that no mistake had been made when Congress voted an appropriation of $50,000 to Langley, for experimental purposes, for which, as you knew, they were criticised. It was hoped to get $50,000 more for this "scientist" Zahm to spend.

Mr. Wilt sent us the Congressional Record for the day of the discussion in Congress. Mr. Mann said that it had been proved now that Langley was the real inventor of the flying machine and that the Laboratory, named in his honor, should have a liberal appropriation—or words to about that effect. Our congressman rose to the occasion by saying that he hoped that "the young Dayton mechanics" would not be entirely forgotten or something about as forcible and discriminating! It remained for someone in Minnesota, Sharp I believe was the name, to say that he had had some doubts about those experiments at Hammondsport, that the courts had just given a decision, sustaining the Wrights in their patents and that Curtiss, who had been conducting those experiments, was the man who had been making money by infringing the patents. He thought they had better be careful, in their zeal to do justice to a dead inventor, that they didn't do *in*justice to the living. The appropriation failed. It was this incident in Congress that made me say that we often wish you were back in Congress. I can imagine that you would have had something to say, besides making a faint plea for the "young Dayton mechanics"! Now I want to watch up that thing in Congress, because those people in Washington are never idle—my brothers' enemies I mean—and it would be so much fun to blow up some of their clever schemes.

We're not jealous of Langley. He was an honorable man and he tried to solve the problem of flight. He didn't succeed but his belief in the possibility of its solution had much to do with my brothers taking up the study and sticking to it. They have always said that they felt under obligation to Langley and that has been twisted to make it appear that Langley's work was the basis of their success.

All this would have taken care of itself, if it had not been for the fight over the patent. The Court of Appeals, in its decision of Jan. 13, 1915, said, "The Wrights may fairly be considered pioneers in the art of flying and therefore are entitled to a liberal interpretation of their claims." It was Curtiss' hope to stir up public opinion so that he would have sympathy in his fight. He is clever and has *no* scruples. He always gets away with his schemes for a year or two, until it can be proved that he is not telling the truth. Then he turns to some new lie.

That Langley fake of last summer was so raw that it seems incredible that it could have succeeded. Curtiss and Zahm got possession of the old machine, took it to Hammondsport, changed it until they thought they had it strong enough so it wouldn't collapse, called in the reporters who knew nothing about the original machine, told them this was "Langley's Folly," told them that it only failed in Langley's day because of a trifling defect in the launching mechanism, told them that they were about to vindicate Langley who had died of a broken heart because his invention had gone to the Wrights, etc., etc., until the proper psychological effect had been obtained. Then the machine was taken out, run along the water, lifted off for a distance of about forty or fifty feet, at a height of three or four feet, when it lost its momentum and fell back into the water. It wasn't a flight at all—only a hop. Lyman Seeley of the Curtiss company now says that the Curtiss Company never gave out the report that a flight had been made. True, the Curtiss Company did not give out the report. Zahm spent three or four hours preparing a statement for the newspapers, explaining at length how Langley had invented the aeroplane, etc. etc., but speaking very briefly and vaguely about the flight. He was afraid to put that down in writing. The newspaper reporters did the rest. The N. Y. *World* man reported to his paper that "Langley's Folly" had sailed round and round at a height of several hundred feet. Others made their stories a little more moderate, in varying degrees. The *Tribune* man reported that there was doubt whether any flight had been accomplished. But the editors all over the country shed barrels of tears over the injustice to Langley. Dozens of them announced on the spot that Langley had really invented the flying machine but the Wrights, by being skillful aerobats and skilled mechanics had stolen the credit, etc. etc.

Now these editors did not know that the machine was not Langley's at all. No one ever thought of that! They did not know that the ribs were made stronger; that the shape of the surfaces had been changed; that the shape of the propellers had been changed; that the trussing of the frame had been changed and greatly strengthened, that the Langley steering wheel had been taken off and the Curtiss steering gear, including the shoulder yoke, which operated the vertical tail (a part of the Wright patent, a thing Langley never heard of!) had been substituted, that the Langley launching scheme had been given up entirely and Curtiss floats substituted.

I think it important to have a few people of sense, force and resourcefulness understand this thing. It seems to me that when the case comes to trial on June 21st, it would be the right time to expose the fraud.

Sincerely,
Katharine Wright

The two brothers and Katharine, the sister, before Wilbur's illness, had made plans for the erection of their home on a seventeen-acre, wooded tract, overlooking the city of Dayton. They called it Hawthorn Hill. It is a chaste and dignified Colonial house. Orville still lives there, the only remaining member of his family. He spends his summers on an island which he owns in the Georgian Bay country, fishing and continuing his research and experiments. He does not enjoy the best of health because of an accident sustained in one of his first flights at Washington. He maintains a very keen interest in what is going on in the world. He has a retentive mind, and nothing in the development of aviation has escaped his notice or understanding. Some day the part he played in developing the system of blind flying may be told. He is rarely seen in public, but goes daily to his office in the city of Dayton. His intellectual activities keep him from growing old.

On the anniversary of the first flight at Kitty Hawk, which is now known as Aviation Day, the government for years regularly sent representatives to Dayton, where they were entertained at breakfast at the Wright home. On one of these occasions, Henry Ford and I were guests. What happened that morning developed into a good deal of a joke of which I was the victim. Orville had once heard me describe the historic flight at Washington and he asked me to repeat it to Mr. Ford. Lieutenant (afterwards General) Benjamin D. Foulois, now deceased, had been designated by the War Department as one of those to make the trip to Dayton honoring his old friend. Describing the great event as Orville had requested, I turned to Lieutenant Foulois and said, "Did you happen to be there to see all of this?" He answered, "Yes, I was there, I was in the ship with Orville." I think this provoked the heartiest laugh of Orville Wright's whole life. The conversation at the breakfast table, of course, was over a wide range.

At the same breakfast complimentary questions were asked Mr. Ford about certain phases of his life, whereupon I remarked that I had often been impressed with something which I had never heard anyone mention. That was that as great as had been the success of Mr. Ford and John D. Rockefeller, Sr., my impression had always been that the greatest blessing that had come to them was their sons. Neither John D. Rockefeller, Jr., nor Edsel Ford had ever brought embarrassment to his parents. They never presumed upon the position of their fathers. They had never sought to shine in reflected glory. They had no disposition to be breaking into print to exploit themselves. They led fine, useful, dignified lives in their own way. When breakfast was over, Mr. Ford took me by the arm over to a corner of the room and said, "Cox, I have thought about that very thing so many times, but no one until now has ever spoken about it."

I first met Henry Ford in 1913. The Detroit Chamber of Commerce had chartered one of the big steamships of the C. & B. Line and had taken its members and some guests to Fort William at the far end of Lake Superior. All kinds of entertainment was provided, including a political evening. Job Hedges, the brilliant wit and orator of New York, represented the Republicans and I the Democrats. Ford had asked me to come to his factory before I left the city, which I did with Hugh Chalmers, the young automobile magnate who had grown up in our city with the National Cash Register Company. Automobiles had ceased to be tested on the public roads because of traffic problems. There seemed to be acres of the little Fords, painted red with square cheeseboxlike hoods in front, scattered all about the factory grounds. The rear of the machine was hoisted, some gasoline was put into the tank and the engines ran until the fuel was gone. That was the new system of testing. Ford remarked that day, "If I were making shoes, I would make the $2 kind because there are more $2 users than $5 users." Obviously, that was the basis of his whole policy. One prediction which he made, however, was not borne out. He said the great future of the industry was not in passenger cars but in tractors for the farmer.

Henry Ford was one of the most loyal supporters of the Wright brothers. He had been impressed with the magnificent way in which they had advanced against adversity to a great triumph. As is well known, he purchased the house in which Orville was born and the old two-story workshop where the first ship to fly was built, removing both to his Greenfield Village at Dearborn, Michigan.

As the years came and went, the honor of inventing the first heavier-than-air ship to fly, so far as governmental recognition went, had been bestowed upon Dr. Langley, and his creation hanging in the Smithsonian Institution carried a tag giving it this distinction. Scientists generally were outraged. The government as already stated had made an appropriation of $50,000 to facilitate Dr. Langley's experiments, but the struggling Wright brothers were ignored. Langley had attempted flights, but without success. The Langley ship had at one time been taken from the Institution to the Curtiss factory where, as we have seen, fundamental changes were made in it to make it fly; but this was long after the Wrights had made many flights. Orville did not resort to the press in his effort to have the right prevail, but he kept diligently and painstakingly at work. He showed the patience of a Chinese philosopher. It was evident, to those of us who played some minor parts in the effort to have a wrong redressed, that he was battling too for the honor of his brother. In 1918 Lord Northcliffe came to Dayton on behalf of the Royal Society of London to present a medal to the Wright brothers (posthumously, of course, to Wilbur) in recognition of building and flying the first heavier-than-air machine. I was governor at the time and Orville had asked me to preside at the exercises which were held in the Memorial Hall at Dayton. At this very time the Allied countries were in breathless suspense. The Germans and Austrians were breaking through into Italy and there was considerable doubt as to whether the line could be held against them. Northcliffe was very noticeably depressed and at luncheon said to me, "This is the darkest hour in all the history of the world." The recognition given by Northcliffe's visit seemed to be a determining circumstance, but the authorities at the Smithsonian still refused to budge. The director, Dr. Charles S. Abbott, very much of a gentleman, was evidently aware that the truth as officially proclaimed cast considerable reflection upon his predecessor, Dr. Walcott. Loyalty to him compelled silence.

On August 19, 1940, the Wright Memorial was dedicated on the hills east of Dayton overlooking the scenes of the Wrights' first struggles in the air. Colonel E. A. Deeds, who had been a loyal and unfaltering supporter of the cause of the Wrights, presided. At the request of Orville, I made the chief address of the day. By a strange coincidence, one hour before the ceremony started the flash came that the Germans had made their first bombing assault on London. Of course, in reciting the contribution which the Wrights had made to civilization, we were very conscious of the fact that their invention was responsible for the tragedy of the hour.

In the course of my speech I said, "We are still thrilled as we recall the day in the autumn of 1918 when Lord Northcliffe came to Dayton as the representative of the Royal Society of London, England. He brought, as an award of that historically distinguished organization, the Albert medal. The final verdict of the world was thus formally rendered. The gentlemen of the Royal Society, famous for their conservatism and impeccable honesty, made their findings after a most thorough and painstaking investigation. Every fair-minded scientist in the world accepted as conclusive the engraved words on the English medal: 'In recognition of the value of the contribution of Wilbur and Orville Wright to the solution of the problem of mechanical flight.'

"It is a sad commentary that the only taint on honor so meritoriously won has been cast in the name of an American institution by a small group of bureaucrats, the type that has so often done discredit to our government. The pettiness of a few officers in the Smithsonian Institution is to be regarded more in pity than bitterness. It is an important fact that the Smithsonian, founded by private benefaction, derives funds from our government for part of its support. It is a private institution when its agents seek to serve their private ends, a member of the government when government aid is asked.

"It is high time that the Congress of the United States inquired into the scandalous conduct of this quasi-official department. Driven by the irresistible force of fact it recedes little by little toward the

93

truth. But it still stands guilty of distortion of the facts. The day, we trust, is near when Orville Wright in self-respect can restore to the nation as a priceless heritage the old Wright machine, the instrument of man's first flight, and now under bomb fire in England."

I did not know at the time that Dr. Abbott was in the audience. I spoke so plainly about the conduct of the Smithsonian Institution that my words might have implied, had I known Dr. Abbott was there, a deliberate affront to him. Happily, he understood the circumstances. In harmony with the facts, not a phrase could have been changed, though perhaps some might have been softened. This speech was inserted in the *Congressional Record* and attracted considerable attention. Soon thereafter, Congressional resolutions were prepared demanding an inquiry into the whole affair. Orville Wright discouraged this, observing that such a procedure ordinarily prolonged controversy. In his wise conception of the status of public opinion, he must have realized that the bloodhounds of truth were in hot pursuit of fraud and falsehood. This seemed to be the case and the Smithsonian Institution gave up its claims in behalf of the Langley machine and announced that the Wright ship, which had been sent to England, would be given the designation it deserved when it was received at the Institution. There now remains the simple post-war detail of bringing back the ship in which the Wrights made their first flight.

CHAPTER VIII

NOTABLES OF CONGRESS, 1909–1913

WHEN THE congressional campaign of 1910 came, the Democratic cause was moving along at high tide. The Democrats carried the House. In our district the campaign was spirited, and very interesting. Our meetings were large and my personal following had increased. The vote was as follows: Cox (D) 31,539, George R. Young (R) 18,730, Harmon Evans (Soc.) 6275. This was hailed as a record majority and attracted attention over the state. Not an inconsiderable factor in the result was our carrying every precinct in the Soldiers' Home.

Governor Harmon had been re-elected by a plurality running close to 100,000. Some time during the summer preceding the election in 1910, Senator Money from Mississippi asked me how Harmon, whom he regarded then as more than a presidential prospect, was making out. I told him I thought he would carry the state by 100,000. "Well," he said, "if that happens, there isn't much use in holding a Democratic National Convention two years from now. It will only be a formality. Harmon will be our candidate." This seemed to be pretty much the feeling all over the country, but the progressive era was dawning and Harmon was to run into obstacles not then apparent.

The Sixty-second Congress assembled with a spirit of great jubilation on the Democratic side. Champ Clark was elected Speaker of the House and Oscar Underwood was made the majority leader. Both men added to their fame. Congress was exceptionally well managed and there was a fine order of harmony. On the other hand there were many evidences of disorganization in the Republican party. Roosevelt was in Africa, but the bleating of the Bull Moose was heard for the first time. Bryan was present when the Democratic House assembled. Speaker Clark gave a luncheon for Bryan in the House restaurant at which I was fortunate enough to be one of the invited guests. Bryan sat beside Mrs. Champ Clark and their conversation developed an incident which seemed minor at the time but which there is reason to believe influenced future major events. Mr. Bryan himself told me about it. Clark, by this time, was being discussed with great favor as the logical nominee in the next presidential campaign. Bryan remarked to Mrs. Clark, "The Democrats have a great opportunity now for service and popularity. Champ should make up his mind to be the best Speaker the House ever had and to think of the speakership objectively and of nothing else." Mrs. Clark was displeased, saying to Bryan that she had always felt he was not in favor of Champ for the presidency and now she knew it. Of course, there was a suspicion abroad even then that Bryan, foreseeing a probable split in the Republican party movement, was becoming convinced that the fates were spinning the presidential web for him. Bryan was never fully trusted by Clark's close followers after this. Ollie James, a devoted friend of both Clark and Bryan, kept the waters tranquil as best he could, but the clouds were beginning to form for the storm which came in the Baltimore convention of 1912, when Bryan's speech doubtless defeated Clark.

The new method of making up the committees of the House had worked very well and while there were some disappointments, the members seemed to be pretty well pleased with their assignments. I was given a place on the Appropriations Committee and sat beside Uncle Joe Cannon. John J. Fitzgerald of Brooklyn was chairman. Cannon's demotion from the speakership back to the Appropriations Committee, brought about by the great upheaval in the preceding election, was not in the least disturbing to him and he attended the meetings regularly. By long service as a member and Speaker of the House, and by serving in important committee assignments, he knew the affairs of the government as well as anyone in Washington. Many a bureau head, contending for increased funds at the hearings, was greatly embarrassed by Cannon's cross-examination. There was a good deal of partisanship in these days, but underneath it all were finer emotions which did credit to a Congress that had many able men in it. There wasn't a member of our committee but had an affectionate regard for Mr. Cannon. When I left Congress he gave me an autographed picture and on it wrote these words, "To my friend Cox. If he weren't a Democrat he would be

a d——d good Republican." Cannon showed what a great old game-
cock he was when he was unseated as czar of the House. He stood
his ground throughout the day and all-night sessions. It was necessary at one time, an hour or two after midnight, to have him resume
his place in the chair. He had evidently been asleep in his office.
With firm step and resolute manner he walked into the chamber,
collarless, the front of his shirt open and what hair remained much
disheveled. Like an old lion, he shook his mane and carried his colors
to the rostrum.

The heavy majority which I had received in the famous old Third
District had occasioned a good deal of comment in Ohio, in the
press and otherwise, on my availability for the next gubernatorial
nomination. Resolutions in my favor were passed by county committees and the movement was beginning to take very definite shape.
There was no neglect of my congressional duties, but I was tremendously flattered and deeply moved by the prospect of becoming
governor of the state of my birth.

Into my memory of the days spent in Congress the names of conspicuous members of the Sixty-first and Sixty-second Congresses fit
as a background. The list includes the names of many able men. Let
us run through it in order that our readers may have a glimpse of
the human side of these statesmen.

One who held the affection of his colleagues was Henry D. Clayton of Eufaula, Alabama. He was chairman of the Democratic caucus and his name is associated with important legislation. He was
appointed to the federal bench at Montgomery, Alabama, by
Woodrow Wilson. In the early twenties, he was assigned to southern Florida to help clear up a congested docket. One evening he and
I attended together a banquet given by the Florida Bar Association.
William Jennings Bryan was present and in the course of the dinner,
so it seemed to Judge Clayton, ate abnormally heavily, on which he
remarked to me, "Bryan is for prohibition. I am against it. I usually
have two or three whiskey toddies a day and yet I am sure that
there is not a day passes that Bryan, with his large consumption of
food, doesn't have more alcohol in his body than I have."

Richmond P. Hobson, the hero of Santiago, had come into the
Sixtieth Congress. He was a man of unusual attainments but after
leaving the halls of Congress he seemed to become obsessed with
the crusading spirit and spent many years lecturing against nar-

97

cotics. He never lost an opportunity to warn this country against the menace of the Japanese. Even then, thirty-five years ago, he said they were preparing for war against us and that when it came they would very quickly take the Philippines, the East Indies and other islands. He was positive they would also successfully invade Alaska. A member facetiously remarked that Hobson every now and then filled us with the fear that a Jap was lurking under every seat in the House. Hobson made a genuinely able speech in the exposure of Dr. Cook, the fake Arctic explorer. The Peary-Cook controversy was then at white heat and it is difficult now to realize what a large following a fraud like Cook could gather about himself.

Admiral Colby M. Chester will doubtless be known historically as the first person to puncture Cook's false claims. Admiral Chester's son, Colby M. Chester, is now the very able head of General Foods. Cook claimed to have gone to the top of Mt. McKinley in Alaska, 21,000 feet high. One of his lectures, I was told by Dr. John Oliver La Gorce of the National Geographic Society, was attended by Admiral Chester. Stereopticon pictures were displayed. In one of them Cook and another man were scaling the rugged heights of the mountain. Admiral Chester knew that Cook had but one guide with him, so he inquired who it was that had taken the picture. Cook then admitted, in great confusion, that they were laboratory specimens. Remembering this, the admiral entered intensively into a study of Cook's claims of reaching the North Pole. He established, to the complete satisfaction of all scientists, that the observations in Cook's report could not have been made without the sun's standing still for twelve days.

The scientific world had become convinced that Cook was an impostor. The lay mind, however, had not. Cook had continued to go through the country on a lecture tour which yielded him a harvest of wealth. Hobson unwound the whole question in words that were convincing to the public. It was a magnificent effort. He threw himself into it, inspired no doubt by his love for the Navy in which he had been a picturesque officer. He construed the attack on Admiral Peary as an assault on the honor of the Navy. The House floor and galleries were packed and the effort of the young Alabaman wound up Cook's career. He subsequently admitted his guilt and died a disgraced figure.

Oscar W. Underwood had been in the House since 1895, and

was known as one of its most levelheaded members. Always tranquil in thought and speech, he was heard with great interest and respect. He was one of the few members who really knew the rules of the House. So complex and thorny is the subject, as anyone will see who studies the seven large volumes of Hind's *Precedents of the House*, that a parliamentarian always sits beside the speaker. Others who had mastered them were Augustus P. Gardner of Massachusetts (son-in-law of Senator Lodge), John J. Fitzgerald of New York, James B. Mann of Illinois and Finis J. Garrett of Tennessee. Another Southerner who was to become as noted as Underwood was Joseph T. Robinson of the Lonoke district in Arkansas. He also had long been in Congress—since 1903. He was a man who grew with every year and every responsibility, and the country vividly remembers how he literally worked himself to death in the Senate, dying at the climax of a brilliant career.

Among the able Georgia delegation was one man of special interest to me—William M. Howard of Lexington. He was one of the most attractive men in Washington. The Sargent portrait of Edwin Booth in the Players' Club in New York is a faithful presentation of Howard in the prime of life. His fine figure, features as symmetrical as if carved from marble, and wavy black hair, touched with gray, made him a man who would attract notice anywhere. He had read the best of the world's literature and was a ripe Shakespearean student. He rarely addressed the House, but when he did his colleagues were conscious of a fine mind. Later he became a member of the Tariff Commission. His defense of Leo Frank in the famous Atlanta trial exhibited his intrepid courage.

Senator Borah of Idaho and I were thrown together a great deal. We lived in the same apartment building, the old Stoneleigh Court. Neither of us went out much socially and from many evenings spent with him I was impressed by the depth and quality of his mind. He has often been referred to as a "lone wolf." When it was announced that he would speak, the galleries in the Senate were always well filled. He rarely spoke from notes, but the subject to be treated had been carefully "kneaded" in his mind. Important passages were written out and then read aloud in order to see if they sounded well. His great ambition was to be elevated to the bench. A year or two before his death, Joseph P. Tumulty, former secretary to Woodrow Wilson and then a practicing attorney, gave a luncheon for me in Washington and Senator Borah was present. He told me that in his long career in Washington this was the only luncheon he had ever attended away from the Capitol. Important personages were there representing both political parties. In my brief response to the compliment implied by the occasion I said that if I had been elected, Borah would have been appointed to the Supreme Court. The man's eyes filled with tears as he expressed his gratitude. After I returned to Ohio, he wrote me a letter expressing the happiness which he had derived from attending the social function.

Mrs. Borah, whom the Senator called "Mamie," was a remarkable woman, perhaps the best storyteller in Washington. She chided the Senator a great deal about his carelessness in dress. This emboldened him to buy what she designated as a new "cheap" suit. He proudly wore it to the Senate and when he came home that evening he remarked, "Mamie, I was told today I was the best-dressed man in the Senate." Mrs. Borah made no reply and he inquired if she wasn't interested in knowing who had made the observation. "I don't need to be told," she said. "Of course, it was Senator Gore." Gore was the blind senator from Oklahoma.

Borah was a speaker of great power and charm. We differed widely in our views of international affairs, but I always felt that he was a sincere man. After the campaign of 1920 on two occasions when I think it can safely be said that I could have been elected to the Senate from our state, he urged me to become a candidate. He lived a cloistered life in Washington and it is doubtful whether there was a more omnivorous reader in either branch of Congress.

Of several of the Illinois delegation I have already spoken: William Lorimer, whose unseating when elected to the Senate heartened all believers in progressivism and decency; the indefatigable "Jim" Mann; and Martin B. Madden, a highly useful member of the Appropriations Committee. Frank O. Lowden, afterwards governor, was one of the most attractive and ablest men of his time. He should have been the Republican nominee in 1920, and doubtless would have been but for the indiscretions of some of his followers in securing Missouri delegates and but for the fear of Senate bosses that he would make a President they could not control. Lowden had great administrative ability, and as governor showed a rare knack of getting on well with the state legislature. In 1940, when nearly eighty, he made much the ablest of all the campaign speeches against the third term.

Conspicuous in the Indiana delegation was Albert J. Beveridge, whose intellectual grasp made it easy for us to understand how he became a great historian. He had a photographic mind. A four-hour speech which he made on the Philippine question was said to have deviated scarcely a word from the written text, at which he never glanced.

Of the Kansans, Daniel R. Anthony—a nephew of Susan B. Anthony—represented the Leavenworth district. Reserved in manner and speech, he was very popular. Of Victor Murdock's unusual qualities I have already spoken. I shall never forget a speech he made in support of a proposal to increase the pay of railway mail clerks. In graphic language he described the exacting demands of the service—how a man in a mail car in Maine, or Florida, for instance, must know exactly how to dispose of a letter so that it would reach somebody in England, or Oregon, or Manitoba, by the quickest route. He made out so compelling a case that the House approved the increase.

The pioneer Anthonys and Murdocks had a discriminating eye for the best Kansas land. As Victor once said to me, his father rode about on horseback locating the areas where the grass grew high. That indicated fertile soil.

Will Rogers, the humorist and philosopher, told me how his father in Oklahoma had followed the fertile lowlands in staking out his claims. As he put it, "The old man found himself in more than one county and the narrow strip even extended once into another state." This was an exaggeration, but it did illustrate how the old-timers could pick their lands. And speaking of Rogers, how badly we need him in these days! Not many Americans have been so much missed. In trying times particularly, he could turn public anxiety into a laugh. The man was clean of mind and speech. I knew him very well and early discovered that he was something more than a wit. He thought deeply, profoundly and clearly and in no man's veins did more patriotic blood flow.

Big, towering Ollie M. James was proud to represent the Marion, Kentucky, district. He later went to the Senate. As a rough-and-ready speaker, he had few equals and campaigned in many parts of the country. In my campaigns for governor, he always seemed glad to lend his help. He spoke once in the mountain districts of Kentucky. In those days, and perhaps even yet, in the rural sections, there is often found a self-assumed leader of thought. A public meeting gives him the opportunity to rise above the intellectual level of his neighbors. James told me of an interesting episode concerning such a person. He was in the midst of a very profound discussion of an economic question, when a tall man rose in the middle of the aisle in front of him. His head and his unbuttoned shirt revealed a prodigious growth of red hair. James's head, tremendous in size, was as bare as a billiard ball. The question proposed was this: "Senator James, how do you account for the unequal distribution of wealth in this country?" Ollie fired back without hesitation, "My friend, it would be just as impossible to account for the unequal distribution of hair."

Augustus O. Stanley came from the Henderson district of Kentucky. He was one of the best-read men in Congress and his earthly god was John Sharp Williams of Mississippi. Stanley was once asked about the natural eloquence of Williams and his ready response was, "When John had a pint of good liquor, he was fine. Give him a quart and he was divine." From Bardstown, where *My Old Kentucky Home* was written, came Ben Johnson, a tall, quiet man who had been successful in business and loved politics. It was often remarked how his profile resembled that of the bust of Lincoln in the corridor of the Capitol. J. Swagar Sherley of Louisville had genuine ability. He would have gone far in public life if he had possessed the amiable qualities of James.

Isidor Rayner had come into the Senate from Maryland on the wave of popularity which followed his able and courageous defense of Admiral Schley in the long controversy over the naval battle of Santiago. J. F. C. Talbott from Maryland was still serving. He had been a delegate to the Democratic National Convention in 1876 which nominated Tilden, and began his congressional service on March 4, 1879. He was still in the House at the time of his death in 1918. George A. Pearre was an able lawyer from the Cumberland, Maryland, district. We served on the same committee. A bill which I had introduced was referred to a special subcommittee which the chairman suggested should be headed by me. I replied that there was a legal question involved and I thought a lawyer should serve instead. Pearre left his place at the table and came over to me with evident surprise, stating, "I have served here with you for a considerable time and I not only thought you were a lawyer, but a good one." He was amused by my reply that he had probably been misled by my remaining silent and looking wise whenever a legal question was discussed.

One of the most charming men of his time, LeRoy Percy, came into the Senate from Greenville, Mississippi. He courageously stood out against the era of cheap demagoguery which swept that state. He owed his place to an appointment by the governor of the state to fill a vacancy. A graduate of the University of Virginia, he was clearly above the level of political opinion in his state and was defeated at the end of his term. His son was William Alexander Percy, whose book, *Lanterns On the Levee*, attracted national attention. Young Percy would certainly have gone to greater fame except for his untimely death, for he seemed to know the Negro question in the South better than anyone of his generation. In the editorial office of the Atlanta *Journal*, we conceived the idea of having him contribute once a week an article on the problems and future of the South. I made the suggestion to him, but the letter arrived the day following his death.

The mere name of Mississippi brings in John Sharp Williams. I have always felt that the two most scholarly men in the history of the United States Congress were Williams and John Quincy Adams. Williams and Bailey of Texas never got on well together. They constantly clashed in the House and sparks flew when they came to oratorical grips.

An interesting story about Williams was told to me by Joseph P. Tumulty, secretary to President Wilson. When the Senator was getting ready to retire to Mississippi, some of his colleagues discussed the propriety of giving him a dinner as a tribute to his long service and a gesture of their affection for him. The idea probably took root first in the mind of Mr. Tumulty and this was characteristic of his thoughtfulness. He was advised to consult Williams and select a convenient date. When Tumulty went to see the retiring Senator, Williams said, "Your invitation is very flattering, but I have only that one last evening available, and I have already made an appointment. I am going to dine with the old bartender of the Senate. He is a man of fine qualities, and I am not going to break that engagement no matter what the temptation may be." The devotion of Williams to Woodrow Wilson, for whom he fought bravely on the Senate Foreign Relations Committee, was beautiful to behold. The isolationism of the Senate under Republican control utterly disgusted him. When he left in 1923 it was with this scorching remark: "I would rather go back to Mississippi and be a hound-dog and bay the moon than be a member of this Senate!"

In the Nebraska delegation were two men of rare qualities, Gilbert M. Hitchcock and George W. Norris. The lives of the Hitchcock family are deeply rooted in the history of Nebraska. The father, Phineas Warren Hitchcock, was a delegate to Congress from Nebraska before it became a state. He came from New Lebanon, Columbia County, New York, became a full member of Congress upon the admission of the territory as a state and served in the Senate from 1871 to 1877. Congressman Hitchcock's wife was the daughter of Lorenzo Crounse, who served as governor of the state from 1893 to 1895 and as a member of Congress from 1873 to 1877.

Very few men are as companionable as was Gilbert M. Hitchcock, publisher of the Omaha *World-Herald*. He and I were together a great deal in our congressional years and usually lunched either in the House or the Senate restaurant. Joining us frequently was a young man, Arthur Krock, then in his early career, now attached to the New York *Times*. In those days Krock was Washington correspondent for the Louisville *Courier-Journal*. A Kentucky boy, born at Glasgow, he was the one who procured from Colonel Halderman an option on the Courier-Journal Company which he turned over to Robert W. Bingham. Merely guessing, I would say he has regretted having done so, for he could easily have financed the project in his own behalf. If he had done so, he would be publisher and editor of the *Courier-Journal*, a newspaper of great tradition. Hitchcock was graduated in law and practiced for a time, but left law because of the lure of journalism. He made a great paper out of the *World-Herald*. After Bryan's defeat for the Senate in 1894, he employed Bryan as one of his editors. A rift in the friendship between Bryan and Hitchcock grew out of Bryan's failure to support Hitchcock for United States senator in 1899 when a vacancy occurred by the death of Senator Hayward. Bryan supported William Vinson Allen, the Populist, who received the appointment at the hands of Governor Poynter. I once asked Hitchcock which profession helped him more in public life, law or journalism.

He said emphatically that the odds were in favor of the newspaper business. Hitchcock had to battle his way in all his contests. He was elected to the Fifty-eighth Congress, was defeated in 1904, but was successful in 1906 and 1910 and served two terms in the United States Senate. He was a courtly, dignified man, but in his fight against the Ballinger regime in the Taft administration he showed that under the gentle exterior was a fighting man. The exposure of the frauds in the Department of Interior was largely the work of Hitchcock, who was then in the House. He was a convincing and effective speaker, a man of rugged integrity and intellectual honesty and courage. As chairman of the Committee on Foreign Relations in the Wilson administration, he showed conspicuous ability. A great many people at the time felt that moderate reservations to the League Covenant, which Hitchcock was willing to approve, should have been adopted. Hitchcock himself was strongly of this opinion. "If Wilson had consented to let us take these reservations," he said to me, "the ground would have been cut from under Lodge's feet. He would not have been left a leg to stand on, and the United States would have gone into the League."

Lunching with us often and joining Hitchcock and myself through the week ends in golf was Martin W. Littleton, the brilliant lawyer and orator from New York. Littleton had no taste for the details of legislation and like many men who preceded and followed him, he discovered that when one enters Congress, one's prestige counts very little; he must make his own place in the councils and debates of the Congress. In the Chevy Chase clubhouse at Washington, he fell to talking one day about the Thaw murder case. He had been the chief counsel for defense and observed that Thaw came very near being a genius. When he was reminded that there is a very narrow division between genius and insanity, he said the point he wanted to make was that Thaw came close to being a sane genius.

Not long ago James E. Lawrence, biographer of Senator Norris, asked me to suggest a title for what is unquestionably a very interesting contribution to our political history. I told him there was only one that would fit and that would be "The Great Liberal." Few men of our times have been responsible for so much constructive, if not pioneer, legislation. On the surface he was tranquil and yet within him were the forces that everlastingly fought to correct what he believed to be social and economic wrongs accruing from faulty or antiquated policies of government. He was more responsible for the revolution in the House of Representatives which took away the power of the speaker to appoint committees than any other man. During the days and nights that the battle raged, he was as placid as though nothing untoward was going on. He was a member of the Committee on Rules and though there were votes enough —so it was thought—to unseat the speaker, Norris prevented the adoption of a rule which would have brought that about. He said there was nothing. personal in the affair and that he would not subscribe to anything except stripping that officer of the power he could wield over the deliberations of the House through the appointment of committees.

When he was defeated for the Senate, an everlasting reproach against his state, President Roosevelt offered him a position in Washington. The reaction to that was characteristic of the man: "I was the author of the lame duck amendment to the federal Constitution and it is not within me to be a lame duck appointee." Friends and supporters in the Tennessee Valley wanted him to spend his days there and it was suggested that an attractive home be provided for him. He would have none of it, observing that he would go back to the people through whose faith in him he had been permitted to play his part.

There was a very picturesque member from New Jersey in the person of William Hughes from the Paterson district. He was a rough diamond, a fine, rugged mind and an adroit politician able to maintain himself on the floor. Senators from New York were Chauncey M. Depew and Elihu Root. A member of our Supreme Court in Ohio told me of Root's arguing a point of law before that tribunal after he had left the Senate. In a quiet, conversational tone, as though he were addressing a jury without the emotionalism which the jury sometimes inspires in a lawyer at the bar, Root exhibited the best-ordered legal mind that this old-time jurist had ever observed.

In the House from New York was J. Sloat Fassett. He was a boon companion of Frank O. Lowden and was a ripe scholar in Greek. John J. Fitzgerald came from Brooklyn. Reference has already been made to his profound knowledge of the rules of the House. After leaving Congress he had a distinguished judicial service in his home state. Francis B. Harrison came from New York City and was a brother of Fairfax Harrison, so long president of the Southern Railway system. Their father was private secretary to Jefferson Davis during the War Between the States and also a member of the Confederate cabinet. While a member of the Ways and Means Committee, the junior Harrison gave the tariff his intensive study and did a capable job. Harrison and I spent many happy days together in the great north woods. He was a very companionable man. For many years after his service as Governor General of the Philippines he lived in the upper reaches of Scotland, indulging in the pleasures and intellectual pastimes of an old-fashioned Scotch gentleman.

A picturesque member from New York, who was also a corrupt demagogue, was William Sulzer. "Old Bill," as we all called him, thought he looked like Clay. In fact there was a marked resemblance —in dress. His hair was given the roach of the Kentucky commoner. He always wore the long, full-breasted coat of the horse-and-buggy days and the large cravat at his throat which was an exact copy of Clay's. He was a man of inordinate and yet not offensive egotism. He would always come into the House through the door beside the speaker's desk with the stride of Henry Irving. If the galleries happened to be well filled he would in some way get into the discussion or debate then going on. On a day when the House was considering a bill introduced by Richard Bartholdt of St. Louis, appropriating $5000 to erect a monument to Baron Steuben, the Prussian officer who had rendered historic service to Washington in the drilling of our raw troops during the American Revolution, Sulzer proposed an amendment, substituting the name of George Washington for Steuben, and under his right took time to discuss it. He insisted that the cause of world-wide liberty would be better promoted if his suggestion was adopted. A point of order was made against the amendment on the ground that it was not germane. Speaker Cannon sustained it, whereupon Sulzer roared, "Mr. Speaker, am I to understand that George Washington is out of order in this House?" Old Uncle Joe was visibly irritated. He brought down the gavel with a swing of his left hand and said, "He certainly is when he is in the company he is keeping today."

Sulzer became the candidate of his party and the governor of his state largely through the fight which he made against the pogroms against the Jews in Russia. He became the idol of the Israelite voters in his state. Addressing a large Jewish meeting in New York City—an enthusiastic audience—he said, "Wherever the name of William Sulzer is spoken to Jewish people they fall to their knees and thank God for his life." Herbert Bayard Swope, the brilliant journalist and protégé of Joseph Pulitzer of the *World*, was on the speaker's stand. He pulled Sulzer's coattail and reminded him that the Jews do not, in prayer, go to bended knee. Sulzer, undismayed, merely observed, "My good young friend, Herbert Swope, says that the Jews do not kneel in prayer. I want him to know that when they thank God for the life of William Sulzer they do go to the bended knee."

Another anecdote about Sulzer: On July 4, 1913, there was a reunion of tens of thousands of survivors of the Battle of Gettysburg at the site of that battle. The federal government and the individual states had arranged for what turned out to be a historic occasion. We had sent five trainloads from Ohio. As governor of the state, I went with them. Woodrow Wilson came up from Washington to speak. During the forenoon, I was sitting in the shade of trees which sheltered a college building. It had been used as a hospital during and following that great engagement. Sulzer came along and we had quite a visit. In the course of it, he said, "Wilson will be here today. This fellow won't do. He can't be elected and he will not be nominated in 1916. I will be the nominee and I have accepted you as my running mate." I thanked him but my smile I am sure had a significance he did not sense. When Sulzer rose from his chair on the speakers' stand to address the great assembly in the afternoon and went to the front of the rostrum, there can be no doubt that he expected his words to take precedence over the immortal speech of Lincoln, delivered November 19, 1863.

Claude Kitchin came from the Scotland Neck district in North Carolina. Short, compactly built, beardless, he had a countenance expressing great resolution. He was one of the readiest debaters in the whole history of the House. A master of ridicule, he delivered cruel blows in a rich Southern drawl, and with a smile that seemed to soothe the blows that he inflicted. His brother was governor of the state at the time. Kitchin often referred to the fact that North Carolina sent more men in proportion to population into the Confederate Army than any other state. His father was in the Army of Northern Virginia with Lee, and his uncle with Joseph E. Johnston in the South. He told me that as each made his way home after the war ended, they met, singularly enough, at the crossroads near the farm where they had been reared. There was not a building left standing. The residence and farm buildings had been destroyed and they were taken in by slaves who had been born and lived with the family. For several days they existed on parched corn. An able man from this state was Robert N. Page, brother of Walter Hines Page, ambassador to the Court of St. James under Wilson. Page served for seven terms in the House, but declined re-election during World War I. He had lost political caste because of his opposition to our going into it. He was a very popular man and his friends were very unhappy over his experience.

Thomas P. Gore and Robert L. Owen were in the Senate from Oklahoma. Gore had been blind since boyhood from accidents in play and had been a Populist before he joined the Democratic party; Owen had begun life as the principal teacher in a Cherokee orphan asylum. Both were able men whose liberal views appealed to me. Owen, for example, had been a staunch advocate of the initiative and referendum and other agencies of direct government. He was one of the men most active in shaping the Federal Reserve legislation. By a sad coincidence, late in life he, too, became totally blind. From Ardmore, Okla., came Representative Charles D. Carter, who had a very interesting family history. In the Indian massacre of the Cherry Valley settlers in 1778, a white child named Charlie Carter was captured by the savages. He was adopted into the tribe, moved westward with it and remained a member. His descendants finally found themselves in Indian Territory, now part of Oklahoma. Carter was born near Boggy Depot, an old fort in the Choctaw Nation in Indian Territory, and got part of his education in the Chickasaw Manual Labor Academy. His sketch in the *Congressional Directory* showed that he was seven-sixteenths Indian. I found him a very interesting man. He bore all the facial characteristics of his ancestors. When government aid for the Indians or other legislation touching Indian affairs was under debate, Carter grew eloquent in championing the red men. We have heard a great deal about the natural eloquence of Logan, Tecumseh and other Indian chiefs, and Carter possessed it in rare degree.

A. Mitchell Palmer, a handsome and able figure on the floor, had just entered Congress from the Stroudsburg district in Pennsylvania. He had been an expert court stenographer in his time and he once told me that in his public or court arguments he carried in his mind notes made in shorthand. He was said to have declined the Secretaryship of War under Wilson because of his Quaker ancestry, but he accepted the Attorney Generalship. His record in that office was unfortunately very illiberal. But he redeemed himself by his share in the authorship of the 1932 Democratic platform, a splendidly progressive document.

A tall, commanding figure with flowing mustachios was James L. Slayden from the San Antonio, Texas, district. He was of Kentucky birth and was appointed by Andrew Carnegie as one of the original trustees of the Carnegie Endowment for International Peace in 1910. He served eleven terms in Congress. He once remarked that at the time of his first election there were forty-eight counties in his district. Distances were great then and in recounting his experience he insisted that he once hitched his horse at the gate entrance of a farm and walked back six miles before reaching the residence of his constituent. He was well grounded over a wide spread of subjects that related to our public affairs. Serving long on the Military Affairs Committee, of which he became chairman in the Wilson administration, he was intimately acquainted with the personnel of the War Department. Mrs. Slayden, a charming little lady born in Virginia, near Monticello, was famous for her Sunday morning breakfasts. To this hospitable board came men of note from this country and abroad. I have always been very grateful for the contacts thus established. There was a strong political enmity between Slayden and Albert S. Burleson, then in the House, later to become Postmaster General under Wilson. In the campaign of 1912, Slayden was a supporter of Governor Harmon of Ohio. Burleson and Colonel House were militantly sponsoring the cause of Woodrow Wilson.

Slayden and I often walked to the Capitol from the northwest section. One morning we were passing through McPherson Park. Standing beside the monument to General McPherson was Congressman Lon Livingston of Georgia, an officer of the Confederate Army. Slayden was a great jokester and as we approached he remarked, "Lon, did you kill him?" He replied, "I did not kill him, Jim, but I saw him fall. He was a brave man and the spectacle has always saddened me. He got beyond his lines and the only way he could escape was to plunge horseback over a stake-and-rider rail fence. His horse made a perfect jump, but at the very apex of the clearance, McPherson was struck. He was a very able soldier and, if spared, might well have been President instead of Grant, and how much better it would have been for all concerned."

None of the books on Sherman or McPherson give the precise details of how the general was killed. Some of the reference books say that General McPherson was born in Sandusky, Ohio. His place of birth was Clyde, which for a long time was the sauerkraut center of the whole country.

Senator Ben Tillman of South Carolina had about reached the peak of his unpopularity in the country. Subsequently he came to be recognized as a sincere man, possessing many personal and official virtues. The Carthage, Tennessee, member was Cordell Hull, the quiet, dignified gentleman that he continued to be. Joseph W. Bailey, for a long time the idol of his state, was in the Senate. Here was a man who, except for his being diverted by interests and activities outside of his public life, would have risen to an enduring eminence. He had great power as an orator and many said he had as good a legal mind as Webster. I remember hearing him speak on the constitutionality of the reciprocity treaty with Cuba. He had attacked it upon the ground that it was a revenue measure and should have been initiated in the House. He was in the flower of his manhood then and the very atmosphere of the Senate chamber seemed to be charged by the dynamic force of his brain and personality. In Texas, he was hated by his opposition, but idolized by his friends. His friends remained faithful to him as long as he lived. On the day of his funeral the trains coming to the city of burial were crowded. At every station through which these trains passed people from every walk of life climbed aboard to pay tribute to the man they admired. Unfortunately Bailey craved wealth and was careless of the means by which he gained it. Rich corporate interests in New York flattered him, he made an indiscreet connection with the Standard Oil Company and he was accused of using his senatorial influence in behalf of his clients. I knew him well and had a high regard for his intellectual power; to me and others it was a tragedy that he did not devote them exclusively to his public duties and so make secure his place as Texas's greatest leader since Sam Houston. Incidentally, he had studied at the University of Mississippi, and had gained his first understanding of the law from L. Q. C. Lamar.

Not long since, Sam Rayburn, present Speaker of the House of Representatives, and I were exchanging congressional reminiscences. He told me of a conversation with Champ Clark in which he reminded Clark of the many statesmen who had passed through the House in Clark's time and asked him to name the two men whose abilities were most outstanding. Without hesitation, he said that they were Bailey of Texas and Reed of Maine.

Albert S. Burleson, member from Texas and later Postmaster General, was a very interesting character. Obviously he was named for Albert Sidney Johnson, whom he always considered as next in ability to Lee in the War Between the States. He often remarked that if Johnson had not fallen at the Battle of Shiloh, there might have been no Grant in the military picture. He lived in Austin, where Johnson is buried with a magnificent statue to mark his grave. Burleson and I served together on the Committee on Appropriations and I knew him well, both in his characteristics and his foibles. He was a great student of our political history, an intense reader and always good company. He played an important part in the campaign preceding the nomination of Wilson at Baltimore and in the convention as well. In at least one respect he was the Neville Chamberlain of our public life, as he always, in fair weather and foul, carried an umbrella and on most occasions wore rubber overshoes as well. He was very individualistic, as might be inferred by the circumstances of his death. He passed away in the early hours of the forenoon and the burial services were at four o'clock the same day. He did not want a fuss made over him. On reflection, I am not sure but what his conception of the propriety of the last scene was sensible.

The wit of the Texas delegation was Jack Beall. His colleagues used to joke him a good deal about the town he came from—Waxahachie. From his face and manner, no one would ever have suspected his humorous side. All the Democratic campaign books of that day carried a speech made in the House by Beall.

Reed Smoot, prominent in the affairs of the Mormon Church, was a senator from Utah. He was a dyed-in-the-wool reactionary, but one of the hardest-working and most affable members of the upper branch. Coming to Virginia, we found James Hay from the Jefferson district. Carter Glass, whose name is known in most households of the country now with a considerable degree of affection, had been in Congress eight years. He was more responsible for the

Federal Reserve System than anyone else. Champ Clark once told me how Glass happened to become a specialist in banking legislation. When Glass first came to Congress, Clark had advised him to take a place on the Banking and Currency Committee, remarking at the time that it had not been considered an important assignment before, but the country was becoming engrossed in a revision of our entire system of finance. He remarked that Glass would be fully occupied serving on that committee if he went to the roots of the whole question. This he did, and the part he played will doubtless remain the most enduring part of his career. He worshiped Woodrow Wilson, and Wilson had great respect for his capabilities as a statesman and his qualities as a man. In a national campaign he was more dangerous to the opposition than anyone in the Democratic lists. He deserved the homage which the country paid him.

Tall, gaunt, certainly very individual in his personal appearance was Francis W. Cushman, member from the Tacoma, Washington, district. It was he who "floored" and wounded the pride of Charles H. Grosvenor, known as "Old Figgers" in political prognostications and as "The Sage" of Athens, Ohio. Senator Jim Watson of Indiana told me this story. Grosvenor was speaking in the House. Cushman asked a question in good spirit, but it seemed to annoy Grosvenor, who turned on the young member in petulance and sarcasm. Young Cushman fought back. He said, "I am sorry to have incurred the displeasure of the statesman from Ohio. From my earliest boyhood I have had great admiration for him. If I were delving into a subject, I could always find that Grosvenor had had something to say about it. If I went far enough in my search, I would find that Grosvenor had something to say on practically every question that troubled humanity. One time he would be for it and later on against it. He is the greatest 'all-sider' in our history." Grosvenor never got over it. He was particularly irked at the laughter from his colleagues inspired by the rapier of the blooming statesman from the Northwest.

Cushman, because of large lumber interests in his section, had tried to get on the Ways and Means Committee, but Grosvenor had always prevented it. In one of Watson's campaigns Cushman made several speeches. He was a guest at the Watson home over the week end and he frankly admitted why he had given so much time to his Hoosier friend. He related the circumstance of his passage of words with Grosvenor and, recognizing the power of Watson in the councils of his party, had felt that if Cushman helped Watson in his re-election, Watson would help Cushman in gaining a place on the committee in question. Matters turned out that way. When the Payne-Aldrich tariff bill was put on passage, the duty devolved upon Cushman, as a member of the committee from which the measure had come, to address the House. He said that his position reminded him of the story of a man out in the western country. He settled on a tract of land and the only animal he had ever been known to purchase was a brindle steer. The cowboys, however, no-ticed that his herd multiplied. They put up with it long enough and then took the cattle thief in a spring wagon under a tree with low-ering limbs, strung up the noose and prepared for the execution. The final act was about to go on when the suspect said that he thought he was entitled to a word, remarking, "I am the most inter-ested person in this affair, but the least enthusiastic." The tariff bill, as it went through the House, had cut the tariff rates on lumber coming in from Canada, but there was an understanding that the schedule would be revised in the Senate. Cushman, of course, could not reveal this to his colleague, but his position on the committee compelled him to say something.

Doubtless the two most popular men in the Senate of this genera-tion were Pat Harrison of Mississippi and Charles L. McNary of Oregon. It was very different qualities which ingratiated them in the affection of their colleagues. McNary, as it has been so justly written of him recently, was a great diplomat and composed differ-ences between the majority and the minority in such a way as to mark his labors as farseeing and constructive. Unlike McNary, Harrison had a great zest for berating the policies of the Republican leaders, but he did it always with a smile. His remarks in the Senate might well be regarded as observations, casual and otherwise, on current political and economic events. In his committee work he had a rare facility in evening the rough edges of a bill and removing thereby, not serious, but annoying, opposition. He enjoyed the com-panionship of his friends and yet was a very hard worker. He ren-dered noteworthy service in the Democratic National Headquarters in New York City in the campaign of 1920 and was a distinct fac-tor in bringing about the final result in the San Francisco national convention that year. Until his death, a large poster likeness of me hung in his office. As he put it, "He is still my candidate."

114

The "Old Home Farm," built by Governor Cox's grandfather, 1817-20, where James M. Cox was born

Gilbert Cox, the Governor's father, and his mother, Eliza Andrew Cox

James M. Cox, the youngest of seven children, at the age of two

Seventeen-year-old Cox became a teacher at West Middletown.

Cox (left) as a reporter for the Cincinnati Enquirer, *circa 1892*

HON. JAMES M. COX.

MEMBER OF CONGRESS FROM THE THIRD DISTRICT OF OHIO, OWNER AND PUBLISHER OF
THE DAYTON (O.) DAILY NEWS AND THE SPRINGFIELD (O.) DAILY NEWS.

Editor & Publisher, *the trade press magazine, took note of the newly elected congressman.*

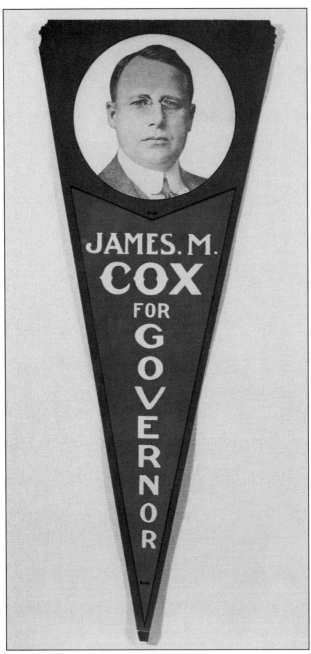

Political progressive Cox was inaugurated as Governor of Ohio in 1913.

King Albert of Belgium was a guest of Governor Cox and the Ohio state government at the end of World War I.

As Governor, Cox (fourth from left) greeted returning World War I veterans of the 37th Division.

Governor Cox's beloved "Trailsend," completed in 1917, was his primary residence until his death there on July 15, 1957. "Tradition has it that this spot overlooking the great Miami Valley was a famous camping place for the Indians.... Reflecting many times upon the pleasure that must have come to the red man at this end of the trail, and being certain, too, that I would live my life out there, I gave the name 'Trailsend' to the place," wrote Governor Cox, pictured there with his wife, Margaretta Blair Cox.

Governor Cox with his daughters, Anne (left), age 5, and Barbara, age 2

"What one has missed who has never lived with horses and known their qualities well enough to love them!" — *James M. Cox*

"My experience [with horses] started with breaking colts on the farm in the springtime, then later owning trotters, which I sometimes drove in matinee races [pictured above], and winding up in the saddle." — *James M. Cox*

The Governor enjoyed visiting the stables throughout his life.

PEACE - PROGRESS - PROSPERITY

FOR PRESIDENT
DEMOCRATIC NOMINEE
JAMES M. COX

FOR VICE PRESIDENT
DEMOCRATIC NOMINEE
FRANKLIN D. ROOSEVELT

When Cox chose Franklin Roosevelt as his running mate in 1920, the two men had never met. Below, presidential candidate Cox (hatless) meets the Washington, D.C., press corps.

Governor Cox was a strong supporter of women's suffrage. 1920 marked the first time women were allowed to vote in a national election.

On the campaign trail, 1920, with FDR

Cox campaigned extensively, visiting 36 states, traveling 22,000 miles by train and delivering 394 scheduled speeches. "Many stops had to be made at railway stations, with the attendant noises which come from freight and passenger yards. It was a common saying that we could tell the politics of the man who was running the switch engine nearby. He was quiet with his locomotive or not, according to his partisanship."

Among 1920 campaign materials were a 78 rpm record, sheet music for a supporting song, campaign buttons and banners.

THE WHITE HOUSE
WASHINGTON

5 November, 1920

My dear Governor Cox:

I hope that you know that no Democrat attributes the defeat of Tuesday to anything that you did or omitted to do. We have
all admired the fight that you made with the
greatest sincerity, and believe that the whole
country honors you for the frank and courageous
way in which you conducted the campaign.

With the most cordial good wishes and,
of course, with unabated confidence,

Cordially and sincerely yours,

Woodrow Wilson

Hon. James M. Cox,
Executive Office,
Columbus, Ohio.

Cox joined President Wilson in supporting the League of Nations, which turned out to be a major factor in Cox's defeat.

To the Sixty-second Congress came Atlee Pomerene as senator from Ohio. In the cross currents of politics, attempts made to stir up a competitive feeling between him and me never succeeded. He was my loyal supporter and I was his. He was a man of great purity of purpose and deeds and labored in the Senate with efficient and conscientious industry. He died before his time; otherwise he might easily have risen to higher honors.

A picturesque figure in his sharply cut cutaway coat, worn in the House and on all occasions, was General J. Warren Keifer. He had been elected to Congress first in 1877, serving in four successive Congresses through the Forty-eighth. He was speaker of the Forty-seventh Congress and here he was back in Congress again when I arrived. He had entered the War Between the States as a private and rose to major general, serving with that title in the Spanish-American War. He had been a close friend of Hayes, Garfield and McKinley and made his way by the sheer power of industry and study. When I met him in 1909 in the House he was seventy-three years old, regular in attendance and vigilantly industrious in looking after the interests of his district, the center of which was Springfield, Ohio. I often invited him to dinner in the old Willard Hotel and always enjoyed his civil and military reminiscences. He was a close friend of the Hayes family. Mrs. Hayes, it will be remembered, was the first mistress of the White House who drove liquor out of it. Keifer said she was a woman of superior mind and fine spiritual impulses who had, he asserted, almost taken William McKinley to raise in the early days of the war. Without elaboration he stated that except for her care McKinley never would have become President.

There was a report, widely circulated once, that President Lincoln had pronounced General Phil Sheridan and J. Warren Keifer the bravest men he had ever known. I asked Keifer about it once and he said that he had often heard of it, but did not know whether there was any truth in it. Keifer died in Springfield in 1932, aged ninety-six years.

All in all, the two Congresses of 1909–1913 in which I sat were an interesting and profitable school of public affairs. We were concerned with public questions of moment: the Payne-Aldrich tariff, the Canadian reciprocity issue, the Mann-Elkins railroad regulation law, the Ballinger investigation and national defense. These years witnessed the eclipse of the standpat conservatism represented by

115

the Old Guard leaders about Taft, and the growth of great new progressive forces—a change which I heartily approved and so far as I could assisted. They witnessed the great split in the Republican party, begun by La Follette and the other insurgents, men whose vision and courage commanded my admiration. I took great pride in the fact that La Follette once went out of his way to commend my course. Seldom in our history have public issues so excited the country as in these years when the Progressives were trying to overthrow Taft, when Roosevelt came back from Africa and began to fix his ambition upon the presidency again, and when Wilson, Champ Clark, Harmon and Underwood were all aspirants for the Democratic nomination. It was exhilarating to be in Congress at that time. We worked hard. The public knows little of the long, tedious, arduous hours that are spent by conscientious members of Congress in the committee room and in anxious study of legislation. Some of us labored up to the limit of physical endurance. But we had our reward in seeing the country move towards more liberal goals.

I should make it clear that my own allegiance had been from the start with the progressive wing of the Democratic party. As a boy I had taken the train to Cincinnati to hear Robert G. Ingersoll. As a young man struggling to make the Dayton *News* a force, I had read all the so-called muckraking literature: the books of Lincoln Steffens, Ida M. Tarbell, David Graham Phillips, Ray Stannard Baker and others exposing the social, political and economic evils of the day. My newspaper activity had naturally brought me into contact with some of the liberal leaders of my section. In particular, I had been an interested observer of what "Golden Rule" Jones and his successor Brand Whitlock were doing to regenerate Toledo, what Hazen S. Pingree was doing in Detroit and what Tom L. Johnson and the bright young men about him were doing in Cleveland. One of these bright young men, Newton D. Baker, became a particularly close friend and in state affairs a political partner of mine.

In Congress I had been glad for the chance to work with the more progressive Democrats. My maiden speech had been delivered within a month after my arrival and while I gave most of my time to committee work and conferences, and looked assiduously after the legitimate interests of my district, I spoke on the floor as often as seemed useful. I have said that I voted consistently for lower tariffs and regarded the Payne-Aldrich bill as an outrage. I was an ardent supporter of Canadian reciprocity. Nothing interested me more than the proper control of trusts and the efficient regulation of railroads. On the latter question I accepted La Follette's idea of the importance of an honest appraisal of railroad values. I took a keen interest in the investigation of the alleged frauds in the Interior Department under Secretary Ballinger and sat right beside Gilbert M. Hitchcock when he was conducting the House fight against Ballinger.

As preparations for the 1912 campaign began, my private hopes were that Woodrow Wilson would gain the Democratic nomination. I first met Wilson at a banquet at the Raleigh Hotel in Washington, where he spoke alongside Champ Clark, Harmon and Hearst, and his intellectual superiority was evident. Publicly, nearly all Ohio Democrats were cómpelled by state and personal loyalty to support Harmon, who would have made a good candidate. He had been one of the best governors in the whole history of the state and his integrity was above question. But Wilson, who was clearly much more in harmony with the progressive trend, had caught my imagination.

Despite my record as a rather advanced political progressive, the fact that I had achieved some measure of success in the business conduct of a newspaper inspired conservative Ohioans with a certain confidence in me. They regarded me as a "safe" kind of liberal. No movement of the time was more important than the remaking of our state governments. After what Tom Johnson, Jones and Whitlock had done for the cities, another group of reformers, including La Follette in Wisconsin and Albert B. Cummins in Iowa, came forward to make state government more honest, more efficient and more responsive to the social needs of the time. For this movement I felt the strongest enthusiasm. It was obvious that no state government needed regeneration more than that of Ohio, so long in the control of reactionary Republican regimes. Its constitution was almost incredibly antiquated in text and spirit; its administrative machinery was full of creaky maladjustments and abuses; all kinds of urgent problems were going untouched. While my second congressional term was drawing towards its close, the opportunity came to me to help bring my own state into the front rank of progress. It was precisely the opportunity that I valued most.

PART FOUR

An Outworn State Constitution

Nominated for the Governorship

Campaigning with Woodrow Wilson

Reforms Bring New Day to Ohio

Pioneer Social and Economic Legislation

The Tragedy of a Great Flood

Defeat and Vindication

A War Governor

First Contact with Coolidge

CHAPTER IX

REMAKING A STATE GOVERNMENT

~

WHEN A state legislature is strait-jacketed by constitutional limitations, changing social and economic conditions cannot be dealt with. It is this sort of thing which breeds discontent and a lack of faith in government. It also tends to the development of radical movements. It provides fertile soil for those who do not want to improve government by orderly evolution. It is not an exaggerated figure of speech to say that our government fields in Ohio were comparable to a neglected farm in the hill sections. As one looks back, he can see how it all came about. We had been a reactionary state, if not a syndicated one. There were evidences of the Mark Hanna machine and its successors in administrative departments, in the legislature and even in our Supreme Court. Recurrently, members of the legislature would attempt to correct conditions in their communities, but if the measure in question did not entirely fit into the blueprints of the outmoded constitution, it was set aside by the Supreme Court. No people ever exhibited finer patience running through the years than ours did. Patience ran out, however, and finally there came a firm and fixed resolution to overhaul our state government completely. It was upon this progressive movement that I came into the governorship in 1912.

Those of us in the movement had but to remind our public that little, if anything, had been accomplished in constitutional change since the convention of 1851. In fairness it might be assumed that at that time the needs were not so pressing. The next convention came in 1873. It was not a representative body and was tinctured with partisanship. What it recommended was rejected by a vote of two to one. A factor in the result, however, was that the convention recommended doing away with the fee system in county offices. This aligned every courthouse with the opposition. Another important issue was the licensing of the liquor traffic. The prohibition element had begun to feel its strength and it used it to good advantage.

The work of the convention in 1873 never took hold of the popular imagination. It was called a lawyers' assembly, which gave rise to the charge that it proposed a technical readjustment of affairs and devoted more attention to vested than to public interests. A majority of the delegates were Republicans, even though the trend was Liberal Republican and Democratic. Grant had been re-elected in 1872, but the very next year things had begun to change. Public resentment rose high because of the Credit Mobilier and the Belknap scandals. Until then the Ohio Democrats were dispirited and discouraged. When they assembled in state convention in 1873, there was so little hope of success at the polls in the autumn that it had been suggested there was no use in putting up a fight. A committee was appointed to take the matter up with Allen G. Thurman, the "Old Roman." He was sitting at home in his rocking chair, in carpet slippers. In thunderous rage he exclaimed that any attempt to bury the Democratic party would not have his support and "by the Eternals, it is not to be buried in this room now." He sounded the war cry of the party, ordered an advance instead of a retreat. William Allen ("Rise Up, Bill Allen") was nominated for governor and elected. This triumph thrilled the national Democracy and helped to set the stage for the aggressive and successful campaign in 1876.

In 1910 both political parties in Ohio had called in their state platforms for a constitutional convention. The spirit of reform was then evident all over the world. It had been manifested in Russia by the creation of the Duma, a parliamentary body of limited powers; in China by the attempted establishment of a republic. In Germany the strong vote cast by the Social Democrats was symptomatic of a desire for change. Lloyd George's reforms in Britain had attracted universal attention. In the United States the Bull Moose movement was gaining headway, and the break-up of the Republican organization was near at hand. Ohio had been profoundly stirred by the revelation of wholesale corruption in Adams and Scioto Counties, about two thousand voters pleading guilty to selling their votes and accepting fines. A revolt against the iniquitously unfair general property tax was also gaining prominence. With Governor Harmon lending encouragement, the 1911 General Assembly passed an act for electing a convention by nonpartisan ballot.

The 119 delegates were duly chosen and met in Columbus on the first Monday in January, finishing their labors on June 6. Politically the Democrats had a majority of the convention, which included two Socialists. One feature of the proceedings was the delivery of important addresses by distinguished men invited in from outside. Governor Harmon spoke, urging that the new constitution contain a clause licensing the liquor traffic. Hiram Johnson of California spoke in favor of the initiative and referendum, woman suffrage and the recall of judges; William Jennings Bryan advocated not only these innovations, but the guarantee of bank deposits. Senator Burton as well as Harmon opposed the initiative and referendum. Both President Taft and former President Roosevelt made speeches which attracted national attention. The convention represented a high level of ability and experience. H. R. Mengert, the veteran state correspondent of the Cincinnati *Enquirer*, said later, "Generally speaking, it was the most inspiring body that has been witnessed in all the years that I have watched affairs in Ohio."

In the end forty-two amendments were proposed and were voted on at a special election in September, 1912, where thirty-four of them were adopted. These changes gave Ohio what was generally regarded as one of the most liberal of all state constitutions. Some of the changes were mandatory, some merely permissive—a fact which made the character of the next administration (which I was destined to head) of vital importance. Thanks to the help of Newton D. Baker and Brand Whitlock, municipal home-rule was written into the new constitution. State-wide primaries were set up. A state-wide civil service system was created. The initiative and referendum, which I had supported, was made a mandatory feature of the government. We often hear that this was intended to be "the rifle over the door," to be used in emergencies and to make the people the sovereign power in fact as well as in principle. It has rarely been invoked, but when it has, good has resulted from it. Reactionary legislatures in the last few years have done some damage to the new device, but I feel certain that future attempts in this direction will fail.

Under the old constitution, a bill vetoed by the governor had to have as many votes in each house as it had on its first passage in order to be passed over executive rejection. In the change made, a three-fifths vote was necessary to override. A change which I had strongly advocated gave to the governor the right to veto any item in an appropriations bill without affecting the remaining sections. Under prevailing decisions of the Supreme Court the General Assembly had no power to pass a mechanic's lien law for the protection of laborers, mechanics and subcontractors. It was necessary to give to the legislature the right to pass laws "affecting and regulating the hours of labor, establishing a minimum wage and providing for the health, safety and general welfare of all employees." Laws of this character had previously been held by the Supreme Court to be void. Full power was given for the enactment of a workmen's compensation law. No power had been inherent in the General Assembly to pass measures providing for the conservation of natural resources. It was practically impossible to remove public officers except upon conviction by the courts. This was corrected, and the change was so constructed that it could not be the tool of petty partisan devices.

A very constructive reform in our judicial system was adopted. The judicial dockets everywhere were badly congested. Suits originating and passing through the lower courts had been taken to what was known as the Circuit Courts and then the Supreme Court. This was changed. The Circuit Court, under the new order, was called the Court of Appeals and no case could go beyond it to the Supreme Court unless a constitutional question was involved. If, however, conflicting opinions upon a given question of law should come from the divisional Courts of Appeal, then final judgment rested with the Supreme Court. The Supreme Court was also given discretionary power to hear any case that involved general policy. Provision was made for the election of a chief justice of the Supreme Court. The practice had been to select this officer under the seniority rule from the members themselves. Civil and grand jury practices were changed. It had been practically impossible to bring a suit against the state without the consent of the legislature. Justices of the peace were abandoned in sizable cities. A woman's suffrage amendment was adopted by the convention but rejected by the voters. A broad primary election system was created and did away with the old-time conventions, under which political parties selected their candidates.

I advocated a further change. Let the state convention recommend candidates for the several offices. Their names would go on the primary ballot as reflecting the judgment of the party in convention assembled with these names clearly designated. Anyone, however, would have the right to become a candidate at the primary elections. This would accomplish two things; it would emphasize the responsibility of the political party, and if the convention made a bad nomination, an independent movement in the form of a non-convention candidacy or candidacies could be inaugurated. In one of the first primary contests a man named Arnold got a surprisingly large vote for lieutenant governor. This was due to the listing of candidates' names on the ballot in alphabetical order. James W. Faulkner, one of the wisest men of our day, remarked about it, "As things are working out, Benedict Arnold would defeat George Washington in an Ohio primary." This led to an administrative change which varied the order of placement of names on the primary tickets all over the state.

It was necessary to amend the constitution to give the General Assembly power to lay down a general pattern of policy and operation in the public school system. It was made clear that local communities could not destroy the unity of a state system. This paved the way for what was, and I think still is, regarded as the most advanced common school code existent anywhere. Sundry state departments were abolished. Power was granted the legislature to pass laws regulating the issue and sale of stocks and bonds. There were many private banks operating without state regulation or inspection. Power was given to control this practice. The rights of women were enlarged. Under the new order they could be appointed as superintendents and board members of those state institutions or any of the subdivisions where the interests and care of women and children were involved. Women could also be appointed as notaries public. State control was granted over the liquor traffic, not only in the issuance of permits, but in the cancellation of them. A civil service system was authorized. The passage of laws regulating and limiting the use of property on and near the public ways and grounds for display posters and advertising was permitted. Greater facility was given for the proposal of amendments to the constitution. Municipal home-rule was given to the cities.

Of course, some vested interests in the state pronounced the work of the convention as the product of radicals. Public opinion, however, was so predominantly in favor of the reforms that the election in September carried overwhelming approval of every important change. The instrument was a creditable production, largely because the convention was thoroughly representative in its membership. Furthermore, the element of compromise entered into the deliberations; there were conflicting opinions in the convention, but they ended usually in constructive compromise. Thus came the new order in Ohio and there are few now who would question the great good that has come from it.

The year 1912 was one of vast political movements, seldom equalled in our history. New political alignments were made. Voters whose forebears would have been shocked by the new political faiths were enlisting under banners not followed before. The Republican party, after four successful national elections, was torn apart and reduced to a state of impotence which lasted for eight years.

The Democratic State Convention assembled at Toledo in the first week of June in hopeful mood. The political omens were favorable. Tickets were to be presented by three major parties instead of two. The Bull Moose movement had attracted men and interests which had been powerful in the councils and triumphs of the Republican party. There was but one opinion as to the campaign lying ahead and that was that the nominee of the Democratic State Convention would be elected governor. Following the adjournment of the constitutional convention, I had spoken for the new charter in as many counties and as many communities as was physically possible. This was largely a campaign of information. The meetings were large and more people than usual seemed to be interested in the changes and reforms which the new order promised. This gave me a very helpful introduction to the state. It enabled me to appear under nonpartisan auspices because the constitutional convention had not been made up along partisan lines, and the new charter was not presented as the document of any political party.

The platform adopted at Toledo harmonized with the progressive handiwork of the constitutional convention. The ablest men in the party were there. Among them were Newton D. Baker, the most active leader of the liberal forces; William G. Sharp, Representative from the Elyria district and later ambassador to France, a receptive if not an active candidate for the gubernatorial nomination; former Governor Campbell; John Peck, a leader of the Cincinnati bar and also a receptive candidate, and Judge Dennis Dwyer, the oldest practicing lawyer of the state. Brand Whitlock, as mayor of Toledo, was in evidence. I found there, in fact, practically every prominent Democrat of Ohio. The counties were called in alphabetical order, and when the last was reached, the convention broke into a demonstration—for my name was the only one presented. Everybody felt that the gathering was naming the future governor. John A. McMahon, dean of the Ohio bar, said in an interview next day, "I regard the nomination of Mr. Cox by acclamation as a compliment of the most unusual character. In the days when a nomination usually meant defeat, there was almost always a struggle for the empty honor. Now when the candidate is almost sure to be elected, all the varied and conflicting interests within the organization have turned to Mr. Cox as the natural leader of the party. Such a tribute is rare, but is well deserved."

In my speech of acceptance to the convention I said: "I stand for a progressive charter, believing that the intelligence, the genius, the ambition and the higher destiny of man should not be retarded by a plan of government long since ill fitted to our needs. If our race is to develop a real genius for government, each generation must play its part in construction. This is not an age for laggards.

"It may be a restless age, but not an unhappy one. We have more schools, more churches, greater resources, as well as comforts and utilities, than our fathers dreamed of.

"It is an age of unrest and why not? It's an ambitious age. The race, spurred on by the greatest civilization in all history, breathes through its nostrils the air of our free institutions and resolves that our government shall be a help rather than a check to our development."

That was the tempo of our whole campaign. No apologies were made for the new constitution. We insisted that it cut the fetters and opened the gate for the adoption of a program of constructive liberalism. Newton D. Baker rendered vast service in this campaign. He and I at that time were often referred to as Socialists, but this didn't last long. We simply bore the brunt of resentment that came from interests which had operated against moral conscience and ethics but under constituted authority for so many years to their own enrichment. We were battling then against inequalities and injustice of the old order when a great many present-day reformers were learning their multiplication tables.

It would be difficult to measure in words the help that came from John H. Clarke, afterwards United States judge at Cleveland and later a member of the Supreme Court in Washington. His unreserved advocacy of our cause was an effective answer to the reactionary charge of radicalism. He was recognized as a just and good man, a profound student of government and of our social and economic questions.

Woodrow Wilson came to Ohio in September, 1912. He, as the presidential nominee, and I, as the nominee for governor, opened the campaign in Columbus. Crowds that assembled to greet him were beyond all precedent in size. In the afternoon at the Hartman Theater he addressed the educators of the state. I introduced him there. In the evening at Memorial Hall, Governor Harmon presented him to a magnificent audience. Wilson obviously was on his mettle that night for he was not only speaking to the voters of the country, but to a distinguished man as well, Governor Judson Harmon, who had been a competitor for the high honor. His address that night will rank with the best he ever delivered. Democrats, he said, see the facts from another point of view than their rivals. To quote:

"They see as clearly as anyone else sees that business must in our day be done upon a great scale, but they know there is a size which is natural and a size which is unnatural in business. The size which is not natural is built upon certain kinds of practices, certain understandings with regard to control which are seldom economical and whose effect is not efficiency. The right and wholesome kind of size comes from natural growth, from the development of a business managed with brains, with the closest study of efficiency, with a sort of statesmanlike knowledge of the markets of the world and that kind of size no wise or well-informed man fears or is jealous of.

"Monopoly is always in the long run weak and inefficient and the leaders of the Democratic party know perfectly well that they are serving the business interests of the country much better, much more intelligently, than the leaders of other parties because they mean to so regulate competition and free the conditions of business in this country as to substitute the efficient for the merely powerful. It is futile to stand for the cause of our present wrongs and weakly to propose to control and moderate the results, and yet this is all that our opponents suggest."

At the luncheon given for him, Wilson sat between Governor Harmon and myself. He seemed deeply sincere in thanking me for the support which I had given to him and said that he had been greatly impressed with the fact that the young men of the party seemed to believe in him. I remarked upon his genius for transplanting what was in his mind into the minds of others in a way that left both understanding and conviction. He replied that that was the very thing he had always tried to do in his classes at Princeton and he had often wondered whether he had succeeded.

A pleasant aftermath of the campaign opening was something reported to me by Mr. Tumulty, Wilson's secretary. When Wilson returned to Washington, as Tumulty put it, he had a great deal to say about the gubernatorial candidate in Ohio, and expressed the opinion that he was a fine piece of material for the future. This was more than encouraging.

If anyone had attempted, not so many years before, to forecast what was to happen in Ohio in 1912, he would have been ridiculed. Here was a son of Ohio, William H. Taft, leading the Republican cause and asking for re-election. As jurist, Governor General of the Philippines, member of the cabinet at Washington and President he had inspired for himself, a native son, universal respect. Now in this campaign the opposition movement within his own party was led by Theodore Roosevelt, the man who had made Taft one of his cabinet advisers. In the opposition front was James R. Garfield, son of a previous Republican president from Ohio. So bitter was the fight between these rival wings that Taft led Roosevelt by a relatively narrow margin. The vote was, Wilson 424,834, Taft 278,168, Roosevelt 229,807 and Debs 90,144. If Roosevelt had received a measurable part of the Socialist vote, he would have led Taft. The vote for governor was Cox (Dem.) 439,323, Brown (Rep.) 272,500 and Garford (Bull Moose) 217,903.

There must have been a much more deeply rooted confidence in the new order in Ohio than we had supposed, and I must have symbolized it. Our campaign had been very astutely managed by William L. Finley of Kenton, Ohio, but without this special enthusiasm for the Ohio reforms I would not have received more votes than Woodrow Wilson. It will be noted that Brown, the Republican candidate, ran behind Taft, and Garford, the Bull Moose candidate, received fewer votes than Roosevelt.

Those who are interested in newspaper affairs will ask how, during all my work as congressman and gubernatorial candidate, my newspaper properties were conducted. Of course I gave them as much attention as I could. I constantly contributed editorials to the Dayton *News*, and kept in close touch with its management even while I was in Washington. It meant much to me to have organs which I could place behind the new progressive ideas of the day. But I was specially fortunate in the conscientious, hard-working and public-spirited manager whom I left in charge while I was absent, Richard B. Mead. He was destined to spend more than forty years working with me, and fully shared my ideals for my papers.

In charge of the news and editorial department was one of the most golden characters I ever knew, Daniel E. Kumler. He came from a family which had made rich contributions to the bar, bench and United Brethren ministry. He was with the paper when we purchased it in 1898 and remained until he died forty years afterwards. He combined the qualities of sound judgment, devotion to the best journalistic ethics and great industry and loyalty.

Following the election in 1912, Congress of course met in December. A Washington dispatch to the Ohio papers carried the news of a luncheon given by Speaker and Mrs. Champ Clark to former Speaker Cannon and his daughter, Representative James R. Mann and his wife, Representative Oscar Underwood and Mrs. Underwood, and myself and my daughter, Helen. The dispatch added:

> Governor-elect Cox received a great ovation when his name was reached on the roll call in the House Monday. There was tremendous applause on both sides of the chamber, Republicans (regular and progressive) joining with the Democrats in signifying their pleasure at the honor he has received at the hands of the people of Ohio.
>
> One of the leaders of the demonstration was the Republican floor leader, Mr. Mann, who afterwards led a procession from his side of the House to congratulate the governor-elect personally on his promotion to the public service.
>
> Speaker Clark, wielding his emblem of order with ever-increasing force, succeeded in breaking two gavels before he had brought the enthusiastic session to a close.

In my incessant speechmaking in Ohio, I had taken the position that the next legislature should give the new constitution complete compliance; that it should put into effect not merely the mandatory amendments, but the permissive powers. Now, as governor, I was to be faced with the task of seeing that the legislature did just this. Mine was the chief responsibility for putting our improved form of government into complete and efficient operation. Fortunately, the spirit of the Democratic party in the state—and of many Republicans—was one of ardent liberalism. We were eager to turn a bright new page.

CHAPTER X

THE CAMPAIGN OF 1912

◆

OHIO FIGURED very prominently in the national elections of 1912. In fact, as soon as the voting began, from our state came the presentation of an issue which, in a sense, determined the nomination of Woodrow Wilson. At the Ohio Democratic convention a resolution was passed applying the unit rule, which bound to Governor Harmon every delegate selected at large and those in the congressional districts. In Cleveland the delegates had been elected as Wilson men. Newton D. Baker, in a very logical and eloquent appeal to the national convention, contended that neither in ethics nor precedent could the will of the state convention be visited upon the delegates from districts where the Democratic voters had plainly expressed their wish. It was one of the greatest efforts of Baker's career. At that phase of the proceedings, Wilson doubtless did not have a majority of the convention, so it must be assumed that Baker's plea carrying the convention prevailed with some anti-Wilson delegates who were moved more by their conception of broad democratic principles than by their presidential preference. Obviously this very adversely affected the chances of nominating Governor Judson Harmon.

Judson Harmon was a man of large physical and mental structure. I first met him and grew to know him well when I was a young reporter on the Cincinnati *Enquirer*. He was a member of the law firm of Harmon, Hoadly, Colston and Goldsmith. The Hoadly member of the firm was the son of a former governor, the Honorable George Hoadly. Serving on the *Enquirer*, I was in Harmon's office frequently. Neither Mr. Harmon nor I could, by any sort of inspiration, have foreseen that the eminent lawyer should become governor of Ohio, to be succeeded by the young reporter who came to his office for news.

It would be unfair to Judson Harmon to assert that he was not a constructive liberal. However, he was not in step with all of the elements creating the swift, progressive pace that was then on. He went before the Ohio constitutional convention in the early part of 1912 and made a speech in opposition to the initiative and referendum. From that hour he had no chance of being nominated for President, for this precipitated the active opposition of William J. Bryan. Whether this was only a culminating circumstance in Mr. Bryan's mind, we do not know. Bryan knew that Harmon, as a member of the Cleveland cabinet, had not supported his candidacy in 1896, but Harmon had risen to full stature as a presidential figure by his demonstrated executive and administrative capacity and without some specific act upon the part of Harmon, Bryan in all probability could not have influenced any sentiment against the distinguished Ohioan. After Harmon's speech to the constitutional convention, however, Bryan could logically oppose him upon broad grounds of principle.

It is doubtful whether any national convention ever witnessed anything comparable to Bryan's dramatic speech against the alleged power of Wall Street interests in the convention at Baltimore. He singled out Thomas Fortune Ryan, long a figure in large financial operations in this country, as a symbol of the force which he felt was menacing the future of the party. It was a bitter invective which Bryan delivered and for a day or two it looked as if he had spoiled what had seemed a certain chance of Democratic success. There can be little doubt that this attack defeated Champ Clark. The votes in the convention, alleged by Bryan to be a part of a conspiracy, were being cast in the main for Mr. Clark. Any inference that Champ Clark, if nominated, would have been influenced in the slightest by vested interests was an aspersion against the character of an honest man. Clark was greatly embittered by what Bryan did and also by the failure of the convention to nominate him after he had received a majority vote.

After Wilson was nominated, Bryan—so Ollie James told me at the time—called James on the telephone, requesting that he ask Clark to accept the vice-presidential nomination. The old warrior from Missouri replied, "Yes, I will, if Bryan addresses the convention and makes a public apology to me."

While state primaries were being held for the election of delegates preliminary to the national convention of 1912, it was often said that Champ Clark injured his chances by a statement made when Canada was about to vote on the Reciprocity Treaty negotiated between that country and ours during the Taft administration. Mr. Clark said publicly that he hoped to see the day when the American flag would float over every inch of the British North American territories. This, many believed, influenced the negative verdict in Canada. After Clark had received the majority vote in the Baltimore convention, his leaders pleaded with Judson Harmon to start throwing his strength to Clark. This Harmon refused to do. He was very much offended because the Clark forces had permitted some of their votes to support the claim of Newton D. Baker that certain district delegates pledged to Wilson in the primary could not be bound by the unit rule adopted by the Democratic State Convention in Toledo which had tied up the entire delegation for Harmon. Recently, H. R. Mengert of the Cincinnati *Enquirer*, who was in close contact with the Ohio delegation during the Baltimore convention, expressed the opinion that this had a great deal of bearing on the nomination of Wilson. His view was that Harmon was naturally more inclined to Clark than to Wilson and if the Harmon votes in the Ohio delegation had been cast for Clark after he received a majority of the delegates, Clark in all probability would have been nominated. The Harmon managers had a feeling that the Clark strategists, in supporting Baker's plea, thought the time had come to ease Harmon out of the picture. At the moment that seemed the expedient thing to do, but it turned out the other way.

CHAPTER XI

A LIBERAL'S OPPORTUNITY

◆

JANUARY 13, 1913, might have shocked a superstitious mind. That was the inaugural date. When I left Dayton Sunday evening, a steady rain was pouring down. It was a sad picture when we arrived in Columbus. Flags and bunting were everywhere. Drooping and wet, they seemed to take on a despondent view of the coming event. Inauguration day, however, dawned clear and crisp and beautiful. The crowds were tremendous. The inaugural parade had been perfected with great care and formed a beautiful pageant. Our distinguished former governors, Campbell and Harmon, were present, as was Newton D. Baker. A future governor, John W. Bricker, marched with the State University cadets.

The oath of office was delivered in the presence of a representative audience in the rotunda of the historic, old, solid stone State house. It had been the practice through the years for the inaugural address of the governor to include recommendations to the General Assembly. In view of the vast legislative program confronting us in compliance with the new constitution, that would have been impractical. I delivered the message to the two houses the next day.

To become the chief executive of a great commonwealth, the state of my birth, brought me a deep emotional reaction. About us everywhere were monuments perpetuating the memory of our great military and civil heroes—men whose works and wisdom had given us a glorious past and supplied bases useful to the projects demanded by modern needs. All of this planted deeply in my consciousness a sense of the responsibility of applying the new state constitution and creating a new pattern of government. From this understanding must have come these words in my inaugural address:

"We are entering upon a new day. The evolutions and processes of time are working great advances in every activity of man. The forces of human intelligence have carried us to a point of higher moral vision, and it would have been a distinct anomaly of history if government had not been carried on in the progress of the time. It requires considerable faith in the righteousness of a cause to turn face from the old order of things, mindful that in the plans and policies of government about to be adopted are involved the hopes and aspirations, the happiness and general welfare of five million human souls.

"I sense therefore the sublime responsibility of this hour."

The progressive movement in our state had come from the needs of the day. That it was not prompted by an impulse of impatience is evidenced by another passage: "We reverence the works of our fathers, and seek to prove ourselves the worthy sons of worthy sires, by making a great development in our time as they made in theirs. Ours is not the creed of the cynic, looking with scorn upon the institutions of yesterday. Civilization is simply a relay race, and unless we take it up with the freshness of spirit with which our fathers began it, the generation is in a condition of certain decay. Mistakes will be made, because government is the creature of man. But if civilization from its beginning had followed the course of least resistance and not approached uncertainty with experimentation, this old world of ours would present a far different aspect."

The message to the Assembly made it clear that its members could not shirk the task which the sovereign power of the people had imposed. Of the thirty-four amendments to the constitution, part went into effect automatically. Others granted the legislature discretionary authority, while a third portion was mandatory and was to be regarded as a command from the electorate. In this connection I said, "There can be no justification for any departure from the intent of these amendments in the detail of legislative compliance. Progressive government, so-called, which means in its correct understanding constructive work along the lines pointed out by the lamps of experience and the higher moral vision of advanced civilization, is now on trial in our state. Every constitutional facility has been provided for an upward step and Ohio, because of the useful part it has played in the affairs of the country, is at this hour in the eye of the nation."

Attorney General Timothy S. Hogan and his assistants rendered fine service. One of his aides, Frank R. Davis, had a mind of crystal clarity in legal matters. We also took the best advice of outside experts that we could get. It was obvious that we had much to learn from Wisconsin, whose progressive experiments I had watched appreciatively. I induced John R. Commons, a public servant of the highest type, and Charles H. McCarthy to come from Madison to Columbus to give us assistance on various points. Nor did I fail to consult with some of the best men on the faculties at our state universities: Ohio State at Columbus, Ohio University at Athens and Miami University at Oxford.

We employed an expert draftsman to be constantly at the call of members of the Assembly and to be used primarily in drawing up measures dealing with provincial conditions. This avoided any possibility of conflict with existing laws or objections that might be raised in test cases before the courts. A few years ago Averell Harriman, now ambassador to Great Britain, remarking about the progressive movement in Ohio, stated that he had heard Raymond Moley on one occasion call to the attention of Franklin D. Roosevelt, who was then President-elect, just what had been done in preparation for our legislative program. That this was not done in Washington was probably the result of the overwhelming weight of responsibilities that fell upon Mr. Roosevelt at the very outset of his administration. Students of governmental affairs will probably agree that it might well have been adopted because there were bills presented in both the Senate and the House whose details had to be filled in, so hastily were they drawn.

In my message, the observation was made that, regardless of the justice of laws enacted and of good intentions generally which lay behind them, thought must be given to our administrative personnel. We found many departments of the state government dealing with the same subjects and responsibility. There was conflicting jurisdiction and too much lack of the system and efficiency to be found in private or corporate industry. To head these commissions we appointed men versed in the theory of government and, to serve with them, others who had had practical experience. We have heard criticism of college professors and doctrinaires in administrative capacities. We made extensive and gratifying use of our state universities, but largely in survey work. The scholars were more useful in research than in administrative tasks but they did make a valuable contribution to our work.

We lost no time in presenting to the Senate a draft of the Workmen's Compensation Law. The author was William Green, then a senator from the Coshocton district, now the head of the American Federation of Labor. Hearings were conducted in the Senate chamber at night and the members of the appropriate committees in both houses were in attendance. This procedure was adopted not only to save time, but to afford ample quarters for the meetings and make it possible for every class of our citizenship to attend. The opposition came from the liability insurance companies. They charged paternalism in the creation of a state insurance fund to be administered by the state. I insisted that meting out justice to the injured workman and to the dependents of those who lost their lives in industry constituted a trust too sacred to be assigned to any corporation, be it insurance company or otherwise. It was provided, however, that any corporation of ample resources could deal directly with its employees, subject always to the scrutiny and control of the state. This was a pioneer piece of legislation and students of the subject say to this day that it is a model instrument.

Many manufacturers were heartily in favor of the law and so expressed themselves at the hearings. A wide public interest was shown by the attendance of citizens. During the course of drafting this law the men assigned to the task had numberless conferences with representatives of labor and of capital and with men who had made a study of social legislation. Out of these meetings had come a measure which we felt would easily overcome any form of opposition that might be brought against it in the House or Senate. Highly appropriate is a reference to the labors of Daniel J. Ryan, general counsel of the Ohio Manufacturers' Association. He was and is still known, years after his death, as a writer and historian of exceptional worth. His task was not easy at the outset because many members of the association had joined the opposition. At that time Don C. Seitz, of the editorial staff of the New York *World*, made extensive inquiry into the character of the legislation which we were enacting. He approved it, but criticized the New York plan. All of this came back to my mind not long ago when a leading editorial in the New York *Times* vigorously contended that fundamental changes should be made in the existing statute in that state.

The Ohio law, long after its enactment, continued to be a matter of widespread interest. In January, 1920, the Ohio State Archaeological and Historical Society requested H. R. Mengert, the veteran journalist, to prepare a document showing the origin of the law, the conditions which gave it birth, the opposition which it provoked and the long contention in the courts. It is a document of great merit and I am advised that it is on file in practically every state library in the country. It brings into very clear outline the whole picture of events. He asserts that it has "been looked upon as the very embodiment of what Theodore Roosevelt called social justice, that it is being copied in other states of the Union and that King Albert of Belgium, upon the occasion of his visit to Ohio, pronounced it one of the greatest pieces of legislation upon the statute books of any country. It immensely improved the relations between employers and employees. The praise of its authors and its friends has been sung by the injured and the widows and the orphans. It stands as a vindication of the great principle that the plastic instrument of democratic institutions can be remodelled to suit changing needs and conditions. Directly and indirectly, it probably affects a larger number of people than any other piece of legislation on the statute books of Ohio."

There had been great unrest in our industrial centers growing out of injustices under the old laws which had been passed when we were an agrarian state. They had been copied from the civil law of England. England had abandoned them in the course of time, yet Ohio and other American states still clung to the old rules. If a workman was killed, his dependents, and if a workman was injured, he himself, sought damages in the courts. There he was confronted with the three common law defenses which ran in favor of the employer. First, if injury or death ensued because a fellow workman was careless, then damages could not be awarded. That was called the fellow-servant rule. Second, if the employee, in a moment of lapsing precaution, were caught in machinery and injury or death occurred, then no compensation could be given because of what was called contributory negligence. Third, if a workman, in the course of his employment, entered upon a hazardous task and death or injury occurred, no damages could be exacted because of what was called assumption of risk.

A case in point may be found in an incident which occurred in the sugar-growing country of northwest Ohio. Gas had generated in one of the large vats or reservoirs and two or three men working there were rendered unconscious. A fellow workman went to their rescue. He hoisted them into the fresh air in time to save them, only to fall back himself and die, a victim of his own bravery and self-sacrifice. His widow went to court for damages. She was not opposed by her employer, but by a liability insurance company which had insured the employer against damages. The attorney for the defense cited the assumption-of-risk rule and the judge did as he was compelled by the law to do, take it from the jury and render a verdict against the widow. Such things happened all over our state. We had become a vast industrial area and the accumulation of so much injustice developed a tremendous public protest.

It was well said, "Attacks on the courts multiplied and the judicial ermine lost the respect which it once held." A further disgraceful development under the old order was the delay in the courts. One of the evidences of this was the ferocity with which, in 1913, the improved Workmen's Compensation Law was attacked. One of those who was loudest in the attack chanced himself to have been a Supreme Court justice during the unfavorable years of the "nadir of the judiciary." When attention was called to the fact that one of the personal injury cases in which he concurred was in the courts for about twenty-one years, or nearly a generation, and was finally dismissed because all parties in interest save the corporation had passed into eternity, his criticisms ceased.

In street-corner meetings soapbox orators went further than denouncing the courts. They contended that this was but a symptom of bad government generally. It afforded fruitful soil for the planting of the seeds of overthrow. In the administration of Judson Harmon, a beginning had been made in affording compensation for personal injury cases, but its scope was very limited. Employers participated in the plan voluntarily. The project demonstrated its virtue, but it could not go far because the old constitution did not permit the passage of a compulsory workmen's compensation law.

One of the very first participants in the voluntary plan was Harvey E. Firestone, who entered his company, the Firestone Tire and Rubber Company of Akron. This was but one instance of the farseeing humanitarian and constructive qualities which made Mr. Firestone one of the outstanding men of his time.

In discussing the proposal of a compulsory measure, Mr. Mengert, in his able document, says, "Succeeding to the governorship in January, 1913, Mr. James M. Cox presented a clear idea of the entire plan. His inaugural message is a landmark in the history of the law." In this statement to the General Assembly on this important subject I made the following remarks: "It would certainly be common bad faith not to pass a compulsory workmen's compensation law. No subject was discussed during the last campaign with greater elaboration, and it must be stated to the credit of our citizenship generally that regardless of the differences of opinion existent for many years, the justice of the compulsory feature is now admitted. Much of the criticism of the courts has been due to the trials of personal injury cases under the principles of practice which held the fellow-servant, the assumption-of-risk and the contributory-negligence rules to be grounds of defense. The layman reaches his conclusion with respect to justice along the lines of common sense, and the practice in personal injury cases has been so sharply in conflict with the plain fundamentals of right that social unrest has been increased. A second phase of this whole subject which has been noted in the development of the great industrialism of the day has been the inevitable animosity between capital and labor through the ceaseless litigation growing out of these cases. The individual or the corporation that employs on a large scale has taken insurance in liability companies, and in too many instances cases which admitted of little difference of opinion have been carried into the courts. The third injustice has been the waste occasioned by the system. The injured workman or the family deprived of its support by accident is not so circumstanced that the case can be contested with the corporation to the court of last resort. The need of funds compels compromise on a base that is not always equitable. Human nature many times drives sharp bargains that can hardly be endorsed by the moral scale. In the final analysis the costs and attorney fees are so heavy that the amount which finally accrues in cases of accident is seriously curtailed before it reaches the beneficiary. These three considerations clearly suggest the lifting of this whole operation out of the courts and the sphere of legal disputation. And then there is a broader principle which must be recognized. There is no characteristic of our civilization so marked as the element of interdependence as between social units. We are all dependent upon our fellows in one way or another. Some occupations, however, are more hazardous than others, and the rule of the past, in compelling those engaged in dangerous activities to bear unaided the burden of this great risk, is not right. An objective to be sought is the fullest measure of protection to those engaged in dangerous occupations, with the least burden of cost to society, because after all the social organizations must pay for it. The ultimate result of this law will be reduction in death and accident, because not only the humanitarian but the commercial consideration will suggest the necessity of installing and maintaining with more vigilance modern safety devices."

Some time after the law had been passed, I called on President Woodrow Wilson in the White House. He made a very complimentary reference to the measure. I told him of the delegations of manufacturers who had been swept into my office under the propaganda of the liability insurance companies and of my difficulty in finding a single one of them who had read the law. Mr. Wilson then remarked, "That is precisely what happened here when so much opposition was made to the Federal Reserve Act. Many bankers came to the White House to voice their protests. Whenever they came, I inquired whether the bill, as perfected, had been read. I was unable to find a single man who would even claim he had read it."

It would be a foolish man who would now make any attempt in Ohio to impair or distort the compensation law. We were fortunate in the personnel of the commission which administered it—Wallace D. Yaple, an able lawyer from Ross County, Thomas J. Duffy, now an attorney-at-law in Columbus and a product of the labor movement, coming from the pottery fields of eastern Ohio, and Morris Woodhull, a manufacturer. Thus we had a lawyer, a very able labor leader and a representative of industry. The finest tribute ever paid to this law was a dramatic incident which attracted attention all over the country. The state line between Ohio and Pennsylvania ran through a manufacturing plant. A workman one day was badly injured. He was paralyzed from his hips down, but his mind was clear and he had strength in the muscles of his arms. His machine was in Pennsylvania. He reached out, took hold of a lathe and pulled himself across the state line from Pennsylvania into Ohio. The case came to me and I ordered an award made to him.

The compensation law was not long in operation before two striking developments were apparent. The rates applied to employers were to be influenced in considerable degree by the number of accidents occurring in the plant. It became the part of good business, therefore, in reducing operating cost of a corporation, to apply safety devices for the preservation of life and limb. Then, too, the judicial dockets over the state cleared up automatically because personal injury suits were tremendously reduced in number. These two beneficent results, added to the common justice of compensation for injury or death, attracted wide public notice and brought general commendation of the new order of things. Liability insurance companies, however, continued their opposition. Within the ninety-day period following the enactment of the law as prescribed in the new constitution, the Equity League, so-called, was organized by these companies for the purpose of carrying the new instrument to a vote of the people. This procedure involved a petition for the submission of the question, signed by a stipulated number of voters. In a number of instances, the circulators of these petitions were chased out of factories by the workmen. Then petitions were manufactured by writing in fictitious names and the forging of others. Investigation revealed the frauds and the Secretary of State, Charles A. Graves, rejected the petition. The question of the legality of this action was carried to the Supreme Court, which held that the officer had acted within the implied discretion vested in him.

Then came a long line of litigation upon one pretext or another. From time to time individual and specific provisions of the law were attacked. Attempts were made to procure the removal of the administrative officers vested with the authority to enforce the law. Then an attack was made upon the actuarial branch of the department. We had the compensation fund carefully audited and found it was solid as a rock. In due time all of this told us the need of completely cutting out any participation by the liability insurance companies. This ended what had been an assault upon the law from every angle and took the liability companies out of the politics of our state. In the campaign of 1918, after our victory was complete, William G. Wilson, the active political head of the insurance movement against me in 1914, came to me with the surprising statement that he intended as an individual to support me, for the reason, as expressed by him, that I had never lied to him.

The rural picture in our state has been much changed. This has been occasioned largely by bringing modern facilities of education to the homes of the younger generation. The history of this change is interesting, as the Ohio venture received considerable attention throughout the nation. The new constitution gave wide powers to establish a fixed standard of education. This was emphasized by these words in my message to the Assembly:

"If the police power of the Commonwealth is to be exercised for the prevention of crime, the protection of property, the preservation of human rights, the prevention of disease and the conservation of public health, then public policy certainly demands lodgment of positive power in the same hands as a guarantee against sectional atrophy or neglect in our educational system."

Attention was called to the fact that Ohio had no uniform school system. Instead, we had a variety of school systems. We suggested that no legislation be passed without a complete investigation of the whole subject. This phase of the situation was epitomized in these words: "If a survey is made in Ohio there will be found such a number of school systems as to index clearly the disorders and incongruity of our present archaic structure."

Pursuant to the plan outlined, a committee consisting of W. L. Allendorf of Erie County, Edith May Campbell of Hamilton County and Oliver J. Thatcher of Clinton County was appointed to make the survey. William H. Allen of the Municipal Research Bureau of New York, who had conducted a like research in Wisconsin, was requested to send to our state an expert in this sort of work. He came in the person of Horace L. Brittain. The survey extended into every county, particular attention being given to the common schools in the country districts.

Their research consumed considerable time and every condition of neglect, provincial and otherwise, was revealed. In order that there might be a complete state-wide understanding of the report of this committee, we set in motion a project by public proclamation that brought impressive results. In it I said:

"There are no two opinions as to the necessity of creating in the minds of our people a thorough awakening on the subject of community life and a modern school system. There is a common conviction also that the remedy can be largely worked out through the school organization. I am so impressed with the opportunity for good to be wrought that the power and influence of the executive department of our Commonwealth is invoked for the purpose of inducing our citizens to lay aside for one day the cares and activities of social, business and professional life, reflect on the dignity and importance of our common school system and analyze the conditions revealed by the survey recently made, in the hope that the legislative changes to be made can voice the desire of every community, which is the only guarantee that correction will be state-wide.

"It is therefore suggested that Friday, November 14, 1913, be observed by every school district in Ohio as School Day, and that teachers, pupils, parents and patrons assemble during the afternoon, and particularly the evening. Speakers will be supplied and literature prepared, with such general supervision by the Superintendent of Public Instruction and the School Survey Commission that conditions throughout the state will be known and remedies can be suggested. Nothing can be more wholesome than adding to this an historic review of the origin and function of our school system.

"What an inspiration will be given the whole movement when the light burns in every schoolhouse in Ohio on the evening of November 14! What a spur it will be to community life to have assembled at the same hour four thousand community meetings at the shrine of the local schoolhouse!

"It is further suggested that an educational congress be held in Columbus on December 5 and 6, 1913, and that the community meetings select lay delegates to the congress. The Teachers' Institute organization will designate delegates from the teaching forces within the counties.

"We ask that mayors of municipalities supplement this proclamation with like official action, and that the fullest measure of cooperation be given by boards of education, teachers' institutes, the Grange, women's clubs, mothers' clubs and labor and civic organizations.

"Let it be a day of genuine awakening. The necessity and opportunity of the hour call for it."

This took hold of the imagination of our people. On the night of November 14, every countryside seemed on the move. The little schoolhouses were lighted up with kerosene lamps. The hope of better things for her children was planted in the heart of many a mother. Some of these meetings revealed that the school buildings had not been opened for any kind of public meetings within a generation. In one instance inquiry was made as to why a flag was not

145

flying over the structure. It developed that there was one, but it was in the basement, covered with cobwebs.

The capital city of Columbus will be a long time forgetting the coming together of the thousands of delegates to the meetings of December 5 and 6, 1913. In all my experience I never saw an assembly of people that moved me so much. Every section—city, village and farm—was represented. From Cincinnati came Dr. John M. Withrow, eminent physician and president of the board of education in his city. He and I were born on adjoining farms. He was graduated from Miami University not far away and became a national figure. A high school in Cincinnati bears his name. Among others supporting us were President W. O. Thompson of Ohio State University, President Allston Ellis of Ohio University and President Raymond M. Hughes of Miami University. Indeed, every educational leader of importance in the state was behind us, and many of them were present.

The report of the commission was fully explained and then came the fireworks. One old fellow from the hill section, with shoes colored by red clay, mounted the platform and said substantially this: "I don't like these newfangled notions. The little red brick schoolhouse was good enough for Pap, it was good enough for me and it is good enough for my children." He represented a considerable, but a wholly uninformed, class of people. A very attractive woman, a retired schoolteacher from New York City, who had been born in Noble County and had returned there to live, went to the corner grocery in the village in which she was then residing and, standing on a nail-keg, read the governor's proclamation, incidentally inquiring what attention was being paid to it. As she stated at the convention, she had some difficulty in working up a good local meeting. This led her to find out what had been going on in that school. Untrained teachers had been employed and in one instance a young man had forged a check to pay for a teacher's certificate and had been sent to prison. It was evident that the project in hand had taken deeper hold upon the women than upon the men. Many of the teachers in remote sections recited that the average attendance in their schools was about six pupils, divided in some instances into four classes.

The great audience in the auditorium in Memorial Hall was thrilled with other recitals. In tearful voice the sad state of things in

146

the rural schools was described. There was no school spirit to speak of, no assembly in numbers such as might develop an enthusiasm for school life. We discovered numberless towns where the leading man in the community was a township officer and the dominating figure in the school board. He was regarded as a man of affairs and in many instances, because of his wealth as measured by provincial standards, conducted a private banking business without any sort of examination or regulation by the state. Some member of his family was the teacher. He was the heart and center of a little empire of his own and such a unit as this was to be broken up by the new order.

I was at the convention every minute, and took part in the discussion, answering as many objections to our plans as possible. It became evident on the last day that it was useless for laggard individuals or communities to try to obstruct the great movement. The report of the commission was enthusiastically adopted, and resolutions were passed urging the General Assembly to enact a general school code. Most members of the legislature attended the convention and it was apparent that the action of the lawmaking body would be favorable and prompt. The appropriate measure passed both houses. A system of training teachers was inaugurated, higher standards were included in the pedagogic requirements, power was given to consolidate districts, county superintendents were provided and connection established between our universities and high schools. It developed that where mergers were effected, even with the construction of modern buildings and the maintenance of better teaching staffs, the educational cost per capita was reduced. New modern structures appeared everywhere. Some of the finest high schools in the state, as someone put it, were erected in the cornfields. Graduates of the high schools, with proper rating, were admitted without further question to our state universities. Thus they were kept at home under parental roof and protection during the formative years of their minds and characters before entering upon college life. This involved both a monetary and a moral gain.

Tied in with this program was the creation of a carefully laid out system of highways and market roads. Prior to this, the building of highways was influenced by politics. In many of our counties, you could easily locate the county commissioners because they lived on good roads. We held a good-roads convention which was as representative in attendance as the school assembly. From the hill counties came delegations with brass bands and they insisted on having some attention. A half-mill levy was voted by the legislature and a determining step was taken in the development of our present system of highways. These two improvements supplemented each other, for in the consolidation of districts and the running of school buses, better roads were highly necessary.

In the highway program valuable aid was given by Dan R. Hanna, son of Mark Hanna, the old Republican leader. This seemed like history repeating itself, and during the course of this movement I often remembered that when Andrew Jackson was seeking to destroy the United States Bank one of his valued aides was the son of Alexander Hamilton.

The diehards who had looked upon the passing of the little one-room schoolhouses as the end of an era that could not be improved sought by ridicule to discredit this great development, but the new order presented a picture which could not be denied. During the construction and after the completion of the new schoolhouses, they were opprobriously referred to as "one of those d——d Cox schoolhouses." But what a transformation they have brought about! Instead of small, lethargic and uninterested groups, we have the larger assemblies of pupils. Under the old system there was not only a lack of interest in the work of the pupils, but there was absolutely no fun. These modern school buildings have become of great utility for farm meetings. They enable the wives of the farmers to get together and discuss questions of interest and profit. There are now basketball, football and baseball teams, to say nothing of fine gymnasiums which are helping to build a more robust youth. In all the work of transforming our state government and our social conditions as well, nothing was comparable to the contribution which our rural school code made to our country life. Once the tide turns back to the farms and villages, I shall be very much surprised if the educational changes made at the beginning of the Twentieth Century in Ohio are not found a means to a happier and healthier rural life.

CHAPTER XII

PRISON REFORMS

◆

ONE OF the most interesting of the reform movements of the time was the effort to bring society to adopt a more humane attitude towards those who broke its laws. Prisons had hitherto been conducted primarily for purposes of punishment; but the principle was gaining ground that criminals are in general the product of heredity and environment, that the responsibility for their evil acts must be shared by society, and that a constructive emphasis must be laid on education, reformation and probation. I had taken a keen interest in the new trends in penology. I had given a good deal of study to systems of parole, probation and the indeterminate sentence as tried in various parts of the country. The movement for farm colonies, the attack of Governor G. W. Donaghey of Arkansas and others on the convict lease system, and the experiment of the Oregon authorities in introducing the honor system into prisons had attracted my attention. Public sentiment for reform was awakening in Ohio as elsewhere, and I was anxious to make it effective.

The prison conditions in Ohio at the outset of our administration were generally no worse than anywhere else; but they were deplorable. Several hundred men in the state penitentiary at Columbus were in the idle house. As I put it in my first message to the Assembly, "Their time is doubtless spent in reflection over their own disgrace and the plight of their families back home." There was no incentive for improvement because even good conduct in prison meant little or nothing for them.

The first Sunday after my first inauguration, I attended religious services in the chapel. I was anxious to know how long some of the inmates had been there. I found one man who was consigned there ten days before I was born. He had fallen into a quarrel with another young man over the possession of a jew's-harp. In a moment

149

of passion he threw a wrench and the injury was fatal. He had been a good prisoner. No effort had been made to have him paroled or pardoned. Only prisoners whose families could employ an attorney had their applications brought to the attention of the Pardon Board and then, too often, favorable action came from political influence. We established a new Parole Board. We sought to protect the interests of society by stern discipline when necessary and to search out prisoners who became criminals due to circumstances not of their making. This new board was in close touch with all of our state institutions of correction. Instead of waiting for a deserving man to employ a lawyer to bring official notice to his good record the board studied the reports of the warden of the penitentiary and superintendents of other institutions. We implanted in the minds of first offenders particularly that they were not beyond redemption. We established a night school in the prison and in addition to this arranged for prisoners to take correspondence courses in specialized subjects. We broke up the old system wherein the judges of courts consigned their charges to specific institutions.

To the girls' reformatory, women of hardened depravity had been sent. To the boys' industrial schools were consigned men who had been previously sentenced. At the Lancaster Home for Boys, youngsters were committed who were feeble-minded. The whole mass of unfortunates were passed to sundry institutions without any idea of segregation, classification of types or otherwise. It is difficult to understand now in the long-range view how such a mess of inefficiency and inhumanity could have existed so long.

Then, too, it was a mistake, as we viewed it, to send habitual criminals back to prison again for a short sentence. We put this question to the legislature in these words: "Our whole system is a plain travesty on human intelligence. It is as much of an outrage to sentence an habitual criminal to three years in the penitentiary as it would be to consign a hopeless lunatic to an asylum for three years. It is as much a crime against society to release from prison gates a known criminal as it would be to turn loose a maniac. At the expiration of a prisoner's term, some constituted authority should pass on the propriety and safety of turning him loose."

Laws were created changing the whole system of imposing sentences. The term of imprisonment was changed to minimum and maximum years. After a given time, the prisoner would be considered eligible for parole. If he behaved while in our charge, he had a chance to escape the long time imposed.

The paroled prisoners were carefully checked by officers of the state after release. The idle house was broken up in large measure by the purchase of a large tract of land near London, Ohio, in the central part of the state. Obviously the prisoners consigned to this institution were regarded as good prospects for reform. We recommended that small compensation be given for useful labor, this to be paid to families of prisoners or kept as a credit until the day of release. We acquired large acreages of land for all our state institutions. We found that even the feeble-minded were capable of rendering labor a considerable part of their time. Their physical and mental condition improved under outdoor life and with light tasks assigned to them. A survey showed that for the food maintenance of our state institutions, hundreds of thousands of dollars were expended for what could, in considerable measure, be produced by our institutions at small cost.

Starting on a modest scale, we established herds of dairy cattle. At the outset we purchased purebred stock. We explained to important breeders all over the country what we were attempting to do and we procured the loan of male animals of standard breeding. In surprisingly brief time, some of our cattle produced world's records in both milk and butterfat.

Both men and women were taught a means of earning their livelihood when their debts to the state were paid. The Mansfield Reformatory makes furniture for the state and other tax-supported institutions; it makes desks and chairs for kindergartens and school auditoriums and for the State University. A shoe factory was installed for state use and metal beds were made for our hospitals. At the London prison farm, in addition to the farm activities and the manufacture of soaps, there is a production of brushes and cotton goods. The women's reformatory at Marysville turns out women's clothing. This whole program took such form at its beginning that there was never any doubt as to its success. The statistics show a continuous growth.

I never pardoned a man from prison without seeing him and talking to him. Nor did I go into his case without having a complete record from the moment of arrest to the time he was committed to prison. In some instances, the subject under inquiry might seem, from the papers filed, to be deserving of his liberty, and yet on personal contact it would be apparent that such a thing was out of the question. The impression is that the worst prisoners are murderers. This is not true. Such crimes as murder are ordinarily committed under the influence of liquor or in violent passion of jealousy or anger and do not represent an habitual attitude. I took a great interest in our new policy and made many visits to our institutions. This was done as a spur to efficient management and to give hope to those consigned to our care. One Sunday, passing through the penitentiary at Columbus, I noticed a fine-looking young fellow sitting in his cell holding the picture of a woman and two children. I went in and sat down with him, remarking that he seemed to be out of place. In deep emotion he said, "Governor, no one ever had worse luck. I killed the best friend I had in the world. I was a madman with liquor in me. One night I was on a rampage and killed my father-in-law. No one ever had been nicer to me than he was."

I sent for his wife and found full confirmation of what the prisoner had said. When sober he was well behaved and took good care of his family. She said it was not the man who committed the murder but liquor. I told her to come back a few days before Christmas and in the meantime I would give full consideration to the matter. He rejoined his family at Christmastime, but he was let out only on condition that he should not touch intoxicating liquor. He never abused the trust.

The type of criminal hardest to cure is the forger. Yet, I remember giving a conditional pardon to a first offender in this class. He led an upright life and distinguished himself in the First World War. He sent me from the battlefields of France some dried poppies pasted to a sheet of paper on which was written the immortal poem, *In Flanders Fields*, by John McCrae.

Warden Thomas and I always felt that one of the most interesting stories of prison life which we encountered was one that I shall now relate. A Negro was sentenced to die in the electric chair for killing a guard in the Cincinnati workhouse. It was our practice for the warden always to check with me a few hours before the time set for execution. The prisoner's mother had visited the warden during the afternoon. The warden had asked a clerk to call the governor's office. While the mother and the warden were talking together the clerk returned with the message, "The governor's office is on the telephone." Then a very unusual thing happened. The mother said to the warden, "Now don't you let the governor save my boy. He has given me a lot of trouble in his time. I have talked with him today and I know that he has made his peace with his God and this is the time for him to meet his God. Let him do that tonight." There was nothing in the case which merited executive interference.

In another matter the Parole Board had had brought to its attention the claim that a man who was supposed to have been murdered had been seen alive in New Orleans. This naturally demanded attention. I sent for the convict who had been sentenced for life for the crime and told him about the report. Here is what he said: "I won't lie to you. You have been too good to us down in the prison. That fellow was not seen in New Orleans. I buried him in a cornfield in Jefferson County. My mother was poor, very poor, in a hill section of the state, and in her distress she married a Negro. I was hunting rabbits one day when I came upon my stepfather beating my mother in a cornfield. I lost control of myself and shot him. I can tell you just where his body can be found." Within the year he was pardoned, of course with the condition of good conduct imposed.

Another interesting case is concerned with a young man in his late teens who had been convicted of killing his mother. He had always pleaded innocence and did not take the stand in his own defense. A lawyer from the county from which he came had carefully but unsuccessfully prepared a brief seeking to show the prisoner guiltless. The man had been sentenced to the electric chair, but Governor Harmon had commuted the sentence to life imprisonment. I had gone carefully through all the papers. The warden brought the young man to the State house. The officer was sent out of the room, for no one was ever present in my talks with prisoners. The young man was a fine-looking youngster. When he first arrived at the prison there was no color in his cheeks, no depth of chest nor width of shoulders. He entered the night school and took a course in engineering; now he was engaged in reconditioning and even building trucks for state use. I asked him how things were going and he replied that a fine feeling had permeated every cell block under the new order of things. I told him that only a few days before I had had the unhappy experience of having one of the boys at the prison tell me a falsehood, and that this, of course, had prejudiced his case. To this the young prisoner replied, "Governor, you

153

are trying to do so much for us down there that any man who lies to you ought to be sent to the chair."

Picking up the papers, I stated that the Board of Pardons had become convinced of his innocence and eye to eye I asked him, "Did you kill your mother?" "Yes, I killed her, Governor," he admitted, "but I have never been able to figure out just why I did it. In the trial they always insisted that I killed her to get the money she had in her purse. She was always kind and indulgent to me and she would have given me the money had I asked her for it, so there was nothing in that. We were hanging curtains. I was at the top of the stepladder with a hammer and she was standing below. An uncontrollable impulse which I cannot in any way account for seized me and I struck her on the head; the blow killed her."

I told him I was proud of him for telling the truth and assured him that no one would ever know what had happened between us and that he should not consider his case hopeless. By this time evening had fallen on the State house. I walked out into a large reception room. Waiting to see me was a member of the State Medical Board, a man respected for his fine character as a citizen and practitioner. Without mentioning names I told him the whole story. He insisted that the boy didn't know how it all happened but that he, the doctor, did. "I have seen cases like this even though murder never resulted," he said. "In your home city the wife and mother of a family called at my office one day in great disturbance of mind. She said they had saved up money to send their only child through college. That was all they could afford. There was unmistakable evidence of an approaching birth and she begged me to help them out of a difficulty they could not surmount. I declined. As she told me afterwards, she tried sundry devices without success. The child was born and before he reached the age of adolescence he attempted suicide three times. Then he became perfectly normal. Many doctors and scientists tell us there is nothing in prenatal influence. I think there is. The young prisoner that you describe, you will find upon investigation, is mentally sound and he ought to be pardoned." The doctor had had a wide experience. Upon the strength of my confidence in him, I pardoned the young man. He went to Detroit, took a responsible position, became an officer in the Y. M. C. A. and about a year afterwards died. The load of unhappy memories was doubtless too much to carry. This story may cause discussion pro and con, on the subject of prenatal influence, but regardless of all that, I have never regretted what I did.

A few years ago John Golden, the playwright, asked me whether I had ever received a letter from a man yet living whose death sentence I had commuted to life imprisonment. Singularly, it so happened just a week before our talk. The facts were these. Warden Thomas of the prison had telephoned me twenty minutes before midnight, the fateful hour, that evidence had been brought to him that would seem to justify my ordering a postponement. This I did, and when we later considered the case, the man's life was saved. He wrote a very intelligent letter to me, stating that he had made a good record in the institution and was hoping some day to regain his freedom.

Among those who took a keen interest in our policies was Clarence Darrow. He never passed through Columbus without coming to see me and exchange ideas. Darrow had a breadth of view and a generosity of spirit which pleased me, and I valued his warm approval of my innovations. He particularly liked my personal attention to pardon cases. In some quarters the policy was criticized as sentimental and unrealistic. These critics failed to realize how grossly many inmates of our prisons had been neglected. Nobody had been interested in separating the many reformable prisoners from the few who were hopelessly criminal. This indiscriminate lumping of the potentially good with the irredeemably bad and the frequent sending of convicted persons to the wrong institution had created a tragic situation. The prisoners themselves were quick to realize what we were trying to do. They soon comprehended that the state meant to help those who by good behavior and otherwise were helping themselves. This created an entirely new spirit.

Illustrative of this is an event which occurred during the First World War. Roy Chapin, Detroit automobile manufacturer and later a member of President Hoover's cabinet, had been assigned by the federal administration to the task of moving trucks and cars to the seaboard. Railroad terminals were glutted with shipments and Mr. Chapin and his organization sought relief by using the highways. The old National road, built originally from Baltimore to St. Louis, was a very direct route and it was in fairly good condition, though here and there were stretches that were impassable during inclement weather. As a part of our highway program, we had, in our first term, laid out a project of paving the part of the historic highway running through Ohio. The movement had caught the imagination of our public and had appealed strongly to the organizations promoting better roads. There was one link covering twenty-seven miles in Muskingum and Guernsey Counties, a beautiful and picturesque section, which provided a real obstacle to the transportation in question. The job had to be done not only quickly but thoroughly. It was not a matter of repairs; the thoroughfare had to be built along modern lines. In order that there might be no delays, I called a meeting at Cambridge in Guernsey County of every local officer under whose jurisdiction any detail of the project might come. We had there the judges of the courts, the county auditors, the county engineers and surveyors and the county commissioners. They all recognized that we had an emergency to deal with and pledged their cooperation. The real problem was not machinery nor supplies, but labor. I consulted Warden Thomas of the penitentiary in Columbus and suggested that we assemble 250 prisoners, selected according to the nature of the crimes they were charged with, the records they had made for good behavior and their physical equipment for a hard piece of work. Without much delay 250 Negroes were assembled. I went to the prison and talked to them, telling them that it was their opportunity to render service to their country and that every man who labored industriously and behaved himself would have that fact registered in his record at the prison. The state bought the materials and placed the whole operation in charge of a brick manufacturer of good repute. The state auditor assigned a competent accountant and the disbursement of money was carefully supervised. How the red clay flew in those hills of southeastern Ohio! The countryside shook from the explosions of dynamite that were tearing away rock and hardpan soil. Nothing interfered with the expeditious carrying out of the project and in surprisingly brief time the automobiles and trucks were rolling eastward. Only one prisoner was guilty of an infraction of the rules of conduct. He was caught by some of his fellows and pretty badly beaten up. They felt that he had brought discredit on the whole group.

In due time the prison reforms were not only understood, but generally endorsed. After I left office there was placed over the gates of the prison farm a bronze tablet bearing these words:

"This institution was builded on the sentiment expressed by Governor James M. Cox in his message to the legislature in which he said: 'As the tides and storms of life bring misfortune and wreckage, let there be governmental harbors in sight. Let our own state government reflect this symptom of our people's desires by the continuance of its welfare work. Let us take away from the crowded city, pulsating from the throbs of intensive industrial life, those who are entrusted to our care, and plant the prison in the fields and meadows where divine manifestations are more manifold. Let us hear the busy hum of machinery inside the walls, and know that employment of time previously wasted is working out human salvation. Let us reward with confidence those whose step is steadier, whose purpose is firmer and whose conscience is easier through the touch of sympathetic contact, by letting them work in the fields as a test of their reform. Let us write in letters of gold over the gates of the prison,

" 'He who enters here leaves not hope behind.' "

The liquor question has always been a ticklish one in our political affairs. Personally, I was opposed to prohibition. If all the liquor in the world could be wiped out with one fell swoop, with no roots left, we would be much better off. However, that cannot be done. It has been often demonstrated that you cannot, by statute, regulate the habits of man. The sensible arrangement seemed to be the regulation of the traffic under strict state control. That was the thought of the members of our constitutional convention.

The new constitution declared that the state and municipalities could provide for the limitation of the number of saloons, and that there should be not more than one saloon in each township or municipality of five thousand population, nor more than one saloon for every five hundred population in other townships or municipalities. Areas that had been voted dry were to remain so. No license could be issued to any person not a citizen of the United States and of good moral character. Any connection between the saloon and brewery was prohibited. Two offenses against the law were deemed sufficient for revocation of license.

My message to the Assembly reached the vital phase of the whole matter in these words: "For years this question in Ohio has been the football of politics. Not only has the so-called wet and dry question been the means of disquieting community life but it has formed divisions in the legislature and occasioned confusion in such measure as to interfere seriously with the proper settlement of strictly economic questions. The action of the constitutional convention was a positive reflection of the public desire to approach and dispose of this subject on the base of common sense, having high regard for the public welfare."

If liquor laws on the statute books of the states had been properly enforced, doubtless there would have been no prohibition amendment to the federal Constitution.

Under the old law, a man coming out of the penitentiary could open a saloon the next day. He could be, as many of them were, attractive to young men to whom he would recite his exploits in crime and his experiences in prison. In no time, gangs of young hoodlums grew up, crime multiplied and there seemed to be no cure for a thoroughly wretched state of affairs. We were determined to have a law with teeth in it and to see to its strict enforcement.

The law worked very well and undesirable persons were denied licenses. Enforcement matched the letter of the law. Certain elements were shocked when the saloons were closed tighter than a drum on Sundays, but I had many letters at that time from wives and mothers who approved the new order. Too many of them to be counted expressed their satisfaction, substantially in the words of one communication which was recently dug out of our files. It said: "Things are different in our house. Time was when there was hardly such a thing as the Sabbath. My husband went to the saloon in the morning, came back in due time filled with liquor, pretzels, liver and onions, and our whole day was spoiled."

Countless unbelievable things of other sorts were revealed as new legislation put a stop to timeworn practices. Private bankers were scattered all over the state. In many instances a rich man, as measured by the provincial standards of wealth, would become the custodian of the savings and funds of his neighbors and the administrator of trusts created by wills. These private banks accounted to no one. They were neither examined nor regulated.

After a great deal of our legislative program had been completed and we began to consider the matter of overhauling our tax system, a quiet-mannered man of wide experience and wisdom said to me,

"Well, your administration has been enjoying its honeymoon. Your troubles will begin the moment you take up the question of taxes." His words were prophecy to be fulfilled. In the administration of Governor Harmon, laws were enacted which did away with a great many inequalities in the assessment of property, and uncovered much that banks and utility companies had not listed. The method of assessing personal property and intangible assets, however, was nothing short of a travesty. This work, in the main, was consigned to the local tax assessor who operated within his home township. He was usually someone of little consequence, a ne'er-do-well or a man physically disabled, usually a Union soldier. If he did his work capably, he was never re-elected. His chances of re-election were determined by the amount of property which he overlooked.

The law regulating the liquor traffic had closed many saloons because the number of such places was determined by population in local subdivisions. It was therefore necessary for municipal, county and state purposes to increase the tax duplicates.

Through the long course of the years, dating back to Governors Foraker and McKinley, commissions had been appointed to study the whole question of taxation. Though with the growth of the state there was an inevitable demand for increased governmental duties, the two governors served in a time when the state was hard pressed for funds. Foraker bluntly said under date of April 6, 1886, "The financial condition of the state needs attention," and he recommended the issue of bonds to pay current expenses. He showed that there was a constant shrinkage of personal property. He touched the morals of the situation in these words: "The idea seems to prevail . . . that there is no harm in cheating the state, although to do so a false return must be made and perjury must be committed. This offense against the state and good morals is too frequently committed by men of wealth and reputed high character and of corresponding position in society."

Times of stress also fell on the McKinley administration. There wasn't money enough for the needs of the government, and a capable commission was appointed to investigate the problem. In its report it said: "A system of public finance must be considered. Not what is theoretically possible, but what is attainable in view of the weakness and greed of human nature, should be the aim of the lawmaker. The system, as it is actually administered, results in debauching the moral sense. It is a school of perjury, it sends large amounts of property into hiding; it imposes unjust burdens on various classes in the community, those particularly whose property is in sight. These burdens are unjust because these people pay the taxes which should be paid by their neighbors."

Yet the years went on and nothing was done. Conditions were indescribable. Their causes and effects were recited by men who knew the subject and suggested a remedy, yet nothing was done. Foraker and McKinley were able men and one wonders why a situation so unfair and scandalous was not corrected. Probably it was because the legislatures were not interested. Tremendous power was held by the Republican party machine. It had the state in its grip for a generation and was unbeatable at the polls because it was supported by most of business, by the colored vote and by most of the members of the Grand Army of the Republic. Closely linked to it, also, was the State Brewers' Association, which gave votes in return for protection. Occasionally things got so bad that a revolt led to political upsets in the state election, notably in the case of James E. Campbell, John M. Pattison and Judson Harmon. Harmon created a state tax commission, the very thing that had been recommended for a long time, and gave it supervision over the assessment of property of public utilities. The real estate duplicate was multiplied threefold.

When my administration came in there was yet much to be done. Neither power nor machinery had been provided for the listing of personal and intangible property. Monies loaned on mortgages had not been adequately put on the duplicate. Both Governor Foraker and the McKinley commission had recommended the appointment of assessors. Since our legislative program had given an unprecedented amount of attention to welfare measures, it seemed not only appropriate but necessary to round out the picture by providing for the financial health of the government. This one phase of taxation had always been regarded as heavily loaded with political dynamite. Many politicians in our party strongly urged against the action.

Subordinate to the tax commission, a county tax commission was now created which in turn appointed the assessors. The ensuing revelations were startling. In my home county of Montgomery, a single township, Madison, had been reporting for taxation in money and stocks and bonds as much as the entire city of Dayton with a population of 200,000. This was an index to conditions over the state. The sum added to the duplicate amounted to a billion dollars. It enabled me afterwards to call a special session of the legislature to repeal the current appropriations bill and pass another carrying measurable reductions. The beneficent results did not run entirely to the state, but to municipalities as well. The elective assessor system was never restored and doubtless never will be.

There was one phase of the law which bore heavily and probably inequitably in certain directions. Citizens in the state owning stocks or securities in corporations chartered under the laws of other states were compelled to list them for taxation. These were assessed at their money value, usually established by market quotations. In many instances, the tax rate too heavily absorbed the income from low-interest- or dividend-bearing securities. It was our feeling that these inequities would make plain the need and justice of an amendment to the constitution giving the legislature the right to pass laws classifying property for taxation. This was later done.

While the legislation already described possessed major importance, our program covered a great variety of other subjects. The State house had been what I once called "a roosting place for lobbyists." Four great interests, the railroads, the traction, electric, gas and other public utilities, the building and loan companies and the Anti-Saloon League, had usually organized the legislature. That is, they combined to control the committees and to make sure that no bills hostile to themselves were reported out of committee. Alongside their lobbyists worked another crew, the peculiarly obnoxious men who got nuisance or "strike" bills introduced in order to be paid for dropping them. This became a profitable industry. Certain interests of course had a legitimate need for representatives who would confer with members and attend committee meetings to furnish useful information. Legitimate agents found no objection to having their names registered. It was the other class that did.

The Democratic state platform had declared for a "short ballot in the selection of administrative officers as a means of securing greater security in the selection of public officials and for fixing and centralizing responsibility." John H. Clarke, afterwards justice of the United States Supreme Court, was the leading sponsor of this reform. There was little opposition to it in the legislature. A referendum was invoked, however, and parts of it were defeated. It was purely a demagogic movement and some public officers, who had been elected on the party platform in question, took a part in it. A new law separated the state and national election ballots on the theory that the issues were distinct. When Mr. Willis became governor, he went back to the old arrangement. He regretted this later, as he thought the change contributed to his defeat in 1916.

I have mentioned the municipal-home-rule feature which Newton D. Baker and others had written into the new constitution; it was a reform essential to the improvement of city government. The state reserved, however, the right to fix limitations on tax rates and debt. For example, if the municipality voted to acquire or create a public utility, the bonds issued to meet the cost, or purchase, or construction should lie as a lien only against the utility and not against the municipality. I always urged that in the operation of municipally-owned utilities, the method of bookkeeping and accounting should be subject to the same examination and regulation which the state imposes in the operation of departments of the government proper, local and state. If a municipally-owned project became enmeshed in politics, it would easily throw expenses into capital investments and thus make the enterprise appear profitable when, in fact, it was not.

Several other reforms were put into effect at this time. A practice had grown up of issuing temporary injunctions in the courts against state officers and department boards. This was often done without notice by the court. It was corrected. Also, several departments had to do with relations between labor and capital. They were merged into one. Again, we had three distinct administrative units dealing with agriculture. They were brought under one unit. In this connection, I urged the state to do what has been so successfully done in Wisconsin—coordinate the energies of the state government and the state universities and to establish a bureau of legislative research for the development of every subject vital to the state and for the legislature.

A mothers' pension law was passed, one of the first in the country, the primary purpose being to keep more children at home with their mothers instead of passing them into public institutions. There had been much complaint about the absence of any supervision over the moving picture industry. A board of censors was created in the face of tremendous opposition which came, however, from outside the state. The wisdom of the law is indicated by the fact that it is still in operation.

An efficient budget system was established. It was long before the plan was adopted by the federal government and we were one of the first states to put it into operation. It put an end to duplication of service. We found that the state had a fiscal year, an appropriations year, a college year, and in the case of one department, a calendar year. We changed both the fiscal and the appropriations years and each now begins July 1 and runs until June 30.

Regardless of the quality or extent of legislation passed by a law-making body, it always seemed to me that there was a sense of public relief when the day of adjournment came. It came in Ohio in the spring of 1913 with considerable surprise. The legislative work of putting the new constitution into effect and instrumenting its provisions with what we believed to be efficient administrative laws, would, in the expressed judgment of John R. Commons, take at least two years. It was all well rounded up long before the time expected by the public. The great flood disaster of 1913 came in March and this retarded the legislative program, yet it was completed ahead of time.

My experience in the Congress had made it clear to me how much time was needlessly lost in legislative procedure. After bills were presented, they were carefully catalogued by Robert S. Hayes, our executive secretary. So systematically card-indexed was every measure that we knew exactly where it was, whether it was in committee or out of it, what progress was being made and what obstructions were encountered. We had a striking illustration of how differences in the committee could be composed by compromises which ordinarily involved the form and not the substance. In the House, with its large membership, the aid of Speaker Charles L. Swain was invaluable. A careful organization was effected under the majority leader, Milton Warnes of Holmes County. He designated captains to head up groups of from twelve to fifteen members. When bills regarded as administrative were up for consideration and passage, the leader and his aides saw to it that there were few, if any, absentees. In this way, matters progressed. There was a steady rhythm of movement. James W. Faulkner, the dean of state correspondents, a profound student of government and a careful observer of events, came into the executive office and remarked, "Last night I put together all the bills that have been passed as you would assemble a crossword puzzle and I was surprised to find that the job here is about done." And so it was.

The legislature which assembled on inaugural day, January 13, adjourned in April—in about ninety days' time. Matters presented at two special sessions in January and July of 1914, the next year, had to do primarily with details. Thus ended what had been a legislative task of somewhat historic importance.

We were blessed with a very fine legislature. In a campaign for their election, the members had stood without exception for the new order. The Senate was presided over by Hugh L. Nichols, the lieutenant governor. He was a calm and tranquil man. His faith in the virtue of bills under discussion carried great weight and he exhibited there the same capacity to keep things moving as he did subsequently when he became the first chief justice to be appointed by the governor. A senator of very versatile ability was Carl D. Friebolin of Cleveland, whose training in public matters with Newton D. Baker, then mayor of that city, had been in the days of intelligent reform movements. He was a psychologist in the truest sense and the harmonious action of the Senate would have been difficult without his devotion to the cause and his aptitude in legislative matters.

CHAPTER XIII

THE OHIO FLOODS OF 1913

◆

THE GREAT Ohio catastrophe of 1913 formed one of the most dramatic chapters of my whole life.

In the days when the Indians roamed the valleys and uplands of Ohio, their forts or settlements were to be found along the rivers, preferably where one or more streams joined. What seem to have been the major settlements were established there. The white man followed in their footsteps in this respect and thus prepared a way for the greatest disaster known to the Buckeye State. At Columbus, Ohio, the Olentangy and Scioto Rivers merge. At Zanesville the Licking and Muskingum Rivers join. At Dayton the Miami, Stillwater and Mad Rivers come together. And so it was that when the great flood of 1913 fell upon our state, the cities of Dayton, Columbus and Zanesville suffered most.

The physical outlines of the state show a watershed extending from the northeast portion southwesterly. In the north, the drainage and flow of waters is into Lake Erie. In the main, this area is made up of lowlands. To the south are most of the vast hills builded by the movements of the ice sheet thousands of years ago. Interspersed strata of sandstone and limestone create the rugged features of the landscape. The Ohio River catches every drop of water that drains south of this watershed, carried there in the main by the Tuscarawas, Licking, Muskingum, Scioto, Olentangy, Little Miami, Great Miami, Stillwater and Mad Rivers.

Over this expanse there fell in March, 1913, one of the heaviest rainfalls in all the history of the United States. The records show only one storm that exceeded it. That was in October, 1910, in eastern Missouri, western Kentucky and southern Illinois. The Ohio rainfall in five days was eleven inches in some sections. The resulting flood came like a flash, but fortunately early in the morning; otherwise the loss of human life would have been multiplied manyfold.

On the morning of the flood in March, 1913, our managing editor in Dayton called me and said that the rivers had broken the levees and that water had begun to flow through the streets of the city. The telephone circuit was cut during the conversation; the storm had begun to take its toll. The day before, the river gauge in Dayton was three feet and it gradually rose to a maximum of twenty-nine feet. Ohio was never thrown into such a ferment of excitement. Wild rumors spread everywhere. The Red Cross wired from Washington a report that the city of Dayton had been destroyed. It was the greatest tragedy that had ever struck the state.

The hope that the storm might subside and the whole thing turn out to be but a violent freshet was not long in giving way to disappointment and despair. The heavens continued to pour out their waters everywhere. From the northwest in Tiffin to the southeast at Marietta, it was substantially the same story. Railroad bridges were swept away, railroad and highway beds disappeared as if they were banks of sand. Farm buildings, in some instances partially filled with livestock or with human beings, were floated down the rivers. Communications by rail, highway, telephone and telegraph were severed.

The suspense which overwhelmed our people and centered, in considerable measure, in the capitol at Columbus would be difficult to describe. One thing which in due time impressed our consciousness was the remarkable capacity of the human being to save his own life. Had the storm broken after schools had assembled and greater numbers of workmen were in the factories, it is difficult to contemplate what the loss of life would have been. The number of known dead was 361, but undoubtedly many more bodies were never recovered. Much sickness and many deaths followed the flood. Thirty-two persons were admitted to the Dayton State Hospital, their commitment papers expressly stating that their insanity was a direct consequence of the flood.

There were twelve feet of water in the ground floor of our newspaper office at Dayton. The basement was flooded and paper rolls weighing over a ton had floated from it into the accounting room. A photograph taken from the top of the *News* building showed a horse and a mule hitched together swimming for dear life. In those days fire engines were drawn by horses. One of them swam several squares and finally landed in the second story of a bank building. In Middletown hogs had floated or swum downstream and had taken quarters in one of the swankiest residences in the city. Men and women in the streets going to their labors were forced to seek safety at close hand. For days their families did not know whether they had survived. In cottages the retreat was first to the attic and then to the roof. Isolated houses were in most instances swept away.

From the State house in Columbus, we could look across the river and see the entire west section of the capital city not only under water but also in the midst of a turbulent river which had broken the bounds of the levee and was tearing through the streets. The worst reports came from Zanesville and Dayton. They were probably the hardest hit of all the communities, although the great Miami Valley from Sidney to a point below Hamilton was so completely submerged that the only means of transit was the few boats that could be found.

In the city of Dayton every known article of furniture was being carried away by the waters, even pianos in wholesale numbers. The storm had broken so suddenly that most families were without water. Some, in prompt precaution, had filled the bathtubs and sundry vessels with drinking water. In many instances families removed furniture to the second floor but forgot entirely the lifesaving contents of the cupboard and refrigerator. The first thought of hundreds of thousands of stricken people was to save their own lives and then to gain food to keep alive.

All units of the National Guard were called out at once and assembled in the armories. I declared martial law and took possession of the telegraph and the railroads. We were unable to get any information from Zanesville. We dispatched an expedition towards that city, but it was unable to reach the place. In a few instances, however, the telephone wires were still above water and in the midst of our great concern over what had actually happened at Zanesville, a skilled lineman of the Bell Telephone Company north of that city had climbed a pole, tapped a wire and called me at the State house. He gave a very comprehensive view of the whole situation and we were thus enabled to get food into that city and the villages in the Muskingum Valley.

Finally about midnight of the second or third day, a report came from above Dayton that the city was on fire. There was no way of combatting the flames and one could easily visualize the complete destruction of one of the most attractive cities in the state. Then again came a lifesaver in John A. Bell, an employee of the telephone company. In an inspired moment when the waters first began running into the telephone building, he removed two or three storage batteries to the top of the structure. After painstaking effort lasting over two days, he finally established a circuit into the governor's office. He told me in detail where the fire was raging. Our guess was as good as his as to how long it would last. It subsided that night and our anxiety, in part at least, was relieved. By Thursday of that week the height of the flood was receding and in all the stricken cities boats were at work rescuing those in peril. But the nights remained dark and the food shortage, in some instances a clothing shortage also, was severe.

When the waters had run out, the desolate scenes told how complete the disaster was. On the streets of Dayton the carcasses of one thousand horses were found. The storm had done a complete job. The Pennsylvania Railroad published a pamphlet soon after the flood in which is to be found this passage: "It was a titanic battle. It mattered little that the enemy was a natural force instead of a body of armed men. Armed men would not have waged war so relentlessly—they might have had some regard for the weak and defenseless, for the women and children. The flood's object was plain destruction, animate or inanimate objects—toward both, its enmity was equally implacable."

The report of the railway company said: "Governor Cox of Ohio, in the early days of the flood, gave out a statement to the effect that the disaster would prove to be a greater one than the San Francisco earthquake. This was regarded, in some quarters, as one of the wild reports emanating from the flooded district. It has proved more than literally true. It should be borne in mind, too, that there was no insurance against losses occasioned by the flood. Even after the abolition of temporary relief some 16,000 families required financial relief in order to return to housekeeping."

Scores of passenger trains were stalled in the floods and the survivors came out with thrilling tales of their rescue. The Pennsylvania Railroad alone had lost twenty-four bridges, and fifty spans were damaged.

The Pennsylvania booklet gives a further glimpse of things in these words: "To have stood in Dayton a week after the waters had subsided, either at the center of her business section or in her so-called "Sealskin" district, the imagination could not conceive a reality of turbulent, swirling water, generally ten and twelve feet deep, rushing through her wide thoroughfares and islanding her city blocks. Yet at this later time, when the Miami River had retreated within its banks—and was not even half filling them—the city was a picture of woe and desolation. It was stamped on the face of every man and woman one met.

"In the streets, on either side, were long ramparts of mud and filth and broken articles of all sorts and description, with a lane between these ramparts for the passage of vehicles."

Once the task of saving lives had passed, the food problem was upon us. Wherever we found supplies, food, clothing or what not, we seized them and turned them over to the relief authorities. At one time, near the city of Marion, we took possession of a carload of eggs. When the clearing-up process had come, Colonel H. E. Talbott in Dayton asked for as many wheelbarrows as could be had. We found two carloads in the freight yards at Columbus and dispatched them to the city. At the request of the newspapers and the press associations, I had given a complete story every day with the understanding that newspapers would render aid in broadcasting the need of funds and supplies. Telegrams poured in not only from all parts of our own country, but from many persons traveling abroad, all wanting to know whether their families, friends and loved ones had been saved. Every message was turned over to the National Guard and the reports received were promptly transmitted by wire.

I appointed a Flood Commission made up of the following gentlemen: John H. Patterson, Dayton; H. H. Johnson, Cleveland; J. G. Schmidlapp, Cincinnati; S. O. Richardson, Toledo; G. W. Lattimer, Columbus. I accompanied the members of this body in their visits to every stricken community in the state. The legislature adjourned for a week for two reasons: the members desired to see the extent of damage that had been done to state property and many of the legislators had themselves suffered heavy property loss.

That the heart of the nation was touched was evidenced by the relief provided. Two million dollars—a good deal of money in those days—came by mail and wire. I was concerned for a time about providing custody for these funds and, until the Red Cross authorities arrived, they were put in charge of General George H. Wood, our adjutant general, and Price Russell, our executive clerk. Someone aptly remarked at the time, "The money is safe. If either one of those men stole a nickel he would commit suicide the next morning." The newspapers, of course, carried stories of the flow of funds and the mayor of Zanesville wired me a request for one million dollars, to be sent at once. I handed the telegram to newspaper correspondent James W. Faulkner, who chanced to be in the room, and his characteristically witty observation was, "Ask him whether he wants it in nickels or dimes."

It would require a book to recite the heroic parts played all over the flood areas. For the first time, so far as I know, a newspaper was printed on the street. The electric system in Dayton was completely out of service and our presses and motors were under water, but Robert F. Wolfe, manufacturer, banker and newspaper publisher of Columbus, found a second-hand press in the capital city, shipped it to Dayton and erected it on the cement paving. He then found in the adjacent countryside a steam engine used in the threshing of grain, and within a brief season papers were coming off the press. Prior to that our news force had put out a paper with the dimensions of a handbill, printed in the Job Department of the National Cash Register Company, which was beyond the flood zone. Mr. Wolfe, when the whole west side of Columbus was under water, had gathered up every boat on Buckeye Lake, about twenty-five miles away, regardless of size or description. They were put to rescue work. For this service, Mr. Wolfe was made a Commodore in the Ohio National Guard, a title which he happily bore throughout his life.

The Wolfe brothers, Robert F. and H. P., were important figures during my entire service as governor. Their careers were impressive illustrations of what can be done in the wide opportunities of America. Their father was an itinerant shoemaker who came from good old stock in the Guernsey County area. In time the brothers became bankers and newspaper publishers. During the panic of 1929 their twenty-one financial institutions weathered the storm without difficulty.

H. P. Wolfe was a part of the original Federal Reserve System and was designated by Paul Warburg, the distinguished financier, as one of its most efficient officers. In the First World War he made a national record in charge of the War Savings campaign in Ohio. Sales amounted to $150,000 in ten months. Stamps were in units from 25¢ to $5.00. Ohio sold many times more than any other state. In three of the larger states the expense of the campaign to the government was more than two million dollars. In Ohio it was thirty thousand.

The state was not long in showing the stuff of which it was made, both in resource and citizenship. Workmen were brought in from other states and there were busy scenes of restoration everywhere. Funds were voted out of the state treasury to building and loan companies for the purpose of affording the financial aid necessary for repairs and rebuilding. These local concerns supplied ample mortgage collateral and paid interest on the advances until they were taken up. The federal government, too, rendered every aid within its power and authority, and General Leonard Wood of the Army visited the stricken cities with our Flood Commission.

Too much cannot be said about the immediate and effective help given by the Red Cross. Miss Mabel T. Boardman, its head, visited the state and assigned as an aide to the Ohio Flood Relief Commission Mr. Ernest P. Bicknell, who had rendered notable service in San Francisco at the time of the earthquake disaster. The money that flowed into the state was used exclusively for relief purposes and was turned over as soon as possible to the Red Cross, which set up local organizations in every stricken area. I had a firm of expert accountants audit every item of intake and expenditure. Every dollar was followed from the time it came to us until it was disbursed by the Red Cross through its local representatives. This audit was submitted in full to the legislature. Mr. Bicknell, at the conclusion of the work, said that this was the largest undertaking ever assumed by the Red Cross and in no instance, so far as he knew, had the work been so systematically done and the financial operations so completely accounted for.

Expressing the pride and reassurance of our people, I issued the following statement once the whole relief movement was under way:

"Ohio has risen from the floods.

"Such a pitiless blow from nature as we sustained would have wiped out society and destroyed governments in other days, but

171

our commonwealth, refreshed by the tears of the American people, stands ready from today to meet the crisis alone.

"We cannot speak our gratitude to President Wilson for federal aid, to the Red Cross, to states, municipalities, trade organizations and individuals, that sent funds and supplies. They will never know their contribution to humanity.

"The relief situation, so far as food and clothing are concerned, is in hand. The legislature has recessed for a week for the purpose of ascertaining the extent of the damage to public works that must be repaired by legislation. The Red Cross, acting in concert with the State Relief Commission, will begin a movement to rehabilitate the homes of the poor.

"The calamity has its compensations—in that the state now knows its resources in vitality and citizenship, and we are conscious that the depths of human sympathy will never be sounded.

"Thankful to her friends who succored her, Ohio faces tomorrow serene and confident."

Later, the following letter came to me from President Wilson:

My dear Governor: December 20, 1913

At the Ninth Annual Meeting of the American Red Cross held at Washington on December 10th, by unanimous vote, you were awarded the society's gold medal of merit. It was a sincere disappointment to myself, the other officers of the Red Cross and the General Board that you were unavoidably detained in Ohio, and that therefore I was unable to have the pleasure of presenting you in person the medal so well deserved and of expressing to you the appreciation it typifies.

It was largely due to your prompt, energetic, and wise measures for emergency relief, to your confidence in the Red Cross, and to your hearty cooperation in its efforts to mitigate the sufferings of the victims of the serious floods that the society was enabled to cope successfully with so great a task. As President of the American Red Cross, I take pleasure in transmitting to you the medal awarded you for your invaluable aid and desire to express to you the gratitude of the national organization.

With earnest and well-justified hope for the speedy recovery of the state from this recent misfortune and with all good wishes for her continued prosperity, I am, my dear Governor,

Yours sincerely,

Woodrow Wilson

172

In running through my files I find an editorial from the New York *World*, written, as he stated to me, by Don C. Seitz, a great journalist of his day. It reads as follows:

AN APPRECIATION

The man who has dominated the situation in Ohio is Governor Cox. He has been not only Chief Magistrate and Commander-in-Chief, but the head of the life-saving service, the greatest provider of food and clothing that the state has ever known, the principal health officer, the sanest counselor, the severest disciplinarian, the hardest worker, the most hopeful prophet, the kindest philanthropist and the best reporter. He has performed almost incredible labors in all these fields, and his illuminating dispatches to the *World* at the close of several heartbreaking days have given a clearer idea of conditions than could be had from any other source.

Reared on a farm, educated in the public schools, a printer by trade, a successful publisher and editor of newspapers, a faithful congressman, a true democrat, a great governor and a reporter who gets his story into the first edition, James M. Cox excites and is herewith offered assurances of the *World's* most distinguished consideration.

From Paris, France, Myron T. Herrick, former governor of Ohio and at the time ambassador to France, sent his felicitations in the following words:

"Please accept my warmest congratulations for the deserved honor conferred on you for your services during the flood."

CHAPTER XIV

THE MIAMI VALLEY PLAN

◆

THE CITIZENS of Dayton, rising from the great flood of 1913 with renewed determination, contributed a fund of two million dollars for the exclusive purpose of conducting an extensive survey of the watershed taking up parts of nine counties. Ultimately, they planned an extensive program of flood control.

When the first meeting was held to raise funds to defray preliminary costs of survey and investigation, probably no more than $100,000 was in mind. Adam Schantz took the assembled group by surprise in stating that at the outset the size of the task must not be underestimated. He proposed that $2,000,000 be raised. This naturally appealed to the imagination of John H. Patterson, who was never shocked by large figures in finance. Mr. Schantz, a born leader, was of great service in the early stages of the project.

Nothing can ever be more to the credit of the citizens of the Miami Valley than their execution of this project without government aid. Their self-reliance stands in marked contrast with the use of tremendous sums of federal money in recent years to carry out such enterprises in various parts of the country. This vast undertaking, to cost almost $40,000,000, was to be planned, built and paid for by a relatively small section of the state. First it was necessary to find out whether it was physically possible to restrain the waters of a flood so as to avoid a tragic recurrence. For this purpose the leading engineers of the country, men with wide experience at home and abroad, were assembled for study and consultation. This inquiry was organized by Colonel E. A. Deeds, a Dayton businessman who had left the National Cash Register Company with Charles F. Kettering to establish a company to manufacture Mr. Kettering's device for the electric starting, lighting and ignition of automobiles;

he was assisted by Gordon S. Rentschler, then a leading business executive of Hamilton, Ohio. The engineers finally agreed that it was possible to build a system which would amply protect life and property. It would be a very costly venture and pioneer legislation would have to be passed legalizing the whole project.

A bill creating the Miami Conservancy District and authorizing the formation of new political subdivisions was drawn by the Hon. J. A. McMahon in close collaboration with the chief engineer, Arthur E. Morgan. A committee made up of Walter S. Kidder and Gaylord Cummins, which had searched for the best engineer available, had recommended Morgan, who had been supervising engineer of the Federal Drainage Investigations in 1907–09 and in charge of the design of reclamation works in the Southern states. He was still only in his middle thirties; a man of forceful personality, rare conscientiousness and an almost intuitive knowledge of the best means of adapting conservancy works to a difficult terrain. When the bill for the Conservancy District was passed, I was drawn into the picture as governor. Mr. McMahon realized at the outset that the administration of the law would be turbulent and require a strong hand. It was necessary to consider all the elements of opposition that might be encountered, particularly from counties that might become alarmed over the possible flooding of upstate lands through the building of retention dams. The law, after we had all agreed upon it, was presented to the General Assembly and finally passed. This was one of the heaviest tasks imposed on me.

Involved in the whole enterprise were the moving of highways and railroads, the diversion of streams and in one instance the removal of the entire village of Osborn, having a population of over two thousand.

The administrative set-up consisted of three commissioners. They were to be selected by the Common Pleas Court of every county involved. While politics in all its meanest and most devious ways was played against the project in its formative stages, the Conservancy District now operates without the least tinge of politics attaching to it. The cost was thirty-nine million dollars. That was a great deal of money, but small compared to the loss sustained during the flood—one hundred and forty million dollars.

The topography of the country was ideal. The retention dams

were built across the valley, joining together the abutting hills. Farmers in the affected areas who desired to dispose of their lands to the Conservancy District were accommodated, and generous prices were paid. These farm lands instead of being damaged were fertilized, and a great many of the owners came back and repurchased.

Bonds financing the enterprise mature December 1, 1949. Not a cent was contributed by the state or federal government. Recently an enterprise similar in nature was carried out in the Muskingum and Tuscarawas Valleys of south-central Ohio, but this was done at public expense on the theory that the dams and reservoirs would restrain waters entering into the Ohio in flood season. Colonel Deeds and Charles F. Kettering erected and gave to the Conservancy District a beautiful building in Dayton which houses accountants, tax experts and engineers. The whole thing functions so well that the communities involved scarcely know that it is in existence. There has been no flood damage and it has been demonstrated that the genius of man can in some measure at least triumph over the angry moods of nature.

A word about Arthur E. Morgan. In the early part of the Roosevelt administration, the President had asked me to come to the White House. I was shown up to his bedroom where he was eating breakfast and going through the morning papers. In the course of our talk, he said that out of our flood experience I must know of a good conservancy engineer. I told him that in my judgment there was one who had outshone all others and that was Arthur Morgan. The President summoned Louis Howe, his trusted aide, and told him to get Mr. Morgan on the telephone. They wanted to discuss the T. V. A. project with him. Mr. Morgan was at the White House the next morning and then and there began the great work he rendered in the South. There can be no question that he met the assignment with great distinction. I know very little about the controversy which resulted in his leaving the T. V. A., but I remember well remarking to the President that Morgan would be honest and efficient but had no patience with politics in matters such as this.

In the very close contacts which it was necessary for me to maintain during the creative period of this project, I saw much of Messrs. Morgan, McMahon and Deeds. The happy culmination of all our combined efforts is shown in the following letter:

February 7, 1914

My dear Governor:

I can scarcely realize that our flood measure is soon to become a law. It is still more difficult to realize that the emergency clause has been re-instated.

I want to thank you personally and for our Flood Prevention Committee and for the people of the Miami Valley, insofar as our Flood Prevention Committee reaches them, for your extreme courtesy to us while in the capital and for your effective support of the measure.

I fully appreciate that without you in the Governor's chair, we would not have had the law under which we will be able to work out the salvation of the whole valley, and whether or not the people as a whole fully appreciate this, I want to assure you that, so far as our committee and those whom we reach and myself are concerned, we do most fully appreciate this.

Again I want to thank you for the great service which you have rendered our community, the State and what I predict within the next five or ten years will be a great service to our whole United States.

Yours sincerely,

E. A. Deeds

CHAPTER XV

A TEMPORARY DEFEAT

◆

THE LEGISLATIVE work of my first term was now completed, every mandate of the constitution had been carried out and the major reforms promised in our party platform had been adopted. Now, with new administrative machinery working in satisfactory manner, the time came to submit it all to the people through the election of 1914. I had said once to William L. Finley, chairman of our state committee, that if I wanted to remain in public life, I would deem it better to be defeated on the first test vote and then to come back to the State house later when the new laws had had an opportunity to demonstrate their worth and with a campaign fought purely on the issue of vindication.

We knew it would be one of the most exciting battles in all our political history. The opposition was well organized and we, too, were eager for the fray. This was the year of the anti-Catholic movement which swept the country. Attorney General Timothy S. Hogan, a Catholic, was the Democratic candidate for the United States senatorship. He was opposed by Warren G. Harding. "Read the *Menace*" was on fences, billboards, freight cars and everything else which could be utilized. In chalk and paint we saw it everywhere and the slogan was,

> Read the *Menace* and get the dope,
> Go to the polls and beat the Pope.

Early in the campaign it became apparent that a great fanaticism was developing. In smaller communities we ran across handbills announcing church meetings. I was urged by a great many to make as few public appearances as possible with General Hogan. This advice I refused. In fact, I asked him to accompany me everywhere, all over the state, even in the strongholds of religious opposition. The Catholic candidates were defeated everywhere. Among others, Governor Martin Glynn was rejected for re-election in New York State. Harding defeated Hogan by 100,000 votes. By about the same figures Harmon had defeated Harding for the governorship in 1910, which would seem to show that in those days Harding was not a conspicuously strong vote-getter. The political story of Ohio shows that a Catholic was never elected United States senator or governor until the election of 1944 when Frank Lausche broke all precedent. As a non-Catholic I cannot regard this past evidence of religious prejudice as worthy of one of our great commonwealths. This religious issue turned countless thousands of voters from giving attention to the only issue that deserved to be discussed—the new order which grew out of the constitutional changes through legislative enactments. Then the wet and dry question, of course, came in. Ohio was the birthplace of the Anti-Saloon League, presided over by Purley L. Baker, its head. I always regarded him as a man utterly without character, a professional prohibitionist, moved by thought of self rather than the public welfare.

The driving leader of the League, Wayne B. Wheeler, who became first its state superintendent in Ohio and then general counsel of its national organization, was a very different type of man. One needed only to look at him to realize that he was a dynamo. A comparatively small man with a big head and protruding brow, he was always busy, always hurried, always completely intent on his goal. He was a likable person, friendly in manner and interested in everybody, even saloonkeepers. Once when he was busy lobbying in Columbus, he accosted the venerable Judge Dennis J. Dwyer, then over eighty years old and still active, who was known as a bitter enemy of the League. "How do you account for your long life, Judge?" Wheeler inquired. "I always take my whiskey straight!" Dwyer roared. But Wheeler would make any combination, would cohabit politically with the devil himself, to win. He was truthful, and his word could always be depended upon; but the end, with him, justified the means. In elections on the saloon issues ministers and bootleggers often voted the dry ticket together. Wheeler fought me bitterly in all my campaigns, but I respected him and I think he did me. Our relations were always cordial.

Frank B. Willis, the Republican candidate for governor, and Simeon

Fess, who was to succeed Harding in the Senate after 1920, were the political children of the Anti-Saloon League. Willis was a jovial fellow, big in heart and body, the kind that never took public service very seriously, and pretty much laughed his way through every day. He was a good speaker, largely following the manner of the religious evangelist. He devoted most of his time to an attempt to burlesque the operation of the new government. It will be recalled that when the constitution adopted the system of licensing the saloon traffic and when the law was finally passed, I had let it be known that the law was to be enforced. Persons of ill repute would not be licensed and both the front and the back doors of the liquor establishments would be locked up on Sundays. To the surprise of a great many, this is precisely what was done; in Cincinnati, particularly, it was a shock. And then came protests and threats of reprisal at the polls. In Hamilton County, the county seat of which is Cincinnati, Willis, the prohibitionist, carried the day without reservation. This was due entirely to our establishing proper observance of the Sabbath Day. After prohibition had passed and we came back to the licensing system, the system which was established in 1913 and 1914 continued. The man who sells liquor on Sundays incurs the penalty of having his license revoked. A sense of self-preservation brought a new standard of conduct with our saloonkeepers.

Under the new constitution, the number of saloons was limited; there could not be more than one to each 1000 people in any community, and this meant that many who applied for licenses were disappointed. Politicians besought me to have the announcement of the list of licensees deferred until after the election, so that the rejected men would not have an opportunity to revenge themselves upon the party in power. I thought this improper, and had the list announced before Election Day. This meant a loss of votes.

The Warnes tax law which has been described brought into the campaign picturesque, if not in some instances grotesque, aspects. Thousands of county assessors who had been elected under the old order were on a rampage. A kingly power, as they put it, established in the State house, had deprived the people of the right to select those who would list property for taxation. During that campaign, on street corners of villages and in the country stores protests were heard. These were usually incited by the old assessor who had been

180

uprooted by modern devices—laws, incidentally, which had been recommended for more than half a century by both Democratic and Republican governors and by able economists. Every now and then there was to be found a wooden leg worn by a disabled Union soldier stamping disapproval. Then there was an inarticulate vote cast against it by those who had been evading taxes and throwing the burden of maintaining local government on their neighbors.

In the attacks on that part of our administrative policy relating to taxation, even English despots were brought into the picture in order to establish a parallel calculated to arouse the unthinking. My files reveal a document from which the following passages were taken:

"The principle of consulting local sentiment in assessing taxes on real and personal property is fundamental in our form of government and has existed from the assessment of the first tax on movables—known as the Saladin tithes—in the reign of Henry II in 1188. It rests upon the 'deepest foundations of political justice—the principle that Englishmen cannot rightfully be taxed except by their own taxing agents selected by themselves.' 'Taxation of the people by themselves'—Henry resolutions in Virginia assembly—'or by persons chosen by themselves to represent them, is the distinguishing characteristic of British freedom without which the ancient constitution cannot exist.' Ignoring this proposition, George III lost the American colonies just as for the same reason a century before Charles I lost his head."

This revealed the general character of the campaign. The local assessor whose tenure was dependent entirely upon his neglect of duty was made a martyr, even though it was very evident, and had been for a generation, that this old system was a part of the democratic processes which did not work.

The new school code set in motion a tremendously active opposition. Most of the small school districts had been little empires. These were broken up and when you added together all of those whose status was disturbed, you had a vast army. Out of this came a rather clever campaign device. Stamps were printed showing in bold relief the little one-room schoolhouse. They were attached to envelopes in the mail and used as posters generally. They were meant to symbolize the good old days and to destroy politically the administration which was attempting to discard their practices. The Conservancy

Act, even though it is now recognized as a beneficent provision, was misunderstood in the counties north of Dayton. There was a general belief, and it was sincere, too, that lands and villages would be flooded by backwater from the dams. This, in some respects, was frantic opposition. At a village outdoor meeting at West Milton in Miami County during this campaign, I asked whether it was fair that the great areas above us should pour their waters onto us in a devastating way. Someone in the audience replied with some spirit, "Nor should you throw them back into our faces." In due time this alarm was allayed, but the election had come and gone long before. The uprising cost us thousands of votes.

Outside of the Anti-Saloon League, the best-organized power asserted against us came from the liability insurance companies. Their agents in every county were active and they were influential members of society. Prodigious funds were provided.

A very curious thing happened during the early part of 1914. An organization was perfected under the name of the "True Democracy." Its founder was Harvey C. Garber. He had a rather unusual career, serving in the state legislature and for many years with the Central Union Telephone Company, a subsidiary of the Bell Corporation. That was in the day when men who had gained a considerable acquaintance over the state through their legislative services and who knew the ins and outs of the State house were often sought and employed by the large corporations. Garber was an astute politician and developed a good deal of influence in support of or opposition to any movement or candidate. He was elected to Congress from what was known as the Greenville district and became a very close friend of William Jennings Bryan. Many of his years were spent in lobbying in behalf of corporations. He was for or against the wets as circumstances determined, and sometimes with and sometimes against Harry M. Daugherty in State house manipulations. He was a factor in the election of John M. Pattison in 1906, over Myron T. Herrick, who was completing his first term. While Mr. Pattison possessed the power of a real and sincere crusader for prohibition, he would not have been successful except for the internal war in the Republican party. The Mark Hanna forces on the one hand and Foraker's followers on the other had come to political grips. Herrick, living in Hanna's home city and closely aligned to his organization, was secretly fought by Foraker, who had a very militant and well-organized force behind him.

Garber never underappraised himself. Sensing the prestige which had come from his leadership in the Pattison campaign, he thirsted for more and more power. He had a Napoleonic turn of mind and read almost everything that had been written about the Little Corsican. He could repeat without end his maxims and made a layman's study of his military strategy. It is my impression that he became estranged from the Democratic cause soon after my election in 1912 because he had hoped to be chairman of the state committee. Mr. Garber subsequently came back to the party and, having a considerable acquaintanceship all over the country, he was very industrious in helping the Ohio delegation in the San Francisco convention of 1920.

The "True Democracy" in the campaign of 1914 was well financed, and disgruntled groups herded themselves under the banner of the new outfit. John J. Whitacre, a member of Congress from the Canton district, was finally induced to be a candidate against me in the primary. The impression at the time was that he had been led to believe that he could be nominated and elected. During the primary campaign he was still in Congress and we once visited and dined together on a train to Washington. He afterwards told me that he was sick of the whole thing at that time, wanted to get out of it and above all things desired that I ask him to retire. This I did not do. In fact, his candidacy was not mentioned. In the general election he supported me and in every campaign afterwards in which I was a candidate he was a very loyal and helpful aide. Another issue with low melodramatic features came from a very silly circumstance. The editor of our Springfield paper, apparently hearing his wife complain of so many canvassers appearing at her door, wrote an editorial asking whether the thing wasn't being overdone. It was immediately seized upon by the Commercial Travelers in the state. It was bestirred by the use of money and from one end of the state to the other many of the members of that organization were very noisy emissaries of the opposition. They certainly made the welkin ring. It was suspected that Harvey Garber put this in motion.

State and national administrations usually have difficulties with patronage. This was not much of a factor in the contest for my first

183

re-election, however, because I had made it a point not to make promises. If an individual or a group called at the State house to urge appointment of some individual or request furtherance of some matter before the state departments, it was my unbroken rule to observe merely that the matter would be thoroughly investigated. Even if it seemed at the time that the answer would be favorable, assurance was still withheld. This policy always paid dividends. Then, too, we made it a practice to turn no one away from the State house who was there on business. The large reception room was on occasions filled to overflowing with individuals and delegations representing sundry interests. When I entered it there was with me a competent shorthand man. I would dictate the substance of the matter presented and if it involved reference to a state department, the secretary took charge of it. There was a psychological advantage in this. With so many things falling to the attention of a governor of a state, the man with ordinary intelligence would know they could not all be carried in the executive mind, but by the practice which I have described, those who came went away knowing that the matter would have attention. A problem of executives, particularly those in the larger states, is to prevent the waste of time. There is nothing more upsetting than to have a delegation whittle away precious minutes reciting facts either thoroughly well known or not at all germane to the subject matter. With state departments in competent hands, the heads can develop, with the assistance of the governor, their own individuality and prestige. This greatly facilitates the flow of official business.

I remember at one time, while lunching with President Franklin D. Roosevelt at his desk, he stated that he had sixteen conferences arranged for that day. I told him I thought that was an impossible situation which Grover Cleveland, for instance, would never have permitted to develop. Instead he would have put his cabinet to work.

It pays to deal in the utmost good faith with the organizations of one's party. If an unworthy or inefficient person were endorsed for an appointment, the chairman of the committee was plainly told why favorable action could not be taken. The committee would be privileged to find someone else and if he did not meet the requirements, then I would act without further reference to the organization. This enabled local units to maintain their prestige at home and they all knew that it was useless to come to the State house sponsoring someone who could not meet proper requirements.

The question might easily arise that if our whole program possessed the virtues which we claimed for it, then why were not more people for it than against it? This brings up the curious phase of human nature as we see it in political affairs. Most of those in opposition were not moved by principle. With them, it was a grievance, and they remained militant until Election Day. There was no need of hauling them to the polls. This type votes early. On the other side, a certain portion, in support of a movement such as we were maintaining, accepted what was done as a matter of course. Believing it was the plain duty of the administration so to do, they held to their political lines. When the returns were canvassed, it developed that we had polled a tremendous Republican vote. Labor was well nigh unanimous because of the compensation laws. The teaching force of the state was actively with us. Many adherents of the dry cause approved of the workings of the liquor licensing law. Even the tax law, although it was decidedly a debit in the situation, brought us more than partisan support. But these elements were not organized.

It was a tremendously interesting campaign. Mr. Willis, the Republican candidate, made a vigorous canvass. We, too, were at it day and night. The practice was to visit villages within a given area by automobile and follow these visits by two or three big meetings in as many county seats at night. With the approach of Election Day the trend was in our favor, and the old-timers around the State house, speaking from experience, said that within another thirty days our cause would have found endorsement at the polls.

Our newspaper support was imposing, certainly never surpassed in any previous campaign in our state and possibly never equalled. Nor was it a perfunctory sponsorship. The Cleveland *Plain Dealer*, the Columbus *Dispatch*, the *Ohio State Journal*, the Cleveland *Press*, the Columbus *Citizen*, the Toledo *News-Bee*, the Youngstown *Vindicator*, the Cincinnati *Post*, our two papers, the Dayton *Daily News* and the Springfield *Daily News*, the Hamilton *Journal*, the Portsmouth *Times*, the Canton *News*, the Cambridge *Jeffersonian* (Independent), the Sidney *News* (Independent)—all of these earnestly supported the new order. Two editors who stood out as able sponsors of the new era and whose services were of great value were Paul Bellamy of the Cleveland *Plain Dealer* and Earle Martin of the Scripps-Howard newspapers. The Cincinnati *Enquirer* did not editorially endorse my candidacy, but the state correspondent, James W. Faulkner, was infinitely more influential in my behalf than any editor at the home office could possibly have been. The part that a few newspapermen have played in the careers of public figures has never in the fitness of things been properly mentioned. I would be singularly lacking in both truth and courtesy not to say that James W. Faulkner was a factor in the overhauling of the state government in Ohio and the building of a public confidence that kept the new order intact.

Faulkner was one of the most remarkable men I ever knew, amazing in his fund of information, attractive in his qualities of companionship, and he will be long remembered for his philosophy. He was a part of the history of our state and the days which linked me with political and official matters cannot be reported without reference to him. He had an encyclopedic mind, and his background consisted of a wide knowledge of political, religious, economic and social movements. He even knew a great deal about chemistry and was an intelligent lay student of medical science. Two eminent judges of our Supreme Court at different times told me that they always profited by a touch of minds with Mr. Faulkner.

A year ago Herbert R. Mengert, who was trained under Mr. Faulkner, wrote of his chief, "In the twenty years that have passed since the death of James W. Faulkner, no one has arisen to be even a near rival to his fame as a newspaperman or 'Doctor of Letters,' the title which Miami University accorded to him. At the time of his passing, in 1923, his Washington associates summed it up when they placed this tribute on his bier: 'He was the only newspaper correspondent in the country assigned to a state capital who outranked a Washington correspondent.'

"And there were notables of the era in which he served, including Louis Seibold of the New York *World*, Richard Oulahan of the New York *Times*, Samuel G. Blythe of the *Saturday Evening Post*, James Montague, versifier of the Hearst papers, Mark Sullivan, Jay G. Hayden, Arthur Sears Henning of the Chicago *Tribune* and others. Henning, Sullivan and Hayden are among the minority of associates of 'Jim' who are still active in the world of journalism."

Fraud and hypocrisy suffered at his hands and even though his pen cut like a rapier at times, he never indulged in personalities. Few

186

people may recall that Theodore Roosevelt brought suit against a trade paper in Michigan which had attacked his personal habits. When the suit was tried, Colonel Roosevelt subpoenaed Mr. Faulkner as a witness because he had accompanied the distinguished American on many of his campaign tours. Apparently the determination of the case turned upon his testimony. He said that on many occasions the Colonel's manners might, to one unacquainted with him, have indicated that he was under the influence of liquor. He asserted that at one time he saw him climb to the top of a freight car and address an impromptu audience. Mr. Faulkner summed it all up in substantially these words, "I saw much of Colonel Roosevelt, but no evidence of bibulous inclinations or habit. When men who did not know him thought that he had imbibed freely, he was intoxicated by his own emotions. His was an intense nature and he experienced moments of tremendous, intense pressure. At those times he was completely under that control. Liquor had nothing to do with it."

Like all men of distinguished mind and character, Faulkner worshiped his mother. Her very name to him was a shrine. At the Republican National Convention in 1920, Faulkner predicted accurately that the Republican party meant to discard the League of Nations if it won the election. He described the skillful speech of Senator Henry Cabot Lodge, which he said concentrated on "arousing the intense antipathy of the throng to President Woodrow Wilson. No array of spectators in a Roman arena ever decreed more definitely the death of a gladiator than when this assemblage of ardent opponents of the chief executive marked their disapproval of his administration and its policies."

Presidents and governors offered Faulkner blank commissions for him to fill out if he would agree to accept an appointment. These tenders were always declined appreciatively but firmly. Perhaps no writer of his time so employed the logic of Holy Writ as applied to persons and events. In his desk was a well-worn Bible. This was presented to me by his sister after his death.

I prize something Mr. Faulkner wrote after my first election to Congress in 1908. He certainly assumed the risk of prophecy, but this is what he said: "Cox's rise is worthy of note. From being a corking good reporter in Cincinnati, he went to Washington as the private secretary to the late Congressman Paul J. Sorg. He worked hard and kept his chief to the front. That's an old story of statesmen and secretaries. Today, he stands the chosen successor of Sorg and at the head of a newspaper of his own. In March he will sit in the seat that Schenck, Vallandigham and McMahon adorned and made famous. Nor will he disgrace it if past performance be any criterion of the future. It is safe to say that the man who accomplished so much in ten brief years will not fail in this newer task."

Mr. Faulkner died at the Waldorf-Astoria in New York and his last hours were characteristic of the man. At eventide, an old newspaper friend, Jap Muma, left the bedside of the sick man, observing that he would see him in the morning. To this Mr. Faulkner replied, without emotion and with seeming anticipation of a pleasant journey, "You will not see me in the morning. I think I will go over the hill tonight." Putting his hand to his heart, he said, "The doctors can't fool me. My race is run and will end before the dawn." I hope that journey was a pleasant one to the richest blessings of immortality.

Former Governor Judson Harmon and I were both honored to be pallbearers.

In the election, the vote was as follows: Willis (R), 523,070; Cox (D), 493,804; James R. Garfield (Progressive), 60,904. It will be seen that the progressive vote including that cast for Garfield and myself totaled 554,708. The Bull Moose party doubtless nominated its ticket in the hope of keeping the party alive. It resulted in a division of like minds which may have determined the result at the polls.

Before I retired from office a message to the General Assembly called attention to the fiscal affairs of the state. In the general revenue fund as of December 31, 1914, there was a sum pronounced then "unprecedented in size." This had come despite unusual and unforeseen expenditures. The flood catastrophe had cost $1,000,000, and a quarter of a million dollars had been appropriated to take care of the long-prevalent deficiency system which gathered up the remnants of the previous administration. Three and a quarter million dollars had been spent for our universities, normal schools, state hospitals and correctional institutions. These betterments during the years 1913 and 1914 cost as much money as had been provided for these purposes in the four previous years.

I had a feeling that there should be settled for all time a matter which had been discussed, evaded and ignored for so many years and in such a way as to come to be a current joke. With all its wealth, the State of Ohio had provided no home for its governors. In the old days, the chief executive was not expected to live in Columbus, coming there only when the legislature was in session. Of course, this was in time outgrown. In 1880 Governor Bishop, on retiring from office, had asked the legislature to make provision for his successors. Governor Foster in 1881 and 1883 had said, "The reasons for this recommendation are so apparent that it is needless to refer to them." Governor Hoadly had asked in 1886 that a home be provided for him. In 1889 Governor Foraker had said, "Aside from the inconvenience resulting from having no fixed home for the executive, it is sometimes difficult to find for rent a suitable house."

During the term of Myron T. Herrick as governor, a bill was passed providing for an executive home. Herrick was a man of large means and that might have prompted him to veto the bill. It seemed to me that the time had come to speak very plainly on the subject and this I attempted to do in these words: "To an Ohioan, at least, the position of Governor of this State is second only in importance to the Presidency of the Republic He who occupies this responsible station should live in a manner befitting the dignity of the place. This entails a considerable cost which the Governor should not himself bear. Living as we are under a liberal democracy, our people frown upon pomp or display; and yet a calculated, deliberate, obtrusive and otherwise mawkish simplicity is more offensive to our sensibilities than gaudy ceremonial. I have gone to the trouble of making inquiry from other states as to what they have done in this connection, and find that 33 commonwealths have provided homes for the Chief Executive. Every state of importance has done so and Ohio should no longer continue an obvious neglect of duty."

Nothing was done that year; but when I came back into office, the necessary legislation was enacted. I appointed three former governors—Campbell, Herrick and Harmon—to administer the fund. The project was carried out, and the state now takes pride in its mansion.

Throughout these years I was a strong supporter of the salient measures of the Wilson administration. The downward revision of the tariff especially appealed to me, while I thoroughly approved

189

of the provisions of the Clayton Act to protect labor, and of the new Federal Reserve Act. In the field of foreign affairs Wilson's ideas and policies commanded my general admiration. While I earnestly hoped that the United States would not be drawn into the World War, I was not for surrendering a single one of the historic rights of neutrals, and I agreed with the President that the unrestricted submarine warfare of Germany could not be tolerated. The great domestic achievements of the Wilson administration in its first two years, 1913–15, gave all believers in liberalism a sense that the goals of which they had dreamed were being gained. I had always thought highly of Wilson, and now his leadership vindicated my faith.

CHAPTER XVI

PROGRESSIVISM VINDICATED

◆

I WENT OUT of office in January, 1915, and by the beginning of the next year a campaign was on for the vindication of our new order. I returned to my newspapers in Dayton and Springfield, but kept very close watch on the trend of things in the State house, being careful to observe that the new administration, which had been elected in opposition to the progressive movement, did not dare touch major features of it. That prepared the way for the next campaign.

In taking up again the pleasant tasks of journalism, I attempted to develop a new idea. It seemed to me that the press was not dealing adequately with the background of the news. Spot news, so-called, was being well covered, but conditions out of which came the drama of human activities had scant attention. To both Kent Cooper of the Associated Press and John N. Wheeler of the North American Newspaper Alliance I predicted that if newspapers did not move into this field, weekly magazines would. Those words were more prophetic than could possibly have been realized at the time. I tried also in vain to have Mr. Cooper put on the Associated Press wires every morning a fresh and comprehensive glimpse of New York, in some respects the great center of our country. My recommendation was that a few words be said descriptive of the weather, the new plays or moving pictures and what eminent critics had to say, along with editorial excerpts from the New York papers on matters of moment, and interesting bits that could be gathered from special cable correspondence and not covered by the press associations. Mr. Cooper even had me write two or three samples. This I did, but he gave the unsatisfactory, although complimentary, response that if I would come to New York and do it, he would initiate the service.

The newspaper fraternity, world-wide, owes much to Kent Cooper of the Associated Press. His book, *Barriers Down*, brought the initial break-up of a system which, in Europe particularly, had been of tremendous disservice to our present day. What he has done, as it is quite apparent now, is a forerunner of the movement now in motion to bring in to the new world ahead of us the complete unshackling of the truth. The public opinion of the world cannot be intelligent or controlling unless it is formed from a truthful presentation of what is going on. Europe has suffered great confusion and worse by dishonest and untruthful propaganda. Out of it came venal newspapers which, under the processes of subsidy and corruption, found a lazy way of making a living.

There could have been no more propitious setting for the campaign of 1916. I had been renominated at the summer primary and the state was not long in realizing that there was a tremendous interest not only in the presidential, but in the state election as well. The state convention of our party was held in Columbus. Under the primary system, the convention is nothing more than a formality, called chiefly for the purpose of announcing the party platform of principles. Newton D. Baker, then Secretary of War, as chairman, delivered in his ablest thought and phrase what one would naturally expect from one who revered the mind and character of President Wilson and held for him deep personal affection. There had been some doubt as to the propriety of having a member of the cabinet present. I had urged it upon the President and in his response he said:

"As you know, on general principles, I have thought it unwise for members of the cabinet to take an active part in pending political contests, but I yield to your judgment. I have been sure all along that you could not have made a better choice so far as the Secretary himself is concerned, who has my most cordial and affectionate admiration."

The Democratic party asked only for the vindication of the administration which had been voted out in 1914. As someone very aptly put it, the election that year came too soon. A number of major operations had been performed on the state government and there was not sufficient time for convalescence when Election Day arrived. In 1916, however, the situation was changed. Every word the opposition had uttered or printed either by speaker or press in attempting to ridicule certain phases of the new order was recalled. The inference had been that if the Republicans gained control in the 1914 contest, the things they had reviled would, of course, be repealed. Two years had now elapsed and the state was reminded that the program stood intact and that the Republican regime had not dared dismember it. The opposition was clearly on the defensive. That was the whole and continuing tempo of the campaign.

National speakers, as a part of the national contest, were assigned by both parties to all parts of the state. Our meetings were enthusiastic and we were not long in sensing the fact that Wilson's keeping us out of war would be a factor in Ohio. This had been emphasized by the speech of Martin H. Glynn, as temporary chairman of the national convention in St. Louis, which renominated Mr. Wilson. It was a noteworthy document. Glynn, running through our history, impressively brought attention to the many provocative episodes which might easily have occasioned war. He gave a careful recital of each disturbance and in each case concluded in these words: "But we didn't go to war." In the calm judgment of time, hostilities, if they had come, would now be regarded as the fruitage of a very ill-advised foreign policy. Time after time through Glynn's speech he thundered out, "But we didn't go to war." This easily developed the strategy of the campaign.

About a week before the election, I was speaking in northeastern Ohio and came into Cleveland while former President Theodore Roosevelt was there. He had been thundering for war without reservation. The Republican candidate, Charles E. Hughes, had assumed a more cautious attitude. Colonel Roosevelt and I spoke the same night in Cleveland and after the meetings when we discovered we were in the same hotel, he asked that we visit together. With a smile he snapped out at once, "I see, Governor, where you have been talking about me a lot." I pleaded guilty to the indictment, but called his attention to the fact that I was simply contrasting his speeches with those of Mr. Hughes. "I hope," said he, "that everyone realizes just where I stand. I can't say so much for our candidate and I am not assuming to speak for him."

As one reviews the battle of Gettysburg, and applies two or three "ifs," he can easily see how the result might have been different. The same is true when the campaign of 1916 is reviewed. The general impression was that it would be a close election and that Ohio

193

might play a deciding part. Vance McCormick, Chairman of the Democratic Committee, placed our state in the debatable list. The Columbus *Dispatch* had conducted a most thorough, painstaking and efficient poll which ran into every county and every class of voters. By the early part of October, the poll showed that Wilson would carry the state. I happened to be shown the accumulated figures, all of which could not be published for some two or three weeks. One Sunday afternoon, I called President Wilson by telephone and told him that if the poll was to be relied upon, and we had every confidence in it, he would have a majority of 100,000 in our state. The cheering effect that this had upon him is evidenced by his words, which were: "This is the best news yet of the campaign." As it turned out, Wilson's majority ran approximately into that figure, ninety some thousand to be exact. While my vote in 1912 exceeded Wilson's, the outcome was just the other way around in 1916. Judge Hughes, the Republican candidate, went to his bed election night believing that he was elected. Wilson was certain that he had been defeated. His secretary, Mr. Tumulty, reported to me about that time that the President was cheerful when he arose in the morning and that while stropping his razor before breakfast, he was whistling. Not long afterwards, the surprising news came. It is a matter of record that our paper in Dayton, the *News*, was the first in the country in a special edition to claim Wilson's election. Judge William A. Budroe, of our city, in my private office, had been carefully compiling all the figures that had come in, particularly in strategic states. About three o'clock in the morning he exclaimed, "Wilson is elected!" Before daylight our paper was on the streets heralding for the first time the news which cheered the Wilson followers.

In all my experience there was never anything quite like inauguration day in 1917. In running through newspaper files, we find that the largest crowd in the history of Columbus had assembled for the event. It was in all respects a triumphant Democratic day. We had been returned to power in the state and Ohio had, as it turned out, elected Wilson.

I look back with some pride upon the general tenor of the first message to the newly elected legislature. We called for no more major legislation. The reform in all its major essentials had been complete, "because in theory it was based upon the philosophy and

194

justice of government and in practice laws passed pursuant to that policy had proved both efficient and humane. Let me impress upon you, however, with most respectful emphasis, that progress is made by two distinct stages, and if results are to justify the basic principle there must be two objectives: first, the drafting of the laws with such forethought as the finite mind possesses, and second, the most vigilant and sympathetic administration of them. Newly cleared ground is more susceptible of rank undergrowth and in this biennial period when your responsibilities and mine are in common, we must, in order to approach the maximum possibilities for the general good, hold to the fundamentals upon which the new legislation was based, and go no further in this session than to provide for accruing necessities. Unrestrained reform would soon turn the thought of the state to reaction and the public estimate would be that we were controlled more by caprice than constructive capacity. The laws that came from the new constitution four years ago have stood the test of time, and they have successfully run the gauntlet of sustained, insidious and artful opposition. They are structurally sound, and we should be sure that the revision made is but the logical adjustment of an unaltered principle to changing conditions."

The message as a whole dealt with processes of refinement. We had gone far enough. This created a very good effect upon our public opinion and brought the reassurance that the laws which grew out of the new constitution would be retained and be so administered as to demonstrate their desirability.

The *Ohio State Journal* in its issue of March 11 said, "Every recommendation of Governor Cox, as set forth in his message of January 9th, has been enacted into law in a two months' session of the present legislature—the shortest in years. Distinctly unusual is the fact that both labor and capital appear to be satisfied with the new legislation affecting them. In a majority of instances the so-called administration bills were passed without respect to party lines."

CHAPTER XVII

THE ONSET OF THE WORLD WAR

◆

THERE WAS no special session during this biennial period. The war fell upon us a month after the legislature adjourned and quite naturally both thought and effort were directed to the support of the federal government. Not long before the coming of hostilities, a railroad strike was threatened which induced the following statement from the governor's office: "If labor and capital are unpatriotic enough to engage in a grapple of strength which will result in a paralysis of transportation that would endanger our food supplies and keep from President Wilson the supplies he needs in this hour of crisis, I will place the state under martial law and suffer the consequences." An appropriation was made to mobilize and equip the Ohio National Guard, before the declaration of war. The guard was soon thereafter called out and placed at strategic points throughout the state.

George H. Wood was appointed to head the Ohio Division, National Guard, with the rank of major general. This became one of the conspicuous units in the American Expeditionary Forces. It was subsequently commanded by Generals Charles G. Treat, William R. Smith and Charles S. Farnsworth, and wrote its name heroically in the war history by its gallant conduct, particularly in the Argonne campaign.

It so happened that when I was addressing a tremendous war meeting in my home city of Dayton, President Wilson sent his message to the Congress asking for a declaration of war. It was read to the audience. From then on things moved very swiftly. Under a draft quota, our state was asked for 687,000 men. This detail was handled by the executives of the states. There were many calls on our time from communities which were sending their young men to training camps. Unlike our experience in the recent war, cities, villages and even farm communities made a gala day of the departure of their sons. The officers' training camp at Indianapolis, under control of General Glenn, was one of the most complete and efficient in the country. The very flower of our young manhood was largely represented there and we visited them upon occasions. Subsequently Camp Sherman, near Chillicothe, Ohio, was established. General Glenn was assigned to command. On one occasion we reviewed 30,000 troops there, fitted out and ready for combat service. When the Thirty-seventh Division was about to sail, we went to tidewater to see it off. We supplied one regiment from our National Guard to make up the Rainbow Division. When this magnificent body of men embarked for their overseas assignment, our unit—the Fourth Ohio—marched on shipboard beside the Fourth Alabama. Both of these were very old regiments and had faced each other continuously during the War Between the States. They were then Federal and Confederate soldiers; now America was one. It was a very moving circumstance.

The winters of the war were very severe throughout the country, and a fuel shortage occasioned great suffering and privation. Things finally came to a point where large shipments of coal tonnage were passing from West Virginia and southeastern Ohio mines across the state, consigned to the Northwest, the headwaters of lake traffic. It could not conceivably be used there until probably the first of May, yet tens of thousands were without the means of resisting the most severe winter in a generation. We appealed in vain for relief. There was considerable controversy with the Fuel Administration, presided over by Harry Garfield, president of Williams College. The public need and protest became so pressing that we finally seized shipments and turned them over for the relief of local communities. President Wilson approved what we had done as it was apparent to everyone that we were attempting to further the war effort rather than impede it.

We were honored by many distinguished visitors during the war. General Pershing gave us of his time and the impression he made was lasting. Certainly no one ever wore the uniform of an American general with more dignity. He possessed the genius of appraising the special fitness of his subordinate officers and assigned them to places where they grew in stature. He was an excellent judge of men. He stood beside the best officers of England and France and did not have to look up to any of them. Let it be said that regardless of the great generals before him and those that are following now, Pershing will always remain a commanding figure. While his services in preparation of troops and their command at the front inspired the pride of our people, still the great thing that he was responsible for, and historians will so write it, was the stand he made to keep the American forces intact. Lloyd George, Clemenceau and General Foch urged with all their power that Pershing recede from his position. In imploring and vigorous words they directed their appeal to President Wilson, but in vain. Let me recall a conversation with President Wilson in the White House. He said, "I am going to appoint Pershing the head of the army. I don't want any politics in this war. He is said to be a Republican, but he is a good soldier and when we give him command overseas, he will be the commander in fact."

This subject should not be passed without a word for Secretary of War Newton D. Baker. No commander at the front ever had the kind of support which Baker gave to Pershing. In our contacts with the War Department, and we had many in those days, I was also tremendously impressed with General Peyton C. March, the Chief of Staff. He met difficult problems with a full understanding of what they meant in the communities. General Glenn, too, in command of Camp Sherman, was one of the best minds in the American Army, but he was of the controversial type and this doubtless interfered with his advancement. In a great war meeting in Memorial Hall in Columbus, over which I presided, Glenn, always apt to say the wrong thing under the impulse of the moment, was leading into a criticism of the War Department. I immediately introduced another speaker and nothing came of the incident although General Glenn many times, in the years to come, thanked me for what I did.

In the early days of the war I had another very interesting experience in the White House. I had been asked to see the President at five o'clock in the afternoon. He remarked that it was always refreshing to see me because I never asked him for patronage. With scarcely a pause, he said, "You have been here for two or three days. Tell me what is going on in Washington as you see it." I told him first of all that he should send his cabinet members back home for at least ten days or two weeks in order that they might know and know thoroughly that the country was behind the President wholeheartedly. They would be strengthened by it. I compared the situation to many scenes I had witnessed in the great forests of the north which I had visited many times. The woodsmen felled the trees and put them on their way to the pulp mills in the rivers. This work was done admirably, but vigilant crews saw to it that there were no log jams. I told the President that everyone conceded the efficient service of the federal departments, but there seemed to be some lack of coordination. I told him I thought he ought to bring in a big-fisted businessman who would watch the flow of operations in order that the President might not have to labor with that task. The man that he selected would report to the executive only the things which could not be straightened out except by the White House. Within a few days he appointed Edward R. Stettinius, father of Edward R. Stettinius, Jr., who figured prominently in international affairs later. Mr. Stettinius, a few days after the assignment had been given to him, stated to a friend of his and mine that President Wilson had recited our conversation to him and that he presumed he had been chosen in accordance with my suggestion.

This brings to mind what happened when President Wilson sent for Charles M. Schwab to take complete charge of the production of submarines. Wilson had a very direct way of dealing with things both with tongue and eye. "Mr. Schwab," he said, "I realize at the outset of our relations that you do not like me politically any better than I like you, but all this is being waived and I am asking you to come with us because I think you are best fitted for this important task." When the great war parade—a tremendously inspiring thing— was moving down Fifth Avenue in New York, it was my privilege to observe one of the striking sides of Mr. Wilson's character. He led the procession on foot. As it passed the Union League Club, perhaps the most strongly Tory organization we have ever known, there was some applause from the windows of the building. Wilson never turned his head nor made acknowledgment. He would not bend in hypocrisy to man or movement.

As the war in the country was taking definite shape, I recommended to President Wilson that he call the governors of all the states to Washington, urging that practical as well as psychological benefits would accrue. It seemed to me that the whole world would gain a clearer perspective of our situation at home if the executives of all the states assembled at the White House to pledge unwavering support to the Commander-in-Chief. The meeting was called and was held in the East Room of the White House. Calvin Coolidge, Governor of Massachusetts, presided at the morning session. It was the first time I had ever seen him. He was attired faultlessly in English morning dress. The states were called in their alphabetical order. Two or three governors trespassed somewhat on the proprieties and were criticizing some of the executive departments. Their spirit was not constructive. It reflected unmistakably pure political cynicism. When called, I reminded our state executive associates of the purpose of the conference and pointed out that unless it were conducted with a sincere purpose to help, the effect abroad would be harmful. "Speaking for the State of Ohio," I said, "I am here to help in upholding and strengthening the arm of our Commander-in-Chief." In the midst of this line of thought, Coolidge brought the gavel down with a resounding whack. It was evident that he was not in sympathy with what I was saying. In a strong voice, he said, "The time of the Governor of Ohio has expired." Someone proposed unanimous consent that I be permitted to conclude what I had to say. There was no objection but Mr. Coolidge was plainly irritated.

The many sides of Mr. Coolidge have become a legend in this country. No one ever so completely dramatized silence as he did. Let me relate a story which is creditable to his heart. Hoover had been elected, the advance guards of the new regime were moving into Washington, but few if any of them came to the White House. Late one afternoon Joseph P. Tumulty, on appointment, entered the executive offices which he had known so well for eight years, serving as secretary to President Wilson. He apologized for his coming, stating that if the President did not know the background of his visit, he might think that Mr. Tumulty was trespassing on the proprieties. He continued, "Mr. President, I am here in behalf of a friend. He is Finis J. Garrett, now about to go out of the House of Representatives. When I say that he is a friend, I want to go further and tell you that he was a friend in my hours of loneliness. When I left the White House and opened up my law office, there was a notable difference in the number of those who came to see me. Finis Garrett came every day. I shall never forget what it meant to me. You, too, will be lonely, Mr. President. You may be now. If so, you will understand what lies so heavily on my heart. I should like him appointed to one of the federal judgeships in the District. He is able and will never cast discredit upon you. He is not of your party, but I would have been false to my better self if I had not come here in his behalf."

Mr. Coolidge was deeply moved and assured Mr. Tumulty that he did himself credit in remembering what this kind of friendship meant. He assured Mr. Tumulty that he would give the matter full consideration. Within a day or two, in his own handwriting, he sent a note by messenger to Mr. Tumulty stating that he had just dispatched to the Senate the appointment of Finis J. Garrett of Tennessee to the federal judgeship, a life tenure.

From a fisherman in Wisconsin I get another story. Mr. Coolidge had gone there for trout. He and the guide got on very well together. The President, in expressing his gratitude for the fine service rendered, stated that when he left he intended to give the guide a present. The man who had steered the presidential boat to the spots where fish were found in abundance had observed the beautiful sets of tackle that had come from the White House and he was wondering which one would be his. As Mr. Coolidge departed, he presented him one of his photographs. The old guide laughed about it and insisted that the American people had little understanding of Calvin Coolidge and that when he left the affairs of the world behind him and buried himself in the pleasures of forest and stream, he revealed a side that was very attractive.

Coolidge was supposed to be a tightfisted Yankee, holding firm the dollars which he could earn, and yet at one time, even after he left the presidency, he refused $75,000 in cash for the use of Mrs. Coolidge's name in some kind of competitive contest to be carried on by a widely advertised product. The offer was made by Albert D. Lasker, a very close friend of Coolidge. Mr. Lasker related the circumstance to me. Mr. Coolidge simply said, "She wouldn't like it." Mrs. Coolidge was a great asset to the President, popular with all classes. She takes rank with the most illustrious first ladies who have presided at the White House.

Let no one have the mistaken idea that Coolidge was politically inept. A story related to me by Senator Borah gives the contrary view. One morning, as Borah was entering the White House, Norris, then in the Senate, was coming out. Borah asked the Nebraskan to wait and they would go up to the Capitol together. A man with powerful political backing was seeking appointment to the federal bench in California, and Coolidge exhibited letters which he had received to the effect that the aspirant was not a proper person for the place. Norris and Borah were quite in agreement with this. They were members of the Judiciary Committee which passes on all appointments to the bench. Coolidge did not want to offend his political supporters in the West and yet he did not want the man to go on the bench. He evidently hoped Borah and Norris would block the appointment which, in a day or so, he sent to the Senate. The two senators were not interested in pulling the President's chestnuts out of the fire. They placed the whole responsibility on the White House and allowed the confirmation to go through.

Coolidge's career, after his governorship in Massachusetts, was due to a freak of politics. When the police force in Boston went on strike, the mayor of the city, Andrew J. Peters, took a resolute stand against it. Coolidge was silent. When it became evident that the turn in public opinion had come, Coolidge, as governor, issued a statement which caught the imagination of the country and Peters' part was entirely overlooked. Except for this, I think it will be agreed among political students, the vice-presidential nominee would have been Irvine L. Lenroot of Wisconsin, and it would have been, at Mr. Harding's death, President Lenroot instead of President Coolidge.

It is probably true that with all men of note, little things sometimes supply a key to the eccentricities of the individual. We get a glimpse of Coolidge's thrift from a story which was recited in my presence by an attache of the White House. It was in the days when the President occasionally went yachting down the Potomac on the *Mayflower*. Coolidge, it will be recalled, was not a striking figure in his admiral's cap, but he enjoyed getting away from things. The trips were usually made on Saturdays. On a given occasion, some checking-up was done by the ship steward with the President the day before. The item of cigars was reached and the steward suggested that they would better lay in another box, to which the President responded, "This isn't necessary. There were three cigars left in that box on our last trip."

In the mountains and valleys of New Hampshire and Vermont, thrift has been a necessary part of the habits of life. One must know that country to appreciate it. I spent summers in both the White and Green Mountains and I have happy memories of them. Between the rugged heights, the valleys are narrow, but fairly fertile. The domestic budget must be carefully conducted. Fields do not yield the cereals abundantly found in other parts of the country. Milk and butter and eggs, raspberries and flowers in the summer, and honey, too, are the attractive contributions to the table of the tens of thousands of visitors. Many able men have come out of these parts, perhaps because of the opportunities for study afforded by the long winter seasons. The houses and yards are neatly kept. The long rick of wood is close by the kitchen door and only a few steps away is the barn, for it is convenient to have domestic animals near by when the snowdrifts are heavy. They are fine, God-fearing people. From the Coolidge tradition can never be effaced the picture, mirrored in the American mind, of the father administering in the light of a kerosene lamp the presidential oath of office to his son.

What Coolidge's place in history will be remains to be seen. Charged against him will be his stubborn insistence on the payment of international debts which had been made impossible by the trade policy of his own party. To those who attempted to work out something constructive, Coolidge was a constant irritant. They felt he had lost sight entirely of the realities of the situation.

The meeting of governors in the White House turned out to be quite successful. The President was very well pleased with it.

Among other distinguished figures who came to us during the war was General Joffre, the hero of the Marne, who, with his taxicab army, had saved Paris in the first advance of the Germans. The welcome to Joffre was in the State house grounds on a beautiful evening. Of course, great adulation was showered upon him. Many women, in the French custom, showered him with kisses and his face was covered with rouge. He enjoyed the performance and the spectacle as much as anyone.

Eddie Rickenbacker, the flying ace, came home and it would have been treason for anyone in the state not to regard him as a hero of the war.

Admiral Sims also came to us with a considerable halo of public acclaim. At a banquet given in his honor, I, as governor, chanced to preside. On my right was Sims, on my left Senator Harding. In the press generally, there was speculation as to coming presidential nominees and for a time some thought that honors might go to military men as they had in earlier days to Taylor, Harrison, Grant and others. Senator Harding was being discussed. I chanced to know that

Admiral Sims was not born in this country, so in the facetious spirit of a banquet table I remarked, turning to Senator Harding, that there was one military hero who would not be in his way because the circumstances of his birth had put him outside the list. When Sims was introduced, it was noted that he laid aside the text of his speech and did not refer to it. On the contrary, he went immediately into reminding us that he was not ineligible for presidential distinction. The matter had apparently been very well worked out in his mind. It seems that his parents were on sojourn in another country when he was born and the Supreme Court once had rendered a decision that the child of American citizens, born when they were out of the country, inherited all the privileges of our institutions. The audience was much amused, and Harding, who had a fine sense of humor, was not unimpressed by the implications of the event.

King Albert of Belgium, with the Queen and Crown Prince, came to our state. It fell upon me as governor to be the official host and I saw a great deal of this charming family. The King was a handsome man, of magnificent physical proportions, and he had quite a complete understanding of the social changes that were going on in this country. He knew a good deal about the recent overhauling of our government in Ohio and asked many questions about our Workmen's Compensation Law. He pronounced it an outstanding humanitarian measure. The Queen, although of German origin, reacted bitterly to the outrages which the Kaiser's army had inflicted upon the people of Belgium. The Crown Prince could easily have been taken for a fine, upstanding, well-mannered American youth.

Another visitor was Cardinal Mercier, the ecclesiastic superior of the Catholic Church in Belgium. He must have been six feet two in height. He won the heart of everyone who met him by his fine spiritual bearing. I accompanied him to Cincinnati, where he spoke in one of the large churches there. During the course of our visits together, he told me much of his experiences during the war. He was hemmed in by German generals. The bounds beyond which he could not go in the city were constantly narrowed and his conveniences diminished in the hope that the cardinal would accept the German occupancy of Belgium. He never relented. An emissary came to him from Kaiser Wilhelm telling him that the war could have but one end, victory to the Prussian army, and that it was use-

204

less to count on support from America. The prelate said, "We'll wait and see." In due time, Cardinal Mercier sent a trusted messenger to two of the great ports of France to see at close hand whether troops were arriving from America. When he came back soon afterwards, he fell into the cardinal's arms and with tears streaming down his cheeks told him that every day more than 20,000 fine American troops were being unloaded on the soil of France.

An interesting visitor at this time was Ignace Paderewski, the eminent musician and Polish patriot. He was our guest in Ohio for several days and he and I spoke together at large meetings in Columbus and Dayton. His very soul was aflame with patriotism and love for his native land. Incidentally, he was a very good speaker.

Reference has been made to General Pershing's stand against breaking up the American Expeditionary Forces overseas. By singular coincidence, the War Department was attempting to do with our National Guard Division, the Thirty-seventh, precisely what George, Clemenceau and Foch were trying to persuade Pershing to do. Our unit was to be broken up and parts sent to supplement the troops from other states. The National Guard had been an admirable organization throughout the years and it was held in pride by every section in our state. We voiced our objections to the War Department, but to no avail. Finally, under date of June 25, 1917, I dispatched the following telegram to President Wilson:

"In the name of Ohio, I respectfully but vigorously protest against the outrage attempted on our soldiers by the regular army officers in Washington. In the period ending June tenth, the Ohio National Guard led the nation in recruiting. In Red Cross contributions, Ohio is second. In percentage of registrations Ohio was second. We have the necessary units for a division because cavalry is not to be used, but if needed the cavalry regiment can be found in one week. The regular army plan is to split our troops and bolster up states that need it. Our National Guard officers who have been faithful through the years see their chances of reward disappear and preference visited upon the inner military circles of Washington. The spirit of our boys is broken and Ohio will resent any policy that denies her rights. We will cheerfully accept the judgment of our Commander-in-Chief, but before forming it, I respectfully ask a meeting with you at the earliest possible day."

We soon had assurance that the division would remain intact. It

205

has always been my impression that when the matter was presented by the President to Secretary of War Baker, he had the department abandon its plan. When Baker first headed the War Department, there was some doubt as to the wisdom of the President's selection. Baker was small in physical stature, had never been interested in military matters, and a few of his political critics had contended that he was a pacifist. His remarkable mind, when set to the consideration of a matter, exhausted every phase of it. In due time, his military aides discovered that they had a man on their hands who knew what the business of war and the creation of an army was. He was in no sense despotic but once he took a stand, he was able to support it with controlling logic. It will be recalled that the Senate created a committee to investigate the War Department. I think that Shields of Tennessee and Chamberlain of Oregon were members of it. Both were strong men. No Secretary of War was ever subjected to such an inquisition. He had an answer to every question and came out of the inquiry in unquestioned triumph. The truth is that he conducted himself so admirably that the committee and its evident purpose were thoroughly discredited. Baker was a tenderhearted man. From our office files is taken a very interesting evidence of that. Mr. Baker had clipped out of a newspaper the very brief announcement of my commuting the death sentence of a Gallia County murderer to life imprisonment. In his own handwriting are appended these words, "May the Lord's Holy Name be praised."

A rift in our national unity came for a time with the refusal of President Wilson to send former President Theodore Roosevelt to France in command of troops. There is an inside story about this, related to me by Mr. Tumulty. Colonel Roosevelt had asked for an appointment with the President. When he arrived at the executive offices, he talked first for a few minutes with the presidential secretary, Mr. Tumulty. He was quite full of his subject and went to it promptly, reasserting his desire to be of service to the Army and throwing out a very apparent bait to Mr. Tumulty himself in these words: "I want to make you one of my staff officers. You can tell your wife and your children that you will be in no danger. I am very anxious to have you go with me." This didn't find favor with Mr. Tumulty and he assured the colonel that if he went into the service at all, he did not want to be assigned to any soft spot. Wilson and Roosevelt were in conversation for quite a time, Roosevelt very insistent, Wilson cordial, but making no committal. After the colonel departed, Wilson walked out into Tumulty's office and said, "I have never met Colonel Roosevelt before. I can see why the man has such a large personal following. He has great force of personality and with it infinite charm." Roosevelt did not go to France because Pershing, probably in hope of keeping politics entirely out of military affairs, did not want him over there. This ruling policy must have been evident to him in his own selection by the President.

Then, too, there was very wide discussion for a time over what some regarded as the ungenerous treatment of General Leonard Wood. I happened to be in New York when the Eighty-ninth Division arrived there for embarkation. Wood was idolized by the men in his command. I knew this from very intimate knowledge because a young officer in the Eighty-ninth was Daniel J. Mahoney, my son-in-law. At the time it did seem a cruel thing, particularly after letting him come East with his command. Wood, of course, was heartbroken and his division seemed to share his feelings. Secretary Baker discussed this with me soon afterwards in great detail. While making an inspection trip with General Wood, he had noticed that Wood's powers of locomotion were badly impaired. While military governor of Cuba, he had struck his head on a chandelier in the government house at Havana. The injury in due time involved the brain and the nerve centers leading to his lower extremities. While Mr. Baker recognized the capabilities of General Wood, he said he could not conscientiously send a man into combat service physically incapacitated. Wood possessed real ability. He had impressed this upon President Theodore Roosevelt and it cannot be denied that the latter was a good judge of men. Wood might have been nominated at the Republican convention at Chicago in 1920, except for the overzealous and indiscreet expenditure of money by members of his political organization in some sections.

Both Marshall and MacArthur must be credited to the account of Pershing. He trained them both and, recognizing their soldierly qualities, gave them their opportunity. The business side of the American expedition was looked after by General Charles G. Dawes. Pershing and he had been friends years before in Lincoln, Nebraska, when Pershing was assigned by the War Department to conduct military training at the University of Nebraska. Dawes, however, was born in Ohio, at Marietta, the first settlement in the great Northwest Territory. In his veins was the blood of old Israel Putnam. Like Secretary Baker, Dawes put a congressional committee to rout when, with his "hell and Maria," he showed his contempt for the puny efforts of partisan cynics to find political capital in the conduct of the war. He had much to do with establishing the federal budget system. The name of Dawes is an illustrious one in Ohio.

The winter of 1917–18 was one of the most severe within the memory of man. Railroad traffic was particularly difficult. Theodore Roosevelt had been asked to make a war speech in Cincinnati. In accepting, he had requested that I, as governor, preside at the meeting. Walter Brown of Toledo, prominent in the Bull Moose movement, came to see me about the matter. I told him I would feel honored to present our distinguished visitor, but quite naturally, and as the colonel himself would understand, I would be embarrassed if he said anything in criticism of President Wilson. It was arranged that he should come. I took the train at Columbus and it so happened that Colonel Roosevelt was a passenger. He invited me into his stateroom and we had a five-hour conversation—because traffic moved slowly. The colonel was an entertainer de luxe and the wide range of his reading, his experience, almost unprecedented in scope, and his incisive manner of speech all made him one to be listened to with great interest and pleasure. He ran the list of our statesmen, found things in Washington to criticize; Jefferson, to him, was a demagogue; Jackson he called a barbarian; Lincoln might have done some things differently and McKinley had the fault of not saying no. Wilson, he asserted, had no use for a man of brains. He was strongly of the opinion, as expressed that day, that the fighting genius of the Confederacy was not Stonewall Jackson, but General Forrest, who, prior to the war, had run a small country store in Tennessee. Roosevelt referred to Forrest's exploit in refusing to surrender with General Buckner at Fort Donaldson. Instead he took his cavalry, swam the river and got away. Roosevelt had a written text of his speech. He handed it to me on the train with the facetious remark, "You can read this. You need not worry about your friend." Only once did he depart from his manuscript to take a hidden dig at the President. I think this was more of a prank than anything else because he immediately turned to me on the stage with a sly wink.

Accompanying me to Cincinnati was George H. Wood, our adjutant general. His father, Thomas J. Wood, was a roommate of Grant at West Point, and a distinguished major general in the War Between the States. General Wood stated that Colonel Roosevelt's appraisal of Forrest was precisely that of his father, which he had heard him express many times. The junior Wood's mother was a daughter of Admiral Greer of the United States Navy. Wood was a great student of military history and, of course, acquired much more of it unwritten from his father. One thing which he told Colonel Roosevelt had to do with the battle of Gettysburg. General Hancock was wounded. The surgeons, in making the probe, found that he had been struck by a nail. Hancock immediately sent word to General Meade, in command, that this showed the Confederates were out of ammunition and he urged that Meade order a general advance—but this Meade failed to do.

When Christmas came in 1917, the War Department was besieged with requests for leaves of absence. The boys naturally wanted to be with their home folks. It was obvious that if this very humane impulse were acceded to the facilities of the railroads would be sorely taxed. There was a shortage of both cars and locomotives, so the order went out regretfully that there would be no leaves allowed. We determined in Ohio that if Christmas could not be enjoyed at home, we would take Christmas to the soldiers of our division encamped at Montgomery, Alabama. We established receiving stations in our important cities and requested that Yuletide remembrances be sent there, carefully labeled. These were assorted and assembled finally at Cincinnati and placed in freight cars. We had a huge Christmas tree and a joyous celebration. Presents were provided for those without families, and at every bed in the hospital was a flower and a gift as a greeting from our state.

I had a very beautiful ceremonial adopted in our state, and nowhere else in the country, so far as I know, was it observed. Every day of the week, including the Sabbath, at precisely the minute when taps were being sounded in the camps of our soldiers overseas, we established a shrine on the State house steps and the bugler sounded taps. Many citizens joined in this communion of spirits, particularly the mothers whose boys were in the service.

Every day until the war ended, usually about the middle of the afternoon, which was bedtime in France, the bugler appeared. The

209

shrill notes of his trumpet could be heard all over the downtown area in Columbus. Men and women, in their offices, dropped their work and in spirit joined the mothers, assembled within the shadow of the famous old stone Capitol building, in prayer.

CHAPTER XVIII

RE-ELECTED AS WAR GOVERNOR

THE OUTSTANDING feature of the campaign in 1918 was the request which President Wilson made for a Democratic Congress. This occasioned considerable disapproval and the polling at the ensuing election clearly revealed the fact. The Republican candidates in our state were greatly elated to have this issue thrust into the campaign. Former Governor Willis, whom I had defeated in 1916, was again nominated by the opposing party. He was at a disadvantage in the campaign for the reason that I made no political speeches, confining myself entirely to the war movement. Meetings held, of course, under the fervor of war excitement, were largely attended and were enthusiastic in spirit. However, I carefully kept away from political contentions. Willis attempted, as best he could, to make it a political contest and that did not help him. In the election I received 488,403 votes, Willis 477,459. The Democrats lost heavily in the congressional elections, several incumbent congressmen being defeated. The legislature was strongly Republican. I was the only Democrat elected on the state ticket.

In January, 1919, I was inaugurated, the first governor in our history to serve three times. The third term would not have been possible except for the war. In the utmost sincerity, I can state that instead of seeking it, I would, in other circumstances, have rejected it. I asked re-election in 1916 purely as a matter of vindication. There had been a complete transformation of our state government, under a program made possible by our new constitution. It had been the fixed pattern of my first administration. The laws had been enacted in compliance with all of this, but an adverse election had come in circumstances already described. There were reasons therefore for standing for a second tenure, but none except those growing out of the war for a third term.

The states played a very much more individual part in prosecution of World War I than in the second conflict. As long as the war was in progress, the executive department, aside from purely detail matters, devoted all of its time to giving to Ohio a war record it would not be ashamed of. In my message to the legislature in January, 1919, I asserted that our state had developed a pride in the order of things created by our revised charter. But there were problems. Prohibition had deprived the state treasury of all the revenues which had come from licensing saloons. The policy of acquiring more lands for our correctional institutions had borne unpredicted fruits.

The Workmen's Compensation Law had established itself in the favor of all classes in the state, and the fact was proudly revealed that the cost of administering the trust was borne by interest derived on our funds, with a yearly surplusage of $43,637.63. It was recommended that if necessary a constitutional amendment be initiated providing that any legislation which would increase taxes could not be legally passed unless provisions were made for new revenues to absorb created expense.

In a special message to the Assembly on April 1, 1919, I dealt exclusively with the danger of teaching German to our children in the grade schools. I had hinted at this the year before, insisting that "the statute books must be purged. Every germ of Prussian poison must be squeezed out of the organic law of Ohio." Facts presented to the Ohio legislature at that time are so clearly applicable to recent conditions that doubtless they can be profitably recalled. That same germ imbedded in the Prussian soul at that time seems to be present still. Every word that I communicated to the legislature was a fact taken from German publications, parts of which were textbooks in our schools. It is most regrettable that a country which displays such genius in useful channels of thought, literature, music, industry and what not should be, through continuous time, afflicted with a feeling of racial superiority and a will to rule the world. A prefatory note is found in these words: "Every man whose judgment is formed by an unprejudiced analysis of events knows full well that the recent world war was its direct result. For generations, the theory of the German superman has been implanted into youthful minds, germinated and developed finally into a conviction so concrete as to exclude any devotion whatsoever to the ideals of America. This doctrine has not only been preached to children in this state, but

212

there was added here and there, as a logical corollary, the suggestions that the German destiny ultimately was the subjugation and domination of the earth."

Charles J. Hexamer, president of the National German-American Alliance, said to its annual convention, "The more the teaching of German increases, the greater will be the number of boys and girls who will be brought to us, and who will receive the keys to the treasure houses of our *kultur*. We have long suffered the preachment that 'you Germans must allow yourselves to be assimilated— you must merge with the American people,' but no one will ever find us prepared to descend to an inferior culture."

Attention was called to the Delbruck law passed in Germany at the instance of the Kaiser himself and providing that "any man leaving Germany and going into another country could take the oath of a new citizenship and still remain a legalized citizen of Germany and a loyal subject of the Kaiser." About this I said, "In other words, he was to make false oath and render compliance by voice only to our legal requirements, concealing within himself, as no disturbance to conscience, the certain knowledge that he was perpetrating a willful fraud in order to profit by the circumstances of his environment."

The inner meaning of this was revealed in a German book called *Das Grosser Deutschland*. In it we found these unblushing words: "The reproach often brought against the German-American that as soon as he goes to America he becomes a citizen, is unjustified, for if the German who intends to remain there does not become a citizen, he has no vote at the elections, no influence of any kind on the conduct of the nation's political affairs. He must become an American; he is permitted, however, and can and ought in heart, thought, nature and act, to remain a German."

If any further insult to our intelligence and patriotism were needed, it was in a German publication entitled *The Quarterly of the League for Germanism in Foreign Lands*. It said, "Political candidates, in order to get the votes of Germans, must promise to carry out their demands. In Ohio, Germanism is, at all elections, the needle on the scales." This brought the menace and peril close to home, and was but a reminder that the German vote had been decisive in many of our elections. It was cast well-nigh solidly against me in the campaign of 1918 because I was the war governor. It also played its

JOURNEY THROUGH MY YEARS

part in the defeat of the League of Nations, but that will be dealt with later.

During the war a Professor Munsterberg, of Harvard University, spoke flippantly of our training camps and said that from them we could not produce an army, asserting further, "An army must begin in the nursery and in the schoolroom." I called attention to what the Kaiser himself had said in defiance to our ambassador, that at his voice and command hundreds of thousands of loyal subjects in America would rise for him and against this republic. The Prussians then, as now, were always talking of "Germany and the next war." This was the title of a book by Bernhardi, who insisted that the German element throughout the world is not to be split, but will "remain united in compact blocs and thus form, even in foreign countries, political centers of gravity in our favor."

Attention was called to forty-three teachers of German in one Ohio city who were called before the superintendent of schools. Sixteen of them were convicted of disloyalty and dismissed. In many instances we found that German students received only half the instruction in geography that the English schools were given and they devoted twenty per cent less time to arithmetic, forty per cent less to history and fifty per cent less to the study of English. We found German textbooks in the schools which spoke disparagingly of Washington and said that Baron Steuben had saved him from defeat. I used a quotation from among the last words of former President Theodore Roosevelt, who said, "We have room for but one loyalty. Loyalty to the United States. We have room but for one language, the language of Washington and Lincoln. The language of the Declaration of Independence and the Gettysburg speech—the English language. It should be the only language used or taught in the schools, primary, public or private. We are a nation and not a hodgepodge of foreign nationalities. We must insist on a united nationality."

If the dates were omitted, one might well think that these words were inspired by a fear of recurrent outcroppings of the foolish creed of the Prussian superman.

The law passed by our legislature barring the teaching of German was set aside by a decision of the United States Supreme Court, where it was joined with a case coming up from the state of Nebraska. Apparently, the fatal sentence in both acts was the interdiction of the German language in the statutes of both states. It seems safe to assume that, had the law provided for the teaching of the English language only, there would not have been an unconstitutional invasion. It is interesting to note that Justices Holmes and Sutherland dissented from the opinion of the majority of the Supreme Court of the United States.

Governors have many unusual experiences. There is a background story which has never been printed about the historic battle between Dempsey and Willard at Toledo, July 4, 1919.

Some time in the spring of that year, I chanced to be in New York. Tex Rickard came to the hotel to see me. I had never met him before. His manner indicated that he was very full of the subject which had brought him there and he lost little time getting into it. Mentioning the approaching presidential election of 1920, he asked who would likely be nominated by the Democrats. I told him that one man's guess was as good as another's. I told him that if he was acquainted with the gamble in politics and the many things that might happen between then and the time of the convention, he would realize how useless it was to hazard an opinion. Then he said, "Governor, I think you are going to be the nominee. I have always been interested in your liberal and progressive tendencies and I want to help by putting $25,000 in escrow to be used in case you are nominated." He got the very quick rejoinder, "No, Tex, that isn't what you are interested in. You want to pull off the big prize fight in Ohio and you have found out that under existing laws this is probably the only place where it can be legally held." In great confusion, he left the room. Newspapermen, who doubtless knew what had brought him there, inquired how he had made out and he assured them, using his own language, that he had completely "spilled the beans." They inquired just what had happened and attempted to assure him that the situation probably wasn't as bad as he thought it was. The next morning he came back full of apologies. He was not reminded of his well-meaning but very indiscreet suggestion about the campaign contribution. I told him that his experience with public officers had probably given him a false impression and that there were many more than he thought who respected the ethics. He was advised that the state Attorney General would be consulted as to the legality of the project and that if Rickard was told to go ahead that would be final. However, he was given to understand very definitely that not a penny was to be spent anywhere to "grease the way"; that we had a sports-loving public and I felt convinced that there would be no outcry from our people. He wanted his mind set perfectly clear about expenditures and I told him that no sheriff, constable or anyone whomsoever was to be subsidized. "Well," said Tex, "it will be a very funny fight. The whole thing is new to me, but I will go through with it as you say."

When construction work on his stands began, a controversy arose between him and the contractor. Tex called me about it and said he had engaged a lawyer and the fee would be $5000. This, of course, was ridiculous and it was cut in two. Dempsey always said, after his triumph, that I had made him champion and he was grateful.

During the second part of our administration, across the screen of public attention and controversy came the picture, *The Birth of a Nation*. Governor Willis, who had defeated me in 1914, had refused to let it come into the state for reasons obviously political rather than ethical. In due time, after returning to my executive duties, inquiries were made as to what our policy would be. There came to my office one of our important political leaders who stated that he could make a fee of $75,000 if I would authorize the Board of Censors to bring the picture into Ohio. I told him there was a law in our state against getting money under false pretenses, and that there was nothing he could do to further the interests of the picture people as I had made up my mind to let it come in anyway. I arranged a meeting with Thomas Dixon, author of *The Clansman*, from which the picture was made. I said that I wanted our people to have a better understanding of the outrages of carpetbag rule in the South; that the younger generation was not being informed by the history books and that the cause of national unity would be promoted if the North knew the terrible days through which the South had lived. I imposed one condition, which was that not one penny was to be spent with any local or state officer and that the whole transaction was to be clean and aboveboard.

CHAPTER XIX

FACING LABOR PROBLEMS

◆

To BE GOVERNOR of an industrial state like Ohio for six years and never be compelled to call out troops in connection with labor problems is something that might need explanation and there may be some interest in it. We had our problems, many of them, but it was never necessary to resort to the militia. Our labor, industry and our public were fortunate in the type of our labor leaders. The gangsters and racketeers had not moved in and if they had attempted it in that day, they would have been put in their place by four men who won public respect by their general conduct of labor union matters. Thomas J. Duffy, a member of our industrial commission, a product of the pottery industry, was one of the ablest men ever connected with the labor movement. He was so recognized all over the country. His name will always be identified with the success of the Workmen's Compensation Law of his state. He represented labor on our industrial commission. William Green, now president of the American Federation of Labor, was a member of the state Senate and ranked high in the counsels of the miners. Thomas Donnelly of Cincinnati had been secretary and John Voll of Zanesville president of the Ohio Federation of Labor. While these men never organized what has come to be known as a pressure group, they were very vigilant in promoting the interests of labor. When a public officer deals frankly with men like these, things get on without serious disagreement.

When the rubber industry began to bulk large in Akron, a strike ensued. A delegation of industrial and business leaders rushed to Columbus, urging that troops be sent at once. They were, I think very sincerely, apprehensive. I called their attention to the fact that a great many of the rubber workers who had moved into Akron came from the mountains of West Virginia and they reminded me a good deal of the Mexicans. In the republic to the south of us when revolutions broke out—and there were many in those days—they took their families with them and regarded the whole thing as a sort of picnic jaunt. I had a feeling that this was, in some measure, the spirit of the young fellows from West Virginia. I asked the delegation to consider well whether or not the rushing of troops into their city would not multiply their troubles and make martyrs of the strikers whether their cause was just or not. They were assured, however, that I would send to their city, without any delay, our adjutant general, George H. Wood. He would watch the situation with great care and if life or property were put in jeopardy, I would not hesitate to take drastic steps. Early the next day, the delegation was recommending strongly that the troops not be called out, regardless of what General Wood might report. It became obvious that negotiations which were already under way would be seriously interfered with if troops appeared.

At another time, there was a strike on in Pennsylvania and the constabulary of that state was dealing pretty roughly with the masses of labor in the affected sections. Not far from the Ohio line a large assembly meeting was broken up by officers on horseback who were expert in the use of the billy or club. The strikers decided to move over into Ohio and the pilgrimage was announced. Pittsburgh and Cleveland newspapers were greatly excited and were nervously using the telegraph and telephone wires inquiring what action the executive office intended to take. My response was that, so far as I knew, the soil of Ohio was not exempted from the provision of the Constitution which gave the right of assembly. The large crowd held its meeting just inside the Ohio border. Spellbinders spent their strength and when the shades of evening came, the movement was on back to Pennsylvania homes. The proceedings were under watch. There were no untoward developments and that ended the whole episode as far as we were concerned.

Mayor Tom Johnson of Cleveland established a place on the public square where speakers were free to exploit their theories without any attention whatever from the police. As he once put it, he just permitted them to blow off steam, and he was positive that by establishing this escape valve he had done very much to allay mass discontent. Hyde Park in London, England, is interestingly illustrative of this theory.

There came a day when Pennsylvania and the Middle West were disturbed by a strike among steel workers. The walkout was quite general. The strikers at Steubenville were enraged because their co-workers in a plant at Weirton in West Virginia, not far down the river, had not gone out. A great mass meeting was arranged for a Sunday afternoon where plans, as we discovered, were to be formulated to move a mob the next morning to assault the West Virginia plant and drive the workers out. Obviously this would have been something more than industrial disorder. If no restraint had been offered by our state government, the invasion of a neighboring state, regardless of what brought it about, would have been discreditable to us. I dispatched Mr. Duffy and Mr. Donnelly to Steubenville. They addressed the meeting and said in words that could not be misunderstood that our government would resent the contemplated action and that in the absence of our state militia, I had arranged for the use of troops to be supplied by the federal training camp at Camp Sherman, near Chillicothe, Ohio. The bellicose spirit subsided and nothing was done.

Cincinnati was a very tranquil community. The people were thrifty, law-abiding and orderly. When a streetcar strike was declared, turbulent scenes came. Motormen and conductors who took the places of the strikers were assaulted, cars were thrown off the tracks and on one occasion a sack of cement was thrown from the top of the Union Central skyscraper building flush into the middle of a moving streetcar. Without delay I ordered all cars to be sent to the barns and to remain there until otherwise directed. Cincinnati's very attractive suburbs lie in the hill lands above the river and foot transportation is very irksome. Recognizing that public opinion plays an important part always in the settlement of strikes, I was convinced that the citizenship afoot would help in bringing about a settlement of the trouble. In three days, representatives of the street railway companies and the labor organizations came to an agreement in the governor's office, where they had been asked to meet.

As long as coal mining had been conducted in our state, miners were paid only for the lump coal which they produced. As the product came from the bowels of the earth, it ran over a screen and the slack coal did not enter into the day's labor. Recurrently efforts were made through legislation to correct what the miners insisted was a grave injustice. The courts held that the lawmaking body

219

had no authority to act. The new constitution, however, provided that the legislature could pass laws regulating this whole operation. Senator William Green prepared a bill. It had been favorably reported out of the committee and had been placed on the calendar for action. I told Senator Green that I felt it was a great mistake to enact the law with our public so generally uninformed on the subject and that until a commission made a thorough inquiry, I would have to be opposed to the measure. Naturally, this provoked a pretty bitter feeling in the mining regions and a tremendous protest meeting was arranged to be held at Bellaire down on the Ohio River. In those days acreage rather than thousands was the term applied to the size of a mining crowd. I arranged to go there and discuss the matter. The speakers' stand was erected under an umbrella-shaped tree. It was an exciting affair and too many people piled on the speakers' stand. I felt the first movement in its collapse and made an acrobatic jump, seizing a limb above my head and thus escaping at least some minor scratches and bruises which were sustained by a good many occupants of the stage.

I told the miners that our public was not informed as to the merits of the case; that under our initiative-and-referendum principle of government, the operators could very easily initiate a referendum election and set up the claim that the law, if passed, would increase the price of coal. They were reminded that there were a great many more users than miners of coal and that failure of the first effort to procure relief would very seriously interfere with their whole program. They were advised of my intention to appoint a commission made up of men of such quality that their opinions would carry great weight with our people. The miners accepted this as a policy in good faith. The commission subsequently named was headed by Judge Philip Crow of the Court of Appeals at Kenton. He was an able jurist, one of the best in the state. The report of the commission was unanimous, favoring compensation to the miners for all the usable coal which they produced. The bill was passed and that ended the whole controversy. Now a great deal of lump coal is pulverized and, in powder form, passes through pipes to the furnaces much like gas.

It was necessary at one time to remove the mayor of Canton. In the midst of labor troubles he had failed to do his duty and paid no attention to the defense of property and life. He was removed and no protest of any moment came from the community. In connection with a steel strike in Cleveland, one of the plants had been surrounded by pickets, and an employee, who had been kept on watch for the sole purpose of keeping up fires needful to the preservation of property and machinery, was without food. It was brought to him by members of his family, but the pickets stopped them. His being there bore no relation to the strike and the whole performance was both absurd and inhumane. We felt certain that it went on with the knowledge and consent of the county sheriff. The plant was located outside the city. I called this officer by telephone and told him that unless he put an end to it, there would be a new sheriff in his place. Before I had breakfast the next morning a telephone message came from the county officer stating that the watchman had a fine supper and breakfast and he would continue to have his meals regularly.

PART FIVE

Nominated for the Presidency

Convention Scenes and Democratic Leaders

The Real Story of Roosevelt's Nomination
for Vice-President

Message from Harding

Historic Visit to Wilson in the White House

The Conspiracy of 1920

Part Played by Theodore Roosevelt

Racial Groups Powerful in Election

CHAPTER XX

THE DEMOCRATIC CONVENTION OF 1920

◆

As THE Democratic National Convention of 1920 approached, there was a wide divergence of opinion as to the probable nominee. William G. McAdoo and A. Mitchell Palmer were members of the Wilson administration. Each had dispensed rich political favors throughout the country, and some thought that the power of patronage would determine the final result. It is an interesting fact, however, that at no time did their combined vote approach the two-thirds necessary to a nomination.

Many interesting theories were expressed as to what might happen in the event of a deadlock. McAdoo and his close followers were confident of victory. The treasury portfolio gave him great political power. He conducted the bond drives and that brought him in contact with many people not connected with political activities. In charge of the railroads he had been generous with labor, and its rank and file in our transportation systems were supporting him.

There was some evidence that Woodrow Wilson desired a renomination. It may be that with recurrent signs of improved health he wanted to continue the fight that he had made for his project, the League of Nations. He was not a man to retreat in the face of opposition. One can understand why he would have liked to remain in the White House to carry his whole enterprise through to success. Carter Glass, in his autobiography, says that Wilson favored the nomination of Palmer. It was well understood at the time that he was not sympathetic towards the McAdoo candidacy, but he must have known at the time that Palmer could not be nominated. Bryan, during his years of flirtation with the nomination after 1908, was always proposing someone whom he himself must have known had no chance. This motive cannot be charged to Mr. Wilson, but the reference by Carter Glass gives color to the suggestion that the President would have liked to be nominated.

McAdoo and Palmer were not politically friendly. Both men were of great ambition and it was natural that their contest for delegates should produce a situation which affected their political, if not personal, relations. Out of this could easily have come the nomination of John W. Davis, or possibly of Carter Glass. Their weakness was that they came from states that are not pivotal. Taking all this into consideration, Edmond H. Moore, who managed the Cox forces at the convention, was positive that his candidate would be nominated.

It has been said and never disputed that Moore's generalship on the floor of the convention had never been equalled. He had a wide acquaintanceship and his forthright method of dealing with men tied them to him. When the drives were made to develop the maximum strength of McAdoo and Palmer, he was never disturbed because he knew that neither one could get the necessary two-thirds vote and that they would never join forces. A great many delegates, bound by promise to Moore, assured him when the McAdoo and Palmer drives were on that by going along with them, when the futility of the movement was evident they would not only come back to the Cox standard but also would bring others with them. This was the very essence of his strategy.

The convention assembled on June 28 and adjourned on July 6. Ohio had never sent a delegation surpassing in quality that which was chosen in 1920. The delegates-at-large were former Governors James E. Campbell and Judson Harmon, Senator Atlee W. Pomerene and Edmond H. Moore. W. A. Julian, now treasurer of the United States, was a delegate from Cincinnati. Congressman M. R. Denver represented the Wilmington district. Others were W. W. Durbin of Kenton, W. S. Thomas of Springfield, M. A. Daugherty, one of the leading members of the Ohio bar, Congressman Alfred G. Allen from Cincinnati, Frank T. Dore of Tiffin, Congressman George White from Marietta, Robert T. Scott of Cambridge, John A. O'Dwyer from Toledo, T. J. Duffy from East Liverpool, Thomas Noctor from Cincinnati, James Ross and Claude Meeker of Columbus. Delegates from my local district were Edward Sohngen of Hamilton and Clarence N. Greer, now postmaster of Dayton. Joseph H. Dowling, a veteran Democrat of Dayton, probably knew as many of the delegates from other states as anyone in the convention.

Special trains from our state were run across the continent to the west coast. The attendance of non-delegates from Ohio set a record. In large numbers delegates and others assembled at Dayton. From here they began their western pilgrimage. While they felt it would be a triumphal one, I was never very much excited about it. Among the visitors from our state were many who were as influential as our delegates themselves. They had wide business and professional acquaintanceships and they were able to bring to the delegation information which supplied successful leads to the votes from other states. The Ohio delegation never wavered. Its vote was the same from the first to the last ballot.

A vast assemblage made up from different sections of our state came to my home at Trailsend, in the country five miles from the center of Dayton. When they gathered together in a great natural bowl which the glaciers had carved, a moraine formation, it made a picture difficult to describe. Many inquired whence came the name "Trailsend." I have often been asked that question. In my travels through the country I have encountered it only in Wyoming. Senator Kendrick christened his home there with the same name. When I was campaigning in his state, he told me why. He had ridden horseback from Texas to his new habitat. It was the end of the trail with him. The genesis of my Trailsend was in some sense the same. Maps of the buffalo trails which the Indians followed show one which winds westward in its serpentine course from Hocking County and ends where I built my residence. Its terminus curls into an almost complete circle. Tradition has it that this spot overlooking the great Miami Valley was a famous camping place for the Indians. Here they gathered after the hunt and perhaps after their battles as well. The residence is of the purest type of French architecture, the designer, Oswald Hering, of New York, having in mind the Petite Trianon at Versailles.

I was too much American to give my home a foreign name. Reflecting many times upon the pleasure that must have come to the red man at this end of the trail, and being certain, too, that I would live my life out there, I gave the name Trailsend to the place where I have lived for almost thirty years.

I was importuned to make the trip to San Francisco, but the suggestion was not tempting. I took the position that a candidate for the presidency had no business participating in the rush and turbulence of the convention. Mr. Palmer did attend. He was a handsome figure and looked a President in every respect. His followers believed that his presence and personality might have a controlling influence. I have never since then attended a national convention except in 1924 when the leaders of the party insisted on my coming to New York when the convention threatened to disrupt the party.

The address of Temporary Chairman Homer S. Cummings, of Connecticut, was notable. If there had been any doubt as to what the major issue would be, which there was not, the course of Mr. Cummings' speech removed it. The accomplishments of the Wilson administration, which had been numerous and vital to the readjustment of our economic and social conditions, were recited. In dramatic words he recalled the invasion of the sickroom of the stricken President by members of the Senate who sought his political death. Republican leaders most active in the warfare against Wilson were reminded of commitments on the League which were made before it became a political issue and which they would have liked to forget.

Senator Joseph T. Robinson of Arkansas was the permanent chairman and his speech became a valued campaign document. The practice of having both a temporary and a permanent chairman can be accounted for only by the fact that it gives an opportunity to pass oratorical honors around. Robinson was a faithful follower of Woodrow Wilson and he devoted most of his address to making plain every step that had been taken from the time the Covenant of the League had been adopted at Versailles until it was rejected by the Senate of the United States. The country had not looked with approval upon the long-continuing debate in the Senate. Of this Senator Robinson said:

"Talk of the Senate! In that body we have what is known as the 'rule of unlimited debate,' which means that when any senator gets the floor he may talk just as long as he pleases on any subject that he chooses, and nobody but God can stop him, and the Lord never seems cognizant of him."

On the morning of the third day, Chairman Robinson announced that "the secretary will now call the roll of states for nomination of President of the United States."

The first name presented was that of Senator Robert L. Owen of Oklahoma. Then in rapid succession were presented the names of James W. Gerard of New York, Homer F. Cummings of Connecticut, Gilbert M. Hitchcock of Nebraska, A. Mitchell Palmer of Pennsylvania and Edwin T. Meredith of Iowa. Kentucky yielded to Ohio, and Justice James G. Johnson of our Supreme Court presented my name. He referred to the fact that although for half a century Ohio was normally Republican, I had three times been elected governor of the state. Kentucky and Mississippi seconded the nomination. Thereupon Bourke Cockran, in a characteristically rhetorical speech, placed Al Smith in nomination, while a Missouri delegate named William G. McAdoo. Several "favorite sons" were added to the list, and Governor John J. Cornwall of West Virginia, one of the best speakers in the convention, found an incentive to his best efforts in proposing John W. Davis.

The platform was presented by Carter Glass, chairman of the committee. Its first sentence conveyed "Greetings to the President of the United States, Woodrow Wilson," and hailed "with patriotic pride the great achievements for country and the world wrought by a Democratic administration under his leadership." It left no doubt as to the party position on the League of Nations:

> The Democratic Party favors the League of Nations as the surest, if not the only, practicable means of maintaining the permanent peace of the world and terminating the insufferable burden of great military and naval establishments.

William J. Bryan of Nebraska was announced and said: "You have listened to one of the strongest platforms ever placed before the country in our nation's history."

Bryan, however, wanted some additions made. That was quite characteristic of him. There was nothing the man loved more than the experience of addressing a national convention. He spoke with great power and eloquence and many thought that he was hoping history might repeat itself and the scene of 1896 be re-enacted. He wanted the party to establish a newspaper to be called *The National Bulletin* and to be published regularly from the capital, for the information of American voters. He had a plank on prohibition and he wanted the party to go on record against universal military training.

The prohibition plank was also discussed by Bourke Cockran for the wets and Richmond Pearson Hobson for the drys, while

E. L. Doheny proposed a statement in favor of Irish independence, T. D. Lyons of Oklahoma brought up the question of veterans' compensation, and Bainbridge Colby spoke. But Carter Glass waved all the new proposals aside and asked for the adoption of the platform as originally submitted. The convention agreed with him.

The first ballot for the nomination of the candidate for President was then ordered and the call of the states began, with the following result:

McAdoo	266	Glass	26½
Cox	134	Simmons	24
Palmer	256	Harrison	6
Cummings	25	John Sharp Williams	20
Gerard	21	Thomas R. Marshall	37
Owen	33	Wood	4
Hitchcock	18	Clark	9
Meredith	27	Underwood	½
Smith	109	Hearst	1
Edwards	42	Colby	1
Davis	32	Daniels	1

Further ballots showed little material change. The tenth ballot: McAdoo 385, Cox 321, Palmer 257, Cummings 18, Owen 37, Glass 25, Davis 32.

On the twelfth ballot Cox passed McAdoo: Cox 404, McAdoo 375½, Palmer 201, Owen, Davis and Glass holding their strength.

The fifteenth ballot gave McAdoo 344½, Cox 468½, Palmer 167. The big swell in the Cox vote came from New York's casting 73 votes for him and 17 for McAdoo, while New Jersey's 28 votes went for Cox.

The thirtieth ballot put McAdoo in the lead: McAdoo 403½, Cox 400½, Palmer 165. The Owen, Davis and Glass vote remained intact. The McAdoo drive was on. The test of whether he could make it was now to be made.

While this rally was going on, the anti-McAdoo forces broke in with a song, *Every Vote Is on the Pay Roll*, sung to the tune of the *Battle Hymn of the Republic*.

For several ballots McAdoo lost votes. On the thirty-ninth ballot, he received 440 votes. Cox again took the lead with 468, gaining 82 votes from the preceding ballot. This was the turning point. Palmer's vote dropped from 211 on the thirty-eighth ballot to 74 on the thirty-ninth.

There was great excitement following the announcement of the forty-first ballot: McAdoo 460, Cox 497½, Palmer 12. McAdoo had lost from the previous ballot 7 votes and Cox had gained 7½. It was plain now that most of the Palmer strength would not go to McAdoo. The McAdoo followers at this juncture might by a very clever maneuver have given up enough of their votes to Davis or Glass to show a way out of the deadlock.

On the forty-second ballot Cox received 540½, lacking but four of a majority. McAdoo had dropped to 427. Davis had 49½, Glass 24. Prior to this ballot, the McAdoo people had moved an adjournment but it was voted down, 637 nays to 405 yeas. The votes cast in favor of adjournment were substantially the entire McAdoo vote.

The forty-third ballot gave Cox more than a majority, 568 votes; McAdoo had 412. Apparently the end was approaching. George R. Lunn, of Schenectady, had been among the 20 votes from New York cast from the beginning for McAdoo as opposed to 70 for Cox; he challenged the vote of New York as announced. It was past midnight. Lunn knew that some of the delegates had left the hall but before going it had been understood and agreed that in their absence the vote would remain as it had been previously cast. There was great excitement in the New York delegation, and much indignation was occasioned by what was described as Lunn's poor sportsmanship. A rugged Irishman named McCarthy rushed up to Lunn with these words: "You withdraw that motion now. If you don't, when you wake up in a hospital you will hear that Cox has been nominated." Lunn then moved an adjournment. This was quickly voted down.

On the final ballot, the forty-fourth, Cox made gains from most of the states.

In a convention, when states begin changing their vote the end is near. Colorado changed to Cox. Connecticut attempted to change, but in the midst of the demonstrations which interrupted the speaker the chairman recognized Samuel Amidon of Kansas, who moved "that the rules be suspended and that Mr. Cox be declared the nominee of this convention unanimously."

There was no radio in those days and I received the returns at the *News* office in Dayton over the telegraph. The nomination was made at 1:50 A.M., Tuesday, July 6. That was 4:50 A.M. in Dayton. Dawn had broken when I reached home at Trailsend, after calling on my dear old friend, the Honorable John A. McMahon. Awaiting me there was a telephone call from Moore. The delegations were inquiring of him my preference for vice-president. I told him I had given the matter some thought and that my choice would be Franklin D. Roosevelt of New York. Moore inquired, "Do you know him?" I did not. In fact, so far as I knew, I had never seen him; but I explained to Mr. Moore that he met the geographical requirement, that he was recognized as an Independent and that Roosevelt was a well-known name. I knew that his relations with the organization in his state were not friendly. With a small anti-Tammany group, he, as state senator, had voted against the Democratic caucus nominee for United States Senator, William F. Sheehan. This made it necessary for Mr. Moore to consult Charles F. Murphy, head of New York's organization, explaining to him what had moved me to this selection, but saying that if it were offensive, we would abandon the idea and go to Edward T. Meredith of Iowa. Murphy had gone to bed but Moore delivered the message. I can quote Murphy's exact words: "I don't like Roosevelt. He is not well known in the country, but, Ed, this is the first time a Democratic nominee for the presidency has shown me courtesy. That's why I would vote for the devil himself if Cox wanted me to. Tell him we will nominate Roosevelt on the first ballot as soon as we assemble."

Mr. Roosevelt knew nothing of all this. The story of his nomination has been so badly bungled by biographers in the last few years that I think it appropriate to put in the record the exact facts.

When the convention assembled on its final day, July 6, the chair announced that nominations for the vice-president would be limited to ten minutes for each nominee and seconding speeches to five minutes. Scattering nominations were first made—Lawrence D. Tyson for Tennessee, Samuel V. Stewart for Montana, E. L. Doheny for California. Then Judge Timothy T. Ansberry of the District of Columbia, formerly a member of Congress from Ohio, named Franklin D. Roosevelt, asserting that he was "an able, experienced campaigner, full of virility and optimism of youth, yet sobered by service as Assistant Secretary of the Navy." Kansas and Indiana seconded the Roosevelt nomination. Governor Ralston of Indiana yielded to New York, and Governor Al Smith rose. He warmly praised the platform; he praised me, saying that I fully typified the principles of the platform; and he spoke with genuine enthusiasm for Roosevelt—"a man who has been active in the affairs of our state, not only in the local legislative reforms that constitute so much of Democracy's record in the great Empire State, but a man who during the present administration has held positions of great power and importance in one of the most important departments of our government."

Other men were nominated—David R. Francis for Missouri and J. Hamilton Lewis for Illinois. But the trend of feeling in the convention was clear. When Ohio was called, it yielded to Washington. A woman delegate from that state seconded Roosevelt's nomination. This showed clearly that the Ohioan running for President wished Roosevelt for his fellow nominee, and a general movement for him began. Texas seconded Roosevelt; so did Vermont. For Wisconsin, Joseph E. Davies made an earnest speech. "Progressive Democracy believes that the battle is to be fought in the East and in the West," he said; "we believe that under such conditions, you must have a man equal in vision, equal in conservative capacity, equal in outstanding vision to the head of the ticket." California and Tennessee fell into line, withdrawing their previous nominations and seconding Roosevelt instead.

Former Governor David R. Francis of Missouri thereupon moved that the rules be suspended, "as all of the vice-presidential nominations have been withdrawn except one, and that Franklin D. Roosevelt be declared the nominee of this convention by acclamation." Amid wild applause, this carried unanimously. The final touch was placed on the proceedings when Josephus Daniels briefly addressed the convention in high praise of Roosevelt's services as Assistant Secretary of the Navy and predicted that "we shall meet in Washington on the fourth of March to inaugurate these candidates and carry forth the great work that has been begun."

233

CHAPTER XXI

BEGINNING THE CAMPAIGN

◆

I DO NOT know what emotions have come to other men under the impact of their nomination for the presidency. I very distinctly remember mine. Following the long contest in the convention, there was a letdown, of course, but I was completely benumbed by what had taken place. Lincoln's remark that he was not fit for the presidency certainly added nothing to my small self-assurance. With the coming of the next day and its flood of telegrams, and with the evidences around me of such a feverish excitement as had never before overtaken our section of the country, I came to realize that the banner of Woodrow Wilson had really been put in my hands. I resolved to carry on with such strength of mind and body as I possessed.

If other men in my place have had a reassuring feeling of divine appointment to their task, in the humility of the moment no trace of such a feeling came to me. A responsibility had fallen upon me, the weight of which I keenly felt.

At sunrise in Middletown, twenty-five miles below Dayton in the Miami Valley, near where I was born and where I spent part of my early years, every church bell was tolling a message of which comparatively few inhabitants, at the moment, knew the import. It was a quick response of a fine community, paying tribute to one whose struggles had begun in a humble way. A homecoming was arranged for that evening, which turned out to be a very happy event.

The first duty of the day was to dispatch a message to the convention, addressed to Senator Robinson, the chairman. It was as follows:

Let me thank you for your felicitous message. I shall accept the standard from the Democracy of America conscious not only of the honor but the great responsibility conferred. As Providence gives to me of strength and vision my firm resolve will be to justify the confidence which has been officially expressed. The shrine of government is in the communities of the land near to the homes that have given service and sacrifice. To them we will carry our cause with the assurance that the faith shall be kept. Please convey to the delegates of the convention my grateful acknowledgment. . . .

The messages which came pouring in were heartening. President Wilson sent congratulations and best wishes. Senator Hitchcock of Nebraska wired that the nomination assured several doubtful states. William Cooper Proctor, manager of General Wood's campaign, offered congratulations. Some came from overseas.

Cordial messages came from Josephus Daniels, Adolph S. Ochs of the New York *Times,* John Paschall of the Atlanta *Journal,* Rabbi Wise of New York, Alton B. Parker, presidential nominee in 1904, Senator Hoke Smith, General Jacob S. Coxey, United States Supreme Court Justice John H. Clarke, Ed (Pop) Geers, the beloved old harness-horse figure, Bernard Baruch, Samuel G. Blythe and others. Champ Clark at his home in Hannibal, Missouri, said in an interview, "I am glad Cox was nominated. He is the best of the lot."

Among the last editorials written by Henry Watterson was the one relating to my nomination. The *Courier-Journal* very thoughtfully sent me the original copy. The text is as follows:

Cox the Unbeatable

To the Editor of the Courier-Journal:
Write it Cox the Unbeatable.

He is a journalist and that means a deal. The lawyer is a controversialist, or logician, a master of doctrines, theories, equities. The doctor is a healer, and more or less a specialist. The journalist is an all-around man of affairs.

That is what we require in a President of the United States. It will not be denied that Woodrow Wilson is a highly qualified man. The record of his administration will read well in history. If I wished to be critical, I should say that he is too much the doctrinaire, too much the humanitarian, too much the phrase-maker.

235

Cox is not of this kidney. He is a man among men. He has shown himself ever a practical man, a man of sense and judgment—who, as the saying puts it, "has studied the eve papers" and ascertained the difference between hawk and buzzard. In a word, he does things.

We want, we need, that sort of man in the White House.

Now comes the chance for the Democrats of Kentucky to get together, to wipe out the old scores and, with a long pull, a strong pull and a pull all-together, to line up once more on the Resolution of '98 and fifty-four-forty-or-fight!

I write it Cox the *Unbeatable*.

Better get aboard the band wagon boys!—H. W.

Jeffersontown, Jefferson County, Kentucky.

This editorial is treasured as one of my valued possessions. From boyhood days, I had idolized Watterson.

The press response was all that could be desired. The Cleveland *Plain Dealer* said that "there will be no sidestepping on Governor Cox's part in the campaign," that "he has made himself a part of the history of Ohio to a greater extent than any other governor this state has had" and that "as governor he has known no fear; as president he will have none." The Cincinnati *Enquirer*, then owned by Ned McLean, a close friend of Harding, declared that "selection of Gov. Cox is the last thing the Republicans wished," adding: "As governor he has faced many new problems in government. He went about their solution courageously and worked them out successfully. If elected, the interests of this country will be safe in his hands." The Columbus *Dispatch* remarked that "the people of this commonwealth have a real affection for their popular governor."

Nor were newspapers outside the state less kind. The St. Louis *Post-Dispatch* remarked that "it is to the credit of Mr. Cox that there is no evidence of subservience to any clique, interest, or class in his record," and went on: "He has handled the problems arising from industrial unrest and strikes without yielding to disorder or lawlessness but with a minimum of force and friction." The Brooklyn *Eagle* spoke of the independence of the convention—"There was no private and all-powerful conference of bosses such as prevailed over the Chicago Convention to bring about the nomination

236

of Harding." The New York *Sun*, a Republican organ, asserted that "Gov. Cox may be expected to put into this contest both speed and power." The New York *World*, the nation's leading Democratic daily, endorsed the nominee as "a leader well versed in the principles of democracy, a candidate who has the pleasing habit of carrying his own state, and a man who in high office has demonstrated his capacity to legislate and govern."

Courtesy naturally marked my relations with Warren G. Harding, the Republican nominee. On the morning of my nomination he telegraphed his congratulations, saying that my victory reminded him of a newspaper cartoon portraying himself and me as newsboys for the White House delivery. To that I replied:

> I accept your message as an evidence of the fraternal impulse which has always characterized the craft to which you and I belong. I heartily reciprocate the felicitous spirit which you have expressed.

Senator Harding also gave out a public statement, saying:

> Governor Cox's nomination is an added consideration shown to our great state of Ohio, for which I am glad, and gives reasonable assurance that finally a newspaperman is to be made the nation's chief executive.
>
> Ohio has accorded to Governor Cox very unusual distinction and he deserved his notable victory at San Francisco. His nomination will not in any way change our activities in Ohio.
>
> It is a great party contest before us, to be fought on great principles involved and neither place of residence nor personality will have any marked influence on the result.

This was characteristic of Warren G. Harding. He was a warm-hearted man with most gracious impulses. He was not one to harbor grievances or deliberately do injury to any man. He had advanced from state senator to lieutenant governor and then to the United States Senate. To him that was the ideal public assignment. He loved to travel, and the senatorial recesses permitted his pilgrimages to other parts.

Many unkind things have been said and written of Mr. Harding. Harsh criticism is the penalty laid upon most public men. The scandals of his administration inspired many an accusing word against

237

JOURNEY THROUGH MY YEARS

his character. That he was amiable to the point of weakness, that he lacked vigilance and that he permitted himself unfit associates cannot be denied. But he was an honest man, and while the conduct of many close to him was reprehensible and even corrupt, his own official record was never tarnished with dishonor. With the ablest men in his cabinet he had much too little intimacy. His preference for cronies of a lower type was his major failing. Out of a sense of loyalty, he was blind to their faults. It was they who brought disgrace to his administration and death to the man they had betrayed.

A day or two after the nomination I returned to Columbus, where I found a crowd waiting on the steps of the State house. I spoke briefly and then went to the Union Station to meet the vice-presidential nominee. Mr. Roosevelt was on his way from San Francisco to his home in New York. I liked him from the outset. His mind was alert and he was keenly alive to the conditions that would bear on the campaign. I was not then conscious of his youthful appearance, which is very noticeable now in photographs taken of us that day. Our relationship during the campaign could not have been pleasanter. He made only one suggestion, which was that I should announce it as my intention, in the event of election, to have the vice-president sit with the cabinet. I was frank in stating my objection to this and gave my reasons. I wanted to get on agreeably with the Congress and felt that if the vice-president were to participate in the counsels at cabinet meetings he might be regarded as a White House snoop.

On a speaking tour through the Far West, Mr. Roosevelt made an excellent impression. When I went to the coast afterwards, I had the most enthusiastic reports about his personality and the intelligence and forthrightness of his public addresses. I developed a very deep affection for him.

The National Committee met at Columbus on July 20. Mr. Roosevelt and I attended. In selection of the chairman of the campaign committee, attention was called to the splendid services of Homer S. Cummings. He made no effort to be re-elected. The prevailing thought was that a new man should be selected and Cordell Hull of Tennessee was suggested. Edmond H. Moore, who had been my manager in the campaign, expressed to me his very strong objection. He had developed, unknown to me, a considerable personal feeling over some misunderstanding in the convention. Hull was my personal choice. Moore was a man whose dislikes were as strong as his likes, and not until recently did I know, and then from Mr. Hull himself, the reasons for his opposition. During the convention, Moore had not got on pleasantly with Chairman Cummings and Secretary J. Bruce Kremer of Montana. Moore, as Mr. Hull put it, erroneously thought the Tennessean was too closely aligned with both Cummings and Kremer. Mr. Hull had been a very popular and useful member of Congress and as chairman of the congressional campaign committee had rendered a commendable service. It was finally arranged that Mr. Moore would resign as the Ohio member of the National Committee and that Congressman George White would succeed him and be elevated to the chairmanship of the committee. Mr. White, who had a wide acquaintanceship and was very popular, was afterwards elected governor of our state. This solution was agreeably accepted by the entire membership of the committee.

In addressing the committee, I emphasized the importance of keeping the public fully advised throughout the campaign, particularly with respect to campaign contributions. After calling attention to what was going on in the Republican Committee, I said that "a campaign fund sufficient in size to stagger the sensibilities of the nation is now being formed. If our opposition believes this is correct in principle, God speed them in their enterprise. It will be an asset for us in this campaign."

Continuing, I said:

"I do not want the publication of expenditures after the election. There is no point in advising the voters what has been done. We want them to be fully advised of every circumstance with reference to the collection and disbursement of funds before the election."

Mr. Roosevelt made a very happy talk. After some compliments to myself, and a prediction that the Democracy in the campaign would prove to be 'a happy ship,' he concluded by saying:

"Yes, we have all our cards on the table concerning campaign funds. I hope that the other great party will see not the wisdom but the good American spirit in not hiding its light under a bushel. I take it we might mix a quotation from the Bible by suggesting to our adversaries that 'he who hides his campaign chest under a bushel shall have it returned to him after many days in ways least expected.' And so the spirit of this meeting is going to be the spirit of smaller gatherings in states and cities and counties all over the nation in the next few months and we as candidates look forward with absolute assurance to the same kind of spirit throughout the country, north, south, east and west, with the conviction, the knowledge, that the people of the United States are not going to be willing in November to slide back down hill but are going forward with all of us in the march of progress up the heights.

"And now we are very long overdue and I would not, if I could, keep any of us longer from that great privilege of meeting the charming lady, Mrs. Cox, who is going to be a very worthy first lady of the land."

The meeting of the National Committee was very harmonious and showed no evidence of any bitterness that might have followed the long-drawn-out convention. The followers of all the candidates apparently accepted the nomination in good spirit. Doubtless Mr. McAdoo's closest political and personal friend was Bernard M. Baruch of New York, now much better known to the American public. He was unsparing of his time and talents in furtherance of our campaign. He loved Woodrow Wilson and was and continued to be an ardent supporter of the League of Nations. Mr. Baruch won Wilson's admiration by the control of our forces of production during World War I. The same order of genius which he exhibited then was also devoted usefully in the Second World War. He has become known as the adviser of Presidents, which is a high compliment and shows Mr. Baruch a patriot, devoted first to the public interest.

CHAPTER XXII

THE VISIT TO WILSON

◆

As a preliminary to the campaign came my much discussed visit to Woodrow Wilson in the White House. Arrangements had been made for Mr. Roosevelt to accompany me.

When Claude Bowers, then ambassador to Chile, was in this country he related to me a conversation with President Roosevelt. The President, who happened to know I was writing this book, said there was one story that should be in it which he wanted to write himself. He related it to Bowers. I requested Bowers to make a record of the interview while the words of our executive were fresh in his memory. This he did and the following letter was the result:

Santiago, Chile

Dear Governor:

The other day when in Washington and with President Roosevelt, I told him I had heard from you and that you had been persuaded to write some reminiscences. "Good!" he said. "I wish you would tell him for me that there is a story never yet told, that he must tell. It is this: After the convention at San Francisco I stopped off for a conference with the Governor in Columbus to discuss the character of the campaign. The Governor advised that he was going to see President Wilson the next week.

"I accompanied the Governor on the visit to Wilson. A large crowd greeted us at the station and we went directly to the White House. There we were asked to wait fifteen minutes, as they were taking the President to the portico facing the grounds. As we came in sight of the portico we saw the President in a wheel chair, his left shoulder covered with a shawl which concealed his left arm, which was paralyzed, and the Governor said to me, 'He is a very sick man.'

"The Governor went up to the President and warmly greeted

him. Wilson looked up and in a very low, weak voice said, 'Thank you for coming. I am very glad you came.' His utter weakness was startling and I noticed tears in the eyes of Cox. A little later Cox said, 'Mr. President, we are going to be a million per cent with you, and your Administration, and that means the League of Nations.' The President looked up again, and again in a voice scarcely audible, he said, 'I am very grateful,' and then repeated, 'I am very grateful.'

"As we passed out we came then to the Executive offices and in this very room, Cox sat down at this table"—and here Roosevelt struck the table—"and asked Tumulty for paper and a pencil, and there he wrote the statement that committed us to making the League the paramount issue of the campaign. It was one of the most impressive scenes I have ever witnessed. Tell Cox he must tell that story."

Sincerely,
Claude G. Bowers

The Honorable
James M. Cox
Dayton, Ohio.

After the White House meeting, President Wilson issued the following statement:

"The interview was in every respect most satisfactory and most gratifying. I found what I indeed already knew and what Governor Cox has let the whole world know in his speeches, that he and I were absolutely at one with regard to the great issue of the League of Nations and that he is ready to be the champion in every respect of the honor of the nation and to secure the peace of the world. Governor Cox will have the vigorous support of an absolutely united party and, I am confident, also an absolutely united nation."

My statement, which President Roosevelt referred to as written in the executive office, follows:

"From every viewpoint the meeting was delightful. The President was at his best, recalling any detail inquired about as bearing upon the international situation and enlivening the whole conference with a humorous anecdote now and then in his characteristic way. We are agreed as to the meaning and sufficiency of the Democratic platform and the duty of the party in the face of threatened bad faith to the world in the name of America. His thought is still of the war and the pledges we gave to those who sacrificed. One easily sees that as the leader of the nation who asked for our sons and our resources upon a very distinct understanding and obligation he is resolved that faith shall be kept. To this his thought and life are dedicated. What he promised I shall use my strength to give."

Mr. Roosevelt, in characteristically gracious phrase, said in his statement:

"I wish that every American could have been a silent witness to the meeting between these two great men. Their splendid accord and their high purpose are an inspiration. I need only add that my regret in leaving my post under President Wilson is softened by the knowledge that my new 'commander-in-chief' will be his wholly worthy successor."

Two biographers have done such violence to the truth of the meeting with Wilson in the White House that the real facts should be presented. There was opposition in certain quarters to my making the trip. Edmond H. Moore, who had managed our campaign before and at the San Francisco convention, thought it would be politically unwise. He insisted that the defeat of McAdoo and Palmer in the convention had been construed by certain elements as a victory over the administration, since both of those men were part of it, and that my seeing Wilson might give offense. The racial opposition to the Democratic ticket in 1920, so violent and articulate later in the campaign, was not yet in evidence. Mr. Moore, an impulsive man and a very strong character, was much displeased when I told him that it was my purpose to visit Mr. Wilson regardless of political consequences. He had made a gallant fight for the cause of peace and the League of Nations and had impaired his health and risked his very life by doing it. As the nominee of our party, the leadership in the campaign passed from him to me. I had the feeling then and still have that as long as world cooperation for peace is an issue in the minds and hearts of the peoples of the earth the works of Woodrow Wilson will be their guiding light. There was some doubt at this time as to whether Mr. Wilson would live long. I would have reproached myself everlastingly if he had passed on without my going to him as an earnest of fealty to the cause which he had led.

This should completely refute the inaccuracies of two biographers who have written that until Mr. Roosevelt and I went to Washington we had been in doubt about making the League the issue. Wilson was confident of our election. He never lost that faith, even up to Election Day.

It was a warm day when we visited him, and the President remarked to me that I would find the White House very comfortable to live in. Not only his words but his manner implied his faith in the American people. One of these biographers was so careless with the facts that he even made me a United States senator, and two offenders against the truth said that I had never met Woodrow Wilson. For eight years we had been in very close relationship officially and personally. During the war, it was necessary for me as governor of one of our large states to be in close touch with Washington, and there were often matters which had to go past the cabinet to the President himself.

Except as purely official matters required my presence at the White House, I never went there save when invited by the President. I once remarked to Joseph P. Tumulty, Mr. Wilson's secretary, how gracious the President had always been to me and that I sometimes suspected that Tumulty had a hand in these invitations. He explained that usually at lunchtime, or immediately thereafter, he had a brief session with the President, in the course of which Mr. Wilson always asked, "Who is in town?" When my name was mentioned, the President always asked Mr. Tumulty to have me call at a specified time. I remember once going to his office at five in the afternoon. To my expression of regret that this trespass was made on his time so late in the day, he said, "You see, Governor, your coming to see me is always like a breath of fresh air because you never come here with matters of patronage. You don't know how much I am bedeviled with this sort of thing. Sometimes even the requests of my good friends are embarrassing."

A word about Claude Bowers. After the death of Frank Cobb of the New York *World*, one of the ablest editorial writers of all time, Ralph Pulitzer of the *World* was discussing with me the difficulty that would be encountered in filling his place. He asked me if I knew of anyone who might be considered and I suggested Bowers. Pulitzer remarked that he had never heard of him and was good-naturedly amused when I told him I was not surprised for most New Yorkers regarded the highlands of Jersey as the western boundary of the United States. Bowers lived in Indiana and that was a long way off. Bowers was afterwards employed by the *World*.

I have always considered him one of the ablest of all our American political historians. I had been so much impressed with his book on Andrew Jackson that after reading Beveridge's masterpiece, the *Life of John Marshall*, I told Bowers that Beveridge had been unfair to Jefferson. He should be answered by him. It was my suggestion that whatever he did should not be designated as a reply to Beveridge but that a life of Jefferson as Bowers would write it would in itself correct the false impressions occasioned by Beveridge. His response was his great book, *Jefferson and Hamilton*. It claimed wide popularity. At a banquet in his honor soon after the book appeared, he stated that I was the godfather of the work on Jefferson because I had persuaded him to write it.

Beveridge was very much upset by Bowers' presentation, and so completely on the defensive that he wrote a 5000-word review of *Jefferson and Hamilton* for the Boston *Transcript*. He afterwards admitted that had he read the Bowers' report before he wrote his *Marshall* he would have had a different treatment for Jefferson. Out of the controversy, however, grew a warm friendship between Beveridge and Bowers which continued until the death of the Indiana statesman.

CHAPTER XXIII

THE GREAT CONSPIRACY

◆

THE LEAGUE OF NATIONS in the presidential campaign of 1920 was to be the overshadowing issue. It could not have been otherwise. We had had our bitter taste of war and our people believed that its sacrifice of ten million lives was a criminal waste which should never occur again. The naked facts demanded ways to prevent further such calamities. The better instincts of mankind called for a bending of their best thought and labor in an epoch-making effort to assure world-wide peace. There could be no mistaking that this was the moving impulse of the world's peoples. America prepared to play its proper part in the fulfillment of the need.

The fact is amazing, as viewed from the present day, that almost from the beginning a conspiracy was in the making to defeat this human hope. What took place was then plain only to students of events. Twenty-five years have brought into clear view the plan and purpose of the conspiracy and the disaster which it wrought. The possible parallel between those events and gathering events of the present time gives our people a deep concern in the great betrayal of that other post-war time.

The cause of world peace was not new. The angels had sung of it two thousand years before with their "On earth peace, good will toward men." Peace among men was at the very heart of the religion which Christ proclaimed. Throughout all time, war had brought recurring ruin to the peoples of the earth. Wise men, sickened by the sight, had long sought a world order under which peace might be insured.

At the Thirteenth Inter-Parliamentary Conference at Brussels in 1905, Representative Richard Bartholdt of Missouri presented a plan for world federation. Andrew Carnegie, in his rectorial address at St. Andrews University in Scotland soon afterwards, expressed the need of such a movement. Later, he assembled a peace conference of 1500 people in New York City in support of it. A detailed plan for a league of peace had been presented by Señor Ordóñey, former President of Uruguay, to the Second Hague Conference. A vigorous sponsor came forward in Theodore Roosevelt; going beyond mere theory, he went into a detailed scheme of organization. Roosevelt had brought about peace between Russia and Japan in 1905. In the midst of this task, the Moroccan crisis between Germany and the Entente powers brought a threat of war. Roosevelt was as insistent that this be settled peaceably as he had been that war should end between Russia and Japan. In the Moroccan matter he employed Ambassador Henry White, and there is little question that he averted war both by the persuasiveness of his words and by the force of his will. In 1906 Roosevelt was fittingly awarded the Nobel Peace Prize. Speaking at Christiania, Norway, in May, 1910, in acknowledgment of the honor, Roosevelt reached the high point in his career. He brought his mind and purpose here to something greater than domestic problems. He could not but have been stirred by the opportunity which had come to him for leadership in a great world movement. He was embarking on a project which should be a turning point in the affairs of men and nations. In ringing words he said:

Finally it would be a master stroke if those great Powers honestly bent on peace would form a League of Peace, not only to keep the peace among themselves, but to prevent, by force if necessary, its being broken by others. The supreme difficulty in connection with developing the peace work of the Hague arises from the lack of any executive power, of any police power to enforce the decrees of the court . . . Each nation must keep well prepared to defend itself until the establishment of some form of international police power, competent and willing to prevent violence as between nations. As things are now, such power to command peace throughout the world could best be assured by some combination between those great nations which sincerely desire peace and have no thought themselves of committing aggressions. The combination might at first be only to secure peace within certain definite limits and certain definite conditions; but the ruler or statesman who should bring about such a combination would have earned his

247

place in history for all time and his title to the gratitude of all mankind.

There was no quibbling here about use of police power for peace; and the ruler or statesman who brought about this organization for peace was to earn, in his words, "his place in history for all time."

But other matters soon engrossed the mind of Theodore Roosevelt. Emerging from his journey into Africa, he declared war on the policies of the Taft administration. He tried for another term in the presidency in 1912 and failed. Then came the First World War, with a slaughter so ghastly that civilized men were ready as never before to put into operation the plan for world order and peace which Roosevelt had so boldly presented a decade before. That the subject again took hold of Roosevelt's mind is evidenced by his assertion in 1915 that the nations in the League of Peace should "not only keep the peace among themselves but prevent by force if necessary its being broken by others."

About this time the League to Enforce Peace, a vigorous forward movement, was formed. The conference in Philadelphia which gave it birth was presided over by former President Taft. The meeting, which I as governor attended, including governors of states and many influential citizens, in Independence Hall on June 17, 1914, was very impressive. In support of this enterprise, Mr. Taft made a tour through the country. I introduced him to a large meeting in our Memorial Hall at Dayton. One could not help seeing the deep sincerity of the man and his devotion to the cause of peace. After the meeting, we visited alone together at the club. There did not appear to be a partisan thought in his mind.

Senator Lodge endorsed the League to Enforce Peace, both the organization and the principles which it enunciated. The League held a great meeting in Washington on May 27, 1916. Wilson and Lodge spoke. Lodge's words can be reflected upon now. He said:

I know, and no one, I think, can know better than one who has served long in the Senate, which is charged with an important share in the ratification and confirmation of all treaties; no one can, I think, feel more deeply than I do the difficulties which confront us in the work which this league—that is, the great association extending throughout the country, known as the League to Enforce Peace—undertakes, but the difficulties

248

cannot be overcome unless we try to overcome them. I believe much can be done. Probably it will be impossible to stop all wars, but it certainly will be possible to stop some wars, and thus diminish their number. The way in which this problem must be worked out must be left to this league and to those who are giving this great subject the study which it deserves. I know the obstacles. I know how quickly we shall be met with the statement that this is a dangerous question which you are putting into your argument, that no nation can submit to the judgment of other nations, and we must be careful at the beginning not to attempt too much. I know the difficulties which arise when we speak of anything which seems to involve an alliance, but I do not believe that when Washington warned us against entangling alliances he meant for one moment that we should not join with the other civilized nations of the world if a method could be found to diminish war and encourage peace.

When the battle against the League of Nations was on, Lodge, in numberless speeches, warned against the danger of "entangling alliances," a glaring hypocrisy, for his original views had been well matured. In this same Washington address, he said:

"It was a year ago that in delivering the Chancellor's address at Union College, I made an argument on this theory, that if we were to promote international peace at the close of the present terrible war, if we were to restore international law as it must be restored, we must find some way in which the united forces of the nations could be put behind the cause of peace and law. I said then that my hearers might think I was picturing a Utopia, but it is in the search for Utopia that great discoveries have been made. 'Not failure, but low aim, is crime.' "

Even Philander C. Knox, Secretary of State under Taft, in addressing a number of conferences on international problems stressed the fact "that the common interest of nations is being recognized as superior to their special interests, and that unity of action in international matters may yet control the unrestrained, unregulated or isolated action of independent states."

Emphasizing this point, he continued:

Independence exists, but the interdependence of states is as clearly recognized as their political independence. Indeed, the tendency is very marked to substitute interdependence for independence, and each nation is likely to see itself forced to yield something of its initiative, not to any one nation, but to the community of nations in payment for its share in "the advance in richness of existence."

With every tale of slaughter overseas came a quickening resolve in this country to accomplish two things: first, win the war; then, see that there should never be another one. President Wilson in all of his addresses made it clear that the best way to protect us against war was to write into the treaty of peace an agreement between nations to form and to maintain the peace. There were no discordant notes. The Republican leaders were here at one with President Wilson and the Democrats. The nation was united upon the greatest enterprise of all time, the building of enduring peace. Who could have dreamed then that the enterprise, so supported, could fail?

Wilson was now approaching the high point in his leadership. The whole world seemed to rise in approval of his Fourteen Points. Former Speaker Joseph G. Cannon said: "The President is always strong in his addresses. I wish this one could be read by every man, woman and child and thoroughly explained in Germany and Austria." Simeon D. Fess, an uncompromising partisan, was "wonderfully pleased with the message. It contains no cheap diplomacy."

Even George Harvey, bitter enemy of Wilson, approved in eloquent words: "Mr. Wilson's declaration was a veritable masterpiece. He has never done, and we doubt if any other living being could have done, better. We particularly liked his definiteness. His numerical summary of the fourteen war aims was tremendously effective." Of Wilson's Fourth of July address to come later, Harvey was to say: "No such Fourth of July address as that of President Wilson at Mount Vernon ever has been or probably ever again will be heard in the country's history. It was one of the most impressive utterances that ever fell from the lips or pen of an American statesman. Never has an American spokesman for the American people risen more superbly to a great occasion. It was simply a masterpiece. As long as generations to come read the history of our share in the great World War, just so long will this 1918 Fourth of July address of President Wilson at Washington's tomb be read and admired as a dominant instrument in our history."

Herbert Hoover said:

I am for President Wilson's leadership, not only in the conduct of the war, but also in the negotiations of peace and afterward in the direction of America's burden in the rehabilitation of the world. There is no greater monument to any man's genius than the conduct of negotiations with the enemy by the President.

On October 2, 1919, speaking at Stanford University, Hoover said:

The League of Nations is an aspiration which has been rising in the hearts of all the world. It has become an insistence in the minds of all those to whom the lives of our sons are precious, to all those to whom civilization is a thing to be safeguarded, and all those who see no hope for the amelioration of the misery of those who toil if peace cannot be maintained.

Victory in the war came fast. Every breeze was freighted with promise of a peaceful new world to come. How that fair promise was broken and betrayed is the bleak record we must here put down.

Theodore Roosevelt might have been expected to welcome President Wilson as a follower—a follower of the Roosevelt faith expressed in 1910. Roosevelt could have claimed priority in presenting the principles which Wilson now proclaimed. Why did he, on the contrary, desert and help destroy the cause which he himself had proclaimed and so strongly and eloquently advanced? We deal here with one of those sad reversals of a human character and attitude with which history is tragically replete.

For Roosevelt and Lodge, those days were a stern testing time. They were both historians, familiar with the movements of the past and of the present time. They knew the lasting political consequences of special great events. They knew that from Jefferson to Lincoln, with but brief interruptions, the Democratic party had held full sway. Why? Roosevelt and Lodge, historians, knew why. It was under Democratic rule that the republic, beginning with Jefferson, had maintained its growth and expanded its democracy.

The Democratic party has presided over every extension of the country's contiguous continental area since the United States became a nation. The treaty of peace after the War for Independence found us a nation extending from Maine to Georgia, and from the

251

Atlantic to the Mississippi, but with the mouth of the Mississippi in foreign control.

Under Thomas Jefferson, first of Democratic Presidents, this area was practically doubled by the Louisiana Purchase. This still left Florida and a strip east of the mouth of the Mississippi in Spanish hands. This area was acquired by the United States in the presidency of Monroe, third Democratic President.

Under Democratic President Polk the extension to the Pacific was completed with the annexation of Texas and the area reaching from Texas to the coast. In the same administration of President Polk a settlement with Great Britain was reached which gave us what is now Washington, Oregon and Idaho, completing the expansion on the northern borders to the Pacific. Even the small area acquired from Mexico through the Gadsden Purchase was acquired in the administration of a Democratic President, Franklin Pierce. In this year was completed the present continental area, exclusive of Alaska, a non-contiguous territory, of the United States. Democratic Presidents led us from the status of an eastern seaboard nation to a nation stretched from Gulf to Great Lakes, from sea to sea. It had been a party of progress and so the people had adhered to it. Another important fact not overlooked by historians Roosevelt and Lodge was the capacity the Democrats had shown for turning great, convulsive social movements, such as those of the time of Jefferson and Jackson, into constructive, beneficent, peaceful channels. The party had recognized new needs unheeded by the reactionaries of their day. They might recognize such needs again to the detriment of existing reactionary interests. Could not historians Roosevelt and Lodge see in President Wilson another Jackson or Jefferson? He had come to the presidency in the midst of a political turmoil growing out of the remissness of Republican regimes. He had recognized and supplied long-neglected needs. Jefferson and Jackson had accomplished hardly more than Wilson in resolving social and economic strains. To his credit stood the first income tax law, the establishment of the Federal Trade Commission, the Smith-Lever Act, the Keating-Owen Labor Act, the Underwood tariff law, the La Follette seamen's law, the Jones Act for the government of the Philippines, the Adamson railway labor law, the Federal Land Bank System, the Overman Act, the Federal Reserve System and the National Defense Act of 1916.

Such leadership could not but impress and direct the mood of the nation for years to come. Roosevelt and Lodge well knew this. If now there were added to these achievements the establishment of world peace, the supreme event in the history of nations, the name of Wilson and the prestige of his party might be as invincible as after Jackson and Jefferson. What but dread of all this could have caused the strange reversal of attitude later to appear?

Lodge had been unhappy with the whole world situation. He mourned in 1914 that the leadership of the Roosevelt era had been lost both in the Old World and the New. "Rightly or wrongly," he said, "they have come to believe we are not to be trusted; that we make our international relations the sport of politics and treat them as if they were in no wise different from domestic legislation." But now under Wilson's leadership, skies had cleared. We, with the other nations, were building an accord which held great promise for the world. But all of this was under auspices which only aroused the partisan envy and wrath of Roosevelt and Lodge.

Roosevelt's partisan interest may have been excited by a surviving hope for the presidency. In 1916, when the Republican leaders at their national convention had tentatively agreed to nominate Charles E. Hughes, they asked Nicholas Murray Butler to get Roosevelt by telephone, advise him what was going on and, if possible, get his agreement. Before Butler could utter half a dozen words, Roosevelt asked him, "What about me?" Butler had to tell him that there was no chance. Roosevelt's speeches during the war, and his whole attitude immediately afterwards, created the impression in the minds of political observers that the presidential bug still lived. The path of politics and the path of peace had, for both these leaders, parted company. They chose the path of politics. This historic conversation was related to me by Mr. Butler.

It is strangely impressive how time throws light on situations not clear at first. Mark Sullivan, writer and historian, said almost ten years afterwards in an article in *World's Work:*

The League as we looked upon it in the Senate fight and in the presidential campaign of 1920, was bound up with the personality of Woodrow Wilson and his political position. It carried the liability of the partisan bias against him and of the unwillingness of the opposing political party to take a step which would have exalted him in history, which would have

253

labeled him as a great leader and his work as a success, and would have implied such an approval of him as should logically have been followed by keeping his party in power. All that burden the League question carried in 1920.

Thus the peace effort of a war-weary world was sacrificed on the altar of partisan politics. There was, moreover, a personal bitterness of the two Republican leaders towards Wilson to add to their partisanship in explaining their desertion of the cause of world peace.

Wilson, seeking to keep politics out of the war, had supported Newton D. Baker's decision not to put Roosevelt in command of troops overseas, thus enraging Roosevelt. Wilson, grievously hurt by a statement made by Lodge in connection with the *Lusitania* affair, had insisted that it was so full of falsehood it could only be deliberately false. He refused later to appear on the same platform with Lodge at a public meeting. From that time Lodge hated Wilson and Wilson held only contempt for Lodge.

At whatever cost, the two men, with their personal grievances and their partisan passion, felt Wilson must be destroyed. The way to destroy him was to discredit and defeat the great project which he had brought to the verge of success. Their own words of former days would come back to belie them, but they were too angry and desperate to care for that. It was a titanic task, but Lodge was a master at manipulating the forces which could be worked to confuse the people and defeat their desires.

A movement to take direction of the war from Wilson was launched. A coalition cabinet was proposed to take the command of our armed forces largely from the President. Then it was urged that a joint committee of both houses be created to "assist" the President. This was a companion piece to the measure his enemies in Congress launched against Lincoln in the War Between the States.

In 1918, Wilson had appealed for a politically friendly Congress. The elements behind Roosevelt and Lodge indulged in a war dance of indignation. The patriotism of the Republicans, they cried, had been impugned. They did not remind the country that long before Wilson's appeal was made in October, plans for a Republican Congress were formed in the previous May. Later in the summer, Roosevelt and Taft, who had re-established cordial relations, both addressed an unofficial Republican state convention at Saratoga, New York. The former Presidents said it was necessary to elect a Republican Congress to stimulate the President, as they put it, on to victory in the war and the reconstruction afterwards. The effort for a Republican Congress even included the joint endorsement by Taft and Roosevelt of the candidacy of Truman Newberry, who afterwards resigned under fire, for United States senator from Michigan.

Lodge wanted a Republican Senate which would make him head of the Committee on Foreign Relations, in position to cut the throat of the League. President Wilson was assailed for not appointing one or more members of the Senate to the peace commission to meet at Versailles. The failure to include senators on the commission was ascribed to Wilson's despotic way with public matters and to this same cause was ascribed the failure of the Senate to ratify the League.

The employment of senators in treaty-making had in fact been tried and discarded by Republican administrations long before. President McKinley had made a practice of including senators on commissions that negotiated treaties. This was cited as a precedent in the League argument. The precedent, in fact, had been abandoned by McKinley himself. In his *The United States and the League of Nations, 1918-1920*, D. F. Fleming, the eminent historian of Vanderbilt University in Tennessee, says:

There was, however, another side to the story not so generally known. Many Senators had keenly resented the appointment of their fellow members as negotiators, on the grounds that the Senate was deprived of the services of important members for long periods and that Senators were thereby made into advocates of treaties when it was their duty to judge them with impartial and open minds. How could a Senator come back and fail to support what he had put his name to? Moreover, when Senate leaders defended their own handiwork on the floor of the Senate was not proper criticism by their colleagues made unfairly difficult? Serious assaults were made also upon such appointments on the ground of constitutionality.

The Senate was twice at the point of taking action to condemn the practice. On the second occasion it was agreed in the Judiciary Committee that Senator Hoar, of Massachusetts, should visit President McKinley and inform him of the feeling of the

255

Senate. He did so and received assurance satisfactory to him that Senators would not receive further appointments as negotiators in that Administration.

The argument that senators should negotiate was another case of sheer mendacity on the part of the conspirators. Both as to Wilson's request for a friendly Congress and as to the criticism for not appointing senators on the peace commission, they practiced deceit and dishonesty upon a public looking to them for enlightenment.

Wilson wisely selected Henry White, an outstanding diplomat, for the commission, a man of large experience and eminent ability. He was a close friend of both Roosevelt and Lodge. He talked with both Roosevelt and Lodge before accepting the appointment. Lodge, violating all propriety, then presumed upon his friendship for Henry White to attempt to undermine the President. He prepared a memorandum of nine pages setting forth in general what the terms of peace should cover. On the subject of the League, he stated, "It need only be said here that under no circumstances must provisions for such a League be made a part of the peace treaty which concludes the war with Germany." As he put it, "The League would have to wait. The President's plan could be considerably amended by the Senate." Speaking as chairman of the Committee on Foreign Relations, he thus attempted to use one of the commissioners in an attempt to impair and befuddle his country's negotiations with foreign states. Lodge asked that the memorandum be given to Balfour, Clemenceau and Nitti. Lodge personally knew these men, but out of loyalty to his duty, as he himself afterwards stated, White "kept the document secret."

The famous round robin was another reckless effort to bedevil the peace and wreck the League. Signed by thirty-one Republican members of the Senate, it had no other purpose than to harass the President in his negotiations for peace. George Harvey spread the assertion that Wilson's purpose in going to Paris was to become President of the League of Nations, and thereby ruler of the world. This canard was widely circulated in Europe. While the peace conference was in session, articles cabled from this country, written by Judson Welliver, appeared regularly in two Paris newspapers, *Le Matin* and *Echo de Paris*. Their purpose was to impress upon the peace conference that the final voice was with the United States

Senate. The purpose was, of course, to weaken the influence of Wilson in the negotiations. Thus Wilson did his country's work in Paris with the partisans of Lodge baying at his heels like hostile hounds. Is there any other instance in American history where political partisans went abroad to befoul and baffle their own country's government as it labored there?

Lodge defended his interference with the President's negotiation of the treaty on the ground that the Constitution provided that the power to make treaties was given to the President with the "advice" as well as the "consent" of the Senate. The round robin in the Senate, the private notes which Lodge sought to have delivered to European statesmen by Ambassador White and the articles appearing in Paris newspapers written by Welliver were based, in the view of Lodge, on senatorial rights. This was in harmony with what Lodge said in his debate with President Lowell of Harvard on the subject of ratification. It was the duty of the President to consult with the Senate even before entering into negotiations. He said this had been done by other Presidents, but he did not cite a single instance. If Wilson had done this, he argued, then the Senate would have presented its views as to what he should do at the peace conference. At this stage of the discussion, the question, as Lodge contended, was not what was in the treaty but the unconstitutional processes of making it at the peace table. The final answer to this argument of Lodge is contained in a speech of this same Lodge on a previous occasion when he had a different purpose to serve. Speaking in the Senate, January 24, 1906, when the Algeciras and the Santo Domingo incidents were under discussion, Lodge said:

No one, I think, can doubt the absolute power of the President to initiate and carry on all negotiations; and after a treaty has been returned to him with the ratification of the Senate, to withhold it from ratification if he sees fit so to do. There is no doubt that the Senate can by resolution advise the President to enter upon a negotiation, or advise the President to refrain from a negotiation; but those resolutions have no binding force whatsoever, and the action of the Senate becomes operative and actually effective only when a treaty is actually submitted to it. *We have no possible right to break suddenly into the middle of a negotiation and demand from the President what instructions he has given to his representative.* (Italics mine.)

257

JOURNEY THROUGH MY YEARS

In the course of that debate Senator Spooner of Wisconsin, recognized as one of our best constitutional lawyers, had this to say:

> From the foundation of the Government it has been conceded in practice and in theory that the Constitution vests the power of negotiations and the various phases—and they are multifarious—of the conduct of our foreign relations exclusively in the President. He does not exercise that constitutional power, nor can he be made to do it, under the tutelage or guardianship of the Senate or of the House, or of the Senate and House combined. . . .
> When he shall have negotiated and sent his proposed treaty to the Senate the jurisdiction of that body attaches and its powers begin. It may advise and consent or it may refuse. And in the exercise of this function it is as independent of the Executive as he is independent of it in the matter of negotiation.

What Senator Spooner had said had such a moving effect on Lodge that he immediately took the floor and said:

> I quite realize that after the manner in which he has dealt with those questions, anything that I may say is in great danger of being an anti-climax.

Thus, in his destructive frenzy against the League, Lodge was ready to employ language in precise and direct contradiction of his previous considered attitude. No word has ever been uttered which attempted extenuation of this intellectual dishonesty.

Lodge could as well have claimed the right of the Senate to "advise" the President on the appointment of postmasters, putting in place of John Doe, the President's appointee, if it didn't like him, the name of Richard Roe, its own favorite.

Wilson, in spite of these hindrances, won a great personal achievement at the peace table. When he went to Europe the American people could not but have been impressed by the homage paid there to the American leader of the great crusade for peace. Clemenceau had said of it:

> I knew Paris in the glitter of the Second Empire. I thought I knew my Paris now, but I did not believe she could show such enthusiasm as this. I don't believe there has been anything like it in the history of the world.

No one at the time could have doubted that the public opinion of this country was behind Wilson. I remember a meeting with Senator Borah, an opponent of the League, when we breakfasted together in Columbus, Ohio. Senator Hiram Johnson was about to begin his tour to the west coast speaking against the League. Borah said of this: "Johnson is very foolish in this. There is no question but that the country is behind Wilson and the League of Nations as well."

All of this was discouraging to those who were conspiring against the League, but they were possessed of the spirit of "do or die." A reshaping of their forces was made. The battle cry was sounded, as might have been expected, by the Chicago *Tribune*. It insisted upon a prolonged debate of the question in the Senate. The advocates of exhausting discussion in the Senate doubtless remembered the gauntlet which the Constitution of the United States had to run before its adoption. This great instrument, one hundred years later, was declared by the English Premier, Gladstone, to be "the most wonderful document struck off at a given time by the brain and purpose of man." Yet at the time of its framing, it barely escaped defeat. When the charter went before the states for acceptance in 1787, a bitter opposition arose. The required ninth state, New Hampshire, did not vote its affirmation till 1788. Rhode Island held out until 1790. In the Massachusetts legislature the vote was 187 for, 168 against; in New Hampshire 57 for to 46 against; Virginia 89 to 79; New York 30 to 27; Rhode Island 34 to 32. The debates before the state legislatures produced the same objections offered a century and a third later to the League of Nations. The old bugaboo of sovereignty, which we still hear much about, was there. As Frank Cobb, the journalist, said, "The Lodges and the Knoxes, the Borahs and the Reeds, the Shermans and Thomases of that generation were as vociferous, as clamorous and as vehement in antagonizing the Federal Constitution. They conjured up the same fears and the same doubts, the same tyrannies and the same oppressions. Nothing has changed except the name of the instrument that is assailed."

Patrick Henry assailed the new Constitution, complaining that it used the language of "We, the people," instead of "We, the state." Senator Borah, in the Senate debate, said that he would not support the League if requested to by the "Savior of Mankind." How often did we hear it said in the Senate that the Covenant was unconstitu-

259

tional! The federal Constitution itself was declared unconstitutional before the Massachusetts legislature.

Confusion and doubt, created in the minds of our fathers, almost destroyed the Constitution by which our national life has been preserved. The same doubt and confusion was promoted in the senatorial debates on the League. Those who spread the confusion and doubt had no purpose but to make the Covenant appear so harmful to the prized sovereignty of our Republic that one-third of the membership of the Senate could be induced to vote against it and thus destroy the plan for peace.

Amendments were proposed but voted down. Then recourse was made to reservations. Some of these were offered in good faith. Wilson met with the members of the Foreign Relations Committee of both House and Senate upon his return. Many questions were asked. He answered all freely and stated that no one should hesitate to ask questions. John Jacob Rogers, of Massachusetts, ranking Republican on the House Foreign Relations Committee, said of the White House meeting in a letter to Henry White quoted in Allan Nevins' life of that diplomatist:

> The White House dinner a week ago tonight was a most interesting one and in most respects a memorable one. I thought the President appeared extremely well. He submitted himself to quite rigorous cross-examination for two hours answering every question, easy or difficult, as fully as possible and with apparent candor. He showed not the slightest vexation, even when Senator Brandegee was pressing him rather closely on certain of the difficulties which to his mind were of importance. I never saw Mr. Wilson appear so human or so attractive as that night. There was no suggestion of a feeling of militant arrogance about him.

In a spirit of compromise, and to meet the wishes of the senators who were sincere in their objections to certain phases of the instrument, Mr. Wilson suggested certain clarifications. No restrictions were to be placed on the right of a member state to withdraw. Article 10 was "to be regarded only as advice and leaves every member state free to exercise its own judgment as to whether it is wise or practicable to act upon that advice or not." The League should have no right to deal with "the policy of any member state with regard to such matters as immigration, naturalization or tariffs."

Article 21 was interpreted to mean "that nothing contained in the Covenant shall be interpreted as in any way impairing or interfering with the application of the Monroe Doctrine in the American hemisphere." These concessions served no purpose of the partisans. It was the ruin of Wilson, not a workable way to world peace, that they desired.

It was about this time that President Wilson's breakdown came. Time and its revelations have shown very definitely and beyond the slightest question that such reservations as Lodge proposed were mischievous and sinister in purpose. Senator James Watson, a strong partisan but always a very truthful man, says in his autobiography that at the beginning of the discussion in the Senate he told Lodge that it was futile to attempt to kill the Covenant because public opinion, influenced by the tragedies of the war, was strongly behind it. Lodge then frankly disclosed the strategy which he had planned for his attack. He would insist that he was in favor of the peace plan in principle—which of course he was not. He said bluntly that he would kill it with reservations. The physical powers requisite for the labors of Mr. Wilson's leadership were impaired. Those who had savagely opposed him with reservations now hoped that Wilson, in his illness, could be yet more completely undone. Roosevelt died as the fight was forming but Lodge and his partisans carried on. Lodge had repeatedly said that he knew just what he had to put into the reservations to make Wilson reject them. By this process, as he boasted, the country would then blame Wilson, rather than the Senate, for the defeat of the League. If, contrary to his expectations, Wilson accepted the reservations, then Lodge could claim to have made it a Republican instrument redounding to the glory of his party and the discredit of the Democrats. A policy of harassment was followed. A committee of senators visited the sickroom at the White House on the pretense of ascertaining the physical fitness of the President. It was suggested that the position of President be declared vacant. Thus savagely to the bitter end the war on the President was waged.

Ratification was finally blocked. The cabal had won. Wilson was destroyed. The Republican party was, for the time being, saved— saved at what a cost these prophetic words of Woodrow Wilson in next to his last public speech attest:

I can predict with absolute certainty that within another

generation there will be another world war if the nations of the world do not concert the method by which to prevent it . . . and America has, if I may take the liberty of saying so, a greater interest in the prevention of that war than any other nation. America is less exhausted by the recent war than the other belligerents. She is not exhausted at all.

America has paid for the war that has gone by less heavily, in proportion to her wealth, than the other nations. America still has free capital enough for its own industries and for the industries of the other countries that have to build their industries anew.

The next war would have to be paid for in American blood and American money. The nation of all nations that is most interested to prevent the recurrence of what has already happened is the nation which would assuredly have to bear the brunt of that great catastrophe.

This was not only prophecy of war but a clarion warning that our nation, by reason of its strength, would finally have to bear the brunt of another war.

Ten days after the defeat of the League, Truman Newberry, whose vote had been necessary to make Lodge chairman of the Foreign Relations Committee and master of the Senate, was convicted of violating the Federal Corrupt Practices Act (later to be declared unconstitutional by the Supreme Court) and sentenced to two years in prison.

It was now for the party leaders to keep the people, till election time, in ignorance of what had been done to them. They must not know the door of hope had been closed to them. The action of the Senate had offended millions of the rank and file. With a presidential campaign to win, the people must be reassured. Lodge drew a plank on international relations and sent it to George Harvey, saying that he was between two fires and would be condemned no matter what he did.

These were unhappy days for the Massachusetts senator. An informative note from Mark Sullivan reveals how Lodge once said that in the passion of that period he had been personally addressed "in language which no man of my age should be obliged to hear." Whenever I mentioned Lodge's name during the campaign of 1920, no matter where or to what sort of audience, it produced a hostile reaction of extraordinary intensity. It was a demonstration of abhorrence and detestation for the man who, for such low ends, had done such violence to the high hopes of humanity.

The artful, innocuous, incongruous and meaningless plank finally adopted by the Republican convention was drawn by Elihu Root. Root was in favor of the League. Perhaps he hoped yet to save it. But the party must come first. From his hands came a platform which would enable a Republican President to go into the League or spurn it as served his purposes or whims—and be justified in either case by the party pledge.

If the Republicans had known the extent of the subsequent racial group opposition to the League, they might not have thought it necessary to indulge in such word-juggling in their international plank.

Once the double-dealing platform had garnered the votes, Harding elected to decree: "The League is dead." This broke the promise of a world to be kept at peace; that "Spirit of Party" against which Washington so earnestly warned his countrymen had triumphed. Theodore Roosevelt, Lodge and their followers, reversing their oft-recorded professions, had put their party above their country and above the world's peace. We now have paid the price in the lives of hundreds of thousands of our best young men immolated on battlefields. It all could have been prevented had a certain few men of politics been willing, a quarter of a century ago, to put good faith above personal spite and partisan interest.

The final act of the shabby drama was now played. The League was dead. It was now for the Republican party to make a separate peace with the enemy, with Germany. We leave the story to a master of words. On October 18, 1921, Frank Cobb wrote in the New York *World:*

> In the midst of impressive ceremonies Gen. John J. Pershing yesterday laid the Congressional Medal of Honor on the grave of the unknown British soldier who lies buried in Westminster Abbey.
>
> The same Congress, however, which so ostentatiously bestowed its Medal of Honor has with equal ostentation abandoned the cause for which that unknown soldier died. The United States Senate is now preparing to vote for the ratification of a separate treaty of peace with Germany which seeks

263

to reduce the War to the status of a damage suit and to limit the aims and objects of the United States to the collection of certain money claims against the democratic successor of the Imperial German Government. . . .

It is fitting that the Congressional Medal of Honor should lie on the grave of the unknown British soldier who is sleeping his last sleep within the historic walls of Westminster Abbey; but if this German Treaty is to be ratified in the form in which it has been submitted to the United States Senate, the medal is not complete in itself. It should bear the inscription, "Decorated but Deserted."

Since the end of World War II the people have given evidence of a resolve not to permit another conspiracy here against world peace. Confusing situations have arisen as was to be expected in the wake of a war in which the whole world has been in turmoil. It should be evident to anyone now that it would have been much easier to bind nations together into a charter for peace under the conditions of twenty-five years ago than it will be now. Yet it can be done. The important thing is to keep going in the right direction with patience and understanding.

CHAPTER XXIV

A BATTLE AGAINST ODDS

◆

THE CAMPAIGN officially started with the notification ceremonies at Dayton on August 7, 1920. This was the old order of procedure when the action of the national convention was formalized by the candidate being officially told that he was the candidate. His acceptance was expected to tell plainly how he interpreted the party platform. With the coming of radio, the old method is passing out; nevertheless, acceptance day as an event took on the appearance and character of a festival day in Ohio at that time. The Fairgrounds provided room for a large crowd, and the parade formed downtown to march there. Mr. Roosevelt and I headed it on foot. Mrs. Roosevelt and Miss Ann, a very attractive young girl in her teens, were our guests at Trailsend. The crowd was estimated at 100,000. Tom Love, of Texas, a very astute politician who had been a McAdoo leader, after witnessing the vast outpouring and demonstration, expressed his opinion that Ohio would go Democratic. That was pretty much the feeling of the militant and perhaps overconfident Democracy.

As I look back upon this day, I see it as significant that the first subject touched upon was the international problem. Moving into it, I said:

> We are in a time which calls for straight thinking, straight talking and straight acting. This is no time for wobbling. Never in all our history has more been done for government. Never was there sacrifice more sublime. The most precious things of heart and home were given up in a spirit which guarantees the perpetuity of our institutions—if the faith is kept with those who served and suffered. The altar of our republic is drenched in blood and tears, and he who turns away from the tragedies and obligations of the war, not consecrated to a sense of honor

265

and of duty which resists every base suggestion of personal or political expediency, is unworthy of the esteem of his countrymen.

The evasive character of the Republican platform was referred to in these words:

As the platform made no definite committal of policy and was, in fact, so artfully phrased as to make almost any deduction possible, it passed through the convention with practical unanimity.

Senator Hiram Johnson, one of the isolationist leaders, said a few days before that Senator Harding, the Republican candidate, "took his stand upon the paramount issue in this campaign, The League of Nations. The Republican party stands committed by the platform. The standard-bearer has now accentuated that platform. There can be no misunderstanding his words."

We pointed out that apparently Senators Harding and Johnson were as one on this question. We did not lose sight of Mr. Harding's promise of a "formal and effective peace so quickly as a Republican Congress can pass its declaration for a Republican executive to sign." We insisted that this meant a separate peace with Germany and was intended to cement the German-American vote. It would be, as we said, "a piece of bungling diplomacy and plain unadulterated dishonesty," since we had fought the war together with our allies and should consummate the peace with unbroken ranks. Calling attention to the ambiguity of the Republican platform, and the spoken words of Mr. Harding, I announced my position in few words. They were: "I am in favor of going into the League."

We had single speaking engagements in Indiana and West Virginia, and then the tour to the West started, to carry the issues of the campaign to the public. We went through Ohio to Michigan, Wisconsin, Minnesota, North Dakota, Montana, Washington, Oregon, Idaho, Utah, Nevada, California, Arizona, New Mexico, Colorado, Wyoming, Nebraska, Kansas, Oklahoma, Missouri, Illinois, Indiana and back to Dayton. The Western trip ended on October 3. Newspaper files show a dispatch by Harry L. Rogers, a correspondent on the train, to the effect that starting at Dayton we had covered twenty-four states. All states west of the Mississippi, except Arkansas, Louisiana and Texas, were visited. Two hundred and thirty-eight speeches were delivered and the mileage covered was 9975. This was a tremendously laborious and fatiguing ordeal.

One car carried an improvised printing shop, where advance matter was provided for the press. As we went through the Western country, I was reminded how little the average citizen of the East, and even most public men, knew about the great Western empire. At one time, I remarked that a condition might well be imposed on presidential candidates that, as a matter of duty, they visit the Western states, get a comprehensive view of their resources and needs and make contact with their thought. Harding, at the insistence of those who constantly attended him at Marion, notably George Harvey, said that his campaign would be made from the front porch at Marion. The implication was that it was undignified for a presidential nominee to make these long speaking trips. I became convinced that this plan would have to be abandoned by Harding. It subsequently was, and the Republican candidate left the front porch for the rear platform, and then the "one-night stand."

One of the bedeviling things in this kind of campaigning was that so many stops had to be made at railway stations, with the attendant noises which come from freight and passenger yards. It was a common saying that we could tell the politics of the man who was running the switch engine near by. He was quiet with his locomotive or not, according to his partisanship. We did not have as many disagreeable experiences in this way as did Mr. Harding.

In Butte, Montana, at that time a hotbed of radicalism, we had our first experience with the I.W.W. It was a night meeting on the public square. The call of the I.W.W. was something approaching the mew of a cat. Most of the members of the order must have been present, but they remained in the outskirts of the crowd, which was large. We soon discovered that when we approached the subject of labor, the uncivil behavior gave way to respectful silence. The I.W.W. had known something about our Workmen's Compensation Law in Ohio. As we went into the subject in some detail, there was a shifting in the crowd and the I.W.W. fellows were nudging their way closer to the speakers' stand. I told them by the ·recital of a simple story, one that I have already mentioned in these pages, the difference between a progressive and a reactionary state. A certain factory was located across the Ohio-Pennsylvania state line. A man working on the Pennsylvania side was injured. He was helpless in hips and legs, but he retained consciousness and pulled himself across the state line into Ohio, where the mishap was reported and recognized under the law. There were no more unfriendly demonstrations.

Campaigning in the Far West presented many difficulties. The three hours' difference in time made it imperative for us to send out advance press notices during the night; otherwise, we would have missed all the next day's morning papers in the East and some of the early afternoon editions, too. This work had to be done after our night meetings. It was not uncommon to be so engaged until two o'clock in the morning. My executive secretary, Charles E. Morris, a trained newspaperman, was tremendously efficient and useful in this detail. He was ably assisted by Senator Carl D. Friebolin of Ohio and Welles Hawkes, one of the best-known publicity men in the country.

Everywhere in the West we were advised of a highly organized movement for the collection of funds for the Republican campaign. The facts were well known because no attempt had been made to suppress them. The method was not unlike that followed in community drives. Many good newspaper stories grew out of this activity and the representatives of the press for a time in their daily reports played them up more prominently than my treatment of the League of Nations issue. This created some uneasiness in the East for a time.

In the Northwest it became apparent that Will Hays, the Republican National Chairman, was sending hecklers ahead of us, one or more of whom attended every meeting. It was soon plain, however, that heckling was more helpful than harmful to me, and the practice was abandoned. An interesting psychology enters into interruptions of a speaker. If no restraint in manner or voice is imposed by the speaker on the heckler, he always seems emboldened to go further than he first intended, and without exception he offends the audience. Then is the time for the speaker to give him an overhauling. If this were done before the heckler offended, the reaction could easily be in his favor. In some instances the hecklers were literally driven out of the meetings. The instance which I recall best was at Baltimore, Maryland.

The cordial spirit everywhere in the Western country proved stimulating. Our meetings were well attended everywhere. It mattered not where they were held, whether in the early forenoon or beginning close to midnight. At no time was the attendance or the reception disappointing. Robert (Red) Smith, of the Chicago *Tribune*, one of the newspapermen who went with us across the continent, was instructed, apparently, to observe developments carefully and advise his central office. In one of his messages to headquarters which Secretary Morris chanced to see he said: "There is something going on in the country. I can't quite make it out. Cox's meetings are enormous and the enthusiasm seems to have a great depth of meaning."

We reached Pueblo, Colorado, on September 26, 1920. We were reminded that on the very platform from which I spoke, Woodrow Wilson, just one year before, almost to the minute, had issued his last words as President of the United States, his fortieth speech in a twenty-two days' trip, not one of which had been prepared in advance. It was a solemn moment. Everyone in the Colorado audience knew the meaning of the anniversary date. A difficult task fell upon me. I dwelt on the message of a great man whose view into the future was beyond the vision of his time. He had given all the strength of body and mind and was to give his life for a cause sacred to him but soon to be rejected. On the day Mr. Wilson was stricken, in part he said:

> On last Decoration Day, I went to a beautiful hillside near Paris, where was located the cemetery of Suresnes, a cemetery given over to the burial of the American dead. Behind me on the slopes was rank upon rank of living American soldiers, and lying before me on the levels of the plain was rank upon rank of departed American soldiers.
>
> Right by the side of the stand where I spoke, there was a little group of French women who had adopted these graves, had made themselves mothers of those dear ghosts by putting flowers every day upon these graves, taking them as their own sons, their own beloved, because they had died in the same cause —France was free and the world was free because America had come!
>
> I wish some men in public life who are now opposing the settlement for which these men died could visit such a spot as that. I wish that the thought that comes out of those graves could penetrate their consciousness. I wish that they could feel

the moral obligation that rests upon us not to go back on those boys, but to see the thing through, to see it through to the end and make good their redemption of the world. For nothing less depends upon this decision, nothing less than the liberation and salvation of the world.

On the day spent in Indiana there were twenty-six meetings beginning in the early morning and ending an hour and a half after midnight, winding up at Fort Wayne. One of the newspapermen facetiously observed to Tom Taggart, who was with us throughout the day, that he had evidently chased me into every county where an incumbent sheriff was in danger of defeat.

Campaigning in those days was very different from now. There was no written speech. What you had to say had to be drawn out of thin air and the draft on one's physical strength never relaxed. Next to the Hoosier experience, the most laborious day was in New England. We started either at Worcester or Springfield before breakfast. The brass band and the crowd were there before I was up. If anyone has never attempted to speak about the hour of dawn before having a cup of coffee, he has but to try and discover just what it means. We moved from Massachusetts into New Hampshire, stopping at every important place. Soon after noon on a beautiful autumn day a meeting was held in the State house grounds at Concord where I was introduced by a Republican, a justice of the Supreme Court who believed in the League of Nations. The next meeting was at Lynn, Massachusetts, where the crowd could only be measured by thousands. The full moon was in the eastern skies and the sun was setting as we traveled on to Cambridge, Massachusetts, where the graduate body of Harvard was assembled. The presiding officer was President Charles W. Eliot. James W. Faulkner, probably the ablest man among all our correspondents, pronounced the speech that night my best of the campaign. Mrs. Sayre, daughter of President Wilson, was in attendance. Winding up the day, I began speaking on Boston Common to a crowd, the size of which it was difficult to calculate, at eleven o'clock at night. The audiences that day were from the shops and textile mills, from college campuses and from the metropolis of Boston.

Harding's vacillating attitude helped us tremendously. I attempted to discuss the League from different angles. If we were in doubt

270

how to proceed on a given day, we had only to look at the morning papers to find some new contradiction in speech or statement from Harding or one of the bitter-enders against the League.

Forgetting what had happened to the Republican party in the election of 1910 because of the offensive Payne-Aldrich tariff bill, Harding moved back into old tracks. One day he would go far enough towards the League to satisfy those who were displeased with the Republican platform. Soon thereafter, he would pronounce the League a failure. Then, to gain ground already lost by previous pronouncements, he would propose an entirely new plan. He was to construct a world association on the framework of the Hague Tribunal. Some features of the League he said would be kept if found "safe and practicable." The Hague Tribunal was only a judicial body. On another occasion, he thought the Convenant might be revised so as to protect national sovereignty. Once he said, in plain words, that he would bring our boys all back home by negotiating a separate peace with Germany. This evidently made trouble and before the week was out he was saying that all that was necessary was a peace resolution by Congress without negotiating a separate instrument with Germany. Harding had evidently given assurances to Taft and Root, both of whom believed in the League and had urged Lodge not to kill it with drastic reservations. Evidently the constant efforts to keep these two men and others of their thinking in line under one interpretation of the platform and then to appease Lodge, Hiram Johnson, Borah, Brandegee, McCormick and other opponents of the League became very tiresome. At such an impasse he would take up matters of business, farming, railroad transportation and what not for a time. He got on dangerous ground once in discussing our hyphenated citizenship. Stating that our meddling in the affairs of other nations would prevent our foreign-born becoming united in loyalty to our government, he extenuated the disloyalty of some alien groups, insisting that the fault was not with them but with our own nation. After he announced his purpose to create an association of nations, inquiry came from all quarters as to just what it was to be. He replied at Baltimore: "I am perfectly frank to say to you that I am without a single program constructive in character about an association of nations. I am not in favor of going into the League. I want an association behind which all America can stand."

271

Finding no favor for his plan to make the Hague Tribunal the basis for an institution for maintaining world peace, Harding announced that he intended to put teeth in the Tribunal. It was not long, however, before he began to see some virtue in the League, the institution with which he had previously said he would have nothing to do. At Marion he went so far as to say that if the League then functioning was so entwined and interwoven into the peace of Europe that its good must be preserved in order to stabilize the peace of that continent, then it may be amended or revised. One week afterwards, he admitted that there was much good in the Versailles treaty and he had no desire to discard all of it. Once he asserted there was no virtue in reservations, even though he had contended for them in the Senate. The League to be useful would have to be revised or reconstructed. He was careful, however, to express his doubt about the use of force in restraining an outlaw nation.

By this time, the strategists of the Republican campaign decided that Harding should have a guard thrown about him. George Harvey was sent to Marion to prevent any utterances that might wreck the Republican campaign. But this was not all. Campaign publicity in the main came from Chicago headquarters where Albert S. Lasker, a genius in publicity and experienced in the moving of public opinion through the printed word, and George Sutherland, afterwards to be appointed to the Supreme Court bench by Harding, were put on guard. With them was Richard Washburn Child, afterwards to be appointed ambassador to Italy by President Harding.

Harding had prepared his speech to be delivered at Des Moines. George Harvey's vigilance for this day had relaxed. Partial distribution of the speech had been made in Chicago when Lasker and Sutherland, the censors, discovered that Harding had carried himself to the very threshold of the League. There was great excitement. Lodge was advised, and George Harvey. The advance copies were called in and the speech was reconstructed.

All of this maneuvering to hold together both the pro-League and the anti-League was unnecessary. The balance of power to be asserted in that campaign was set without regard to argument. Leaders of three racial groups, German, Irish and Italian, had gone over to the Republican side. The Germans were angry with Wilson because of the war. The Irish were inflamed because Wilson did not make the independence of Ireland a part of the Versailles treaty. The Italians were enraged because Fiume had been taken away from Italy. The Italian vote was practically solid. It would be unfair not to explain that it was largely the "professional Irish," whose hate of England was most bitter, that led the opposition from that angle. They did not take with them the entire Irish vote, but they mustered enough to be effective.

In the Democratic organization down to the precincts were many fine, loyal and efficient young Irishmen. They did their best but they were battling against terrific odds.

The articulately active Germans were those associated with the German-American Alliance and other societies which had maintained close relations with the fatherland. This racial lineup insured the electoral vote of states like Massachusetts, Connecticut, Rhode Island, New York, New Jersey, Pennsylvania, Ohio, Indiana, Illinois, Nebraska and others. No matter what the candidates might say or do, the die was cast.

The Springfield, Massachusetts, *Republican* in its issue of October 30, 1920, said:

> An Italian newspaper in New York exhorted its readers that "not to vote for the adversary of Cox, the legatee of Wilson, is a betrayal of the mother country. Let Italians bear this in mind and consider the day of the presidential election as a day of sacred and imperative revenge."

The *Literary Digest* in September quoted the New York *Sun* as saying:

> Not one prominent German daily stands behind Governor Cox . . . and against him are added hundreds of German weekly and monthly periodicals which are rapidly coming into the field again.

George Viereck, the militant pro-German, had this to say:

> German-Americans were doubtless opposed in great numbers to the League as a matter of principle, but most of them were drawn into the fight not by that proclaimed motive but by the unproclaimed motive of punishing Wilson.

273

The adverse Irish movement was led by Dan Cohalan, a New York lawyer. He was a dominating personality. He was made to order for revolution and he did his work well.

When we came to Baltimore, I called by invitation on Cardinal Gibbons, an able, pious, kindly man who would have graced the high place in Rome. In his presence one was conscious of a spiritual uplift. I had met him in Dayton at the residence of Frank J. McCormick, Sr. The cardinal was visiting the McCormick and Gibbons families, cousins of his. The cardinal was not a part of the militantly anti-Wilson Catholic oligarchy, but their influence spread to most parishes of the country. One could understand their feeling. For generations, Ireland had been a downtrodden country. In view of the outrages perpetrated against them, we can realize how men, women and children grew up in hatred against the English government. Prayers for the freedom of the Emerald Isle had rung through the centuries. With the end of the war and the making of the peace at Versailles, the Irish hoped that in the new world there and then to be created, Ireland would take her place as an independent nation. Wilson was blamed for not presenting the cause of Irish freedom at the peace table. They overlooked the fact that it would have been an interference with the internal affairs of England. It probably would have thrown completely out of joint the harmony necessary in the peace conference to the creation of the League, the passion of Wilson's life.

We were mindful of the adverse currents that were running against us. President Wilson, remarking about the opposition of the racial groups, said that he knew they were after him and not Cox and reminded him of something which happened in Ireland long ago. The Governor General, presiding in Dublin, was a very likeable man. A plot was formed to have him assassinated. A warmhearted young Irishman wrote him a note saying: "We like you here and that's why I am writing you. I want you to know that in your assassination, which will not be long delayed, there is nothing personal intended against you."

The newspaper polls were not reassuring to the Democrats. They were not surprising to those who knew the sundry groups which had been gathered into the Republican fold, without regard to the merits of the League question. Mark Sullivan, on one of his visits

to our train, remarked that he was surprised to find no discouragement. The uplifting character of our meetings kept us going. Our
supporters believed in the principle for which we fought. There was
an emotional aspect to the campaign. Mothers who had lost their
sons in the war were in every assemblage. At one time it looked as
if the women's vote might come almost solidly to our cause, but a
strategy which developed late in the campaign at Republican headquarters made inroads on the women's vote. Far and wide they
spread the declaration that if we entered the League, we would have
to help maintain an international military force and that from time
to time our sons would be fighting again on European soil. European
troubles, as it was put, should be settled by Europe, which was in a
turmoil. Women have always abhorred war more deeply than men
and the campaign to scare the mothers of the country met with
some success. The colored vote was, in those days, solidly Republican. Those business interests which profited by high tariffs were
always opposed to the Democratic rule. They contributed more
lavishly than ever before. As I pointed out, the money which they
advanced was an investment to be paid back in the form of a license
to establish such prices as they wished on their products, protected
under the wall of a high tariff.

A drift our way seemed to start when the campaign reached the
East. A heartening letter came from President Wilson:

29 October, 1920

THE WHITE HOUSE
Washington

My dear Governor Cox:

As the campaign approaches its climax, I want to give myself
the pleasure of writing to say with what admiration I have followed your course throughout the campaign. You have spoken
truly and fearlessly about the great issues at stake, and I believe
that you will receive the emphatic endorsement of the voters of
the country. As one of those voters, and as one of your fellow-
citizens, I want to express my entire confidence in you and my
confident hope that under your leadership we may carry the
policy of the national government forward along the path of
liberal legislation and humane reform, until the whole world

275

again sees an illustration of the wholesome strength of democracy and the happy fruit of what the founders of the republic purposed when they set this great government.

Allow me to sign myself

Your gratified and loyal supporter,

(signed) Woodrow Wilson

Hon. James M. Cox
Columbus, Ohio

Our meeting in upper New York, either in Syracuse or Rochester, was held in the middle of the forenoon. Samuel Gompers, president of the American Federation of Labor, and Norman Mack, the Buffalo publisher and Democratic leader, were present. Many members of college faculties were there and they asked interesting and intelligent questions. Gompers and Mack were so impressed with the general character of the meeting that they called national headquarters and insisted upon a change in our itinerary. They expressed their belief that if three or four more days were added, we would certainly carry New York State. After the Baltimore meeting which was attended by several men from Republican National Headquarters and which was a tremendously moving event, Senator Smith, then running for re-election, made the same request on our Democratic headquarters that they had received from New York. The Senator stated with enthusiasm that two days more of campaigning would certainly swing Maryland.

I was not conscious at the time of being under inspection by an eminent American. Theodore Marburg, writer and author who had given much of his time and thought to great world movements, attended the Baltimore meeting with a special purpose in mind. The story of it is told in the following letter:

Baltimore   November 5, 1920

Hon. James M. Cox,
Executive Offices,
Columbus, Ohio.

Dear Governor Cox:—
I enclose you my swan song as a member of the Maryland Democratic Campaign Committee, and am giving myself the pleasure of congratulating you on your truly wonderful cam-

276

paign which I believe will go down in history as the most brilliant single-handed political fight in a just and losing cause which has ever been fought anywhere. I can't tell you how greatly the people of Baltimore and Maryland were impressed by your really magnificent speech at the Fifth Regiment Armory; and, of course, my son Andrew and I will always remember our personal meeting with you. I am going to take the liberty of quoting to you a *real* appraisal of your speech.

You will remember that Mr. Theodore Marburg, the former Minister to Belgium, left the Republican party on the League issue. He had been North all summer; and in spite of his enthusiasm for the League he had absorbed a little bit of doubt about you personally. I took the trouble to get him a seat on the platform at the Fifth Regiment Armory meeting; and in a hastily scribbled note of thanks after the meeting—which, of course, was not intended for publication and, therefore, represented his sincere personal impressions—he used the following language:

"I was deeply impressed by the great speech of Governor Cox. I never listened to a speech of such length which was so absolutely free from political buncombe. He is evidently a man of great understanding as well as a man of great ability. He is a brilliant speaker and he has—what is a great asset for a speaker —great dignity of manner. When I add to this his fine record as governor of Ohio I feel no doubt that as a man he is 'presidential timber.' "

I believe Mr. Marburg's impression was the impression of our entire community, Republican and Democratic. I am proud, indeed, to have been associated with you.

Faithfully yours,
(signed) Francis King Carey

It came as a distinct surprise to us when a group of prominent Republicans, whose sponsorship of the League war was known, issued a statement to the effect that the best guarantee of joining the League in the circumstances then existing would be the election of Harding. The document was projected by Elihu Root. He had written the League plank in the Republican platform and he knew full well that it had not satisfied the sincere friends of the supporters of the Covenant. One hundred and twenty-one Republicans and Progressives had declared against Harding. Root, fearing that the League Republicans and Independents who were supporting the League might bring a serious defection in Republican ranks, came forward with his declaration. No doubt some of the signers were perfectly sincere. They knew that much of the opposition in the Senate had come from pure political partisanship and they would be more apt to change their position if we went into the League under Republican auspices. The Democratic senators were already committed. Some presidents of prominent colleges signed the Root document. Dr. H. N. McCracken, president of Vassar, declined "for the reason that the names of those signing it will not in my opinion have influence on Senator Harding's foreign policy after election." It has been generally supposed that former President Taft signed the Root declaration but the records do not show that he did. However, he supported the Harding candidacy, doubtless feeling that as a former Republican President he could not go against his party. I have never been able to believe that Taft would have acted in bad faith with the American public. It has always been my feeling that Wilson should have appointed him one of the peace commissioners. He would have brought the prestige of a former President. There was no doubt whatsoever of his deep and sincere devotion to the League. He would have been helpful to Wilson at Versailles and probably more effective in persuading Republican senators to accept the Covenant. Taft had warned the Republicans after they carried the Senate with the aid of Truman Newberry not to build up a Committee on Foreign Relations upon the basic design of destroying the League. During the peace conference, he had communicated to Wilson several suggested changes that should be made to meet objections at home. Incidentally, three of Taft's four proposals were adopted, although it required all the force of Wilson's eloquence to secure the amendment protecting the principles of the Monroe Doctrine. The French bitterly opposed it. Taft insisted after the election that the result was not a mandate against the League. Coolidge at one time expressed the same view, stating that the League was not a super-state but a pact.

There can be little doubt that this document brought back into line many wavering Republican voters. Harding at this time was having a great many prominent Republican callers, who wanted to support their party nominee, but in so doing did not want to destroy the League. Harding, however, was giving assurances to both

278

sides. On one occasion he said to Professor Irving Fisher of Yale University that he was for a league but that the Wilson instrument would have to be changed. Permission was given to Mr. Fisher "even in this campaign to tell your friends." It was more or less a common saying among the doubting Republican leaders that the pro-League half of Harding was really the better half. These waverings reminded someone at the time of that pauper in *The Hoosier Schoolmaster* whose head, as he himself proclaimed, was half " 'tater" and who warned his hearers that while he might be talking sense at the moment, he could never tell when the 'tater side would take command.

Taft's real state of mind with respect to the events and personalities figuring in this struggle is revealed in a confidential letter written from Salt Lake City on Washington's Birthday, 1919, to Gus J. Karger, long a devoted friend of the former President and Washington correspondent of the Cincinnati *Times-Star:*

> As I write I look out upon the desert of Nevada, and it suggests the waste that war makes, and when I think of the vicious narrowness of Reed, the explosive ignorance of Poindexter, the ponderous Websterian language and lack of stamina of Borah, the vanity of Lodge as an old diplomatic hand on the Foreign Relations Committee, the selfishness, laziness and narrow lawyerlike acuteness of Knox, the emptiness and sly partisanship of Hale, with the utter nothingness of Fall, in the face of this great world's crisis, I confess I don't see where we have any advantage over the women—at least in this juncture.

Two tremendous and impressive meetings held in Chicago and New York revived the spirits of the Democrats. The New York meeting, in Madison Square Garden, was one not to be forgotten. There were present men and women who knew the subject of the League thoroughly and were there to evidence their high favor for the Wilson plan for peace. On the stage and in the audience were great numbers of distinguished people. Dr. Henry Van Dyke pronounced the demonstration the most moving that he had witnessed in his time.

It was remarked that in Chicago no such quality of enthusiasm had ever been witnessed. After the meeting was over, James W.

Faulkner, who traveled with us throughout the campaign, walked to the hotel with Gus J. Karger of Charles P. Taft's *Times-Star* in Cincinnati. Faulkner and Karger had served together as reporters in their young days and were close friends. The meeting apparently had been a great surprise to Mr. Karger and he inquired of Faulkner whether it was an index to those that had been held elsewhere. Faulkner remarked that in every section at any hour of the day and long into the night the crowds had been surprisingly large and emotionally excited over the League. Karger then confided to Faulkner that he thought Harding was beaten. The turn, as he put it, had come two weeks before. The Chicago meeting was on the Saturday night preceding the election. Our train came into Dayton early Sunday morning. Emmanuel Church is not far from the station. Its bells were tolling. Faulkner came out of his berth and, for the first time in our long acquaintance, his eyes were filled with tears. He said, "Those bells tell me that at this very moment my mother at early mass in Cincinnati is praying confidently for your election, and you haven't a chance. It's a damn shame."

The election brought an overwhelming Democratic defeat. I immediately wired Senator Harding as follows:

Warren G. Harding
Marion, Ohio

In the spirit of America, I accept the decision of the majority, tender as the defeated candidate my congratulations, and pledge as a citizen my support to the executive authority in whatever emergency might arise.

James M. Cox

Harding's reply was:

As the successful candidate, I thank you for your message of congratulation and support.

On returning to the governor's office in Columbus, I issued the following statement:

For the first time in ten years the Republican party is in complete control of the legislative and executive branches of the national government, therefore policy as to statute and administration is with it. Its task is no longer that of the critic, but the constructor. It is my hope and firm belief that the Democracy of the nation will not attempt political sabotage. The country has seen quite enough of that. We are in the midst of emergency and the nation's every resource should coordinate in behalf of the things that are helpful. So long as government exists, hopes will gather. Talk of a new party is absurd. One might as well discuss the destruction of human emotions. As essential as it has been to the welfare of the country in the past, the creed of Democracy is more needed now than ever, because recent events have made it distinctly the American party. In spirit I am as proud as when the fight started. I would not retrace a step nor yield a single jot in principle. It was a privilege to make the contest for the right in the face of overwhelming odds. There is a distinct difference between defeat and surrender. The flag of Democracy still flies as the symbol of the things more enduring than the passions and resentments that come with the aftermath of war.

A prized message came from the White House. It was:

THE WHITE HOUSE
Washington

5 November, 1920
My dear Governor Cox:
   I hope that you know that no Democrat attributes the defeat of Tuesday to anything that you did or omitted to do. We have all admired the fight that you made with the greatest sincerity, and believe that the whole country honors you for the frank and courageous way in which you conducted the campaign.
   With the most cordial good wishes and, of course, with unabated confidence,
                              Cordially and sincerely yours,
                                   (signed) Woodrow Wilson

Hon. James M. Cox,
Executive Office,
Columbus, Ohio.

Henry Van Dyke, the esteemed author and litterateur, was very gracious with his observations, which were:

281

H. V. D.
Avalon,
Princeton, N. J.

Nov. 10, 1920

My dear Governor Cox:

Will you accept a letter from a comparative stranger who feels that he knows you well?

Your record as Governor commanded my confidence. Your conduct of the Presidential campaign drew my esteem. The two speeches that I heard you make, at Princeton and New York, on the League of Nations, called out my instant and warm admiration. You argued the good cause as a master, and won every open mind. I am sure you feel no personal disappointment and no real discouragement. This battle was lost, not the war. Victory is coming. The ark of the Covenant survives the Deluge and America will climb aboard. Then you will be glad that you helped mightily towards the triumph, and you will go on for many years doing great work for our country.

Sincerely yours,
(signed) Henry Van Dyke

To Governor
James M. Cox.

Another eminent writer, John S. Bassett, wrote:

The Century Association
7 West Forty-Third Street
New York City

Oct. 31, 1920

Dear Gov. Cox:

I am closing up my office tonight and leaving New York for my home in Northampton, Mass. But before I leave I wish to tell you how much I feel it an honor to have been one of those helping you in your fight for the League of Nations and good government in general. You have made a brilliant campaign and I devoutly trust that victory will crown it. The signs of a great popular awakening seem to foretell it. But whatever the result of the election, you have won a great moral victory. Those of us who write history will have to say that you have done what few have done before you—You have made your own campaign and led the way—and made us all hope for victory, where victory at first seemed impossible.

Please accept my best wishes for your success and happiness. Yours sincerely,
(signed) John S. Bassett

An interesting review of the result was contained in the following editorial in the New York *Times* of November 4, 1920:

GOVERNOR COX

Governor Cox is as good-natured and philosophical after his defeat as he was ardent, energetic and resourceful in his campaign. Never was a political forlorn hope led more gallantly. His intellectual keenness and readiness, his clearness and vigor of exposition and argument, above all, the passion and the strength of his appeal for the League of Nations, were cumulative. Instead of diminution or exhaustion, he showed new power, which increased steadily till the end of his canvass. Quickness, wit, continuous and sharp attack, the gift of pleasing and stirring multitudes—he has the gifts, unsuspected by the public before his nomination, unknown probably even to himself, of an effective popular orator.

An irresistible combination of reasons, unreasons and opponents bore him down. If he had been Jefferson plus Jackson he would have fared no better. Metaphysically speaking, it was not he who was defeated; it was a composite figure of many illusions, legends, errors, dissatisfactions, grudges; a Mumbo Jumbo who represented to some high prices and taxes, to others a certain fondness for slow delivery in Mr. Burleson's department, and so on ad infinitum. There is nothing personal to Governor Cox in the result. He did all that could be done and more than most men could have done. He has won the thanks of the Democratic Party and the liking and respect of the country.

CHAPTER XXV

DAWN AFTER DEFEAT

—◆—

THE ELECTION over, telegrams and letters came in large numbers. All of them reflected disappointment and sorrow, many of them bitterness. High hopes had risen in the hearts of many that civilization was now to protect itself against another world war. The common feeling was that the decision did not come from consideration of the merits of the League. The man in the street was aware that partisan politics and racial prejudices had turned the election. Many could not believe that an adverse decision had been rendered. Mrs. Emmons Blaine of Chicago, daughter-in-law of James G. Blaine, wired me to order a recount. She said that such a thing as turning down the League by the American people in the exercise of their suffrage right could not be possible.

As for me, my only unhappiness was in the conviction that Harding and those above him meant to wreck the League. Now, twenty-six years after the election, I can say without reservation that the sting of defeat did not touch me. I had the feeling that I had been honored much beyond my deserts by our party. To have been given the banner of world peace from the hands of the stricken Wilson and to have carried it unsullied was happiness enough for any man. In defeat I would not have changed places with Harding. There was inescapable trouble ahead for him. Contradictory committals had been made and no matter what he did he would be accused of bad faith. I had not evaded the great issue nor had I dipped the colors of our cause to gain a salute from disloyal elements. In the circumstances, defeat had no sting for me.

I think it will be pretty generally conceded that never from 1920 until this day have I given evidence of personal disappointment or bitterness. A wrong reaction then could have ruined my life. And the only occasion I can recall in which the subject was raised, I was introduced to a nonpartisan meeting by a noted wit who referred facetiously to the 1920 campaign. My response was that I could easily understand how a humorist had been moved to such a joke. But I thought that the country now knew that as things had turned out the joke was not on me but on the country. So far as I recall, that is the only reference I ever made in public to what to some men would have been a disaster. A great many men have retired from public life defeated and brokenhearted. Others, out of sheer homesickness for the activities they were compelled to forego, have shortened their days by disappointed broodings. I had this great advantage: I was still in public life, even though it was my resolve never again to seek or to accept a public office. I had my newspapers. The procession of events interested me deeply, and our own publications gave me the outlet for my convictions. And so I turned back content to my private affairs, confident that civilization would in time be compelled, if not by conviction, then by sheer necessity for self-preservation, to join together the nations of the world as a protective instrument.

William Jennings Bryan once said to me that his defeat in 1896 brought great sense of relief. He had been sensitive to the heavy responsibility that would fall upon him if he were elected. He was frank enough to say that he was without administrative experience and had often viewed the executive task with no pleasurable anticipations. I had no such feeling as this; but that can be explained by my appreciation of the many men of outstanding ability whose help would have been available in carrying out our plans. There were Al Smith, John W. Davis, Newton D. Baker and Bernard W. Baruch, of New York; Carter Glass, of Virginia; Claude Kitchin and Josephus Daniels, of North Carolina; Joseph T. Robinson, senator from Arkansas; Swagar Sherley, of Kentucky, prominent member of Congress; David F. Houston (Newton Baker once told me that Houston was the ablest man in the Wilson cabinet); Gilbert M. Hitchcock, of Nebraska, once chairman of the Senate Foreign Relations Committee; Oscar Underwood, senator from Alabama and formerly chairman of the Ways and Means Committee of the House; Senator Thomas J. Walsh, of Montana; Franklin K. Lane, member of Wilson's cabinet; Senator Robert L. Owen, of Oklahoma, and Frederick W. Lehman, of Missouri. Mr. Lehman was an independent in politics but a man of marked ability. This array of men of great ability was

285

very reassuring. In ordinary circumstances, most of them would doubtless have been unwilling to serve in the cabinet, but if the great project of going into the League was by common mandate entrusted to us, I had no question that any one of these gentlemen would accept the call of duty.

We all were fearful that the verdict at the polls might bring an early end to Woodrow Wilson's life. He was confident of victory up to the counting of the votes. A day or two before the election, he had so expressed himself. Postmaster General Burleson, who foresaw the result, expressed his opinion to Mr. Wilson and was frowned upon for such a defeatist spirit, and an argument ensued. But, great man that he was, Wilson accepted the decision calmly. He felt that the nation had disgraced itself in the eyes of the world, but was mindful that it was not easy to lead a nation so variously constituted as ours to accept quickly a new forward step such as the League of Nations was. The people would have "to learn" now by bitter experience, he said, just what they had lost. Someone suggested that all he needed to do to put Harding and the Republican party in a hole was to return the treaty to the vice-president's desk. Wilson resented this. It was too serious a matter to be a plaything of politics. He wanted to help the President-elect and hoped that all citizens would be moved by a like impulse. He was heartened by the functioning of the League at Geneva even in the face of the discouragement from our refusal to join. He never wavered in his confidence that the nation would in time see the necessity of joining in a world cooperation for peace.

Woodrow Wilson's farewell utterance came on November 10, 1923, the eve of Armistice Day. He was sadly broken in health. The stroke he had suffered had paralyzed his left side and for a time interfered with his speech. His words, which were brief and prophetic, have still a burning significance:

> The anniversary of Armistice Day should stir us to great exaltation of spirit . . . although the stimulating memories of that happy time of triumph are forever marred and embittered for us by the shameful fact that when the victory was won—won, be it remembered, chiefly by the indomitable spirit and ungrudging sacrifices of our own incomparable soldiers—we turned our backs upon our associates and refused to bear any responsible part in the administration of peace or the firm and perma-

nent establishment of the results of the war—won at so terrible a cost of life and treasure—and withdrew into a sullen and selfish isolation which is deeply ignoble because manifestly cowardly and dishonorable.

This must always be a source of deep mortification to us and we shall inevitably be forced by the moral obligations of freedom and honor to retrieve that fatal error and assume once more the role of courage and self-respect and helpfulness which every true American must wish to regard as our natural part in the affairs of the world.

That we should have thus done a great wrong to civilization at one of the most critical turning points in the history of the world is the more to be deplored because every anxious year that has followed has made the exceeding need for such services as we might have rendered more and more evident and more and more pressing, as demoralizing circumstances which we might have controlled have gone from bad to worse.

Each day encroached upon his strength, yet he held on to life because he continued to think of the day when a great wrong would be righted.

By invitation I called on Mr. Wilson in the White House once after the election. As I walked forward to greet him, he said, "Stand up, I want to look at you. I don't see how you ever went through the campaign. I marvel at your strength that lasted until the battle was over." It was a pleasant and yet a sad and tragic visit. At times his mind flared up with the clarity and brilliance of old. We discussed the conspiracy. When Lodge's name was mentioned, he said, "I don't like to say it, but I have always had an intellectual contempt for the man." He still had faith in the ultimate wisdom of our people.

I never saw Woodrow Wilson after this visit in the White House, but in my memory his words, spoken then to me, still burn:

When the final referendum has come, although in the meantime the cost in human life may be too great even to think about, civilization will do what it has to do to save itself. I do not know how long it will be delayed but it is as certain to come as the rising of the sun.

The whole world knows how completely time has vindicated Wilson's prophecy.

287

PART SIX

A Tour of Europe

Suggestions to President Harding About
Reparations Settlement

Is Not America Responsible for Hitler?

Visits with Lloyd George, Poincaré and Dr· Wirth

Entering the Newspaper Field in Florida

Campaigns of 1924 and 1928

Newton D. Baker, John W. Davis, Alfred E. Smith

CHAPTER XXVI

STUDIES OF EUROPE

◆

In 1922 I decided to have a firsthand view of conditions in Europe. In this country things seemed to be going fairly well. The administration at Washington apparently felt secure in our financial position. We were the largest creditor in the world. All nations owed us. We had their certificates of indebtedness and promises to pay. All this, no doubt, convinced the powers in Washington that by slipping back into normalcy and re-establishing high protective tariffs, prosperity would endure. I was thoroughly convinced before going to Europe that the danger in the whole international economic situation was not sensed by the administration. If Germany could not pay to France and England the reparations imposed after the war, it was hardly likely that those two countries could pay us. The burden which had been placed upon Germany was the inevitable fruit of the bitterness of war. The Republic of Germany under Dr. Wirth was making an effort to work its way out from under the load. If it failed, the Republic would fall and that would be disastrous to all hopes of European stability. On leaving America, I felt that the impasse must be broken. Something must be done to revise reparations which had been imposed largely by war bitterness.

I made the trip with Judge T. T. Ansberry, James M. Cox, Jr., my son, and a young friend of his, Ernest H. Rice. By the courtesy of the French government, we had very comfortable quarters on the old steamship *Ile de France* and found like accommodations on our return on the *Ile de Paris*. We landed at Havre and there took a motorcar in which we traveled exclusively while on the Continent.

Our itinerary was Paris to Vichy, south across the mountains to Avignon, then to the sea, then eastward to Genoa, Milan, Rome, Venice, back to Milan and across the Simplon Pass into Switzerland. I spent two or three days at the headquarters of the League in

Geneva. A luncheon given for me there was attended by representatives of thirty governments. We then went by way of Lausanne and Luzern to Oberammergau. Entering Austria at its western frontier, we went to Vienna, then to Prague, Dresden and Berlin. Thence we passed through Holland and Belgium and across the Channel to England.

An officer of the French army was assigned to us and he guided us to the points of war interest in France. At Rheims we lunched with the dear old Cardinal Lucon who had said prayers in the cathedral even while the roof was being struck by shells and shrapnel. Three stories underground we dined with the commander at Verdun. He had lost an eye and a leg in defense of that fortress. There were abundant signs of devastation everywhere.

Soon after arriving in Paris a dinner was given for me by Raymond Poincaré, Premier of France. It was a beautiful affair. In the course of the evening, Poincaré and I slipped away from the guests and discussed the situation which had come as an aftermath of the war. He seemed interested in the purpose of my visit to Europe. I told him I was convinced that the whole world economy was concerned in some sort of settlement of the reparations question. I was convinced that Germany could not pay what she had been asked to, that the republic in that country might fall and that then there would come a general repudiation of all obligations imposed by the Treaty of Versailles. It was not how much Germany ought to pay for damages inflicted, as I expressed it to the French Premier, but how much she could pay. It was apparent that Poincaré wanted to make an open response but in the face of a public opinion still enraged against Germany, he could not do it. He finally said, "I cannot say." The next morning I was called to the telephone by the wife of Jean Herbert, who was regarded as closer to Poincaré than anyone else in France. She extended an invitation to dine at their home that very evening. The Premier had great confidence in Herbert and listened to his advice. Herbert was a man of intellectual attainments, possessed of enough wealth to live well. As an intellectual diversion he wrote the leading editorial in each issue of Le Temps. In after years, he served as ambassador to Russia. He was an accomplished and attractive man. As I came into the Herbert house, he said to me quite aside: "When the other guests go, I wish you would remain. There is a matter I would like to discuss with you." About a dozen people attended the dinner. It was altogether an interesting evening. I remained with Mr. Herbert, and as soon as we entered his study he told me that Poincaré had told him the question I had put to him. The Premier could not answer and Herbert would have to do so, but in the utmost confidence. Substantially these were his words:

Your analysis of the situation is clear and sound. Germany can't pay what has been imposed upon her, and if the terms stand the German Republic may fall. The common sense of the situation is to ascertain what she can pay. The Premier and I both know this but we feel that we are helpless in the situation. If we should suggest a revision in the terms, our government would fall in ten days. You see desolation everywhere in the provinces and our public is still bitter. If Germany should propose a compromise and it should be substantially the figures which I have quoted to you, we could not accept because the French people would not favor it. If the proposal came from England, the French would oppose it. Some way must be found to break this deadlock and I am delighted that you are giving it your attention.

Just at this time, Lloyd George was having a dispute with France and had asserted the English position so incisively that considerable feeling in France had resulted. I talked to Ambassador Meyer, representing in Paris the German government. He and I went over the same ground covered by Herbert and myself, although I could not tell him in detail what the French journalist had said to me. The Ambassador said that conditions were becoming serious in Germany and that Chancellor Wirth was very much worried about them. He expressed in figures what he thought Germany could pay.

We had luncheon a number of times at the home of Maurice Bunau-Varilla in Paris. Poincaré and his advisers often assembled there for the noontime meal. Old Bunau-Varilla had the finest wine chest in France. He was owner of the newspaper Le Matin and of a group of banks and smaller newspapers scattered through France. He had probably the largest collection of Napoleonic souvenirs in the country. A dressing table used by Josephine had a large oval mirror on it completely surrounded by rich jewels. There was a miniature of one of Napoleon's eyes made into a small clasp, back of which was a lock of the emperor's hair. Josephine is said always to have worn this over her heart. Napoleon's bed was in his collection.

293

The dining room must have been eighty feet long and more than half as wide. There wasn't a square inch of wall space that was not covered by beautiful tapestries. At the far end of this room there was a rock garden with a stream of water constantly running through it. The old Frenchman was a great entertainer and he, I felt, was very curious about what I was doing in France. He convinced me that the solid opinion of that country would endorse any plan that would break up the financial deadlock but he insisted that neither France, Germany nor England could take the initiative.

In Germany, I had dinner with Dr. Karl Helfferich who was the German Kaiser's last Minister of Finance. We talked together until long after midnight. He was a very attractive man. When he referred to the policy of unrestricted submarine warfare, the thing that brought us into the war, he closed his eyes and shuddered. He said he had always opposed it. Helfferich, who was the son-in-law of the head of the old Staats Bank, told me that the Kaiser was never entitled to credit for building the railroad to Bagdad. The bank had done it. Helfferich was with the Kaiser at the front the night before the day when the Germans expected to enter Paris. The Kaiser was in high fettle and said that this advance would end the war, that he would go into history as the great peace emperor. He intended to have a bridge of gold built at some appropriate place on the boundary line between France and Germany—a literal bridge of gold that would stand, as the Kaiser expressed it, as a symbol of the peace that he had brought to Europe. I inquired whether the Kaiser had any notions about newly created frontiers between the two countries. Smilingly, he replied, "Probably some refinements." Helfferich was enthusiastic over the suggestion that something be undertaken to help Germany meet her obligations. I asked him bluntly what she could pay. He told me. The following summer Helfferich's train, passing through a Swiss tunnel, was wrecked and the car in which he was a passenger was burned. I thought he was a very able man.

The next day I called on Chancellor Wirth and told him what was in my mind as a solution of existing troubles. I revealed my plan to be presented to President Harding. Briefly it was this: Since neither England, France nor Germany could make the first move there was only one country whose voice would be effective. President Harding would be urged to send Mr. Hoover, then Secretary of Commerce, to Europe and summon the interested powers, explaining to them the potential danger which lurked not only over the continent of Europe but potentially over our country and the whole world.

Hoover was suggested because he was a member of the government and knew the official personnel of Europe, and for the part he had played in the distribution of food in Europe. He had been free from political controversies. The United States could say that it entered the war unselfishly and came out of it unselfishly. It had asked for no territory but had given abundantly of its wealth. As the largest creditor nation it could insist that something be done since the matter vitally concerned our whole world economy. Wirth, a serious and apparently sincere man, burst into tears and begged me to cable the proposal from Berlin. I explained that this would be a very serious psychological mistake and in our country and elsewhere the feeling would be that it had been inspired by my environment in Germany. Besides, it was desirable to consult with Lloyd George before anything was done. Wirth told me what he thought his country could pay. Wirth, the liberal, and Helfferich, the conservative, were substantially of the same mind.

I then went on to England and had a three-hour visit at breakfast time with Lloyd George. A photograph which he sent me bears this inscription: "In happy remembrance of a memorable conversation, Aug. 27, 1922.—D. Lloyd George."

It was plain to see why Lloyd George had played so dynamic a part in the First World War. He was a man who could see the course of logic and had the administrative force to follow through systematically and effectively. In the course of my visit with him, he took me into the cabinet room which, as he put it, was where war was declared against the American colonies. Pointing to a picture of Lord North on the wall, he said, "That's the damned old fool that made the trouble." It was around the same conference table that war was declared against Germany in World War I. In discussing bygone days, reference to Washington brought this observation from him: "Washington shouldn't have done it. He was one of us. He should have known better. I like Lincoln better than Washington."

I gave him every detail of my interviews in France and Germany. He was interested in the estimates that had been given to me and said they were not far off. Here now was an amazing fact. There was so little difference in the opinions expressed in the three interested European countries that it seemed to me the whole thing could be adjusted in brief time. It was a simple task. There was no question but that the governments of the three countries mentioned would have looked not only with favor but with enthusiasm upon the enterprise. I consulted with Reginald McKenna, head of the Great Midland Bank which had approximately two thousand branches in the British Isles. He said something had to be done and this seemed to him to be the best way to do it. Later, I met Wickham Steed, the leading editor of England, and Colonel E. M. House, who chanced to be in London. Steed said that Harding would have to accept the plan. He didn't see how he could avoid it. House felt the same way. In the afternoon, House called on Lloyd George at 10 Downing Street. I saw House that evening and he reported that Lloyd George had spoken of our visit together and then had said with a good deal of warmth, "Colonel, your politics must be meaner than ours. I don't see many Democrats over here. Most of my callers are Republicans. I guess they are more able to travel. A great many of them have talked to me about Cox. Everything they said as to what sort of man he is, he is not, and everything they said as to what sort of man he is not, he is. Too bad that politics anywhere has to become so bitter as to be unfair."

From London, I cabled my proposal to President Harding and supported it by an interview with the New York *Times* London correspondent, which was published in its issue of August 26, 1922, as follows:

Copyright, 1922, by The New York Times Company
Special Cable to THE NEW YORK TIMES.

LONDON, Aug. 26.—Ex-Governor Cox of Ohio gave THE NEW YORK TIMES the following summary of his conclusions on the economic situation in Europe and the attitude he thinks the United States should pursue toward it:

"The storm centre of the economic world is Central Europe. Those who have visited Austria and Germany are of one opinion as to the state of things now and the tragic point to which both countries are drifting. Austria has reached the stage of almost complete dissolution. The approach of Germany to the same condition is steadily marked by every passing hour.

"The nations of Europe are deadlocked on the reparations question. There seems to be no relief on this side of the Atlantic. No decision by England seems likely to be accepted by France. The French Government will not sanction a proposal from Germany which might approximate a readjustment of the figures now in the minds of French statesmen because that circumstance might be regarded by public opinion in France as a surrender to Germany. There the matter rests, and every hour is fraught with danger.

"It is well to summarize the contentions of both France and Germany. Since the end of the war France has sold approximately ten billion dollars' worth of bonds to her own people upon the representation that she would be reimbursed by Germany in compliance with the terms of the peace treaty. Germany says that she has lost one-fourth of her grain lands, four-fifths of her ore and altogether one-tenth of her territory. She issued about twenty-five billion dollars' worth of bonds during the war, and a deficit of ten billions remains as a floating debt. It will be seen at a glance that the fiscal state of both countries, without economic stabilization, portends but one result. . . .

"Germany has 20,000,000 more people than she can sustain except under high industrial stress. When the mark was 100 to 200 to the dollar there was a certain trade advantage accruing to Germany, but in the present circumstances the banks of Germany cannot finance the industries of that country in the purchase of raw products and foodstuffs. Unless relief is granted the shops will soon be closing, millions will be out of employment and the winter will bring the threat, if not the certainty, of starvation.

"With the economic collapse, the Government will go down, too. If Germany fails, France is without reimbursement, and she cannot sustain the loss involved without serious consequences. Within the last week I had a long interview with Chancellor Wirth in Berlin. He summarized the situation by saying with the deepest emotion: 'Unless the United States interests herself in European affairs within a very short time all in Germany is lost, and all in Central Europe as well.'

"Recognizing that this statement broke the fetters of diplomatic usage, I asked authority to repeat it in Dr. Wirth's name to the people of the United States. It was given without reservation. It is not too late to prevent disaster. Our Government, taking the initiative on behalf of our country, can do it without any inconsistency with its

JOURNEY THROUGH MY YEARS

existing policy. It is represented on the Reparations Commission. It should designate Herbert Hoover, now a member of the Cabinet, to serve in the reparations task. He holds the confidence of Europe. Peoples and Governments trust him. He can analyze the economic situation of Germany. His decision as to what Germany can pay beyond much question of doubt would be accepted by France—and that means by all the parties interested. I believe every Chancellery in Europe would welcome his coming. The mere announcement of his selection would stabilize things.

"With reparations adjusted, Germany and France—both in need of large loans—would be given credit, and Austria, too. Then would come the dawn of a new day. Mr. Hoover is not of my political party, but anyone in as close touch with Continental conditions as I have been is thoroughly stripped of every partisan thought.

"The question of the inter-allied debt need not be considered—it is not necessary. Europe recognizes that its discussion in America is ill-timed now.

"Three considerations will cover every shade of American public opinion; first, if from a moral awakening we desire to relieve distress, the opportunity is presented; second, if our desires are purely practical, and a market for our products is to be gained, the necessary rehabilitation is a guarantee; third, if our policy is to insist upon the ultimate payment of inter-allied debts, we must remember who the world's debtors are and realize that if some of them are permitted to go to ruin now there is not even a remote chance of collection later.

"The fate of the world is in the hands of America. Days wasted in procrastination now will bring years of self-reproach later. From Europe, the base of our early ancestry, prayers go up that America will understand and, understanding, will not falter."

Ex-Governor Cox breakfasted today at 10 Downing Street with Premier Lloyd George and had a long chat with him. Colonel Collins, a member of the Government of the Union of South Africa, was also a guest. Mr. Cox, when he returned to the Carlton Hotel, was reticent as to the subjects of his conversation with the Premier. It is understood, however, that Mr. Cox gave Mr. Lloyd George a full account of his observations of general and economic conditions during his trip through Europe. Speaking to THE NEW YORK TIMES correspondent, Mr. Cox said:

298

"It would be obviously improper to tell you what were the subjects I discussed with Mr. Lloyd George, but I was very much interested to meet him. He is, you will remember, the only war Prime Minister still in office. I was particularly struck by his color of health. I should think he is the sort of man who when he goes to bed gets to sleep at once. He has a bold and agile mind, but he does not worry. That is how he has done such great things."

One characteristic of the Premier reminded Mr. Cox of Abraham Lincoln: he seemed to find without effort a homely story to fit every point which came up. "He is a very great man," Mr. Cox declared. "I should say he is a great man not only of this time but of all generations." ...

Then he began to describe the incidents of his visit to Downing Street.

"If I felt any self-imposed restraint—and I don't say I didn't—in breakfasting with the British Prime Minister, when he swung round in his chair and lit his pipe I felt quite at ease," said Mr. Cox. Mr. Lloyd George took him for a little while into the historic room where every British Cabinet has deliberated since the eighteenth century. He showed him with a great deal of pride the presentation made to him by some American women's organizations. It is one of his cherished possessions and consists of silken flags of all the allied countries grouped together within an embroidered border. A similar gift was made to Marshal Foch.

Mr. Cox has been invited by Lord Grey of Fallodon to visit him at his country house in Northumberland. He is especially anxious to see him, he explains, because of his work for the League of Nations. The Government of the Irish Free State has renewed to him its invitation to cross over to Dublin, which fell through on account of the deaths of Griffiths and Collins. Mr. Cox is afraid, however, that he will not find time to take the trip before he sails for home next Saturday.

My proposal, however, did not commend itself to the Harding administration. A Washington dispatch in the same issue of the *Times* quoted the President as saying that "in an informal and consistent way the American Government is keeping in touch with European affairs and is awaiting the time when it can take a more formal part in the restoration of financial stability abroad. The time

299

is not ripe for the United States to participate in any international conference looking toward a solution of financial problems."

So the reparations deadlock was allowed to drift into the French occupation of the Ruhr, in 1923, which in turn led to the complete extinction of Germany's currency and the deep embitterment of Franco-German relations.

At the London Conference in 1933, Hjalmar Schacht, the eminent financial authority of Germany who attended as a delegate from that country, made the observation to me that if Harding had acted upon my suggestion eight years before, there would have been no need for a conference. Vice-President Charles G. Dawes once said to me that Harding made a tragic blunder in not making the settlement which could so easily have been effected then. It has always been my opinion that if reparations had been leveled off to the logic of conditions at that time, the Republic of Germany would have lived, and if it had lived there would have been no Hitler.

Hitler, it is important to remember, came upon the scene only when the republic was about to collapse because of the world economic depression which our false economic policy generated. Hitler made the bold declaration that no debts would be paid, for, as he claimed, Germany had not been responsible for the war. This broke the dam. The German people followed, feeling that they had nothing to lose. What Hitler might take them into could not be worse than what they had been passing through. Debts forgotten, and with many public improvements made with loans secured from American banks, Hitler started upon his insane career. It is safe to say that if there had been no Hitler, there would have been no war. Another opportunity had been given to the Republican administration to avert the ghastly conflict which finally came. The opportunity was rejected.

In his book, *The Time for Decision*, Sumner Welles has a page which strongly supports my belief that the Harding administration should have done something about reparations.

He says that no republic in Germany "attempting to govern a people unaccustomed to and uninclined toward democratic institutions, could carry on successfully in the face of the insuperable obstacle which the Allied handling of the reparations question represented."

He continues that the men who were directing our policies were

300

fully aware of the danger, but that "popular fear of becoming involved in the 'disputes of Europe,' added to the belief that official
participation by this country would also result in the refusal of the
European debtor nations to repay their war debts, created an issue
of such magnitude that the Harding administration" officially held
aloof from the controversy.

Then Welles continues immediately: "It was not difficult to forecast the outcome. Not only did the treatment of Germany in the
matter of reparations make it far easier for German militarism to
consolidate its grip upon the German people, but it was also one of
the reasons why the war debts owing to the United States by the
Allies later fell into default. If in 1921 the United States government
had been willing to take an official part in deciding the reparations
question, particularly since we had renounced all reparations for
ourselves, the course of events in Europe would have been greatly
modified."

Time has revealed that another opportunity was yet to come and
again was missed. Harding was increasingly distressed by accusations
of bad faith made by Republicans who had accepted the plea of
thirty-one prominent men in that party to support Harding as the
surest way to get into the League. This feeling apparently resulted
in a temporary decision on Harding's part to move strongly towards
the League of Nations. In Harry M. Daugherty's book, *The Inside
Story of the Harding Tragedy*, there is an account of a struggle
with him before one of his messages to Congress was delivered.

Daugherty relates that when he was called to the White House he
found a distinct tension between the President and Mrs. Harding
over a passage in the proposed message. Daugherty agreed with Mrs.
Harding that the paragraph would "lead us straight into the League
of Nations, destroy the policy of our party and ignore the pledge
of the last elections." Secretary of War Weeks also agreed that this
would be true but several hours of argument did not convince
Harding.

The next day Daugherty and Weeks sat together in the House
chamber gripping each other's hands as the dreaded passage approached, but instead Harding read a substitute paragraph which
Daugherty had left with him. Once again politics had triumphed over
principle.

CHAPTER XXVII

THE OHIO GANG

◆

MANY TIMES in different parts of the country I have been asked about the "Ohio Gang." What was it? Who was in it? The scandals which gave rise to the term became nationally notorious, and since it operated within my eye and in opposition to my own program of reform in Ohio, it can hardly be left out of this narrative.

The central figure in it was Harry M. Daugherty, and the climax came when he was appointed by President Harding to a place in his cabinet. It is no exaggeration to say that the Ohio Gang was a political underworld which came into being under cover of the long period of Republican party ascendancy following the Civil War. The elements of corruption in politics tend to gravitate into the party with power to serve them, and the Ohio Gang was a manifestation of this fact.

Daugherty was a product of Fayette County, where he was early caught in a cheap trick to best the local gamblers. He and his brother, Mal Daugherty, had set up, a few miles from Washington Court House, an equipment under a culvert to tap telegraph wires and get sporting news in advance to be used in sure-thing bets. This was exposed by Harry M. Weldon, later with the Cincinnati *Enquirer*, and long regarded as the ablest sports editor in the country. From his earliest days, Daugherty did not respect the ethics of public life. One might in charity overlook early indiscretions if his pattern of conduct had changed in mature years.

Not long after he was admitted to the bar, young Daugherty was charged with unethical conduct in his law practice. The grievance committee of the bar which considered the case found the charges true. The case was about to be filed with the Clerk of the Court when Judge Maynard directed the clerk not to permit the procedure to go on. The judge later admitted that he had exceeded his powers but explained that he sought to protect the reputation of a young lawyer. Later, when Daugherty controlled the Ohio legislative machinery, John P. Maynard, this judge's son, held the position of Clerk of the House of Representatives. Daugherty was operating as a legislative lobbyist, and it was notorious that as bills were introduced into the legislature, Maynard would report them to Daugherty and Daugherty would indicate the committee to which they were to be referred. If the bills were in any way inimical to Daugherty's clients, they were to be buried.

The times in which Daugherty operated were peculiarly favorable to his kind of activity. A distinguished group of leaders furnished prestige for the party under cover of which he worked. There was John Sherman, distinguished as member of Congress, senator, Secretary of the Treasury under Hayes and finally Secretary of State under McKinley. Sherman was first elected to Congress in 1854, yet he lived to be associated with Presidents Hayes and Garfield and at last McKinley, and this brought him to the days of Daugherty. Sherman resigned from the Senate to become Secretary of State in McKinley's cabinet under the presumption this was done in order to pave the way for the appointment of Mark Hanna to the Senate in his stead.

Joseph B. Foraker, elected as governor in 1887, was an audacious character and never popular with Sherman, Hanna or McKinley. There were no tears when he was defeated in 1889 by James E. Campbell for the governorship. The Republican feud, involving Sherman, McKinley, Foraker, Hanna, Governor Herrick, Governor Bushnell and Boss Cox, of Cincinnati, raged for years. Daugherty found ways to use this conflict for his own peculiar ends. With friends in the legislature, he had influence which naturally was sought by the contending forces. When a contest approached Daugherty was always noncommittal but he never remained so. In the end he was actively aligned with one cause or the other. Sometimes he was suspected of attempting to make terms with both sides. After his defeat for the governorship, Foraker became a candidate against Sherman in the senatorial election of 1893. Senators were then elected by the legislature. Daugherty, a member from Fayette County, declared for Foraker, by whose organization his own election campaign was financed. The Fayette County Republican Convention, however, endorsed Sherman. Daugherty appeared on the stage and pledged himself to support this action. That same evening, he met Charles J. Kurtz, Foraker's manager, in Columbus, and assured him of his allegiance to Foraker. As Kurtz afterwards remarked, for some strange reason he did not see much of Daugherty after this. The federal patronage was thrown against Foraker and he was beaten.

At this time an article in the Columbus *Press-Post* told that William M. Hahn, Sherman's manager, had procured from the Deshler Bank several crisp five-hundred-dollar bills, one of which later appeared in the possession of Harry M. Daugherty. A young teller in the bank, with a penchant for sleuthing, had deftly inked the letter "W" on the bills. Other members of the legislature were linked with Daugherty in the newspaper article and this led to an investigation by the House of Representatives. The author of the newspaper story appeared before the committee and did not retract a single word. The committee reported, nevertheless, that it was unable to fasten guilt upon any member of the Assembly. D. K. Watson, Attorney General at the time and afterwards a member of Congress, later referred to the action of the committee as a pure "party whitewash."

Following his retirement from the legislature, Daugherty openly engaged in lobbying activities. William Gear, an old-time member, used to say publicly that Daugherty was "paymaster for the boys." After the General Assembly of 1900 was organized, Daugherty wrote a number of insurance companies saying that both branches of the legislature were controlled by his friends, that undoubtedly bills inimical to their interests would be introduced and they should have someone on the ground to protect their interests. He offered his services to each company for fifteen hundred dollars. One of these letters fell into unfriendly hands and led to considerable discussion around the state capital. "Milker" bills, introduced to extort money from the interests threatened, were Daugherty's specialty. The anti-cigarette bills then springing up in practically every state legislature were commonly of this intent. It seems significant that the last measure of this character was introduced in 1905 by L. M. McFadden, a member of the House of Representatives from Daugherty's home county of Fayette.

When the Columbus Savings and Trust Company failed, Daugherty's name appeared in connection with a number of questionable transactions. The company was formed by former State Treasurer

Cameron, a political intimate of Daugherty's. Daugherty was a member of its Board of Trustees. The closing out of the assets of the institution ran through several years, until I became governor. There were threats of indictment and Attorney General Timothy S. Hogan believed that Daugherty, with others, should be prosecuted for the misuse of depositors' funds. Daugherty came to see me about it. I was never a believer in purely political indictments, intended to influence political campaigns. Inquiry had convinced me that Daugherty could not be convicted. I told him frankly what my feelings were in such matters, and that I had already so advised the Attorney General. I told Daugherty very pointedly, however, not to consider himself under the slightest obligation to me.

It was almost ten years before I again saw Daugherty. President Harding's social group, including Ned McLean, Senator Frelinghuysen, Secretary of the Interior Fall, Jess Smith and Daugherty, came to Miami on a pleasure trip. On a fishing expedition to Cocolobo Key, forty miles south of Miami, the party was photographed and the large picture still hangs over the fireplace in the club. There is a strange thing about the picture which many people have remarked. It shows a pronounced shadow over Secretary Fall, and another, but not so pronounced, over Daugherty. The superstitious could call this a prophecy. Both Fall and Daugherty were compelled to leave the public service under a cloud. I was in Florida at the time and had a long talk with Daugherty. He was in unusually high spirits due, I felt at the time, to his own consciousness of the power he was exerting in the administration. I remember remarking to a discreet friend of mine later that I thought I saw considerable mental instability in Daugherty at that time.

In Washington, the "Gang" made its headquarters at what came to be known as the "little green house on K Street." Charles Kinney, Ohio Secretary of State, was a Daugherty supporter and his Assistant Secretary, Howard Mannington, of Urbana, became identified with the Daugherty crowd in Washington and figured prominently in the gossip and scandals concerning it. Mannington, who lived at the "little green house," made a trip to Europe at a time when the wealthy Grover C. Bergdoll was attempting to obtain permission to return to this country. The names of Bergdoll and Mannington were linked in the gossip of the time, but after Daugherty's departure from the Department of Justice nothing more was heard of Mannington

305

in connection with Bergdoll's case. Daugherty knew perfectly the game he was playing. He was always able to draw about him a group of loyal aides. He could develop skillfully the situations out of which a profit could be coined. He was generous with his assistants and this tied them to him.

Daugherty had made a killing under the Taft administration out of the pardon for Banker Morse. He induced an army surgeon to certify that Morse was suffering from "cardiac dyspnoe" and that, even if released, his life expectancy was not more than six months. Taft, a ruggedly honest man, was imposed upon. The pardon was granted but Morse did not die in six months or six years. After his release he went on a pleasure trip to Europe. On his return he was interviewed at the ship's dock by news reporters. He recited the items of the high cost of his liberty, one of which was a liberal payment to Harry M. Daugherty.

Warren Harding and Daugherty were close personal and political friends. As a member of the state Senate, Harding certainly knew of Daugherty's lobbying activities and of his checkered political background. One could go further and say there was no politically sophisticated person in the state who did not know of Daugherty's record. For several years Robert F. Wolfe, owner of the *Ohio State Journal* and the Columbus *Dispatch*, the two leading Republican papers of Ohio, constantly referred to Daugherty's sinister influence on the Republican party. Even in the days of Harding's ascendancy, Mr. Wolfe, a very strong and positive character, never grew friendly to Harding because of his intimate relationship with Daugherty. Harding's instinct alone should have told him that Daugherty was not entitled to his trust. But in the national convention of 1920 it was Daugherty who brought together the elements which put over Harding's nomination and Harding was mindful of his debt. Daugherty had made widespread contacts in the pre-convention campaign. He was of an engaging personality and got on well with the type of politician who was as ethically inept as he was. Harding doubtless had a feeling that Daugherty could relieve him of the annoying details of dispensing patronage. In this respect, Daugherty doubtless made himself appear as indispensable to Harding. Certainly that was the feeling of Mrs. Harding, who had great influence with the President.

Daugherty had organized what became known as the "Ohio

306

Following the deadly floods that struck the Dayton area in 1913, "The Miami Valley Plan" was devised to allay such future disasters. The three men most responsible for the plan were (left to right) Col. E. A. Deeds, who served as chairman of the new Miami Conservancy, Governor Cox and attorney John A. McMahon, who authored the law governing the Conservancy District.

Governor Cox enjoyed the company of Lord and Lady Astor. He visited them in England, and they cruised with him in the Florida Keys.

Top: Governor Cox with one of the
great political figures of the early
20th Century, William Jennings Bryan

Right: Thomas R. Marshall, vice
president under Woodrow Wilson,
visited Governor Cox at "Trailsend."

Top: Bernard Baruch, known as "the adviser of Presidents," was a valued friend to Governor Cox.

Right: Ignace Paderewski, the eminent musician and Polish patriot, visited the Governor in Ohio. Cox said of his guest, "His very soul was aflame with patriotism and love for his native land."

Orville Wright would never speak in public, not even for his "loyal friend" Governor Cox when he dedicated his first radio station, WHIO in Dayton.

The Governor and Orville Wright (center) accompanied President Roosevelt (left) on a campaign tour in 1940.

Governor Cox made the chief address on August 19, 1940, at the dedication of the Wright Memorial on the hills east of Dayton, where the Wright brothers developed their flying machine.

Governor Cox, an enthusiastic golfer, with (left to right) legend Bob Jones, William Danforth and golf pro Willie Klein

Al Smith, governor of New York and 1928 Presidential candidate, relaxes with Governor Cox after a round of golf. At right, an inscribed photo from golfing great Ben Hogan

In June 1933, with the world in economic turmoil, the London Conference was convened to address free trade and international tariffs. The U.S. delegation was chaired by Cordell Hull (left) and vice-chaired by Governor Cox.

Tariffs on tomatoes was one of the issues of the day.

WESTERN UNION

Send the following message, subject to the terms on back hereof, which are hereby agreed to

Dayton, Ohio, August 9, 1934

PERSONAL
Hon. Cordell Hull,
Secretary of State,
Washington, D. C.

MY DEAR CORDELL FLORIDA SEEMS MUCH AGITATED OVER THE SUGGESTED ARRANGEMENT
UNDER WHICH CUBAN TOMATOES WILL COME INTO UNFAIR COMPETITION.(STOP) YOU KNOW
HOW I FEEL ABOUT THE TARIFF QUESTION GENERALLY BUT AS LONG AS OUR POLICY IS
TO BE NATIONALISTIC I SUPPOSE EACH COMMUNITY WILL HAVE TO PROTECT ITS OWN
DOORYARD (STOP) FRANKLY THE EFFECTS OF THE CHANGE UPON FLORIDA WOULD BE
RUINOUS

James M. Cox

Straight wire- Charge News

1206-A.

CHECK

ACCT'G INFMN.

TIME FILED

WESTERN UNION

R. B. WHITE PRESIDENT   NEWCOMB CARLTON CHAIRMAN OF THE BOARD   J. C. WILLEVER FIRST VICE-PRESIDENT

Send the following message, subject to the terms on back hereof, which are hereby agreed to

Dayton, Ohio, May 12, 1937

Hon. Neville Chamberlain,
10 Downing St.,
London, England

WORDS CANNOT TELL YOU HOW DEEPLY MOVED WE HAVE BEEN BY THE SOLEMN AND BEAUTIFUL

CEREMONIAL OF THE CORONATION (STOP) SOMEHOW I FELT IT TIED THE NATIONS AND PEOPLES OF

A COMMON IDEAL INTO A CLOSER BOND WITH A QUICKENED SENSE OF DUTY (STOP) TO ME A VERY

HIGH NOTE IN ALL THE PROCEEDINGS WAS THE APPEAL OF BALDWIN FOR SERVICE TO THE WORLD

(STOP) IT MUST HAVE STIRRED EVERY HEART UNDER YOUR FLAG AND OURS (STOP) ALWAYS KIND

REGARDS

NA 258 Via RCA - CD London 34 13

Cox

May 13, 1937

Hon. James M. Cox,
Dayton, Ohio

DEEPLY TOUCHED BY YOUR SYMPATHETIC UNDERSTANDING MESSAGE I BELIEVE OUR TWO COUNTRIES
ARE DRAWING NEARER TO ONE ANOTHER SINCE WE HAVE SO MANY IDEALS IN COMMON OUR KINDEST
REMEMBRANCES

Chamberlain

Dayton, Ohio, January 30, 1934

Hon. Franklin D. Roosevelt,
White House,
Washington, D. C.

MY DEAR FRANK MRS COX AND I SEND HEARTIEST FELICITATIONS AND WISHES FOR MANY
HAPPY RETURNS OF THE DAY (STOP) MAY GOD PRESERVE YOUR STRENGTH VISION AND
COURAGE (STOP) BY THE WAY I CAN GIVE YOU THE FIRST STRAW VOTE FROM OHIO ON
THE BIRTHDAY BALL (STOP) CHAIRMAN E E WATSON OF COLUMBUS HAS RECEIVED ESTIMATES
FROM HIS ONE HUNDRED AND SIXTEEN LOCAL CHAIRMEN THEY GUARANTEE AN ATTENDANCE OF
TWO HUNDRED THOUSAND

James M. Cox

Stra

Governor Cox remained active in national and international issues, as evidenced by numerous telegram exchanges with Britain's Prime Minister Neville Chamberlain and President Roosevelt.

Governor Cox, Ohio's first three-term governor, and Governor Frank Lausche, Ohio's first four-term governor, before the 1945 PGA Open at Moraine Country Club

Former Gov. James M. Cox, of Ohio, presents a copy of his autobiography, "Journey Through My Years" to his son, James M. Cox, Jr.

Governor Cox with President Harry Truman in Dayton, 1948

Cox bought The Atlanta Journal *shortly before the 1939 premier of "Gone With the Wind." Author Margaret Mitchell was a former* Journal *reporter.*

Below, Governor Cox is congratulated by Dr. Howard Bevis, president of Ohio State University, after receiving an honorary degree.

James M. Cox Jr. (left), Governor Cox and his grandson, Jim Kennedy (aged 9), gather for the 1957 dedication of a new Dayton Daily News *building. Governor Cox died less than a month later.*

Noted political cartoonist Ned White remembered the accomplishments and contributions of Governor Cox at the time of his death.

James Middleton Cox, March 31, 1870 - July 15, 1957
(Painted by noted English-born portraiturist Douglas Chandor in 1949)

Gang" prior to 1920. Once he was in Washington, in high favor with the administration, he gathered together a group to play the game on a national scale as he had played it on the smaller scale in Ohio. The barter and sale of government was to be a nationwide enterprise.

Howard Mannington was there, Jess Smith, Gaston Means, a new recruit, and others whose names became familiar at the time. Jess Smith, the most publicized of Harding's stooges, was simply an errand boy ready to do anything Daugherty asked him to do. He committed suicide in his hotel when he knew that Daugherty was spending the night at the White House and that the stench around the administration had about reached the explosion point. Smith knew of the part Daugherty had played and did not want to live to see him in disgrace.

"The little green house on K Street" with the peculiar doings there was investigated by a committee of Congress and the revelations were very discreditable to the administration. So niggardly an appropriation was made to conduct this inquiry that self-respecting Republicans added to the fund from their own resources. That was not sufficient to finance the work of the committee, and it came to nothing.

Daugherty's operations thrived when Ohio was in the grip of a Republican regime which had succeeded so long at the polls that it felt it could not be dislodged. Conditions became so intolerable that the state revolted and brought to the governorship that eminent executive, Judson Harmon, a Democrat. The Republican party remained in ill odor in Ohio till the chance to return to power came with the rise of Ku Kluxism in 1914. The Democratic candidate for senator that year, Timothy S. Hogan, was a Catholic and the flames of fanaticism ran fiercely against him. It was out of this Ku Klux revival that the political resurrection of Warren Harding came. He had been defeated for governor in 1908 by Judson Harmon and his days in public life seemed at an end. But now he entered the Republican primaries against Foraker, a political cripple. The oil scandals had besmirched Foraker, and Harding defeated him by a small majority. Daugherty had helped Harding to this nomination, and in the election campaign Daugherty played the part which he knew so well of keeping the fanatical frenzy of the time alive through large contributions of money.

The Republican party fell into disrepute after this campaign because of its affiliation with Ku Kluxism. This doubtless helped my return to the governorship in 1916 for a second term and my reelection in 1918 to a third term.

The Ku Klux movement brought Harding back into politics and Daugherty came with him to remain his chief aide and confidant. Thus the "Ohio Gang" which Daugherty headed, essentially a political underworld, came to Washington in 1921 with a place at the right hand of the President. There followed promptly the public scandals which make up the sad story which ensued.

CHAPTER XXVIII

UNDER MIAMI'S PALMS

A CURIOUS TURN of circumstances brought us into the Miami, Florida, newspaper field in 1923. It had its beginning, as a matter of fact, in Dayton. Next to our newspaper plant was one of the first automobile garages in the country, run by Earl Kiser, who was known internationally as the champion bicycle rider of the world. Possessing great muscular strength, the eye of an eagle and the heart of a lion, and being a fine judge of distance, he made his competitors look commonplace. It was natural that he should turn to automobiles and automobile racing. He had given room in an unoccupied story of his building to Fred Avery, who had conceived the idea of supplying gas from a tank to the front lights of an automobile. Until then oil lamps had been used.

Another bicycle and automobile racer, Carl Fisher, resided in Indianapolis. He was an admirer of young Kiser and in one of his visits to Dayton saw what Avery was trying to do. After Avery had demonstrated to his own satisfaction the feasibility of his device he sought funds to start production. Ten thousand dollars, he figured, was what he must have. He had urged Earl Kiser to join him. The elder Kiser, a quiet, conservative man whom I had grown to know very well, advised the son that he would put up $5000 if I would advance a like amount. I had not been in business long and $5000 was a matter of great magnitude to me. Besides, we needed everything we could scrape up to keep our own business going. Kiser was greatly disappointed.

Not long after this Fisher made another of his recurrent trips to Dayton and was told of the proposal that Avery had made to Kiser. Fisher was positive that there was a great future ahead for automobiles and this was the one thing at the moment most needed to make driving more pleasant and safe. He told Avery he would advance the

309

money. When he returned to Indianapolis, he told a friend of his, a banker, James A. Allison, that he had purchased for Allison and himself a two-thirds interest in something that would make them rich and it would only cost Allison $10,000. Allison's immediate and characteristic response was, "Where in the hell are you getting $10,000?" Fisher answered: "It is this way, Jim. A two-thirds interest costs $10,000. You not only put up half of that, but I am charging you the same amount for letting you into a good thing." Allison, something of a plunger himself, accepted the proposal.

That began the career of Carl Fisher as a national figure. Many stories have been printed about him, but this one, I am sure, has never before been told.

Within a year Avery was paid $100,000 for his one-third interest and the two Hoosier boys owned the business completely. They made a great success of "Prestolite." Fisher not only had great imagination, but his sustained efforts were constructive. Someone once said of him that he could sell bonds to finance a highway to the moon. As a matter of fact, Fisher never made a deal with anyone except in the utmost good faith as to values. Fisher and Allison took $8,000,000 in dividends out of the business and then sold it to the Union Carbide Company, taking cash and marketable securities, but unfortunately no common stock. For this they were pointed out as smart fellows, for in those days when combinations were being formed everywhere, small businesses turned into a consolidated unit and usually, in numberless instances to their later regret, took common stock. I took pains recently to find out from the president of the Carbide company, Mr. Benjamin O'Shea, what the result to Fisher and Allison would have been if they had taken common stock and held it until now. It would be worth over fifty million dollars. Fisher, however, had no regrets. The beautiful empire which he built in the Southland, the magical Miami Beach, meant more to him than all the money in the world. Free from business, he was forty years old and had fifteen million dollars in the bank.

Fisher was the type that required outlets for pent-up energies. Boats and boating gave him what he needed. He had several craft built. The one in particular which determined the major enterprise of his life was called the "Eph," after his pet dog. It had been built by the Seabury Ship Yards in New York City and shipped by freight to Cairo, Illinois. His first adventure was to go down the Mississippi

River and then across the Gulf to south Florida. He induced John Levi, later mayor of Miami Beach and then manager of the ship company, to make the trip with him. At Mobile they ran ashore. Fisher, in disgust, took the train back to Indianapolis. Levi, with the aid of an amateur navigator and a couple of sailors, finally made his way around Cape Sable to Miami. He wired Fisher to join him and in mentioning the suggested destination said that it was "a pretty little city."

Fisher at the time was attending an automobile show in New York. Without much enthusiasm he headed south. With him came Harry S. Lehman, then a young man, whose mind was filled with engines and automotive possibilities. He later made his millions as a distributor in Cincinnati and is now chairman of the board of the First National Bank and a very useful citizen of Ohio. He spends his winters at Miami Beach.

There is something in the Miami scene that takes hold of everyone. Seen for the first time, it doesn't seem possible that it is a part of the United States. Fisher's imagination, great lover of nature that he was, was stirred.

In the office of Frank B. Shutts, an Indianan who had come to Miami as receiver of a bank, he was asked whether he would like to buy some bonds on a wooden bridge that was being erected across Biscayne Bay to a beach skirting the sea. Fisher laughed at the idea, but it wasn't long before he was surveying the reefs, islands, inlets and bays of the area served by the bridge. Here he fell in with John Collins, who I think can properly be called the father of Miami Beach. Collins had come from New Jersey, bought a strip of the island peninsula running north and south about eight or nine miles long and conceived the idea of establishing a cocoanut oil business there. He planted thousands of nuts, but as soon as the shoots came up they were eaten by the rabbits. Then he turned to growing avocado pears and did well at it. The fruit could be delivered across the bay only by oar-driven boats, and so he conceived the idea of erecting the wooden bridge.

Collins himself must have had the power of graphic description, for Fisher took the remaining part of the bond issue and received as a bonus 150 acres of swampland along the beach. The bonds paid out dollar for dollar. Then the dream began to unfold. Scrub trees in the mangrove swamps were cut, bulkheads were built about and

311

beyond their edges and dredges were put at work pumping sand and silt from the bay onto what was soon to become high, dry land. They did more than that. In order to get enough dirt for their purpose, they cut canals through the marked-out area and every cubic foot of excavation was used for fill. Most people laughed at it then. It is easy now to see how practical the whole operation was. In 1914 I visited Miami and by houseboat and small craft went through the canals to Lake Okeechobee and then down the Caloosahatchee River to Fort Myers on the Gulf. I was told of Fisher's activities and, even though we were close friends and I would have enjoyed meeting him again, the whole project seemed so fantastic that I didn't want to hear of it.

The canals brought great beauty to the picture. The tide keeps the waters pure and when one looks now at Miami Beach with its waterways, the boulevards planted in oleanders, hibiscus and the whole profusion of tropical foliage, one does not wonder that visitors from all over the world pronounce it in many respects one of the most beautiful spots on earth.

In due time, Allison joined Fisher in the enterprise and Collins brought into it for construction and later administration his son, Irving Collins, and his son-in-law, Thomas J. Pancoast. The younger generation of the Pancoast family makes the Beach its permanent home. Both Fisher and Allison were men of large benefactions. Allison built a beautiful hospital which in time was turned over to the Sisters of St. Francis.

Fisher, this enterprise a great success, felt he had yet other worlds to conquer. As he envisioned the future, Montauk Point at the east tip of Long Island would become a great shipping terminal. He bought thousands of acres, erected boulevards, hotels and residences and was engaged in the fulfillment of his second dream when the depression following 1929 came. Of his own funds, he had advanced about $3,000,000. Subsequently, he floated two bond issues running into the millions. As evidence of his confidence in the worth of his securities and his faith in the enterprise, he guaranteed payment of the bonds. This led to his financial undoing. What he possessed on the Beach was taken over by the bondholders. He was given a comfortable salary to carry him through to what Fisher felt would be a favorable turn in his affairs and, as his interests on the Beach were liquidated, any balance ensuing would be given to Fisher. The property in question has all been disposed of in the last few years. Fisher's debts were paid and two or three years after his death a comfortable competency was turned over to his widow. His life was a romance of constructive enterprise. If you review the history of any great project you will find behind it a personality whose struggles and triumphs and even failures make a story truly stranger than fiction.

Fisher had importuned me to come to Miami. I finally did, in 1923, and fell completely in love with the place, confident that it would grow into a great city. Living in a hotel was always an intolerable experience for me. When I made up my mind to spend a part of each year in Miami, I realized that to find happiness there, I must get something to occupy my time. Carl Fisher suggested that I purchase the only afternoon paper, the Miami *Metropolis*, the oldest paper in this region. It was owned by Bobo Dean. Fisher arranged a meeting for me with Mr. Dean. We came to terms quickly and the deal was made for cash. Before going back North in the spring I purchased land on the Beach and had a residence erected during the summer of 1923. At that time the Nautilus Hotel and our house were the only structures north of the Biscayne canal. Now the city is built solidly more than six miles beyond to the north. To judge by appearances, there will soon be very little unoccupied area between Miami Beach and Hollywood and then on to Fort Lauderdale.

The *Metropolis* was operated in a small place on Flagler Street. Believing that Biscayne Boulevard would become the Fifth Avenue of south Florida, I purchased a lot overlooking the bay and erected on it one of Miami's first skyscrapers, 279 feet in height. I also changed the name of the paper to the *Daily News*.

The land boom was brewing then. The nature of it can be seen by our experience in purchasing the plot of ground for the News Tower building. We found a mortgage on it for a relatively small sum that had been given to an undertaker. It had been paid off, but the records did not show it. On inquiry it developed that the owner had died with a great deal of real estate, but not money enough to bury him. The undertaker took the mortgage in payment. The Bank of Bay Biscayne was administering the estate, and one million dollars in cash was turned over to the heirs.

While making my survey, I chanced one day to visit the Miami docks and ran into a man of Canadian birth, Captain Len Lewis, who was in charge of the affairs of the Clyde Steamship Line. I asked him whether Miami had any chance of growth. This was his reply: "The people back behind us here on land haven't the faintest idea what everything you see about you here will grow into. This will be a big city. It is a jumping-off place for the West Indies and South America. Ships some day will come in here from all over the world." His prediction is proving true.

When the hurricane of 1926 hit south Florida, the first news to the North came from a steamship in the harbor at Mobile, Alabama. A dispatch stated that the News Tower was leaning thirty-three and a third degrees. We fell to wondering whether, in the construction, rubber had been used rather than steel. Adolph S. Ochs once paid our building a treasured compliment by asserting that no newspaper in America had a business office comparable to ours. On the main wall in this part of the building is a large painting symbolic of Florida as known by the ancient and embryonic maps of the 16th century. A curved and scrolled shield at the center encases a poem written at my request by Edwin Markham. On the left is Juan Ponce de Leon holding a stylized staff from which curls the elongated blue, yellow and orange Spanish banner and on the right, that most brazenly betrayed of American Indians, Osceola, holding a staff with seven eagle feathers afloat from its tip.

These figures round out the effect of the central nucleus of curves which broaden out over the whole mural, as ripples of centrally disturbed waters form widening curves. Beyond these central figures on either side are the rounded maps of the two hemispheres, the one of the New World symbolically on de Leon's right.

The Edwin Markham poem runs as follows:

Here once by April breezes blown
You came, O gallant de Leon,
Sailed up this friendly ocean stream
To find the wells of ancient dream—
The fountain by the poets sung
Where life and love are ever young.

You found it not, O prince, and yet
The wells that made the heart forget
Are waiting here—yes ever here
With touch of some immortal sphere,

For here below these skies of gold
We have forgotten to grow old—
Here in this land where all the hours
Dance by us treading upon flowers—

Our building was dedicated in 1925. The blow which can properly be called the master hurricane fell upon south Florida less than a year later. The desolation was food for pessimists, and predictions were made that this was the end of the dream city.

In due time Al Capone, the Chicago gangster, arrived on the scene, attracted no doubt by the easy money to be found in gambling operations. The *Daily News* found itself in the very center of an interesting but trying battle. Capone purchased a commodious residence on one of the islands adjacent to Miami Beach. The hoodlums in his criminal entourage were recurrent visitors, and yet the community seemed little aware of it. Under assumed names they were playing golf on the municipal course on Miami Beach several times a week. A foursome observed a car on a street skirting the golf course. The car came to a stop. The four golfers jumped into a bunker and pulled sawed-off shotguns from their golf bags. This was the tip-off. The *Daily News* made the exposure and gave the names of the notorious assassins there, most of whom have been killed since in gangster wars. Capone was at once pronounced a public enemy.

The Capone outfit spread money like water at a time when business in every channel was depressed. Governor Carlton from the State house in Tallahassee gave warning to the whole commonwealth and issued orders to sheriffs and other officers of the law to stop Capone and his gangsters at the Georgia and Alabama lines. The legality of this was doubtful and nothing came of it, but it did reveal the high character of the Florida executive.

Capone made large contributions to the campaigns of candidates for office. It was the law-enforcing branches of the government, of course, which claimed his attention. It was pretty well established that to one candidate he donated $30,000. The best elements of the town joined in the movement to get rid of the pestilence.

One day a well-dressed gentleman walked into my office and laid down a certified check for $500,000, stating that he represented clients who wanted to present this as first payment on the purchase of the *Daily News* for $5,000,000 in cash. The property was not worth that amount at that time, and there was not the slightest doubt in my mind that the Capone interests were behind the offer. This proved later to be the fact. The emissary did not stay long. I told him that he looked like a gentleman and I wondered if he felt proud of his clients. He was told that no amount of money would be tempting, that it would not be a matter of disposing of a newspaper but selling out a community which was in sore need of protection. He seemed very much embarrassed, expressed regret that he had been drawn into the offer and departed. I never saw nor heard of him afterwards.

To rid the city of the Capone gang, it was decided to enforce a local ordinance against vagrants. The first Capone criminal picked up by the officers had $15,000 in cash on his person. This made a good deal of a travesty out of this procedure. An appeal was made by me to a man very close to President Hoover. The plea was substantially in this form: "The Capone gang is attempting to break down the legal and moral restraints of this community. Money is not a consideration. The millions at its disposal are acquired, as you know, through the violation and defiance of our federal statutes. We are still suffering from the results of the hurricane and the best within us must be asserted to rebuild a city. The federal government is apparently paying no attention to the situation. We are fighting here with our backs to the wall and the situation is not creditable to the federal authorities."

The reply was, "What can we do?" The answer was "Taxes." That was the beginning of Capone's end. In due course he, with other members of his crowd, was on his way to prison. The *Daily News* was left to make this fight alone. This should not imply that the other newspaper was at all in sympathy with Capone. In too many places, if one newspaper begins a bold and necessary crusade, its competitors deny the movement either sympathy or support. The fact is not creditable to the profession, but it is a fault which will be admitted, I think, by most publishers and editors.

There is nothing truer than that every seeming disaster brings compensations in due time. This was true of Greater Miami. The task of reconstruction after the storm and the end of the criminal regime was an inspiring one.

When Carl Fisher arrived here, Miami was already a most attrac-

316

tive place. Clean, well laid out, abounding with flowers everywhere and with glimpses of the sea through the cut between the reefs, it was a beautiful picture. Some things about Miami should be said that the public in general knows nothing of. Its glamorous side has been well publicized, but behind the gay life of winter, the night clubs, racing, golf and water sports, is the life of a community which could never have been built without pioneers who will take high rank in the view of the historian. The pleasure side of Greater Miami would never have been possible without a continuing year-round population. Attractive stores, adequate public buildings, well-run banks, a fine school system, an impressive church life, all of these, on their own account, had created something to which Miami Beach and other suburbs could tie themselves. Through the construction of fine harbors it has become a great shipping point. This was the contribution of E. G. Sewell, who gave to this development more than any other person. Nature had given her wondrous touch. The sand and salt of the seas, and the sun which gives so abundantly of the ultraviolet ray, have spread the fame of this section as a health-giving place. William J. Bryan and I once addressed a gathering here and I remarked that Miami, as I saw it at that time, was "America's greatest human dry dock." Bryan seemed tremendously impressed by this observation.

As you view the citizenry, you find that families of physicians, lawyers, bankers, professors and scientists have come here for the health of someone in the family. Restored health begets happiness as nothing else can. Out of all of this has come a large element of the population—useful men and women who love Miami because here they gained health where health had failed in other sections. Retired naval and army officers have found it a haven for their remaining days. Cultural interests have grown apace with the development of the community. This kind of citizenship has kept its heel on the hoodlum development which has been attracted by the resort phase of the life here. It has risen to every challenge. It once uprooted a corrupt regime in the city hall. It cleaned out Tropical Park, a racing resort, under a drive assisted by Governor Holland and at the continued insistence of Senator Ernest Graham. M. O. Annenberg, known well throughout the North, squandered uncounted thousands of dollars to establish himself here. Rebuffed, he pulled up stakes and moved away. For the part which our newspaper, the *Daily News*, played in ruling out subversive interests it received the annual Pulitzer award.

Many scientists find this not only a happy place to live, but a fruitful field for their labors. Dr. David Fairchild and his wife, the daughter of Alexander Graham Bell, are citizens. His contributions to the semi-tropical sections of America are widely recognized. The avocado and mango, now prized products, were semi-wild plants in Central and South America when Dr. Fairchild brought them here.

Dr. Charles Torrey Simpson is another man who has made large scientific contributions. There is also a great development of musical interests here. A symphony orchestra ranks high. The demand for musical ventures has brought the world's great musicians. These musical events have seldom a vacant seat. Little short of a miracle has been the development of the Miami University. George E. Merrick, in the adventurous days when he was developing Coral Gables, donated 160 acres of land for the beginning of an institution of learning. The hurricane upset the building program, but classes were started wherever vacant buildings were available. The University was opened in 1926. The burden of financing and administration fell upon the shoulders of Dr. Bowman F. Ashe, who subsequently became president. He found strength and faith to keep things going. Increasing contacts with Latin America helped keep the spark of life. The registration, in 1944, had reached 2200 students. A school of engineering and a bureau of tropical research are about to be established. Attention is being given to the study and treatment of tropical diseases. The University has a college of liberal arts, a school of business administration and schools of law and music. Recently Edmond Hughes gave $1,000,000 to the University and an equal amount in addition is now being publicly subscribed.

The Catholic Church, too, has added to the educational advantages of the community. Monsignor William Barry founded St. Patrick's Church and parochial schools in a group of buildings given to him by Carl Fisher. They had been used as stables for polo ponies. Through his efforts, they have been displaced by a beautiful edifice, surmounted by dome and chimes, and extensive and attractive school buildings. This is not all. The Barry College for Women, situated above Miami between Miami Shores and Opa Locka, is an impressive institution.

One could write a book on the significant men who have been

318

attracted here. Henry M. Flagler early foresaw a great future. Mrs. Julia Tuttle, one of the pioneers, gave him, to encourage his enterprise, every second block in the city, comprising two square miles and consisting of 640 acres. Joseph A. McDonald, a Scotchman of strong moral fiber and character, was, in a sense, the father of modern Miami. It was he who induced Mr. Flagler to make deeds of land to churches of every denomination. He did more in building and developing young men than anyone else. Charles H. Crandon, who has done much in furtherance of musical interests, can be regarded as the father of the county park system which is expanding now into impressive dimensions. It was he who induced Hugh M. Matheson not long since to give a two-mile-long strip off the Matheson Key, across Biscayne Bay, to the county for a beach and park.

Not far to the north of Matheson Park is Fisher's Island. William K. Vanderbilt, one of the world's greatest yachtsmen, selected its southern tip for his winter home. Carl Fisher, who owned the island, offered to give Vanderbilt a sufficient acreage for his purpose in exchange for a boat which Vanderbilt owned and Fisher greatly admired. The genius of Maurice Fatio, one of the best architects America ever produced, developed a small village for the Vanderbilt estate. There were spacious grounds, comfortable quarters for domestics and gardeners and even a fire department and a large hangar for Mr. Vanderbilt's seaplane. Vanderbilt, himself his own skipper, sailed the seas of all the earth. He loved Miami and though he was a retiring, self-effacing man, he was a large contributor always to community movements for service and development. The last time I saw him, he was very unhappy because the Navy, for physical reasons, would not let him enter the service as he had done in World War I. He turned over all his ships to the government in accordance with the patriotism which had marked his life.

A banking achievement attracted the attention of financial men all over the country. During the real estate boom the deposits of the First National Bank had grown to $70,000,000. When things flattened out, they had shrunk to $8,000,000, and yet the institution was never less than eighty-eight per cent liquid. The president, Ed Romfh, had come to the Miami area as a youngster from the state of Arkansas. He still ranks as one of the best financial minds of the country. The real estate boom and the hurricane left much wreckage in their wake. Miami needed a process of financial stabilization. Romfh headed this movement with J. N. Lummus, James Gilman, C. D. Leffler and J. I. Wilson, bankers and businessmen, as his associates. This brought confidence in the securities issued by the city and was a distinct contribution to the community.

When the history of this war is written, particularly that part which relates to the tremendous movement of preparation, the production of war essentials and the training of men and women for military service, the country will be surprised to learn the part which south Florida has played. When everything was hurry and bustle, with rising need of quarters for training personnel, I advised Washington authorities of the possibilities in the south Florida area. They were told that in Miami Beach alone there could be supplied within three months hotels and apartments capable of furnishing 140,000 beds. Both north and south of Miami the terrain was made by nature for aviation fields. In a week's time the coral rock underlying the shallow sand can be crushed and oiled and you have a fine runway. The Army and Navy quickly glimpsed the possibilities, remembering what it was that brought Glenn Curtiss here. He was training fliers in the First World War under Florida skies. He told me that for one hundred consecutive days he had been able to fly. There were intermittent showers, but at some time during each one of the one hundred days there were good flying conditions. Mr. Curtiss became a citizen of Miami and developed the Hialeah section.

The early scenes of war preparation in the Miami area were unforgettable. Golf courses, vacant areas and boulevards were full of marching men at the very crack of dawn. Five hundred thousand young Americans came to the Beach to be trained and then classified for service elsewhere. Fifteen thousand young officers were trained for the Army Air Corps. These stalwart youths exemplified the human resources which make the nation's strength. General Arnold of the Air Forces characterized it as the West Point of the air. All up and down the coast great airfields were built with runways in some instances miles in length. The airplanes and blimps were to be seen and heard day and night.

On the Miami side was the large submarine chaser school and other activities common to the naval preparation. Brazilians and even Russians were trained there. Technical schools were established. Admirals Kauffman, Monroe, Benson and Anderson gave service that

320

will long be remembered as an indispensable contribution to the war movement.

The Brazilians were trained to take charge of ships turned over by our government and were in command of Commander Harold R. Cox. His father was English, his mother Portuguese. He had under him a thousand officers and enlisted men of the Brazilian Navy.

The Coast Guard won high praise for itself. While merchant ships and tankers were being sunk along the Florida coast almost daily, this arm of the Navy became a very efficient defensive and at times offensive unit. It was supplemented by volunteers from the Miami area; businessmen, bankers, physicians, citizens of the highest rank, submitted to training and were subject to call day or night.

There was something beyond all this that appealed yet more to my imagination. It told us how a democracy, for all its slowness to move when war approaches, carries overwhelming advantages. Young wives of the men, and in some instances children and babes, were transported to the vicinity of their husbands at government expense. Young women who had lived at home in more than comfort happily took residence in single rooms to be near and with their husbands before they went overseas. The churches were crowded with weddings. Young matrons labored with the Red Cross to the hour of going to the hospital for confinement. Hospitals were taxed to capacity.

I talked to many of the men under training and often asked them if they believed in marriage for men leaving for the war. They always answered yes, that they wanted something of their own to tie them to the country they were fighting for, something to carry on after them the life they were fighting to maintain.

Proud fathers carried their babes in their arms. It was to me a picture of solemn importance. This little mite was one of the things that he was to fight for. Mothers and fathers came in by every train for last visits with sons who were expected soon to be in foreign parts. With tears of both pride and anxiety, they stood by thousands watching their sons graduate as officers in the Air Corps of the Army. This was democracy at work to preserve the blessings that we enjoy in a democracy. It must have surprised the cynic, the fascist and tory.

An officer who gave long service on the Beach was Brigadier General Arnold M. Krogstad. He was appointed to West Point from Minnesota by an old congressional associate of mine, James A. Tawney, Chairman of the House Appropriations Committee. Krogstad was a fine military figure—from his shoulders up a replica of Woodrow Wilson. It was a sad day that brought his retirement for reasons of health. He has purchased a home and will reside permanently in Miami. It is safe to say that now, with peace restored and the hard days of "boot training" forgotten, men in large numbers will turn back in happy memory to the scenes of their military beginnings and locate there.

At present thousands of invalided members of our armed forces are being cared for in Miami. Many interesting facilities, not only for recreation of men in their training but now in the work of rehabilitation, were created. The most notable is the transformation of a vast pier building which had been run out into the ocean by Tex Rickard and some of his associates. Here the women of Greater Miami came into the picture. The movement was led by Katherine Pancoast, who brought to the setup, created largely by her own vision, real qualities of administration. Her account of what was done and how follows:

"In 1942 when military forces moved into this area, first in trickles and then in floods, a sudden strain pressed the community. Municipal government, housing and business made lightning adjustments. It was fitting that women should play the age-old role of their sex and provide the necessary hospitality for the servicemen who were here in such numbers and whose leisure hours added up to such a staggering total. Rolling up their sleeves, some ten thousand of them transformed a crumbling municipal structure, previously dedicated to the burlesque of Billy Minsky, into one of the largest recreation centers in the country, the Miami Beach Servicemen's Pier. Supplemented by branch centers flung the length of the Beach and extending into the sister community of Coconut Grove, they entertained in two years well over two and a half million guests. During one six-month period, over sixteen thousand sailors received instruction at the Pier and passed the swimming tests which could mean life or death to them in the perilous days to come. It was a thrill indeed to watch men of twelve different nationalities, reduced to anonymity through the medium of bathing attire, lean fraternally on each other's shoulders, and to hear young voices from all parts of the world blended in the melody of *The Star-Spangled Banner* in honor of the country which sheltered them for the moment. The estimated work hours of those first two years, approaching half a million, proved conclusively to a doubting public that volunteer energy and ability can not only be harnessed, but, with a forceful enough incentive, can be sustained."

The whole picture of the Florida east coast might have been changed if George E. Merrick, the founder of Coral Gables, had made his start just south of Palm Beach. It can easily be seen where, with Fisher expanding to the north and Merrick to the south, with the natural growth which has continued towards the Florida cape, there would exist today almost a solid settlement for over a hundred miles. Merrick had his real-estate beginning in a citrus grove of good-sized acreage which was left him by his father. At the height of his success he believed that the center of Greater Miami would be at Coral Gables and he tried to persuade me to build the News Tower building there instead of on Biscayne Boulevard, overlooking the ocean. That Merrick's dreams were not entirely shattered was due to the entrance of Henry L. Doherty. He made large purchases and carried out extensive developments. After his death this was continued by W. Alton Jones and the Marquis George MacDonald. The Doherty interests have all been liquidated in south Florida and have yielded handsome profits.

On returning North in the early summer of 1923, I must have been in a very expansive state of mind because I immediately purchased the Canton, Ohio, *News*. This city was very different from others in which we operated. The steel industry of this region attracted a large alien population which is centered about the metropolitan Cleveland area.

In due time, a new structure to house the paper was erected, one of the most beautiful and best-arranged buildings I have ever seen. It is no reflection upon a fine community to say that on mature consideration I was not very keen about our investment. It became apparent that the city could not properly support two newspapers. Gangsters organized and carried out the murder of our editor and when the Brush-Moore Company submitted a handsome offer for the property, we accepted, although our paper, the *News*, was given the annual Pulitzer award for the most distinctive service rendered by any newspaper.

323

CHAPTER XXIX

JOHN W. DAVIS AND AL SMITH

◆

NOT LONG after my return from Europe in 1922 the issues of the approaching presidential campaign were taking shape. The Teapot Dome oil scandal which finally culminated in the conviction and imprisonment of Secretary of the Interior Albert B. Fall gave hope of success to the Democrats. This confidence may have been responsible for the spirited convention contest which ensued. I consented to the presentation of my name by the Democracy of our state, mainly because I was opposed to the nomination of William G. McAdoo and was determined to hold the vote of our state solidly away from him. McAdoo had gone cold on the issue of the League of Nations for which his father-in-law, President Woodrow Wilson, had died. Besides, he remained silent at the sponsorship of his cause by the Ku Klux Klan. There was not only tacit consent to the Klan's support, but it was apparent that he and his major supporters were conniving with the Klan. McAdoo entered the Ohio primaries and presented a ticket in every congressional district. He was led to believe that he could carry the state aganst me and counted on the onus of my defeat in 1920 to strengthen him. The Klan was solidly behind him and the Anti-Saloon League forces as well. The vote in the state was Cox 74,183, McAdoo 29,267. Every Cox delegate in the congressional districts and at large was elected.

In wet-and-dry elections the bootleggers always voted with the Anti-Saloon League. That was the invariable practice, for the obvious reason that illegal dealers in liquor thrive best in prohibition areas. The worst form of hypocrisy this country has ever known was manifest in the contest over liquor. It is doubtful whether the growth of gangsterism under prohibition was more abhorrent to the decent sense of the country than the crop of hypocrites which prohibition made. At a certain Democratic State Convention, Senator Pomerene and I had made addresses in which we contended that prohibition was a fraud and destructive to the moral fiber of the country. The candidate for governor, an articulate dry, made a dry speech. The Senator and I returned to the hotel for the night and went to bed on a bottle of milk each. The dry candidate joined a convivial party which drank bootleg liquor till the small hours of the morning. This sort of thing played its part in bringing about the repeal of the prohibition amendment to the Constitution.

In prohibition days I accepted an invitation to speak at a political gathering in one of our western Ohio counties. Before the meeting, a delegation of local leaders came in to insist that I should not mention the subject of prohibition in my speech. As they argued, they passed around liquor from bottles brought with them. I spoke to a packed house that night and had my say on the question which the local politicians would have tabooed. The hall was filled and the audience demonstrated its approval of what I had said with such enthusiasm that my local advisers disappeared after the speech. Professional politicians rarely raise the flag of principle. With them, everything is expediency, and in their devotion to expediency they commonly miss the currents of public thought which give life and final success to politics.

The second choice of this state would have been Governor Al Smith of New York.

The convention assembled in New York City on June 24 and did not adjourn till July 9, after 103 ballots were taken. It ran so long and so much bitterness was manifest that the country lost interest, and in the protracted deadlock the prestige of the party was seriously impaired.

It was not so much a contest between the two leading candidates, McAdoo and Smith, as between the issues which had developed. The strength behind McAdoo came from the anti-Catholic Ku Klux Klan and the prohibitionists. Governor Smith was the idol of the American Catholics and he had never side-stepped the question of prohibition. He not only opposed it but predicted the ills to which it afterwards led. No Democratic National Convention, with the exception of that of 1860, brought about such a clash of irreconcilable opinions and personalities. My close friends knew the purpose of my candidacy and were sympathetic with it. We were not long in discovering that the votes of Ohio and the influence of its Democracy as well would prevent the nomination of McAdoo. It was equally apparent in due time that Governor Smith could not procure the necessary two-thirds vote. Before the balloting for candidates, there were prolonged debates over the platform. It was proposed that the Ku Klux Klan be condemned by name. This failed, but by the close vote of 541 and 3/20 for and 542 and 3/20 against. It gave an index to the acrimoniousness of the contest which would come when the balloting started for the nomination of the presidential candidate.

William J. Bryan was again prominent in the debates. It was his last national convention and this experience was not a happy one for him. There were unfriendly and discourteous manifestations from the delegates. The prestige of the onetime idol of the party had sunk to a very low level. He had not supported the nominee in 1920 and would not have done so in 1924 except for the nomination of his brother for vice-president. One takes no risk in asserting that he would have opposed Governor Smith in 1928. The part that he had played in popularizing reforms advocated by him and later adopted by the Republican administrations was remembered with gratitude, but the masses of the party had come to think of him as one grown intolerant, who would support the party only if he had his own way.

The debate over the platform was spirited. Some words then spoken might better have remained unsaid. Newton D. Baker, in a magnificent oration, pleaded without success for the insertion of a plank which called for going into the League of Nations. Baker threw his whole soul into this effort. He not only believed in the international principle but he loved Woodrow Wilson. The platform, as adopted, endorsed in principle the League of Nations, contending that "there is no substitute for it as an agency working for peace." In order to take it out of the list of political issues, it recommended that a referendum election be held officially under an Act of Congress. This was an evasion intended to lift the question out of the coming campaign. It was county courthouse sentiment which ruled the convention on this question. That happens in a good many national conventions and it is surprising how many local politicians place more importance upon the election of the county ticket than of the President of the United States.

The selfish motive is understandable. We had suffered defeat in

1920 when the League of Nations was regarded as the predominant issue. The Republican administration had settled into a state of smug complacency. Business was fairly satisfactory and the most of the Democrats were more concerned in victory at the polls than they were in the future peace of the world. Even if I had entered the contest to get the nomination for myself rather than, as was actually the case, merely to prevent the nomination of McAdoo, I could not and would not have accepted the nomination on the party platform as it was finally formed.

On the first ballot McAdoo had 431 votes, Smith 241, Governor Ralston of Indiana 30, Glass 25, John W. Davis 31, Underwood 42, Cox 59, Robinson 21, C. W. Bryan 18, G. S. Silzer of New Jersey 28, Governor Ritchie of Maryland 22, Pat Harrison 43. In all, nineteen candidates were voted for. On the thirtieth ballot Smith had 323 and McAdoo 415½. McAdoo reached his early peak on the fortieth ballot with a total of 505½, Smith having 317½, John W. Davis 70. McAdoo's highest vote in the convention was 530 votes on the sixty-ninth ballot, when Smith had 335. On the eighty-sixth ballot, Smith passed McAdoo: Smith 360, McAdoo 353½. For days this tedious process went on. I was at my home in Dayton. By telephone and telegraph came appeals to go to New York in the hope of breaking the deadlock. Until a nomination had been made I was still titular leader of the party and this fact might have been recalled when I urged upon the convention to do something which had been entirely forgotten—send a message of condolence to President and Mrs. Coolidge over the loss of their son. I made the suggestion to Cordell Hull, who was chairman of the National Committee.

By July 5, it was necessary to give some attention to the appeals that were coming to me. On that date, I sent this message to former Governor James E. Campbell, chairman of the Ohio delegation:

> Whenever in your judgment the withdrawal of my name from the consideration of the convention will promote harmony and bring the existing deadlock to an end, I trust you will, without delay, take such action as you then deem advisable. I have no personal ambition that arises above my devotion to the Democracy, and this message to you is prompted by a desire to serve the cause that has honored me.

Many persons who remember that I am the titular leader of

327

the party until a nomination is made have asked that counsel and advice be given. This is not necessary because the good sense and patriotism of the delegates can be depended upon. Nor would I think of visiting proscriptions against the names of honored and honorable men whose states have proposed them as worthy of a nation's trust. It is an impertinence for anyone to conceive he has a right to do such a thing under the guise of leadership or sincere purpose.

The choice of the convention becomes my choice and my time and strength will be given to his support the moment he is nominated.

Matters grew worse and out of a sense of duty to the political party that had so honored me, I finally went to New York. Arriving there, I gave out a statement in these words:

I have come to New York at the urgent request of prominent members of the party, who have expressed to me the belief that a trying emergency has arisen and that the offices of the titular leader of the Democracy should be extended with a view to bringing about harmony.

At the outset let it be understood that not only am I not a candidate but that I will not accept the nomination if tendered me. I do not know whether I can be of any service but my sense of gratitude and duty tells me that I should try.

It was plain then that some means had to be found to break up the deadlock. The delegates were weary and the prolonged and futile sessions had produced a bad reaction in the country. The Ohio delegation was assembled. Wendell Willkie was a member. I stated it as my opinion that the first move should be to increase the vote for John W. Davis. In every national convention of either party there are many able lawyers. It was my opinion that in both the McAdoo and Smith delegations there were members of the legal profession who regarded Mr. Davis as the leader of the American bar. They would be attracted to him more than anyone outside the two leading contestants. Therefore we planned to increase the Davis vote little by little on ensuing ballots. As an evidence of the trend, we would give him some votes from our state, because I intended to withdraw my name. There was some doubt in my mind, however, as to whether Mr. Davis, because of prejudices running against his corporate connections in New York, could be nominated.

328

If we gained him enough votes to break up the deadlock, and then he could not reach the necessary two-thirds, it was my suggestion that our whole Ohio vote be cast for Carter Glass.

The Davis tide worked perfectly. The delegates had a deep respect for Mr. Davis and they were anxious to bring matters to an end and go home. Once it became apparent that neither McAdoo nor Smith could be nominated, state after state changed its vote and the end came quickly.

If Davis had not been nominated, Glass most certainly would have been. My name was withdrawn on the sixty-fourth ballot and until things took shape in accordance with the plan agreed upon, Ohio's vote was cast for Newton D. Baker.

McAdoo did not receive the vote from Ohio at any time during the convention. Mr. Bryan's brother, Charles, was named for vice-president. In agreeing to this incongruous make-up of ticket, the old Commoner lost more ground in public respect than ever before. The result of my efforts brought complimentary references from the press and prominent Democrats. The following will give some idea of the favorable reaction:

Newton D. Baker—
"I do not feel that I can close the book of the recent convention without putting in your files a word of the loyal and affectionate gratitude for all you have done and made possible in the recent emergency."

George Foster Peabody—
"I am of those who are grateful to you for so promptly responding to the appeal and for taking hold to pull things together as you did."

Gov. Albert C. Ritchie of Maryland—
"Please let me congratulate you on the very important part you played in the fine outcome of our convention, and incidentally thank you for the very sound and wise advice you were kind enough to give me."

James E. Campbell, former Governor of Ohio—
"The Democracy of Ohio can never realize the debt of gratitude it owes to Governor Cox, whose leadership is directly responsible for the nomination of John W. Davis of West Virginia.

"The situation in the convention was hopeless until Governor

Cox, emphasizing his unselfishness, asserted the leadership which was his and brought order out of chaos."

Charles Michelson in New York *World*—
"No small percentage of the credit for restoring harmony to the convention and therefore encompassing the nomination of John W. Davis goes to James M. Cox, the standard bearer of 1920, who was summoned when the deadlock between Smith and McAdoo was beyond the power of the leaders on the ground to break and proved equal to the task. Cox was among the first to receive the thanks of the successful candidate."

Robert T. Small, correspondent of Consolidated Press—
"When the inside history of the record-breaking Democratic National Convention of 1924 comes to be written, the part played behind the scenes and the final distributions by former Governor James M. Cox will perhaps form the most interesting and important chapter. He arrived in New York at the psychological moment when affairs seemed all but hopeless for the party. He knew all the leaders, had been associated with them in campaign and conference, had no axe to grind, no selfish interest to serve."

The campaign of 1924 had not progressed far before it was apparent that the independent ticket headed by Senator La Follette of Wisconsin would divide the liberal vote. In such a situation President Coolidge was an ideal candidate. He had dramatized the virtues of silence and of thrift. He never mentioned the Ku Klux Klan issue. An unaggressive man, he held together the conservative vote. That was sufficient in the face of the division among the liberals.

If the Almighty ever created a finer man than John W. Davis, I never knew him. He possessed every quality of statesmanship. On one occasion, he, Newton D. Baker and I were the speakers. In the midst of his admiration for Mr. Davis's speech, Mr. Baker said to me, "If I knew I were to be born again, by some process of reincarnation, and I were permitted to write out the specifications for my future being, I would ask to be given the legal mind of John W. Davis." Mr. Davis and I came into Congress on the same day. He captivated the members of both branches by his dignity of manner, his intellectual courage and the penetrative qualities of his mind. My opinion is that he would have given an able, liberal ad-

330

ministration as President. His keen sense of justice would have balanced well the equities as between classes and no man would have met his responsibilities with better understanding. The social and economic disturbances of the coming depression years had not yet appeared. Under the conditions then existing, if he had been elected, he would have left a record in our best tradition.

In the campaign of 1924, most of my speaking assignments were in Ohio, Indiana, Kentucky and Tennessee. The Democratic managers in the last-named state had sent me a letter, in the early part of the contest, stating that they had decided to bring in no outside speakers and would confine the discussions to Tennesseans. It was apparent that since I was more or less symbolic of the issue of the League of Nations, it would be better to keep me out of the state. About three weeks later, however, an urgent call came asking whether I could revise my itinerary and give them some time.

Their campaign was dragging and a change in tactics was required. I cancelled meetings in other states and went to Tennessee. At the first meeting, where a magnificent audience had assembled, I stated that I would discuss whatever they most wanted to hear about. The response brought an awakening to the local politicians. They asked me to address myself to the subject of isolation. After that, the Tennessee leaders insisted on my sticking to that text. Austin Peay, the Democratic candidate for governor, was elected in the midst of a Republican landslide.

In Kentucky the year before, a like request had been made to keep away from the question of the League. I told them that would put me in a false light and as long as the breath remained in me, I would preach the gospel of world peace maintained through international relationships and by force, if necessary. At the first meeting in Louisville the reaction of the audience was as demonstrative as in a presidential year. It was so significant that I wrote Woodrow Wilson about it, feeling that in his sickness the fact would be heartening. His reply was as follows:

2340 S Street, N. W.   Woodrow Wilson,
                                     Washington, D. C.
My dear friend: 16 November 1923

Your kind letter of November thirteenth, which I have just greatly enjoyed, affords me the opportunity to express my very sincere admiration (which I am sure is shared by all true Democrats) for your steadfast advocacy of the League of Nations. It constitutes the great and only issue worth fighting for, and I know of no one who has been more true to the faith than you have. May I not,—both as a Democrat and as a private individual,—thank you from the bottom of my heart.

It may interest you, as it has interested me, to reflect that the only nations associated with us in our refusal to take part in sustaining civilization are Turkey, Liberia, Mexico and Germany.

With warm regard,

Cordially and Faithfully yours,
(signed) Woodrow Wilson

Hon. James M. Cox,
Dayton, Ohio

As the campaign of 1928 approached, Governor Al Smith of New York had caught the imagination of the country. In the truest sense a self-made man, he had risen to high place in public confidence. He had come up the hard way, but the resistance of adverse circumstances had only increased his stature. He had come through New York politics unsmirched. Brought up in the fish-market region of the lower East Side, he had surmounted an environment holding temptations that would have been the downfall of many a youngster. He got on well with his neighbors. A fineness in his character and sensibilities gained from his fellows both respect and a feeling that he was destined for an outstanding career. He passed through precinct, ward, municipal, county and state politics without a whisper against his integrity. He knew every angle and phase of government.

I first met him when, on my way to the St. Louis Democratic National Convention in 1916, I stopped off en route at French Lick Springs in Indiana. Al Smith was there with Charles F. Murphy, the head of Tammany, and Robert F. Wagner, now United States Senator from New York. Smith was fresh from his triumphs in the State Constitutional Convention at Albany. There he had reaped the harvest of his diversified political experiences from the bottom up. As Charles F. Murphy put it, Smith had "tied lawyers into knots" in the convention. We had also passed through constitutional changes in our state and between the New Yorkers and me

332

there was an exchange of views as to just what had been done in the two states, and why. I remarked to Mr. Murphy that Smith seemed to have a positive genius for government. Murphy replied that George W. Wickersham, former Attorney General in Taft's cabinet, had remarked to him that if Al Smith were a lawyer, he would pay him $25,000 a year and give him a place in his New York legal firm. "But," Murphy had replied, "if Al Smith were a lawyer, he wouldn't be Al Smith." What a true observation that was!

Smith's mind was not confused by the legalisms of the lawyer. His philosophy of government had come from his contacts with almost every branch of government in New York State. His quaint observations and his unaffected democracy caught the fancy of the average man. He had both legislative and executive experience, including four terms as chief magistrate of our greatest commonwealth. If one focuses his mind upon the years of Al Smith's executive tenure, he must admit that here was an era of unprecedented progress in New York. His business administration was notable. He dealt with social needs in a way which marked him as an outstanding liberal. His was a composite accomplishment. The state government under him was made an instrument that touched every phase of human development and promoted the well-being of society. It created in the ranks of the great heterogeneous masses, and of business and professional men as well, a feeling that a democracy in good hands can meet every challenge of changing times. He knew the lot of the underdog and the vicissitudes of common life. In short, he had demonstrated that he was admirably fitted for the highest office in the gift of the American people. It was not surprising that the Democracy of the nation was practically a unit for his nomination for President. Our Ohio delegation enthusiastically supported him and the national convention at Houston was just register of the wish of his followers throughout the country.

The campaign which followed was one of the most disgraceful in our nation's history. The sheer cussedness of most of our presidential campaigns has always been a reproach to our republic. Well put was the remark of an English visitor years ago. Apparently, he said, our political parties pick the worst men in the country as their candidates for President. So he judged from the fact that he never heard anything good of them in the campaigns. I do not speak from personal experience. In the campaign of 1920, the opposition left me, as to the skullduggery of rumor-mongering, pretty much alone. My religion, Episcopal, was misrepresented and an attempt was made to show that I imbibed heavily of liquor. So many people knew the absurdity of this latter charge that it didn't go far. My friends regarded it as a joke and no attention was paid to it.

The major opposition to Al Smith was based on religious bigotry, as historians will record. It was the most unworthy exhibition in our history. For the first time a Catholic had been nominated for the presidency and he was rejected, not because he was lacking in character or ability, but because he grew up in the church of his mother. It has been difficult for me to understand this prejudice. In the South, it was largely inherited from the French Huguenots. No doubt much of it grew out of old conflicts between state and church in Europe. It deserved no place in American thought. Perhaps the nearest answer came from a homely experience in the autumn of 1928. While the campaign was at its height, I spent an afternoon in the countryside where I was born. An old boyhood friend, as we strolled along the sycamore-lined banks of a creek, looked about him to see that no one was in hearing and said to me: "Are you going to vote for Al Smith?" I told him I was and I was proud of it. It was evident that he had been wrestling with the problem in his own mind. He was emotionally stirred as he said, "My father would turn over in his grave, and my grandfather, too, if I voted against a Democratic presidential candidate, but I am worried. Catholics regard the Pope of Rome as second only to Christ. The Pope is a foreign power and I am afraid that a Catholic President might be unduly influenced." I told him that his conception of the whole thing was wrong; that in this country the church bore no relation to the state and that the attachment of the American Catholic to the Roman Church was spiritual only and could not in any way influence the political thinking of a Catholic officer in our government. I asserted that if any church interference in our political matters ever were attempted, Al Smith would be the first to condemn it.

Some of the happenings of that campaign seem like fiction. As I was campaigning in Tennessee, I was told this story, which was literally true. In one of the remote county seats it had been a practice through the years to run a streamer across the street when a

334

circus was coming to town. A farmer drove in one October day during the campaign with three hogs for market. He could neither read nor write, but he did guess the meaning, as he thought, of the piece of canvas stretched across the street. He inquired when the circus was coming and was told that it was a political meeting, not a circus, and that Pope (a prominent Democrat and once a candidate for the governorship) was speaking soon. In obvious excitement the country man inquired: "Pope, did you say? Well, I have been told right along that fellow would be over in this country, and I'm taking my hogs right back to the farm." Such was the fanaticism of rabble-rousers in that campaign. It resulted in Smith's losing some of the solidly Democratic states.

I proudly gave our candidate every available day. Just before election I delivered a radio address on *The Humanity Engineer*, in which I pointed out that social engineering is a great deal more complicated, difficult and important than mechanical or civil engineering, and that Al Smith was master of a higher art than Herbert Hoover. Just as one engineer, Goethals, had built the Panama Canal, I said, and as another, Gorgas, had abolished malaria and yellow fever over great areas, Al Smith as human engineer had taken a great state full of corruption, maladministration, boss politics, privilege and monopoly, and given the ten million people of New York honest, efficient, humane government. His was the greatest type of achievement. I also pointed out that much of the current campaign of bigotry was inspired by selfish economic interests. "These interests have for a generation preached hatred between North and South in order to keep the people divided and conquered," I said. "Now, for a like purpose, they preach hatred between alien and native, between white and black, between Jew and Gentile, between Protestant and Catholic, in the hope that our wars among ourselves will divert our minds from our economic ills."

In the end, I was distressed not more by Smith's defeat than by the measures which had been employed to bring it about. Al Smith was something more than a great American. Few men in all our public life had such outstanding traits of personality and few had his versatile qualities of mind and character. He could settle a controversy with a few words of common sense. He well-nigh destroyed Hearst as a political figure when he designated Hearst's support of an opposing candidate in New York as "the kiss of death."

He never spoke a demagogic word, and his name will be remembered when those of some of our Presidents are forgotten. I had an appointment to meet him in New York in the summer of 1944 when the presidential campaign was just getting under way. In a letter to me he said, expecting the visit, "I think there is enough left in the world for us to talk about." He was taken ill but a few days before the time we were to have had our meeting and from this sickness he did not recover.

PART SEVEN

The New Deal—Would Roosevelt Have Been Elected
If He Had Outlined It During the Campaign?

Herbert Hoover, High in Purpose, but
Inept in Politics

Achilles Heel of Administration

The London Economic Conference

Secretary Hull, a Distinguished Figure

A Glimpse of World Statesmen and Economists

Why the Conference Failed

CHAPTER XXX

THE NEW DEAL

◆

THE NEW DEAL was not the creature of any one man or set of men. It, or its equivalent, was natural and inevitable. It presents, superficially, a striking political paradox. If its measures had been specified in the Democratic National Platform of 1932, it is doubtful whether Mr. Roosevelt would have been elected. And yet, as the major, if not almost the only, issue in the campaigns of 1936 and 1940, it was overwhelmingly endorsed.

We find historic parallels for this. If Jefferson had declared his intention to purchase Louisiana, would he have been elected President? If Jackson had announced his purpose to destroy the United States Bank, would he have been chosen? If Lincoln had confided to the public what must have been in his mind, to issue a proclamation freeing the slaves, might not Douglas instead have risen to the presidency? Yet if the Democratic platform of 1932 be construed as broadly as the Supreme Court has interpreted the general welfare clause of the Constitution, then there is little or nothing in the New Deal that was not implicit in that party declaration. Lincoln said, "Movements make men, men do not make movements." The New Deal was but the legislative form of necessary measures to remedy the greatest economic and social convulsion since Andrew Jackson's time. Franklin D. Roosevelt merely instrumented the need of the hour and the demand of our public that it be met. The days were dark and ominous. The closing of the banks, to mention but one aspect of the crisis, made imperative the establishment of a sound base of operations upon which banking could be resumed. The ensuing measures were not products of any man's theorizing but of practical necessity.

Singularly, I find that in January, 1932, two public pronouncements based upon existing problems and expressing some vision of the future were made by Governor Al Smith of New York and myself. We spoke together at a banquet in the city of Washington. Governor Smith proposed a vast program of public works as a remedy for pressing unemployment, a program supported by the sale of bonds to the public. He put the principle in the clear-cut Al Smith way: "If it is all right to put the credit of the government behind business, let the credit of the government be used to keep the wolf of hunger away from the door mat of millions of people." "Made work" was the essence of Governor Smith's plan.

In my turn I called attention to the fact that well-managed corporations set aside a surplus to meet a possible future decline in business and profits. I suggested: "If capital is so protected against the rainy day, why should not capital and labor together provide for the same rainy day that comes to both?" This was the essence of the social security measures.

I made reference to the stressful conditions that were upon us then in these words:

> We have nothing in the future, as we survey the achievements of the human race, to fear. The genius of man has carried him through every crisis. He will come out of this with a better mind and a better heart. He will learn that no industrial structure can stand unless its foundation is a just and contented social state.
>
> As we seek a safe course through this dark time the faith of Jefferson shines forth like a beacon in the seas. Why hark back to Jefferson in this modern day? Because the base of his philosophy is justice. So long as people live in communities there must be an instrument of government. If it is to thrive, there must be justice in human relationships.
>
> There is nothing simpler than justice, and its principles never change. Justice yesterday is justice today and forever. If Jefferson's philosophy is charted in the human heart, there is no doubt of a happy destiny for our people.

The election in 1932 was determined chiefly by the severe panic and depression which had come under the Hoover administration; the Democratic majority was increased by the party demand for the repeal of the Eighteenth Amendment. The Democratic campaign was conducted with great skill. It brought into our national picture James A. Farley, who will always be ranked as one of our greatest political strategists.

Herbert Hoover became a political casualty largely because he was inept in political matters. I do not think any man ever came to the presidency with a higher purpose, and he seemed admirably fitted for the place. He had operated in different parts of the world as a capable engineer, and ordinarily the training and experience of a competent engineer insures his success at any administrative work. This fact is very apparent now in the aftermath of war, and we are able to see what the technical schools and their graduates contributed to the success of our military forces.

Mr. Hoover's political status, however, was unstable. There is no doubt that he was willing to be regarded as a Democrat in 1919 when a movement originated by Frank Cobb of the New York *World* to make him the 1920 Democratic candidate gained considerable headway. Eight years later, he qualified as a Republican. That would not have been possible if Harding had not appointed him to the cabinet, thus giving him a distinct political status. That appointment resulted from a strange combination of circumstances. Harding wanted Hoover in his cabinet. Philander Knox and Boies Penrose opposed Hoover but were anxious to have Andrew Mellon made Secretary of the Treasury. Harding acquiesced in their desire on condition that they withdraw their opposition to Hoover. Unfortunately for both Hoover and the country, he allowed political considerations to play too large a part in his conduct as President and in this field he was lost. On numerous occasions when he was urged by economists and men of good judgment both in business and politics to do an obviously desirable thing, he pleaded the need not to disturb party solidarity. On an occasion when conditions were threatening, a close adviser urged him to do something about the bad situation of the railroads and to veto the Smoot-Hawley tariff bill. Hoover said it would disturb things politically and refused. If he had struck out boldly at this time as Theodore Roosevelt did in his time, the severity of the panic would have been diminished and his party might have been saved from the crushing defeat which ensued.

Hoover, by disposition a liberal, became President by grace of a party in reactionary mood and under reactionary control. In his effort to keep his standing in that party, he cut himself adrift from his own traditional nature, a ship without a rudder. This made him, in a time of national crisis, a perplexed and ineffectual pursuer of a vain expediency into the chasm which yawned for him in 1932.

The seeming prosperity which had come under Harding and Coolidge was in large measure synthetic. We were sending billions of dollars to Europe and in most instances imposing the condition that the money be spent in purchasing our goods for export. This course could run only so long, and a factor in ending it was the sale of worthless securities to our public. The financial crash came in 1929 but the climax of its social effect was reached in 1931 and 1932. The far-flung consequences of the panic, reaching every household in the nation, were not foreseeable when the Democratic platform was written in 1932. It seems fair to assume that the New Deal measures to come later were not in Mr. Roosevelt's mind during the campaign. There were evidences of depression in every part of the country that he visited during the campaign, but it is doubtful whether at that time anything approaching a specific program could have been outlined in his mind. That arose with the wholesale failure of banks in early 1933. This threatened complete prostration of business and the need of applying hasty and drastic measures was as pressing as the calling of the fire department when a great conflagration rages. So clearly pressing was the need that the measures which came later to be known as the New Deal were little opposed when in process of enactment. Even the present critics do not condemn them in principle. In fact, the Republican platform in 1944 implied an endorsement of most of them; it was only the administration of the laws which it criticized. The claim is made among certain classes that the New Deal was a formula conceived by an organized cult surrounding Mr. Roosevelt. The truth is that there is not very much that is really new in the New Deal. There was a storm of ridicule and irony when Mr. Roosevelt recalled the "forgotten man." There was nothing new about that. Its birth was in a lecture delivered by Professor William Graham Sumner of Yale fifty years before. The man overlooked and ignored by society was described in these words:

Wealth comes only from production, and all that the wrangling grabbers, loafers and robbers get to deal with comes from somebody's toil and sacrifice. Who, then, is he who provides

342

it all? Go and find him, and you will have once more before
you the Forgotten Man.

You will find him hard at work because he has a great
many to support. Nature has done a great deal for him in giving him a fertile soil and an excellent climate, and he wonders
why it is that, after all, his scale of comfort is so moderate. He
has to get out of the soil enough to pay all his taxes, and that
means the cost of all the jobs and the fund for all the plunder.
The Forgotten Man is delving away in patient industry, supporting his family, paying his taxes, casting his vote, supporting
the church and school, reading his newspaper and cheering for
the politician of his admiration, but he is the only one for
whom there is no provision in the great scramble and the big
divide.

Such is the Forgotten Man. He works, he votes, generally
he prays—but he always pays—yes, above all, he pays.

England passed the first of her social security laws almost forty
years before we entered upon this course. First, old age pensions
were made compulsory. Unemployment insurance and insurance
for widows and orphans came in 1925. It is well to remember the
type of statesmanship which saw the need and devised this progressive program. In the cabinet responsible for it were Asquith, Lloyd
George, Winston Churchill, Haldane and John Morley. The crusader of the movement was Campbell-Bannerman, and history will
not class him as a radical. At the beginning of the Twentieth Century, with business at a high tide in England, Campbell-Bannerman
was impressed with the fact that one-third of the population was
still in distressful circumstances. This did not make sense to him.
He recognized that if such injustice were continued there would
certainly be dark days ahead for his country.

As we were behind England, so England followed in the footsteps of Germany by more than twenty years. This was an important factor in the industrial strength of Germany which brought
the Kaiser close to victory in the First World War.

Looking back on the panic of 1929, we find it hard to understand why our country permitted the speculative gambling in stocks
and securities to go so far and so long. It brought more distress
to our people than almost anything else. The New Deal included
the Securities Act and the Securities Exchange law of 1934. If

343

such measures had been passed a few years before we should have largely escaped the economic demoralization that fell upon us in 1929. The Banking and Currency Committee of the Senate reported that $1,700,000,000 of perfectly worthless and fraudulent securities were sold every year. Our new securities laws were based in principle upon English practices prevailing for a generation.

One morning as I was leaving my residence on Miami Beach for my office in Miami, a representative of one of the largest financial houses in New York came to me very much worried. He predicted all sorts of unseemly things if the regulatory measures then under consideration were adopted. He appealed to me to try to bring some influence to bear upon Washington. I told him that I could be of no help because he and his associates would not do what I should propose to them. He replied that he would come back to see me in a week and that he thought I could be confident that my advice would at least be given thoughtful consideration. When we resumed our discussion I asked him whether legislation was not badly needed. He agreed that it was. I can quote substantially my words:

> The trouble with you men in New York is that in the face of a much-needed reform you do little or nothing to help the Congress pass helpful laws. At the mere suggestion of a change you organize your opposition, develop a lobby and attempt to frighten the country. In other days, when scarlet fever was a much-dreaded disease, medical science went at it the wrong way. It attacked the fever and from this came a reaction on one of the special senses. Children were blinded, made hard of hearing or otherwise afflicted. Now scarlet fever is regarded as a minor ailment. The doctor facilitates the course of the fever and lets it run its course. It is rare indeed that we have the deplorable consequences of earlier practices. The old way with scarlet fever illustrates just how Wall Street ordinarily acts and what harm results to its own interests. If you will approach this in an understanding way, giving full recognition to realities, there may come a law which would do a vast amount of good.

I recommended that he employ Joseph P. Tumulty, a very able lawyer in Washington, onetime secretary to President Woodrow

344

Wilson, and then send to Washington John Hancock, better known now than he was then. He didn't belong to the Rip Van Winkle Club in Wall Street and he was highly regarded in congressional circles both for his ability and sincerity. I told him that Mr. Tumulty would do no lobbying and would not go to Capitol Hill. Tumulty was a rare composite, as skilled a political psychologist as I ever knew and an idealist as well. It will be remembered that he opposed Woodrow Wilson for governor until he knew what was to be done with the controlling bosses of Wilson's political party in New Jersey. Tumulty would recommend nothing that he did not think was in keeping with progressive principle. Hancock's thinking was far in advance of his associates in New York. He knew the subject well and was generally accredited with intellectual honesty. He was advised that the chairmen of the responsible Senate and House committees were not only able men but fair in their judgments. This recommendation was followed to the letter, and the law finally passed has put the stock brokerage business on a sound basis and prevented speculative excesses. If the old order had continued, not many brokerage houses would have been left. Nor would there have been the current flow of sales which are necessary in the operations of our corporations and of business in general. Within the last year the banker with whom I had my conversation recalled the circumstance. He said that no lobby had been employed because it was found not necessary. Out of it had come a lesson which had been profitable to him.

We hear a great deal about regimentation. If the control of products and of acreage is regimentation, then we have had a very mild dose of it as compared to England. Under the Conservative regime preceding World War II, the government of Great Britain became convinced that the public interest required individual acceptance of certain restraints. Much has been said here about "killing little pigs," a plan which came originally from the farm organizations themselves. In England there was established a Pigs Marketing Board to handle both distribution and price. The raising of beet sugar was subsidized. The same practice was followed also with wheat, and potatoes could be sold only by growers who were registered with the marketing board. No one could produce more hops than the quantity allotted to him. The cotton textile industry in England suffered from overproduction, and Parliament passed an act mak-

345

ing every spinner cut down the number of spindles he was operating. There are no two opinions about the great good which has come from our housebuilding movement. Untold thousands of families have been able to gratify the wish, inherent in all of us, to own their own homes. What has been paid in rent now amortizes the cost of the house. There is not a hamlet in America but what has been made more attractive and wholesome by this housing policy. Yet there was nothing new about that. The Federal Housing Administration Act is practically a copy of the Housing Act in England. The English had experimented while faced with the problem of a shortage of workers' homes. Out of this came England's Housing Act.

In 1933, when the New Deal arose, half of the mortgages in this country were in default. It would be difficult to overstate the number of people who would have lost their homes if nothing had been done to correct this tragic situation. It is extremely doubtful whether, in that case, any life insurance company in this country would have escaped bankruptcy. What was true of home owners in the cities was equally true of farms. Scores of thousands of farms were saved to their owners by the New Deal laws. There was a corresponding saving of banks. Credit must be given to William Jennings Bryan for his advocacy in 1908 of the guaranteeing of bank deposits, but there is nothing new about even the reformation in the conduct of our financial institutions which has made our bank failures inconsequential; at this, too, England preceded us, and the records show the last bank failure in the British Isles was in 1878 in Scotland.

The Achilles heel in the New Deal has been the method of dealing with the labor problem. To it must be added the very unwise conduct of FEPC. In labor, as in most of our social reforms, we were again behind England. Following the general strike in 1925 in that country, public opinion demanded that laws fair to industry and labor and the public interests be enacted to prevent repetition of that disaster. Parliament acted accordingly and no further trouble ensued. In our own case, we have moved from one extreme to the other, as we did with prohibition. We do not take heed of dangerous social and political bacteria until the disease has run to an epidemic. Evils are not corrected until they become extreme and intolerable. First we tolerated the disgraceful open saloon, unlicensed and uncontrolled. In my first term as governor, I reminded the legislature and our public as well that it should not be possible for a man to come out of the penitentiary one day and open a saloon the next. No attention was paid to proper observance of the Sabbath by the saloons. This was much the order of things in most of our states. We let things become so bad that when the pendulum swung, it swung to that other extreme, prohibition, which brought us an era of gangster rule.

We followed the same course with labor. The Employers' Association and its black list, I regretfully relate, had its source, in part, in my home city, Dayton. I fought it from its beginning in the face of threatened social and business reprisal. It started when one of our manufacturing enterprises imported a colony of Hungarian laborers and erected a stockade in one of the suburbs to house them. These aliens were ruled despotically by their own masters inside the walls. I condemned the thing as un-American, a disgrace to our industry. That form of slavery was broken up, only to be succeeded by the black list. If a man in any of our factories fell to discussing the welfare of his coworkers, he was tagged as an agitator and discharged and placed on a black list supplied to other employers. If he applied to another factory for work, he was turned away, a marked man. If he had saved his money and bought a home and was rearing his children in this community, he was compelled, in order to live, to move elsewhere. Even then it was an equal chance that he would be pursued to his new location and black-listed there.

The practice spread over the country and in defense against this injustice collective bargaining arose. The momentum which it acquired inevitably affected our politics. In many elections, labor held the balance of power. This power is now in many cases abused by labor bosses, who spring upon us evils to match those of the old labor-oppression days. There is enough common sense in America to control any such excesses in time. Too often that common sense is annoyingly slow in asserting itself. In the reformation which must be made and will be made, labor must play its part and I am sure it will. There must be reforms within its ranks.

Thoughtful conservatives assert often that it is the administration of the Wagner Act, rather than the law itself, that must be held blamable for most conditions complained about.

How intolerable some of these conditions are is illustrated by the following incident. A transmitter was being installed in the stu-

347

dios of a radio station. The wiring connections were as numerous and as delicately assembled as the veins and capillaries of the human body. The most skillful hand is required in the work of installation. Once the plant is in operation, the telephone company is expected to keep it functioning. The Electrical Workers' Union claimed the right to put in the plant. The telephone company, knowing that the union which obtruded itself could not do the work, refused to be responsible for what would happen afterwards. There was no way to proceed except to leave the work to the telephone experts while the electrical workers sat idle, yet compensated for their time. This mild form of brigandage has gone on more or less all over the country. It has opened the way to local labor leaders, often graduates from the criminal gangster class, to levy tribute on industry. There is no need to elaborate further. The public understands it.

We have some very able labor leaders in America, men who are entitled to rank as high in our affairs as the labor leaders in England. They will bring about a house cleaning, but it will not be an easy task. But we must go further than that. The labor laws should be refined according to the terms of experience and the dictates of fair judgment. Not only the employer but the labor union itself must be made amenable to law. There is much good in the English law.

The present conflict in industry between labor and management, with the public a trampled battleground, presents the severest test our democratic order has faced in eighty years. Under another rule the strong arm of dictatorship would decree a settlement. That way is repugnant to our democratic sense and will not be tolerated here.

It is an unhappy weakness among us that we do not grapple with menacing situations till they grow utterly unbearable. That stage in the present case has now been reached. The time has come when the nation must assert itself against new powers grown too dangerously great to be allowed ungoverned sway. The conflict must be brought within the rule of law. The nation cannot be subordinated longer to the power of such private groups and interests.

In the past, industry has employed tremendous sums of money for the control of politics and government. Great aggregations of labor, some of them under irresponsible control, reach now for a like control of politics and government. We see the working of these powers in a Congress warped this way and that by the pressure of arrogant interests. This makes a patchwork of our laws. Not principles of democracy and justice, but provisions put on by the power of special groups, tend to make up the content of our statute books. A government so prostituted cannot thrive. The time has come when the people as a nation must in self-defense assert themselves and put these overweening private powers in their place. Till that is done, the people are a prey to usurping interests.

At every such critical stage in our nation's history the answer has come in the emergence of a great leadership. The American statesmen whose names rank highest in our reverence make a roll of leaders who, standing above sordid and divisive strife, have called the people to join in raising the nation and the larger good above the claims of scrambling interests. When men like Washington and Lincoln have raised this banner, the people have always gladly followed them. They will follow again, I firmly believe, when the chance is given them.

The war, almost by necessity, intensified the race problem in America. The Negroes were called on, as citizens, to bear their equal share in the military services. They felt, not unnaturally, that this entitled them to their equal place in our economic and political life. The shortage of labor with the increased bargaining power which that conferred brought additional pressure from them. The overzealousness or want of discretion of the FEPC further sharpened the problem.

The issue had to be met. That was inevitable. I have no disposition to evade it but I think it is most unfortunate that events brought it to a head in the midst of war. It could be more tranquilly and satisfactorily settled when the country is more at rest emotionally. Things "in the blood" are not easily uprooted. Human feeling cannot be changed by edict. To deny the Negro the right of suffrage is to violate the Constitution. Nor should he be deprived of the deserts of his mind and character in the making of his own life. His place in industry and business is to be made by him. He must not be held down by prejudice, but neither can he be elevated by fanaticism. The sensible Negroes understand that it takes time to remove deep-rooted prejudice. They are entitled to the assurance, however, that the time required will be diligently, intelligently and progressively employed. While there is headway, there is hope. The FEPC has not sensed the deep meaning and implications of this

349

whole question. Its purpose seems to be revolutionary where only an evolutionary course is possible. In the North we are frightfully ignorant of the race problems of the South. Someone long ago said very wisely that the North has a sentimental interest in the race while the South has a sentimental interest in the individual. I think the case has been put as well as can be by William Cole Jones, chief editorial writer of the Atlanta *Journal* and one of the sanest minds in the South. About a year ago, when this subject was very much under discussion, he wrote me as follows:

"Good sense and good will together can work out the race problem in the South. It is partly an economic problem, and wholly a human one.

"Since Negroes make up a third of this region's population, a third of its wage earners and spenders, their productive and consumptive capacity must be increased so that they can contribute their due part to the common weal, if the South is to prosper as it should. This means that they must have the opportunity to get a useful education, to earn a decent living, to enjoy the health of sanitary and comfortable housing, and to share justly in the essentials of democratic government. Good sense tells us that to leave them in ignorance and penury would be a deadly drag on our progress and a stupid mistake from the standpoint of the white man's self-interest.

"But the right-hearted majority of the South, the real Land of Lee, has more than a merely prudential interest in its Negroes. It has good will toward them, a sense of responsibility and an understanding born of old acquaintance. Admittedly, there are obstacles and pitfalls. There are demagogues who traffic in prejudice and passion. There are long-distance doctrinaires who clamor for a mushroom millennium, forgetting that real reforms are the harvest of a gradual growth. And there are extremists who would burn down the house to exploit their social theories or fry their political fat. In spite of such confusions and impediments, the sanest and best minds in the South, with the co-operation of the best and sanest elements of our colored people, are moving toward feasible goals in a spirit of justice and Christian kindness.

"They cannot see the end. But they have a reasonable faith that as they go forward patiently, step by step, with good sense and good will, the clearer the light ahead will shine."

CHAPTER XXXI

THE LONDON CONFERENCE

◆

DID ROOSEVELT wreck the World Monetary and Economic Conference at London in 1933? That has been a much-mooted question over the years. The perspective developed by time gives a clearer view of the general economic situation at the time and its relation to the results of the conference. There was at that time an unprecedented ebb in the flow of commodities between nations. The aftermath of war had brought dislocations in trade. Instead of doing something to remedy this, the nations of the world outdid themselves in the adoption of stupid and destructive policies. They practiced economic nationalism in the most virulent form. No attention was given to the factors entering into the situation. They seemed to have forgotten that behind the creation of this planet was an Infinite Design, an inescapable law.

Climate and soil scatter and diversify the products of nature and this is the basis of our commerce. These products are so abundant in some sections as to create a vast surplus for which there is a great need elsewhere. This leads to a natural flow of trade to the common benefit. If we displace this very natural arrangement with a synthetic plan, we go counter to the laws of nature, and that is always dangerous. We could grow tropical fruits in the temperate climes by artificial means, but the extra cost would vastly exceed the expense of transportation from their natural habitat. Artificial devices to develop unnatural industries in this country were due more to corporate selfishness than to a broad view of our national welfare. Certain initial phases of it were temporarily helpful, but by and large, trade barriers led to price conspiracies with the building up of unearned fortunes and the creation of special interests which controlled our politics for more than a generation. Whether the international malady which stalled the world's economy originated with us or in a human nature much the same all over the world,

351

particularly in the controlling impulse of selfishness, the result was all the same.

An international conference to break the jam should have been called by Coolidge or Hoover. It was too late in 1933. If President Roosevelt brought the London conference to a precipitate end, that was only to hasten the inevitable. The President might have adopted a happier method, but the situation was an impossible one, a product of the untimeliness of the conference itself.

Millions of workers were everywhere unemployed. Wholesale commodity prices had declined one-third since 1929. Raw material prices were off from fifty to sixty per cent. The total value of world trade in the third quarter of 1932 was only one-third that of the corresponding period in 1929. The exchange of goods between nations had diminished twenty-five per cent. National incomes were down in many countries by more than forty per cent. Our loss in foreign trade exceeded that of all the rest of the world combined. Our exports in 1929 aggregated five and a quarter billions; three years later they had shrunk to one and two-thirds billions. Our imports in 1929 were four and one-third billions; in 1932, one and a third billions. Our 1932 exports and imports were the lowest in over twenty years. At the very beginning of the depression, there was an upward lift in tariff levels everywhere and emergency restrictions on international trade were imposed. This was oil on the depression fire. We curtailed our foreign loans in 1929 and this checked our exports and increased unemployment. The Allied debt and reparations hung like a pall over the international scene. Coolidge, asked about collecting the debts to us, replied, "They hired the money, didn't they?" His unbudging position discouraged efforts to break up the economic impasse.

Foreign nations, in an effort to meet their obligations, hoarded their resources and hopelessly tried to raise the level of their balance of trade. In a word, they crept into their shells. The confusion wrought by our misconceptions of the implications of the reparations and the Allied debts grew worse and worse. I cannot refrain from the opinion that we would have had a more wholesome situation if President Harding had adopted in 1922 my suggestion for starting the mass of reparations towards an orderly liquidation.

To meet the emergency which arose in every country, various restrictions were applied—quotas, import licenses, import surtaxes, increased duties and embargoes, administrative restrictions and control of foreign exchange. The preparatory commission of the League of Nations, which sought to bring the world to a quickened sense of something to be done, pointed out that "a general lowering of existing barriers to trade by all countries is unmistakably desirable if conditions of world prosperity are to be restored." Let it be emphasized that it further called attention to the imperative necessity of enabling debtor countries to pay their debts. This imposed upon the creditor nations the obligation to let the debtors pay in the only way that was humanly possible, with goods and services.

The new frontiers created by World War I increased the number of separate customs units in Europe from twenty to twenty-seven. The newly created states adopted a policy of self-containment and, as they thought, economic independence, by high tariff barriers. The older nations had made great gains in industry during the war. They unwisely concluded that these could be maintained by raising tariff rates. The result was not only economic rivalry, but political ill will.

We must confess with shame that it was the United States which led the way in tariff increases. Our Fordney-McCumber Act in the Harding administration was bad enough, but the Smoot-Hawley tariff of 1930 was far worse. This brought the duties on our imports to the highest level in American history. More than half the nations of the earth protested and retaliated by imposing restrictions on our exports. Switzerland was embittered when a handful of watch and clock makers in this country procured the passage of a schedule harmful, if not almost destructive, to the Swiss industry which had given the world an unrivalled craftsmanship. The Smoot-Hawley Act led to a political overturn in our country. The Democrats in 1930 elected a majority of the House of Representatives. This body promptly passed a resolution suggesting international action to reduce excessive duties and eliminate destructive and unfair trade practices. Even the Senate, then Republican, accepted it, but it was vetoed by President Hoover. The Democratic measure vetoed by the President requested also the taking of steps to create an international economic conference and authorized him to negotiate reciprocal trade agreements. His veto completed the circle of economic isolation.

353

Where we had led the way, other countries followed. During 1930 six European nations made general upward revisions in their tariff and all other Continental states but two made changes, though not in all instances so drastic. Only three Continental countries reduced their tariffs. British policy took the form of almost complete abandonment of free trade by the United Kingdom. Then was added the colonial arrangement based on Empire preferences. The British government attempted to induce several Continental countries to make a twenty-five per cent reduction in their duties on the promise that the British would not increase the levies on noncompetitive products which had remained on the free list. This effort did not succeed. England then tried other devices but the tendency constantly ran in the direction of higher rates. The Ottawa agreement, tying closer the trade relations of the mother country and the colonies, occasioned great concern in America. It was predicted that the seventy per cent of the imports into Great Britain from the United States which were free of duty would shrink under the new arrangement to twenty per cent. The English government recognized that this situation would be a bar to the success of the London conference. To meet this, Neville Chamberlain, then Chancellor of the Exchequer, stated in a speech before the House of Commons a short time before the conference assembled, that the quotas would have to be reduced, if not removed, and prohibitively high tariffs, as well, if any good was to come of the conference.

When Great Britain went off the gold standard in 1931, France led the way on the Continent to reviving the system of quotas on a broad scale. Many European states followed. Such was the sorry picture presented at the beginning of the London conference. If the mad rush towards national self-sufficiency, which started at the time of the administrations of Coolidge and Hoover, had been stayed and all nations had been assembled then to foster international trade, we would have had a different world.

For several years, an international economic conference had been discussed by economists, bankers and others, but it remained for the League of Nations to give the project form. A preparatory commission was appointed to make a survey of world economies and present an agenda for the conference to come.

Not long after the inauguration of President Roosevelt, foreign economic authorities and statesmen came to Washington, notably

354

Ramsay MacDonald of Great Britain and Edouard Herriot of France, to discuss the conference plan. Their presence at our capital attracted a great deal of newspaper notice, and for a time it seemed that America was assuming the leadership in an enterprise which held every prospect of success. Mr. Roosevelt and his advisers made it clear at the outset that the question of the Allied debt could not and should not be brought into the conference. After the presidential election in 1932, President Hoover had communicated with President-elect Roosevelt, stressing the importance of initiating some movement to clarify the problem of the international debt. Roosevelt and Hoover were in agreement that if the obligations of our debtors were merged with consideration of tariffs and other economic questions a bad odor would be given the whole procedure. If concessions were made by the creditor nation these might be regarded as having been used in a trading process to gain concessions which otherwise would not have been made. The wave of confidence, following the visit of statesmen and economists from overseas, was checked by developments not long delayed. President Roosevelt, in his inaugural address, had said that while tariff reform must be regarded as an imperative objective of the future, his major concern was building up our national economy. It soon became apparent that what he had in mind was stimulation of trade by lifting the level of prices. To those who were watching the current of events understandingly this had a plain meaning. The program outlined by the agenda prepared for the conference would conflict with what was taking form in the mind of the President. While the conference was in session commodity prices were increasing in our country. This was encouraging to the President. The bank program, the NRA, the AAA and other measures resorted to were, temporarily at least, dispelling the clouds of depression. The President was getting a fine press and in his second fireside speech, on May 7, he made it clear that he was more than satisfied with the policies which he had inaugurated, even though they all pointed to our going it alone, at least for the time.

In America, our preliminary arrangements for the conference were not orderly. That they were not well matured was due to the tremendous task which had fallen upon our government at the beginning of the Roosevelt administration. The halls of Congress and the White House were engrossed with tasks which our economic emergency had thrust upon them. The conference assembled only four months after inauguration day and the delegation was made up in May. The rush of events made better plans and understandings difficult.

The delegates selected were Cordell Hull, President and Chairman; James M. Cox, Vice-President and Vice-Chairman; United States Senators Key Pittman, of Nevada, and James Couzens, of Michigan; Samuel D. McReynolds, Chairman of the Foreign Relations Committee of the House; and Ralph W. Morrison, of Texas, who had a very successful business career in his state. The delegation was not properly put together, as President Roosevelt later recognized. The Executive Officer was William C. Bullitt; Financial Adviser, James P. Warburg; Legal Adviser, Fred K. Nielsen; Chief Technical Adviser, Herbert Feis. Among other technical advisers were Henry Morgenthau, Sr., and Frederick E. Murphy. Their assignment was primarily to see what might be done to control the international surplus in wheat. Mr. Murphy was publisher of the Minneapolis *Tribune* and was thoroughly familiar with the facts and conditions of the northwest wheat belt. The wheat problem had long interested the senior Morgenthau.

Also named as adviser was Ray Atherton, attached to the United States Embassy in London. He had a fine career in the diplomatic service and is now serving as our ambassador to Canada. He met regularly with the delegation. James Clement Dunn, long an attaché of the State Department in Washington, was Secretary. Among assistants to the delegation was H. R. Mengert. The press officers were Charles Michelson and Elliott Thurston, both capable newspapermen of long experience.

Not finding it convenient to sail with the delegation, I took a later ship, the *Olympic,* leaving New York on Decoration Day, 1933. With me were Mrs. Cox and my two daughters, Anne and Barbara, now Mrs. Louis G. Johnson and Mrs. Stanley C. Kennedy, Jr., respectively. On the same ship were Mr. Warburg, George L. Harrison, president of the Federal Reserve Bank of New York, and Oliver Mitchell Wentworth Sprague. The last two were to give specific attention to the stabilization of world currencies. Mr. Warburg was to serve with them and was to be regarded as adviser to the President. While Mr. Warburg was to acquaint President Roosevelt with the developments in London, Bernard W. Baruch, it was understood, was to advise with the President at the Washington end. Baruch was definitely of this impression when I talked with him before sailing. Raymond Moley, however, is on record with an entirely different report. He insists, to put it in his own words, that Baruch was to sit in and advise with the President in Moley's absence and that it was Moley who was to be the President's adviser. Evidently the two men labored under different impressions. Baruch, however, was a man practiced in finance and business, while Moley was without training in either.

To newspaper reporters I said before sailing that the conference would be a success if the world had gained some sense out of its terrible experience in the war. If the loss of life and wealth and the disjointed state of our international economy had not removed prejudices and shaken us loose from traditional policies now outworn and useless, then there was little hope of accomplishment in London.

In the cheer of sunny skies and English hospitality matters shaped quickly for the beginning of the conference. Premier Ramsay Mac-Donald was the presiding officer. The delegations were welcomed by King George V, and there was fine heartiness in his greetings as he spoke for about half an hour. He was not a commanding personality in the same sense as was his father, King Edward VII; yet though he possessed little power under England's democratic arrangements, still he looked like a man who had formed convictions and might yield them with some degree of stubbornness. He gave the members of the conference a distinct impression that their presence at the center of the British Empire was a highly esteemed compliment.

The preparatory commission of the League of Nations had recommended a presiding officer in general charge of the conference and the establishment of an Economic Commission and a Monetary Commission as the two main branches. M. H. Colijn, Minister of State and Prime Minister and Minister of the Colonies of the Netherlands, was chosen to head the Economic Commission. He was a man of unusual industry and well grounded in matters affecting international economy. My name was proposed by our delegation to head the Monetary Commission, and France presented the name of Georges Bonnet, Minister of Finance. It was the rule in these international assemblies that all decisions must be unanimous. Notwithstanding this, the delegates from our country and those from France continued to press Bonnet's name and mine. Bonnet was very eager for the place. I was naturally complimented by the proposal of my name but would not have been greatly disappointed if I had not been chosen. Bonnet could not speak English and I could not speak French. He was an impetuous man, well versed in finance but not popular with members of the conference. Some events of the past war have since brought discredit to his name. He did not respond to the challenges of the hour as did the patriots who held true to their principles throughout France's recent trying days. Bonnet and I conversed through a very attractive member of the French delegation, one of the most popular men in the conference, J. J. Bizot. He was one of the Governors of the Bank of France and an accomplished linguist. Through him, Bonnet, speaking to me one day, observed, "France will not look with favor upon the selection of someone to head the Monetary Commission who comes from a country which has recently gone off the gold standard." My response was, "Nor will the United States look with favor upon the election of a man presented by a country which has repudiated its debts." This exchange was picked up by the press and given worldwide publicity. Not long after this, Bizot withdrew Bonnet from the contest and I was selected. I was far from expert in matters of finance and recognized my chief duty as keeping the Monetary Commission and its committees and subcommittees in motion and in hand as well. It was a pleasant assignment and not a single unpleasant incident came from it. At the last session of the Monetary Commission, Neville Chamberlain stated that in all his experiences with international gatherings, he had seen nothing superior to the way in which the Monetary Commission had been handled. With seemingly great sincerity, he assured me that his observation was not to be taken as a perfunctory gesture.

I never could quite understand why President Roosevelt tendered me the position of head of the Federal Reserve Banking System, which I declined. He had also offered me one of the ambassadorial stations in Europe, which I did not accept. In explanation of his first suggestion he stated that he wanted a businessman rather than a banker.

It is doubtful whether there was ever a more representative body of men assembled anywhere. Every organized government sent delegates. If one were to point to the most commanding personage there, he would probably pick the Right Honorable Jan Christiaan Smuts, Minister of Justice from the Union of South Africa. Smuts had been a warm personal friend and adviser of Woodrow Wilson in the days of Versailles and afterwards. No one, although he was a world figure, was more modest in this gathering than he. He brought with him thirty delegates and advisers.

Dr. Hjalmar Schacht, president of the Reichsbank, was the foremost representative of Germany. I came to know him well. In personal appearance, there was nothing unusual about him unless it was the very high collar he wore. He was regarded as the ablest banker in Europe but not the most ethical. His hobby was raising hogs on his farm and, singularly, his pride was in the Yorkshire breed, an importation from England. In one of the plenary sessions of the conference, when all delegations were assembled, he was scheduled to speak. Ramsay MacDonald from the chair announced that Schacht's address would be in German. Without a word of explanation, Schacht spoke in English, and perfectly. The Secretary to the German delegation was Otto Furst von Bismarck, grandson of the Iron Chancellor. He was attached to the German Embassy in London, a handsome man of agreeable manners. He and his beautiful wife, a Swede by birth, were very popular socially.

Australia was properly proud of its Minister in London, the Right Honorable S. M. Bruce. He had served long in that station. He was a very able speaker and his outlook on and comprehension of economic matters were wide. On the subject of wheat, its surplus and conservation, he was the leading authority. The ill-fated Engelbert Dollfuss, Federal Chancellor of Austria, was the ranking representative from that country, the future of which at that moment was in doubt. There had always been a question as to whether, in the breaking up of the Austro-Hungarian state, Austria as then constituted was a logical economic unit. A most excellent associate of Dollfuss was Victor Kienbock, chairman of the National Bank of Austria, not a brilliant nor a showy person but a man of long experience in banking and head of one of the most important subcommittees of the Monetary Commission. Schacht, in discussing Austria with me, said it could not make its way and that Germany was just waiting to catch it as it fell.

359

The delegation from the United Kingdom, headed by the Right Honorable J. Ramsay MacDonald, Prime Minister and First Lord of the Treasury, was outstanding. MacDonald's chief personal assistant was Col. Sir M. P. A. Hankey, Secretary to the Cabinet and to the Committee of Imperial Defence. The Right Honorable Neville Chamberlain was MacDonald's main dependence. He leaned, too, on the Right Honorable Sir John Simon, Secretary of State for Foreign Affairs. Young Malcolm MacDonald, M.P., was an attaché assistant. The Right Honorable Sir Philip Cunliffe-Lister, Secretary of State for the Colonies, had a world-wide acquaintance; he and his wife gave many small but very attractive luncheons during the noon adjournment hours. The Right Honorable Walter Runciman, President of the Board of Trade, was prominent in the councils of this delegation. A specialist in agriculture was the Right Honorable Walter E. Elliot, Minister of Agriculture and Fisheries. Sir F. W. Leith-Ross, Chief Economic Adviser to His Majesty's Government in the United Kingdom, spoke for the Bank of England and was in close touch with Messrs. Harrison, Warburg and Sprague of our country.

The Canadian Prime Minister, Richard B. Bennett, seemed equally at home in the British or American delegations. He was conservative in type, a thoughtful, gracious person. He was a bachelor and eminent lawyer. Among his clients was a maiden lady who, on her death, left him a large fortune with the condition imposed that as long as he lived he was to continue in the public service. He now resides permanently in England.

China had a strong delegation headed by Dr. T. V. Soong, Minister of Finance in his own country. Japan was already beginning to show her rapacious designs. I discussed this with Soong and I shall never forget his response: "The Chinese are the most patient people in the world. We look unceasingly to the future and never lose sight of ultimate objectives. It may require ten years, or fifty years, or one hundred years, but it matters not how long, China will drive Japan into the sea." Dr. V. K. Wellington Koo, another delegate very well known in this country, was then Minister to Paris. China had a multiplicity of representatives.

A very picturesque figure was tall, gray-haired economist Gustav Cassel. He came from Sweden. He looked like a rare old print. He must have been taller than Lincoln. He was a progressive and not very far removed from Keynes' saner ideas. Cassel died not long

360

ago. While he was best known as a student of the problems of money and foreign exchange, his thinking carried him into other but more or less related fields. It is interesting to observe that in the decade following the international conference he held and expressed very positive convictions against the theory of a Planned Economy. One of his last observations was, "Planned Economy will always tend to develop into Dictatorship." His words of warning should be preserved, bearing in mind that his native country, Sweden, leans strongly to Socialistic tendencies, and because of this I quote further from his statement:

"The existence of some sort of parliament is no guarantee against planned economy being developed into dictatorship. On the contrary, experience has shown that representative bodies are unable to fulfill all the multitudinous functions connected with economic leadership without becoming more and more involved in the struggle between competing interests, with the consequence of a moral decay ending in party—if not individual—corruption. Examples of such a degrading development are indeed in many countries accumulating at such a speed as must fill every honorable citizen with the gravest apprehensions as to the future of the representative system. But apart from that, this system cannot possibly be preserved, if parliaments are constantly overworked by having to consider an infinite mass of the most intricate questions relating to private economy. The parliamentary system can be saved only by wise and deliberate restriction of the functions of parliaments. . . .

"Economic dictatorship is much more dangerous than people believe. Once authoritative control has been established it will not always be possible to limit it to the economic domain. If we allow economic freedom and self-reliance to be destroyed, the powers standing for Liberty will have lost so much in strength that they will not be able to offer any effective resistance against a progressive extension of such destruction to constitutional and public life generally. And if this resistance is gradually given up—perhaps without people ever realizing what is actually going on—such fundamental values as personal liberty, freedom of thought and speech and independence of science are exposed to imminent danger. What stands to be lost is nothing less than the whole of that civilization that we have inherited from generations which once fought hard to lay its foundations and even gave their life for it."

The Prime Minister of France and Minister of War as well, Edouard Daladier, stood at the head of the delegation from France. Second in command was Georges Bonnet. Daladier seemed young for his important place in the affairs of the French nation, but he zealously guarded the gold standard cause. I regarded J. J. Bizot, a career man and one of the Governors of the Bank of France, and M. Charles Rist, also of the bank, as the most useful men in the French list. Bizot spoke several languages, knew the question of money and economics, and no one in the conference drew to himself more friends.

One of the strongest men in the conference was Guido Jung, Minister of Finance in Italy. Hitler had not up to this time invested Mussolini with his hatred of the Jews. Jung was a Jew, born in Baden-Baden, in Germany. The attention which he received from Ramsay MacDonald was noticeable. MacDonald often told me of his high personal regard for the man and conceded him a high place in international fiscal affairs. Joe Nathan, representing the Bank of Italy and the National Institute of Exchange, was a hard-headed, calm, industrious member of the conference. I asked him how he compared Mussolini with Napoleon. This was his reply: "Napoleon would not come up to his bootstraps."

Noticeably self-conscious were the delegates from Japan. That country was then following its conquest of Manchuria under the critical eye of the world. Their representatives seemed bent on being ambassadors of good will. The significance of their general demeanor was clear.

Ranking with Nathan of Italy and Bizot and Rist of France for high efficiency and conscientious labors was M. L. J. A. Trip, President of the Netherlands Bank.

Dr. Eduard Beneš, Minister for Foreign Affairs in Czechoslovakia, attracted much attention. Czechoslovakia, a child of the treaty of Versailles, seemed to be sentimentally regarded with special favor.

The work of the conference started off smoothly. Every plenary meeting of the conference was well attended. MacDonald presided with great dignity and with tact except in one instance. In opening the conference he made reference to international debts. It had been definitely understood that this subject was taboo. Secretary Hull was very much displeased at this.

The subcommittees of the Monetary and Economic Commissions settled down to their work as assigned by the two chairmen, and there was scarcely a day when interesting and informative discussions were not heard. An era of good feeling prevailed. Bitterness towards Germany was not in evidence. That feeling did flare up in one of the subcommittee meetings, induced by the introduction of a very indiscreet resolution by one of the German delegates. He was promptly put in his place by Leon Fraser of the Bank for International Settlements.

Maxim Litvinoff of Russia mixed freely with the delegates. He was indeed an ambassador of good will. Doubtless sensitive to the fact that the Soviet government had not been generally recognized by other nations, he was modest and diplomatic in his approaches. I saw a great deal of him, for I was anxious to know as much as possible about what was taking place in his country. He addressed the conference in one of its early sessions and made a fine impression. He opposed trade barriers and urged good feeling among nations.

As a part of the routine of the conference, a small group assembled every morning at eleven o'clock in MacDonald's rooms. Colijn and I sat on either side of him. Neville Chamberlain was always present, as was Jung of Italy. At different times chairmen of the various delegations were brought in either at their own request or by invitation of Prime Minister MacDonald. Sir Maurice Hankey was always there. I think it safe to say he did not miss a single session. The absence of anyone at the appointed hour did not delay the meeting. MacDonald started on the minute. Colijn and I reported whatever of interest was developing in the work and deliberations of our subcommittees. In the Economic Commission the economists, trade specialists and statisticians were helpful in the general discussions.

It was soon apparent, however, that most of the countries were holding out against disturbing the tariff schedules which gave their own countries an advantage. The gospel of economic freedom had at that time very few supporters.

Everyone wanted to know what progress was being made towards the stabilization of currencies. The Americans assigned to this subject, Messrs. Harrison, Warburg and Sprague, were industriously and vigilantly devoted to their task. They wisely kept their own counsels while striving to gain an agreement.

I became convinced early in the conference that one of the soundest minds was Leon Fraser, connected with the Bank for International Settlements. His administration of the affairs of the bank had brought close and wide contact with world economy and finance. He was attached to the Monetary Commission, and I saw a great deal of him. He never spoke without knowing what he was talking about. His mind was as clear as crystal in its comprehension of vital matters. When I returned from London, I said to Gordon Rentschler of the National City Bank in New York that if I were running a financial institution in this country, I would lose no time in employing Mr. Fraser. He became president of the First National Bank of New York. His tragic death not long since is a great loss to the country. In the early autumn of 1944 he and I had a long visit at my hotel in New York and recalled events and personalities of the London conference. Just a few days before his death we had some correspondence on the subject of the International Bank recommended at Bretton Woods and it is well to put down what was probably his last observation on this subject. In part he said:

"My own feeling is that the Fund is much too big and too theoretical and will not give the expected results. However, the world will not come to an end if it is adopted, as now seems probable, and it will give a temporary fillip to international trade at a time when our problem will not be to get the trade, but to get out the production. Furthermore, our enthusiastic friends forget that credit is debt and the real question is whether we do not have enough debt in the world already plus some more which is coming and which is unavoidable."

In the perspective of time, it is very apparent just what put the conference on the rocks. Basically, the reason was, as already stated, that it came too late. Too many obstructing arrangements were now to be overcome. It would have been better if a complete understanding had been arrived at between the President and Secretary of State Hull. The Secretary was left under the impression that the President would ask Congress for such delegation of powers by the Senate as would enable the conference to regard our decisions as final. Other nations had had experience with the processes of our democracy and had discovered that treaty agreements made by the President were often not approved by the Senate. The crime of the senatorial cabal of 1919–1920 was still fresh in memory. While the conference was in session the President cabled Secretary Hull that he was not going to ask the Senate for such delegation of power. The President and almost everyone else knew Secretary Hull's theories on international trade.

In the first days of the conference, premiers from the important nations and even many of the smaller nations delivered addresses. Secretary Hull cabled the text of his speech to the White House in advance. It came back drastically revised.

This was disquieting. It would also have been better if the President had reduced to comprehensive form and in more or less detail to the financial advisers, Harrison, Warburg and Sprague, just what was in his mind on the subject of stabilization of currencies. These three gentlemen doubtless felt that they knew how far the President would go if concessions had to be made. It must be said to their credit that they were unsparing in their efforts to implement the wishes of the President so as to avoid disagreement with other nations. It was a great mistake for Raymond Moley to go to London. In the view of the conference, his coming discredited Hull. With the President's rejection of the plan tentatively agreed upon for stabilization, the whole machinery of the conference was put out of gear. Prime Minister MacDonald asked that Secretary Hull and I come to his office at 10 Downing Street at four o'clock in the afternoon. He was both hurt and angry over what had happened, observing that he had left the President not a great while before and he thought that in all essential matters they understood each other, not only as to the need but the work of the conference. At eleven o'clock the next morning, the usual group assembled in the Prime Minister's office. MacDonald formally advised us of the cable which had come from the President. Colijn, of the Netherlands, was very explosive, even vitriolic in his comments. When he finished, the entire group turned their eyes on me. It was a tense moment. I reminded my associates that a few days before Colijn had shown temper over a seemingly trivial matter which had come up. He apologized in good spirit and remarked, "At times, we Dutchmen are a little hard to get on with." Looking at Colijn, who had precipitated a rather trying scene, I reminded him that the man who had exploded the "bombshell" came from ancestors of Holland birth, and for the moment at least we should be as forbearing towards our President as we had been of Colijn. This occasioned a general laugh, and then as best I could I sought to explain the situation at home out of which had come the disturbing development.

We were not a homogeneous people as were other nations. Millions of workmen were walking the streets, products of the farm were not meeting the cost of production, factories were closed, as were many banks, and we were attempting to work out of a desperate situation. It was a critical moment for the President. He had gained favor at home by the handling of the bank situation and now that that was over, measures equally effective dealing with our trade conditions were expected of him. It is apparent that his first objective was to raise the price levels on commodities. A cheap dollar obviously would be helpful. Stabilization at the moment would upset his plans. Obviously the President was intent, for the time at least, on keeping us self-contained. He wanted to bring some measure of order out of confusion at home before going into projects outlined for the conference. The President, in his talks with Mac-Donald, Herriot and others in this country, could not have foreseen the conditions which came so fast. Roosevelt wanted the conference to go on. He even suggested a recess. While he did not say so, it was clear that things in London were moving too fast for him. By slowing them up or bringing about a recess, he hoped that the measures which had been taken here would have time to make such headway that stabilization could then be brought about with no harm.

Nevertheless, there was a feeling in London that the President was not dealing frankly with the conference. There was an impression that he had deliberately sought to break it up. One's hindsight is always much better than his foresight. Looking at it from the vantage of the years, it would seem now that the President might well have made frank acknowledgment of the difficulty he was in. Again, he might have felt that the conference could accomplish nothing in the way of a better economic order and that stabilization could be brought about at any time without the aid of a conference. The central banks and the governments of a few countries could easily accomplish that. This, as a matter of fact, is virtually what happened in the beginning of 1934. Aside from the stabilization of currencies, a great deal of time was needed to put into effect what the conference in its wisdom and through its surveys might have agreed upon as the solution of economic ills. During the course of the uncertain days after the receipt of Roosevelt's disrupting cable, he sought to impress upon the conference through his representatives that it should take a longer-range view. This but confirms my contention that he was playing for time. Most statesmen in his place might have done the same thing.

If stabilization had been achieved, the conference would have ended in very much better humor and the chances are it would not have been generally pronounced a failure. The gold block countries, France, Holland, Switzerland, Germany, Italy and Belgium, of course felt that if the currency situation was not remedied they would be forced off the gold standard. Our financial advisers were caught between two fires, the position which the President held to and the apprehension of the gold bloc. Men expert in finance are not agreed even now that stabilization, particularly bringing the dollar and pound to a new ratio, would have interfered with Roosevelt's domestic program. Money is a very involved subject at best, and it is pretty difficult for experts dealing with it to arrive at a common ground. This fact was very apparent to the lay members of the conference. One group was following the original Keynes theory. Another group followed his revised formulas and yet the two groups did not concur for the simple reason that Keynes himself within the course of the year had changed his views. John Maynard Keynes was pretty generally regarded as an extremist. Certainly this was the more or less common appraisal in England. That the Bank of England, that conservative body which so long ruled the destinies of currency, departed from its traditions and accepted more progressive ideas is evidenced by the fact that Keynes became a member of the Board of Governors of the Bank of England.

One reason given by the President for his opposition to the stabilization agreement was that it dealt only with a few large countries, probably meaning England and the representatives of the gold bloc. His insistence that the small countries should be included was not taken seriously. Few of them had a central bank and time would have been required to make them eligible. Besides, his contention that a balanced budget was a prerequisite to stabilization was not taken in good grace.

Moley's going to London, as I have said, was a mistake. Hull and he were unfriendly. Hull was an orthodox Democrat and did not agree with parts of the New Deal; Moley, as measured by the terms of those days, was radical. Hull was highly respected in the conference, not only because of the position he occupied with the leading nation of the world, but also because his sincerity and his manners, those of a courtly Southern gentleman, put him in high favor. If Moley had gone to London more unostentatiously, there probably would have been no feeling among the delegates that he was seeking to discredit Hull.

Moley contends even yet that he was asked to go to London in order to ascertain what had gone awry with our delegation and to see whether he could not straighten things out. Hull claims he was never sent to London. Moley states specifically that when he left Washington to meet the President on a ship in Canadian waters he did so with the full knowledge and consent of the Executive. The President told a different story.

When I returned from London I did not go to Hyde Park as other members of the delegations had done but advised the President that if he wanted a report from me I would be very glad to come to Washington at his pleasure and convenience. He finally indicated a time. We had dinner together alone in the White House. He seemed highly entertained on learning of some developments and episodes that had not been reported to him. He was kind enough to say that I had given him the best word picture he had had and that as soon as I returned home to Dayton I should dictate as nearly as possible what I had said to him and have it locked up.

The President, as it was reported to me, was turning off the lights in his ship cabin in Canadian waters before retiring when a wireless message came from Moley that he would see him in the morning. The President tossed in his bed, wondering what could have happened in Washington. Nothing but an emergency, surely, would have prompted Moley to make such a trip. The President greeted Moley before he had time to set foot on the craft, with the question: "Ray, what has happened?"

Moley replied, "I came to say good-bye."

"But," said the President, "I said good-bye to you before I left Washington."

Newspaper reporters and the moving-picture men as well, doubtless advised in advance, had gathered to take the whole thing in. It smacked of stage-setting to make the trip to Europe more spectacular and more impressive to members of the conference. It is my judgment that this was the beginning of the break between Roosevelt and Moley. Moley in most respects was unquestionably the ablest member of the "brain trusters." Whether he possessed the political genius of Louis Howe is another question. He could have been spoiled by the deference which the President gave to his opinions in the beginning of their relationship and the degree to which the President leaned on him in making important assignments. Another fact bearing on the case was that the man was thoroughly tired out, mentally and physically. His inordinate industry was well known to those familiar with what was going on in Washington.

If a Messiah, to use a term born of current comment at the conference, were to appear, vested with the powers of compromise, then Moley's arrival was well timed. The wheels of the conference had practically stopped. The delegates believed that since a cable from Roosevelt had brought an end to things, here now came a man very close to him to render judgments which would prevail. There had been a great deal in the papers about the cross-purposes of members of our delegation. It was even said that a good deal of quarreling was going on. This was not true. A false impression was created by some of the Americans who talked too freely to newspapermen. To put an end to this, Secretary Hull insisted that nothing should be given to the press without his approval. Admittedly, uncontrolled publicity had done harm to the purposes of the conference and yet we now find criticism in this country of a lack of publicity at international conferences. The Fathers who framed our Constitution worked behind closed doors, knowing that conflicting views in the convention published at that time would have magnified differences and created distrust generally.

Moley expressly stated to the press when he arrived that he did not come with delegated powers or specific instructions. He was there only to render such aid as he could to our delegation in the conference.

All of this was taken with a grain of salt. When Moley arrived, he did not take quarters with the delegates. Instead, he went to the American Embassy, the English seat of our American government. There most of his conferences were held, conferences in which Hull was not included. Ambassador Robert Bingham was not at all pleased with this arrangement. He told me from the outset that Moley's coming was a mistake. He could not reject the request that Moley

369

make quarters at the Embassy. In mid-ocean, so Bingham advised me, Moley had sent a cable asking that he be permitted to bring with him his financial adviser, Herbert Bayard Swope. Bingham felt that he could do nothing but acquiesce in that. A day or two later came another cable asking whether Moley could also bring with him Arthur Mullen, Jr., of Nebraska, son of the Western politician. This Bingham flatly refused.

Moley had only such contacts with Hull as courtesy required. This might have been justified in his mind by presidential instructions to Hull when he crossed the seas to have nothing to do with the question of stabilization. But Moley was not long in getting in touch with Warburg, Harrison and Sprague and monetary representatives of other governments. Hull knew of these conferences and was humiliated by what was going on. It was then and still is my opinion that if Mrs. Hull and I had not induced the Secretary to spend a week end in the country in this trying time, Hull would have forwarded his resignation to the President. What Moley conceived to be important messages to Roosevelt were sent by himself. Occasionally, Hull was asked to transmit certain dispatches but they were conceived and shaped by Moley. Before Moley arrived it looked as though there could be an agreement on stabilization on the base of four to one between the dollar and the pound. This, Mr. Roosevelt rejected. Then Moley embarked upon a new departure, hoping that it would have the endorsement of the President. Hull was disturbed. I asked him simply to be patient and await Moley's disappointment, sure to follow. We knew what Moley was about, and as I put it to the Secretary, "He will have the trap door sprung on him just as it was on you." That is what occurred. What Moley proposed was the vaguest sort of declaration, in which the various nations would piously affirm their desire to return ultimately to a gold standard of some sort. It was in no sense a stabilization. It was merely a vague declaration of intent to stabilize at some time in the future.

That there was an entire misconception in London of the purpose of Moley's visit, as expressed by him, is confirmed again in his written word. It relates to Moley's first meeting with the President when he came back. Moley observes: "I doubt that anything anyone might have said to him (the President) that morning would have ruffled his egregious satisfaction and good humor. He made no comment about what had happened to me except to say that it was too bad *we* 'couldn't have foreseen that I would be greeted as the Saviour of the Conference.'" Moley's reference to Louis Howe was this: "Louis was less subtle when we met that day, with the air of a man who felt he had administered a resounding spanking to someone who badly needed it. He said, 'Well, what happened to you over there? Did they take *you* into camp?'"

Hull, faithful to his charge, attempted to keep the conference going. A meeting called for the specific purpose of adjourning the conference was addressed by Hull. In a moving speech he succeeded in avoiding a termination of the conference so soon after the presidential "bombshell." It was a fine effort and a temporary triumph which he must even yet hark back to with pride. There was no heart in the conference, however, after this. In a plenary session of the whole conference, Colijn, the head of the Economic Commission, spoke of the future, but less hopefully than did I. I insisted, because I believed, that the day would come when the nations of the world, more mindful of the mistakes in national policies, would recognize that some sort of international agreement must come about. The conference was about to end when I remembered that there had been no resolution of thanks either suggested or adopted in courtesy to the English government for the magnificent and hospitable entertainment it had provided. I stepped up to the chair of Ramsay MacDonald, who was presiding, with my suggestion. He asked me to draw a resolution quickly. I did so, including a reference to the Premier himself for the way in which he had played his part as the official head of the conference. The reference to him compelled his leaving the chair, which he yielded to me. I put the motion and then, turning to MacDonald, who had resumed his place, I said: "Mr. Chairman, I beg to report that upon *this resolution* the conference votes its unanimous approval." Perhaps I did not intend emphasis on "this resolution" but, be that as it may, the delegates got the point and I think it was one of the happy moments of the conference.

CHAPTER XXXII

SIDELIGHTS ON THE CONFERENCE

◆

Ramsay MacDonald liked to discuss the relative merits of the forms of government maintained by the United States and by Great Britain. He insisted that the advantage lay with Britain. Theirs, he thought, was a more genuine democracy. He called attention to the important fact that in our country a statesman in the Congress can be retired by a minority group with a balance of power between other groups. He doubtless had in mind such groups as the Anti-Saloon League, labor, agriculture and business blocs. In England, the government might fall and the members of the ministry remain in Parliament. Over there, a regime that proved neither competent nor popular could be ousted at any time. Here, administrations hold for a fixed term of years.

One evening when MacDonald, Chamberlain and I were discussing the two forms of government, I said that according to my observation the English operated much like Knute Rockne, the great football coach. He had first, second and third teams. This seemed to be a part of the English process. I remarked that in looking over the English, I felt I could pick out two Prime Ministers for the future. Both MacDonald and Chamberlain seemed much interested and asked who they were. I named Anthony Eden and Walter E. Elliott. Eden had hardly risen above the horizon at that time. He was not even a delegate to the conference. He was Parliamentary Under Secretary for Foreign Affairs with the London government, much of his time being given to disarmament problems that were then under consideration at Geneva. He was in and out of the conference and I saw a great deal of him.

Elliott had married the youngest daughter of H. H. Asquith, who became Lord Oxford. He was a Scotchman and a clear thinker and he could tie thought and phrase together cleverly. I think he is still in the government. Not long after this, Ramsay MacDonald and his daughter gave a luncheon for Mr. and Mrs. Hull and Mrs. Cox and myself at Chequers, the summer home provided for the Prime Minister. I chanced to be seated beside Mrs. Anthony Eden, a beautiful woman. I told her of my conversation with MacDonald and Chamberlain. For a moment she did not seem interested, then turned on me scornfully and said, "The thing about you Americans that I don't like is that you indulge in such obvious flattery." When Anthony Eden was in this country not long ago, a friend of both of us related to him the conversation between his wife and me. He was much amused and said he hoped that I would have it out with her on my next trip to England.

While MacDonald lived at Lossiemouth, in North Scotland, he was not given, like Chamberlain, to piscatorial pleasures. Fishing was the latter's great recreation. That reminds me that when I saw President Roosevelt before leaving for the conference, he told me that when the date of the conference was under discussion, MacDonald had told him it must not interfere with the grouse-shooting season. Roosevelt remarked on the binding force of English habit.

MacDonald had the touch of eloquence. I saw him every morning regularly in his office and at luncheons and dinners. William C. Bullitt, who was assigned as Executive Officer of our delegation, irritated MacDonald. The Premier told me that during the contest for the presidency of the Monetary Commission between Bonnet of France and myself, Bullitt went to 10 Downing Street with the ultimatum that if the English did not join in support of the American delegation it would take the first boat home. MacDonald said further, "He snoops around too much. He takes my secretary out, gives her a good dinner and thinks he is gaining the secrets of 10 Downing Street." Bullitt, who had spent a good deal of time in Europe, offered advice one morning to the delegates with a sophisticated air. They should not leave papers lying on their desks. "Everything should be locked up," he said. "We should all be very careful with whom we talk and make sure if important matters are discussed that no Dictograph wires are exposed in the room." I told him that if I believed this about the English I would be disposed to leave London at once.

Neville Chamberlain and his wife were lovers, with beautiful devotion, all their lives. Whenever he was to speak in the conference, she would be in the audience. One day he invited Premier Bennett of Canada and me to lunch at his residence. We were the only guests. In the hallway was a fine portrait of Mrs. Chamberlain, made in her younger days. Both Bennett and I remarked upon it with enthusiasm. Whereupon Chamberlain said with impressive earnestness, "Yes, that is a beautiful portrait, but, you know, to me Mrs. Chamberlain is more beautiful now than she ever was." When Chamberlain failed at Munich the fact was due entirely to his imputing his own honesty of purpose to others. He was a forthright person, but one had to know him well to reach the depths of his fine character. We had considerable communication with each other after the conference through letters and cables.

Mrs. Cox and my daughters, Anne and Barbara, and I did not remain long in the hotel. Ray Atherton, with the American Embassy in London, remarked to Lady Fitzgerald, who owned Warren House near Stanmore, that we were looking for a place in the country. She had been greatly interested in my campaign for the League of Nations and since she did not intend to occupy the place that summer, she offered it to us. It was a beautiful estate of about one hundred acres. Among its attractive features were all sorts of fruits grown under glass, a fine herd of black Surrey cattle and a private golf course which had been laid out by Joyce Wethered, England's greatest woman golfer. We could look down on the red tile of London by day and its lights at night. Warren House had many times entertained King Edward VII, the grandfather of the present king. The story was that he liked to be invited there by Lady Fitzgerald because he rated the chef as one of the best in the country. We gave a dinner one evening for MacDonald, Chamberlain, Bruce of Australia, Bennett of Canada, Forbes of New Zealand, Cordell Hull, Ray Atherton, Leith-Ross of the Bank of England, Sir Maurice Hankey and others, including two of our neighbors at home, Mrs. Robert Dun Patterson and Mr. R. H. Grant. Seating of the guests at dinner had to be determined according to rank by Ray Atherton. He decided that in accordance with custom it would be necessary to employ two tables in the large dining room. As the guests were leaving, Neville Chamberlain paid what I accounted a great compliment, coming from one as conservative with words as he, when he said,

374

"It seems as though Governor and Mrs. Cox have lived here with us always."

After the dinner at Warren House, MacDonald, Chamberlain and I somehow got shunted off into a corner where we were free to discuss public matters. The recurring eruptions on the European continent came up and I predicted that unless Germany and Italy, with their dense populations, were given more elbow room there might be another war. Said MacDonald, "That is more easily said than done." I ventured the suggestion that the problem might be solved by inducing Portgual, a traditional ally of England, to give up Angola on the west coast of Africa. It is twice as big as Germany in area, has good natural products and varying altitudes which afford a diversity of climate. It seemed especially desirable, as I stated, because it is out of the line of communication between England and India. It was populated almost exclusively by Negroes and they were by no means making the best out of the country. Chamberlain did not reject the idea and said that it might be done. Somehow Schacht, the German financier, heard about the conversation and mentioned it to me, at the same time suggesting that if that were done Germany would not ask for the return of her colonies. It was interesting a few years ago when the question of finding a home for European refugees was discussed to note that B. M. Baruch, in his farseeing way, proposed Angola as the place.

Of course we saw much of Nancy Astor. Even though Ramsay MacDonald once spoke of her as "that wild woman" I must insist that she is a remarkable character, an able person of fine spiritual qualities who is devoted objectively to what she believes best conserves the cause of humanity. Our first contact with her was unusual, as measured by the customary social amenities of England. Not long after we arrived in London, Mrs. Cox and I were preparing to go out for dinner when Lady Astor came to our rooms to extend what she called a "very informal invitation to dine." She called up her cook and inquired what she was preparing for the evening meal. It was brook trout, but there would be one short. "Well," said the irresistible Nancy, "I don't care much for trout anyhow, so we'll have enough and I am going to bring the guests along."

375

Through an interesting evening our talk ran on long after midnight. At a garden party at Cliveden, the historic country place of the Astors, Lady Astor told me that during the First World War, when the place was turned over to the government as a hospital, 23,000 soldiers had been treated there. She took me to the little burial ground which she had provided for those who had died there. It was an unusual nook. Nature had embellished the borders of the area with a natural wall of rock and had provided an opening with a view of the waters of the Thames. By a singular coincidence, the first marker we came to bore the name of a young soldier from my home city of Dayton. He had served with the Thirty-seventh Division, which I had put together while governor, out of our National Guard units.

Lord Astor is more than Nancy Astor's husband. I golfed and fished with both the Astors in Florida and found him a man of good mind and with an outlook by no means merely national.

One of the most attractive social functions was a dinner given by Lord and Lady Astor in compliment to the American delegation. There must have been four hundred guests placed at two large tables. The present Duke of Windsor was seated between Lady Astor and Mrs. Cox. It was noticed that he ate very sparingly and he explained in these words, "Recently I ran through the pictures of the Kings of England and I certainly don't want to develop the physical proportions of many of them."

In a conversation last winter with Nancy Astor she made what I thought was a very smart remark. She said: "The way to make Russia a part of the world would be to put a five-and-ten-cent store in every town over there."

An unusual Englishman was Sir Maurice Hankey, later Lord Hankey. For over twenty years he served as liaison officer between the cabinet and the King. He was at the Peace Conference at Versailles and the only man permitted to be in the room with Wilson, George, Clemenceau and Orlando in this closed conference. Wilson would permit no one but Hankey to keep charge of his papers. When anyone called on the Prime Minister, Hankey was sitting beside him taking notes. With his long experience, what a fund of reminiscences he must hold! When he and I lunched one day at the Service Club the table was immediately under a handsome portrait of Sir Douglas Haig. I told Hankey that Haig had not only caught the imagination of the American people as a military leader but that there seemed to be about him that gentility of character which endeared him to everyone allied to our cause. I told Hankey that when Haig made the solemn admission, "We are fighting with our backs to the wall," it sent a thrill of increased determination into the heart and soul of America. Hankey remarked that the last time he saw Haig they lunched together at the very table where we were. He told a thing that I have never seen in print nor heard, that Lloyd George and he were to have accompanied Lord Kitchener on his fateful trip to Russia. The orders were canceled half an hour before the battleship sailed. How that canceled order altered the history of the world! England and the Allied cause would have suffered heavily if the dynamic force of Lloyd George had been lost to the war effort then. It was Maurice Hankey who first recommended Neville Chamberlain to Lloyd George. An assignment of importance was to be made and George was unable to make a choice. Hankey told him of the fine service Chamberlain had rendered in the municipality of Birmingham and George selected him. Chamberlain at first did not do well but he quickly found himself and developed into one of England's greatest Ministers of the Exchequer.

I asked Hankey if he had preserved all of his papers. He said he had. I then inquired whether he intended to have them published. He replied that a mercenary motive might be ascribed to him and that he hesitated to do it. He could fill in many blank places in history and I urged that he should write his memoirs as a matter of duty to his and succeeding times.

This story can be told because MacDonald himself once asked me to relate it. When MacDonald became Prime Minister as head of the Labor party, the Tories regarded him as a dangerous radical and at the outset the social attentions paid to him were not up to the traditional English hospitality. But those who met him were charmed by his personality and his conversation. He had inherent refinement and his qualities were particularly noted by Lady Londonderry. She and Lord Londonderry entertained the new head of the government and invited such of the aristocratic groups as were interested to come. This was followed by other social attentions. Of course they gave rise to the rumor that the Tories were attempting to take over

377

MacDonald by the subtle means of social entertainment. He and Lady Londonderry, because of their intellectual congeniality, became fast friends. The Londonderrys gave a dinner and reception to all the delegates of the conference. The Londonderry home occupies almost a square in London. It seemed to be built around portraits; I have never seen so many outside an art museum. The portrait of Viscount Castlereagh, a treasured ancestor, must have been twenty feet in length and twelve or fifteen feet in height. The Viscount, also known as the Second Marquis of Londonderry, had played an important part in the Continental affairs of Europe after the fall of Napoleon. Some act of his which greatly pleased the Czar of Russia prompted a prodigal gift of what was said to be the choicest set of jewels in Europe.

On the night of the reception, Lady Londonderry stood on the landing of the great staircase gowned in a very simple white satin dress with a long train. She carried an enormous green feather fan and wore her famous jewels. They consisted of a tiara, in the center of which was a huge emerald set in a sunburst of diamonds, several bracelets of emeralds and diamonds, a ring and earrings of the same and a most amazing necklace of emeralds set in diamond sunbursts and ending about halfway to her waist in one great emerald set in the same sunburst style. She was a picture one could never forget, though I must admit that the detailed description of costume and jewels was given to me by Mrs. Cox.

The next morning, at the conference in MacDonald's office, always attended by Colijn, the head of the Economic Commission, and by me as head of the Monetary Commission, Jung, the Minister of Finance of Italy, had brought with him an economist from one of the Italian universities. MacDonald submitted a statement on some subject which he was going to give out and the Italian intellectual, in running through it, suggested irrelevant and foolish changes in the phraseology. MacDonald was very much upset by the incident and his petulance lasted through most of our meeting. Finally I leaned towards him and said, "Ramsay, wasn't that a grand occasion last night, and wasn't Lady Londonderry a figure of indescribable beauty?" His face brightened with a smile. His manner changed and the meeting wound up in the pleasantest way.

Not long after, at a dinner given by the Belgian ambassador to London, MacDonald took me by the arm and presented me to Lady

378

Londonderry with the words, "I want you to meet my good friend, Cox, from America." I told her I wanted to acknowledge my debt to her for being responsible for a little turn that she had given to a meeting which involved the fate of nations. I then asked Ramsay whether I should tell her. Enthusiastically he said, "Yes." I then told her of the change the mere mention of her name had brought to the great Prime Minister of England. She blushed in pride and Ramsay was overjoyed that I had told her about it.

Margot Asquith bobbed up in many of the affairs incident to the conference. A niece of hers, a Mrs. Beck, reputed to be one of the most beautiful women in the British Empire, gave a dinner for Mrs. Cox and me. As we came in she said, "Aunt Margot will be here tonight. She is a mean person although I love her dearly. The way to get on with her is to treat her precisely as she treats you." In due time we were introduced and I remarked that I was one of the few persons in America who had read her book. She remarked that I was probably the only person. I told her I wouldn't go so far. She was pleased, however, at my challenge, and saying she was positive I had never read it at all, dared me to "tell one thing in the book." I recalled her description of a week-end holiday spent on her father's estate which bordered the sea. She had taken her lunch in a basket, mounted her favorite saddle horse and was off for the wilds. At lunchtime a shower came up. To get out of it she went under a ledge, almost a cavern, which had been gnawed out by the action of the waves. She discovered a tramp who had also taken refuge there. She shared her lunch with him and found him interesting to talk to. When they were through, the sun was shining. He told her how much he had enjoyed the lunch and started to go. She wanted to know where he was going. He said he never knew. "Don't you know," she inquired, "when you get up in the morning what destination you will aim at?" "No," he said, "I always travel with my back to the wind, just a human derelict, tossed about by the elements as a derelict ship is tossed about by the currents and tides of the sea."

Another such challenge which might have been very embarrassing happened in this country. Soon after William Lyon Phelps had published his autobiography, a production of great merit, I introduced

379

him to an audience and made reference to his book. In his facetious response he said he was positive that I had never read the book. I arose from my chair, waved him aside and told him I thought I could relate to the audience a most unusual incident mentioned in the life history. William Lyon Phelps and Mrs. Phelps were entertaining Edna Ferber at their home in Connecticut. In keeping with family tradition, he had asked the blessing at the dinner table. His wife remarked, "Billy, I never heard a word you said." To which he replied, "Well, dearie, I wasn't speaking to you."

The library at Warren House was very unusual. Great rows of books, including even the printed debates in the old Irish Parliament, were there. I found a half-dozen volumes relating to Coke of Norfolk and remarked to Lady Fitzgerald, who was showing me through the place, that Coke was one of my great enthusiasms. Proudly she remarked that she was a direct descendant of his. I asked her how old Coke was when his last child was born. She admitted she did not know, and wondered how an American should have that intimate information. She asked me to relate the facts, which I did.

When Coke's wife died without leaving a son, under the English law of primogeniture the family title fell to a nephew. Coke was naturally interested in the young man's future. He was courting an attractive young woman who had been almost constantly with Coke's daughters at Holkham, the family residence. The nephew was making no headway and the uncle was much disturbed about it. Coke finally asked her why she was unwilling to marry the heir to his title. She replied that it was for the very good reason that she was not in love with him.

Gruffly he blurted out, "Is there any objection to the Coke family?" She replied that this was a silly inquiry, that the Cokes had been conspicuous in English history and had provided one of the great Lord Chief Justices.

As a last resort, Coke went to the heart of the matter by asking, "Is there someone else?" Yes, there was. Getting very personal, he wanted to know whether the lucky person knew it. Her triumphant response was, "No, he is too dumb."

His curiosity thoroughly aroused, the distinguished Englishman insisted on knowing who it was.

"It's you, you," the young woman echoed.

Well, they were married and "lived happily ever afterwards." He was eighty-one years old when his last child was born.

LadyFitzgeraldwas charmed with the story and asked me to tell her some more things about him. It was he who introduced in the House of Commons the resolution acknowledging the independence of the American colonies. The House had labored with this disagreeable subject for a long time. On the first test of strength there were 194 No's to 193 Aye's. The question was brought up again and carried by 178 to 177. Coke was a great admirer of George Washington. They exchanged notes on their experiences with certain kinds of livestock on the farm. Several animals were shipped to Mount Vernon by Coke.

The King and Queen gave a reception to the members of the conference at Windsor but the most attractive function was the garden party in the grounds at Buckingham Palace. A path was made through the crowd for their majesties, who walked down to the tea house nestled in a young forest of flowers. As they passed, Bizot of France and I were standing together. He said, "Look at that little man. Stripped of his robes, he would be regarded as merely an average man. But here he is, the center and symbol of the British Empire, and as such he commands the affection and reverence of its millions of people. This is a tremendous fact, a great credit to his people and a compliment to the democratic spirit that no one can describe in words."

Ambassador Robert Bingham was ill during the conference of a sickness which afterwards caused his death. I visited at his bedside a number of times. He was well liked in England and Mrs. Bingham was beloved by everyone who knew her. She met in an admirable way all the requirements of her station. A reception was given at the Embassy one evening for our delegation. There I was talking with an Under Secretary and we fell into a discussion of the First World War. I reminded him of the pictures printed at the time in the London *Illustrated News* of the fine young men who had fallen in battle. It seemed that the very flower of England's young manhood had been sacrificed. He said: "England will be a long while

381

making up what she has lost. Every member of my class at Cambridge except myself lost his life in the war. I was the poorest student in our group, and here I am an Under Secretary."

Among the many American newspapermen at the conference one showed pre-eminent ability—Walter Lippmann. He worked hard to enable himself to do a superb job of reporting and interpreting. He saw everybody in the various delegations and in the London financial and political world who could throw light on the problems he discussed. Nor did he merely ask information and ideas; he contributed both. He proved as well grounded in many of the problems before the conference as any of the delegates, and his judgment was worth having.

It was at the conference that I met Frank Knox for the first time. Even though we had been fellow publishers for a long time, our ships had never touched. He and Senator George Moses of New Hampshire had come to London to see the show. The Senator, by the way, told me that upon his return he intended writing the life of Mary Baker Eddy of Christian Science fame. He had known her for many years. Just why he abandoned this project I do not know.

Moses had a brilliant mind and a sharp tongue. At the noon recess he, Knox and a group of other Americans and I were lunching together. Someone remarked to the Senator that the wittiest observation he ever made in the Senate was when he referred to Senator Royal S. Copeland, of New York, as the "Lydia Pinkham of the Democratic party." The New Yorker had come East from Michigan, where he had started in the practice of medicine. He had a very engaging personality and started writing health articles for the Hearst papers. At one time he must have had millions of readers. In this way he became so well known that he was elected to the Senate from the Empire State.

I grew very fond of Frank Knox and saw a great deal of him in his last years. When he returned to this country from his last vacation, spent in Cuba, he spent a day with me at Miami Beach. He was devoted to golf, and I gave a luncheon for him at Indian Creek Club, attended by kindred spirits of the fairways and greens. In referring to his relations with President Roosevelt, he said, "He has been kind and considerate to me and he has never mentioned politics once." It was a denial of the charge often heard that Knox, a Republican, was made Secretary of the Navy in order to gain his political influence for the administration.

I recently read Raymond Moley's account of the London conference. In his reference to the delegates he said that while he was associated with the Council of National Defense in Ohio, he knew me and assisted me occasionally with my speeches. This was news to me. He never did it nor did anyone else. In my six years in the governor's office at Columbus, I never saw Moley. Recently, in order to be certain that my memory was not at fault, I had this fact confirmed by Charles E. Morris, who was my secretary at the time. Mr. Morris said that Moley was employed by Fred Croxton, who was the head of one of our state organizations, formed to keep things moving during the war.

PART EIGHT

Newspaper Dream Comes True in Atlanta

Move into the Field with "Gone with the Wind"

Why Wilson Was Not Buried at Arlington

Bryan Regrets His Conduct in Campaign of 1920

Portraits of Wilson, Bryan, Roosevelt, Eleanor
Roosevelt and Willkie

Roosevelt Joins the Immortals

CHAPTER XXXIII

"COVERS DIXIE LIKE THE DEW"

◆

IT WAS THE rounding out of a dream when, in December, 1939, I purchased the Atlanta *Journal* and the *Georgian*, both afternoon papers. The *Georgian* was discontinued, which left the city with the *Journal* in the evening and the *Constitution* in the morning. Both these papers have fine traditional backgrounds.

This was not the mere acquiring of another newspaper property. Atlanta fitted perfectly into the picture of our operations between Dayton and Springfield in Ohio and Miami in Florida. This gave us three climates and the "air" from the Great Lakes on the north to Latin America on the south. The Atlanta *Journal* owned WSB, call letters expressing the sentiment, "Welcome South, Brother." This was a 50,000-watt station which, joined with WHIO in Dayton and WIOD in Miami, provided a wide coverage. WIOD was established at Miami Beach at a time when a great deal was being said of the wonders of this little-known section of the country. The call letters brief the sentiment, "Wonderful Isle of Dreams."

We had hoped for a long time to get into the Atlanta field but there were persistent difficulties. The majority of the common stock in the *Journal* was owned by the heirs of James R. Gray. There were a number of them and they were not newspaper-minded. The Hon. Hoke Smith had at one time owned the paper but he disposed of it in 1900. Publisher James R. Gray won the admiration of the American press during the trying and exciting days of the famous Frank murder trial. He was an intellectually honest man who followed his duty as solemnly imposed by the best traditions of the newspaper profession regardless of consequences.

Atlanta was a highly competitive field. In 1912 William Randolph Hearst had acquired the *Georgian*, which had been founded six years before by Fred L. Seeley, son-in-law of the well-known E. W.

Grove of St. Louis. In the twenty-seven years of Mr. Hearst's operations, he introduced lively business policies and in the process of
losing over ten million dollars in the venture he made the going
hard for the *Journal* and the *Constitution.* It is highly creditable to
both of these long-established dailies that they remained solvent
under the stress.

There was a romantic flavor to our anticipations in going into
Georgia. The state has had an unusual history and in its confines,
made up of 159 counties, it formed a small empire in itself. One of
the oldest commonwealths, it is in some respects the newest. This
was taken into account by us because it offered a rare opportunity
for service and development. Geographically, its place in the life
and affairs of the country is very much like that of Vienna, in old
Austria. The traffic from London, Paris and Berlin to Constantinople
was routed southeastward through Vienna, and that from the vicinity of eastern Germany and western Russia to Rome and the regions
of the Adriatic Sea came through Vienna from the northeast. Vienna
formed a hub. So it is with Atlanta. Movements from Detroit, Chicago, Cincinnati, the northwest and St. Louis to Florida come southeastward through the Georgia capital, and that from New York,
Philadelphia, Washington, Baltimore and Richmond, Virginia, flows
southwestward through Atlanta. Eight railway systems provide fifteen main lines. It is the third largest telegraph center in the world
and the largest telephone center in the South; it ranks fifth or sixth
in air-mail volume. Fifteen hundred manufacturing concerns maintain distribution offices in Atlanta. Residentially, it has a charm
peculiarly its own. Its environs are built in the foothills of the mountains and the beauty and dignity of the fine forests there are scrupu-
lously preserved in the erection of attractive homes. During the
days of reconstruction, the South held, although tenuously in places,
to the old way of life peculiarly its own. Many sections, however,
were unable to do so. Atlanta held successfully to customs that, of
necessity, had been abandoned by others. When the amazing Coca-
Cola Company brought its fabulous wealth to Georgia, Southern
life, as it had been known through the old days, was re-established
in some of its forms. It has always seemed to me that country life in
England prior to World War I and that in the pre-Civil War South
were unlike that to be found anywhere in the world. A changing

388

world has brought its complete disappearance—a change not without grounds for some regret.

Dealing with the subject of Atlanta without showing how much of a factor the Coca-Cola Company has been in the growth of the city and state would be like discussing the great dramas of Shakespeare without mentioning Hamlet. In 1919 a syndicate headed by Ernest Woodruff paid $25,000,000 for the business then headed by Asa Candler. The skeptics shook their heads. This was a bold piece of business, but the farseeing Mr. Woodruff must have known what he was about. The amazing history of this corporation is probably known by comparatively few people. It reads like fiction rather than fact. Ten million dollars in preferred stock was issued, but retired from profits by 1926. The issue of common stock was 500,000 shares. This was split two for one in 1927, making 1,000,000 shares outstanding. In 1929 one share of three-dollar Class A Stock was issued as a dividend to every share of common stock. In 1935 the common stock was split four to one making it 4,000,000 shares. Subsequent to the issue of 1,000,000 Class A shares as a stock dividend, the company purchased and retired 400,000 shares of that issue. The company's capital as of April 1, 1945, was 600,000 shares of Class A three-dollar stock and 4,113,665 shares of common. The present market valuation of its securities exceeds a half billion dollars.

The senior Mr. Woodruff died quite recently at the age of eighty-one. A considerable part of his fortune, as bequeathed by his will, goes to philanthropic purposes. A modern hospital was built by him as a memorial to Mrs. Woodruff. The son, Robert W., one of the most dynamic industrial figures in the country, became and still is the leading spirit in the corporation. He envisioned almost a world-wide perimeter in his plans of development. He and Harrison Jones, present chairman of the board, gave of their time and talents unsparingly in the war movement. At the present time, Mr. Jones is one of the best minds applied to post-war planning. Ralph Hayes, a protégé of Newton D. Baker, became vice-president in 1933. A. A. Acklin, president of the corporation, was a Georgia country boy who demonstrated his finesse in finance.

I once asked Bob Woodruff whether Hayes was chiefly assigned to the task of public relations. He made a very interesting reply, which was, "Everyone connected with our company is a public relations man." There is a great deal of meaning in this.

389

The Coca-Cola Company buys from other corporations everything it needs in the making and marketing of its product. Mr. Woodruff is opposed to over-consolidation of interests and likes to feel that he is helpful to small enterprises. This may be one of the answers to the great problem of demobilization.

There were many heirs of the Gray family and common stock of the *Journal* was also held by families of men who had at one time or another been associated with Hoke Smith and Mr. Gray. The Grays owned the majority stock but every minority holder was paid precisely the same as the majority received. Mrs. Cohen, widow of the onetime publisher, brought her holdings to Mr. Brice, who had managed her affairs, and said she hoped to get $250 a share. To her surprise she was told that all were to be treated alike and that she would receive $450 a share. This policy of treating all alike cost us an estimated $700,000 but it was a wise investment.

Mr. Hearst was opposed to the sale of the *Georgian* but the trustees of his interests persuaded him to dispose of the property.

We came into Atlanta with *Gone with the Wind*. The premiere performance came a day or two after we took possession. Some editorial wit remarked that we had bought the *Journal* in order to be sure of getting a ticket to the show. Peggy Mitchell, author of this renowned piece, had spent her reportorial days on the *Journal*. She still fraternizes with her old associates and they hold her in deep affection.

Miss Mitchell once said to me, "If *Gone with the Wind* has a central theme, I suppose it is the one of survival. What quality is it that makes some people able to survive catastrophes and others, apparently just as brave and able and strong, go under? I do not know what it was that made our Southern people able to come through a war, a reconstruction and complete wrecking of all their social and economic systems. I only know that the survivors used to call it 'gumption.' "

Peggy Mitchell, now Mrs. John Marsh, grand little woman that she is, was one of the hardest workers in the war movement in her section. Every moment she could spend from the bedside of her ailing father was given to the Red Cross.

Coming into Georgia brought a renewal of my friendship with Judge Price Gilbert, long a member of the state Supreme Court and now living comfortably and pleasantly the life of a seer and philosopher. So far as I know, he was the first Cox supporter in that state prior to the presidential nomination in 1920.

We found the *Journal* with a fine organization which was soon supplemented by some very capable newspaper people from the *Georgian*. After we had been operating three or four months, Dr. M. L. Brittain, head of Georgia Tech, whom I happened to meet socially, said he was coming in to meet our new editor. He was surprised to learn that there had been no changes in editorial personnel.

John A. Brice, a cousin of Hoke Smith, had been associated with the *Journal* for over forty years. He was a happy connecting link between the old regime and the new. He knew the people of Georgia, their temper and traditions, as well as anybody, and was greatly beloved throughout the state. He was made president of the company and served until his death in 1945. He has been succeeded by George C. Biggers, who served as general manager under Mr. Brice. Mr. Biggers' experience has familiarized him with both the news and business departments. He is recognized as one of the ablest of Southern publishers. Mr. Brice liked to call attention to the fact that the publishers of the *Journal* have included Hoke Smith, governor and United States Senator from Georgia; John S. Cohen, United States Senator from Georgia, and myself as governor of Ohio and Democratic nominee for the presidency in 1920. He contended that this is a distinction enjoyed by no other American newspaper.

Horace Powell, the circulation manager, is recognized as one of the best authorities in his field in the country. The paper has been especially happy in its controller, Hedley B. Wilcox, in charge of finance and accounting. Under both Hoke Smith and Senator Cohen the editorial page was given special attention, and we have worked hard to maintain its fine liberal tradition. The editor when I became owner, John Paschall, continued to serve, and is now editor emeritus. His judgment and experience and his broad outlook upon men and policies were invaluable. His successor, Wright Bryan, made a brilliant reputation in Europe as a correspondent covering the Second World War. He gave over the radio the first eyewitness report of the invasion of France. He went through bitter experiences in Poland and Russia as a German prisoner of war and came out of the conflict with a thrilling background. Associated with him as editorial writers are William Cole Jones and Edwin Camp. Mr.

391

Jones, who was once on the faculty of Mercer College, is renowned for the purity of his style and the choiceness of his diction. Mr. Camp, a son-in-law of Joel Chandler Harris, knows the history and spirit of Georgia through and through. Both men can write very incisive editorials.

My conception of the function and duties of a newspaper was stated simply in my first announcement in the *Journal:*

It should tell the truth as only intellectual honesty can discern the truth. It should do what is in conscience needful and right. To try by vague and pointless preachment and evasion to please everyone is bad faith. Persisted in, it pleases none and exposes a lack of character which the people will soon appraise.

In our civilization the interests of the classes are organized and guarded by their own skilled agents. The masses are not so protected. The press should never be unmindful of this fact. It should hold itself above the partisanships of classes and groups, for its right function is to bridge these gulfs with the tolerance and reasonableness of the strong while yet protecting, without coddling, the weak against abuses of power—that is the everlasting labor of self-government. In the field of this labor lies a peculiar opportunity and obligation of the press.

It had never been my intention to create a highly centralized form of "chain journalism." Now that I had newspaper properties in Ohio, Georgia and Florida, each journal was encouraged to maintain its own personality under its own staff. Each paper, I may add, had the personnel to make this easy and natural. In Miami, the *Daily News* had in D. J. Mahoney one of the best public relations men and sales executives in the country. Associated with him as controller was R. A. Reeder, who came to us with the old Miami *Metropolis* and whose service was always highly valuable. The business manager, Charles Coffin, was a man of successful experience in the advertising agency business and developed a fine grasp of newspaper operation. As capable editorial writer, we shortly employed Francis P. Locke, who came to us from Harvard. In Springfield, Ohio, three highly competent men controlled the evening and morning daily: Edgar Morris, assisted by Bert Teeters and Barr Moses. It was my policy to give all these men a helpful general supervision but never to fetter their initiative. I need not say that it

COVERS DIXIE LIKE THE DEW

was a great satisfaction to me when my son, James M. Cox, Jr., after his graduation from Yale University, began to assist me. He entered the naval air service in the Second World War, rising to the rank of lieutenant commander but returning at the close of the conflict to be my chief aide. From newsboy at fourteen to business manager of the Dayton *Daily News* has been the career of Glenn L. Cox. He bears no relation to our family. In all my experience, no member of our organization has shown a more impressive development. A Dayton veteran of forty years' service, Jerry Connors, is still laboring efficiently there.

One associate deserves a special word—Walter Locke, editor of the Dayton *Daily News*. I take a modest pride in my perspicacity in discovering him. Reading various magazines, I repeatedly came upon his name attached to articles marked by pithy common sense and real penetration. Finally a discussion of the McNary-Haugen bill which he published in the *New Republic* spurred me to action. I wrote Charles Merz, then on the *New Republic* staff, asking, "Who is this brilliant man Locke?" Merz replied that he was on the Nebraska *State Journal*. Thereupon I extended my inquiries to Harvey Newbranch, editor of the Omaha *World-Herald*. He replied, in effect, "I have long been thinking of writing you about Locke. He is one of the very ablest men I know. He would long ago have been drawn off to Chicago or New York but that he feared losing his editorial independence." I at once took steps to bring Mr. Locke to Dayton, and for more than twenty years now he has been a pillar of strength to the *Daily News*, giving its editorial page a special luster recognized throughout the Middle West. To anybody who knows that page, it would be futile for me to speak of Walter Locke's broad knowledge of literature and history, his humanity and tolerance, his understanding of common folk and his liberal courage in fighting for them. His *Trends of the Times* runs in all of our papers. Many high schools in the three states use it in both English and history classes.

Here a brief observation on the part that commentators or columnists play in present-day journalism may be appropriate. They have aroused wide interest. Whether this will continue rests with the writers themselves. Their value to the public lies in the diversity of the views which they express, in their sincerity and in their devotion to truth. If a commentator writes only to please the publisher he serves, or to appeal to the prejudices of his readers, he is worthless. If he is selling his own spleen, he will not be long in bringing discredit to his kind. The evolution of the commentator will be one of the most interesting phases of journalism to watch.

It is important to recall that Joseph Pulitzer and Adolph S. Ochs, who will always hold high place in the traditions of journalism, did not need commentators to give either interest or influence to their newspapers. Pulitzer first caught my imagination when he was making great strides with the New York *World*. Even as far back as a country schoolteacher, and later a newspaper reporter, I never missed an issue of the *World*. I did not know the man whom I admired so much. With Ochs it was different. I knew him very well and regarded him not only as an able and constructive publisher but as an eminent citizen of the world. He was a rare composite of all the elements that made him a commanding figure both in this country and abroad.

"The *Journal* Covers Dixie Like the Dew," a most attractive slogan, adopted years before, was highly prized. The *Journal* bore an excellent reputation. People believed in it. It had always dealt with them in good faith, and this made it a tremendously useful instrument in the governmental reforms that the public interest gravely required. We soon found ourselves in the midst of an intense political contest. I doubt whether in all the history of our American commonwealths there was ever a more dangerous and disgraceful regime than that of Eugene Talmadge, who served long as governor of Georgia. He was seeking to have his tenure prolonged four years more. He controlled every cent in the state treasury, and money could be shifted from one fund to another and disbursed as he saw fit. He had had given to him the power to discharge anyone on the pay roll, even officers elected by the people, and in exercising this power he ousted the State Treasurer, the Comptroller General and five members of the Public Service Commission, all of whom had been elected at large. In true Gestapo fashion, he declared martial law around the state capital through the State Highway Department. The ousted State Treasurer had set the time lock on the safe in his office, but with a blowpipe Talmadge's emissaries burned their way into the vaults and gained custody of the state's funds. He seized control of the public school system by having himself elected Chairman of the State Board of Education. Then he reached out for the state colleges and universities, removing enough mem-

394

bers of the Board of Regents to gain control. Seven respected members of the college faculties were dismissed for the expressed reasons that they favored educational and social equality of the races. Ten institutions in the state university system lost their accredited standing among Southern and national schools. With his unchallenged control of state moneys and the power of patronage, he had gained for himself despotic powers through legislative enactment. An amendment to the state constitution was put through, extending the executive term four more years. In the manner of Huey Long, he was one of the country's great rabble-rousers. The level of the man's mind was demonstrated when in a public speech he referred flippantly and unkindly to the physical infirmity of our nation's chief executive.

Talmadge's abuse of the parole system brought shame to the state. Criminals caught red-handed regularly turned out to be men whom Talmadge had pardoned. For some reason, certain business interests supported Talmadge both in funds and influence. The state employees permeated every community in his behalf and public improvements were dispensed with a view to the enhancement of his political interests. He believed he had an impregnable political machine.

We were urged by good friends not to enter upon a political contest that had no chance of success. I told them I had no use for the newspaper that entered into a fight only when it was certain to win. The alumni of the colleges in every county were resentful at Talmadge's efforts to degrade the educational system of the state and were eager to fall in behind any campaign for decent government.

In this country, the hazard usually produces the man. In this case it was Ellis Arnall, a vigorous, honest, courageous young man of thirty-five years of age. He had had excellent training, knew the affairs of the state and its government, and made a brilliant campaign. He had served two years in the House of Representatives and was speaker at both sessions. He was appointed Assistant Attorney General and had been advanced to the Attorney Generalship. He was elected to this office without opposition. A graduate of the University of Georgia, he was regarded by the alumni of the state colleges as the ideal leader in the battle which could not but be a bitter one. The college elements were organized by Marion Smith,

395

the son of the late Hoke Smith. Mr. Arnall announced a platform framed to correct every abuse. With both candidate and issues presenting an augury for a better day, the *Journal* endorsed the candidacy of Mr. Arnall and his platform. The *Constitution* did the same seven months later. Old-timers said that not within their recollection had these two newspapers joined in a great political movement. Hoke Smith, heading the *Journal*, and Clark Howell, the *Constitution*, had been bitter political rivals throughout the years and, at one time, opposing candidates for the governorship.

Arnall never deviated from his platform. He announced that he would attempt to have it adopted by the legislature ahead of any other measures. The contest attracted national attention and election night was eagerly awaited. In some counties the polls closed early. Rural districts which had fallen victim to Talmadge's harangues on race hatred supported him strongly. When the returns came in from the precincts of the county seats it was a different story. Talmadge was defeated. Then came a record of legislative action which caught attention and won approval throughout America.

Governor Arnall was inaugurated on January 12, 1943, and the bills formulating his program were introduced the next day in both houses. The measures to reorganize the State Board of Regents and restore the accredited standing of colleges passed without a dissenting vote in either branch. The same happened to a companion measure giving constitutional status to the Board of Regents and thus preventing removal of the members by any future governor. That same security of tenure was given to members of the state school board. The parole system was reorganized. The law which gave the right of removal from government office was repealed. The State Finance Commission was set up to control the budget. It took from the governor the power to strike off the pay rolls any member of any department. The governor was removed from all boards and bureaus except the Budget Board. A retirement system for teachers was created and a non-political wild life department was created within three weeks' time. Subsequently, an extra session of the Assembly was called to clean up a disgraceful prison situation.

The legislature, under the leadership of Governor Arnall, adopted a new constitution, which was submitted to the voters and approved. This was a tremendous step forward for Georgia. Governor Arnall's success in bringing the federal Supreme Court to decide in favor of the equalized and equitable freight rates which had been denied to the South has attracted the attention of the whole country. His stature grew by his courageously espousing the repeal of the poll tax. No governor of a Southern state within a generation has had wider acclaim. He is regarded by the leaders of the Democratic party as a most promising political figure.

Politics in Georgia is perennial. At least a year before the state election, the political lines are forming. The public had had a very understandable exhibition of the difference between good government under Arnall and bad government under Rivers and Talmadge. The new constitution forbade more than one term of four years. In the old charter, Talmadge, while governor, had made the chief executive eligible to succeed himself. Governor Arnall, as a member of the Constitutional Convention, had favored that part of the new instrument which would have prevented his running again. When the legislature assembled in May, 1945, there was such a demand for Arnall that a resolution was proposed which would remove the bar. This required a two-thirds vote of both branches of the legislature. In the Senate it received 38 votes against 12 opposing. The necessary number was 35. In the House the vote was 127 for, 68 against. It failed by 10 votes. The demand for Arnall continued and when the legislature assembled on January 15, 1946, the effort was renewed in behalf of Arnall's continuance in office. In the Senate the vote was 36 for, 13 against, the required number still being 35. In the House the vote was 126 for, 74 against; this was 11 votes short of what was needed.

In both tests of strength the organized opposition came from the political supporters of Talmadge and Rivers, aided by Roy Harris, Speaker of the House. All three were casting their eyes on the governor's chair. The railroads were displeased over Arnall's successful prosecution of the suit to equalize freight rates in the South and public utility companies did not like the home-rule provision in the constitution, which Arnall had insisted upon. Failure of the two-term movement took Arnall out of the lists. There remained, in so far as personal ambitions governed, Talmadge, Rivers and Roy Harris, Speaker of the House of Representatives.

Harris had for years been looked upon as the head of the "Cracker party" in Augusta. That organization had ruled that community for years with a ruthlessness that had become well known all over Geor-

397

gia. In the 1946 primary election to select members of the legislature, Harris was overwhelmingly defeated. This automatically took Harris out and left Talmadge and Rivers in the field. The progressive elements which heartily supported Arnall in his reform joined in supporting James V. Carmichael, whom Arnall had endorsed.

Carmichael has a fine reputation in the state. He is a lawyer of ability, a man of rugged integrity, who made a splendid record as a member of the General Assembly a few years ago. He was largely responsible for the location of the Bell bomber plant at Marietta in the suburbs of Atlanta and finally became the head of that institution. Eighty-four per cent of its pay rolls, running into uncounted millions of dollars, was distributed in the state of Georgia. He met the race problem in that vast plant with notable success and has also got along well with labor. As a liberal progressive he seemed to be the ideal candidate.

The result of the primary election in Georgia on July 19, 1946, came as such a surprise, if not a shock, to the rest of the country that I feel the subject should be dealt with in some detail. In order to give a true perspective, I would particularly like the people in other states to know just what happened and how and why. Rivers, Talmadge and Carmichael were the three candidates. There were two or three other aspirants but they cut no figure. Measured by the circumstances that ordinarily determine political results, there seemed to be no doubt of the nomination of Carmichael. Rivers' administration had been disgraceful. Six indictments had been returned against him, three for the embezzlement of public funds amounting to $144,000, three for conspiracy to defraud the state. In the state court he was tried on one charge and a mistrial resulted. This was in November, 1942. The war was on and the state's attorney dismissed the cases on the ground that the material witnesses were in military service.

In the Federal Court, Hiram Wesley Evans was indicted for violation of the Sherman anti-trust law by maintaining monopoly in asphalt sales for highway construction. He entered a plea of nolo contendere and paid a $15,000 fine. In the state court, Evans was sued for $390,000 as treble damages under the Sherman anti-trust act. This was carried to the Supreme Court on the plea that the state had no right to sue. The decision was adverse to Evans. Then Evans and two asphalt companies paid into the treasury $37,000 which

398

they admitted had been taken illegally. Evans was Imperial Wizard of the Ku Klux Klan, the national leader. Rivers was Grand Secretary. Grand juries in sixty counties of Georgia passed resolutions of condemnation of Rivers for his indiscriminate pardoning of criminals. In four years, the Pardon Board under his control released 7800 prisoners. By executive order of the governor himself, 2700 were released. In the last four months of his term, 717 were let loose; in the last two weeks, 229; on the last day, 68. It was published in the press throughout the state that on the night preceding the inauguration of Rivers' successor, the governor's office had worked until dawn making out pardon papers. Naturally, no one of any political discernment could concede Rivers a chance in the election. In the last two years of Talmadge's term, 7000 prisoners were released.

Talmadge's record as a dictator, arrogating to himself powers not inherent in the governor, has already been stated. The announcement of the candidacies of these two men brought quick response all over Georgia. Photographs were published showing, among other things, plug-uglies controlled by Rivers beating and carrying out of his office the Chairman of State Highways. This officer had refused to approve the crookedness in the construction of roads. Pictures were also reproduced showing how Talmadge had used a blowpipe to open the vaults of the state treasury in order that he could control all disbursements. The legal custodian, as already stated, he had removed.

The press was practically unanimous, one hundred and seventeen of the state's papers declaring for Carmichael. These included the *Journal* and the *Constitution* of Atlanta. Talmadge was very much embittered and constantly referred to "them lyin' newspapers." He was especially vehement against the *Journal*. There were but twelve papers for Rivers, nine for Talmadge.

The friends of good government were confident of victory. The so-called teen-agers were happy over the voting privilege given by Arnall to all over 18 years of age. The alumni and students of the colleges and universities were a militant force because Talmadge had taken these institutions off the accredited list. The teachers in the common schools perfected organizations in every county. They had not forgotten Talmadge's major affront to them. Just before going out of office he had asked the State Board of Education to purchase $1,200,000 worth of schoolbooks. The board insisted emphatically that they were not needed and that this disbursement would look strange since the teachers' fund was depleted. Talmadge, in his imperious way, said he would give the board five hours to render to him a decision. They gave it to him in less than the prescribed time and the decision was adverse.

The tide was clearly towards Carmichael. Then came the decision of the United States Supreme Court, giving Negroes the right to vote in the Democratic primaries. In due time, in the exercise of this privilege, they began to register. This was the signal for Talmadge. He said it would only be a matter of time until white supremacy would come to an end. Negroes would be filling the courthouses and would occupy the positions in the schools and colleges. Talmadge is a great showman. In the words and manner of a tragedian, he painted a picture of the plague that was to fall upon the state. He decried and defied the courts, spoke disrespectfully of the judiciary in every speech. He warned the Negroes not to register. After the last day of registration had passed, he warned them not to vote. He promised that, if elected, he would do away with the existing election laws and establish what he termed a white primary, to be conducted under the exclusive control of the Democratic State Committee. It would select the election officers, count the votes and be free from any charge of irregularity, because there could be no recourse to law.

It is an interesting coincidence that such a law was once on the statute books and Talmadge claimed that, under it, he was counted out in his race for the United States senatorship. When he became governor, he had it repealed. In the so-called black belt in southern Georgia, where in many counties the colored population exceeds the white, Talmadge immediately caught the attention of the white voters. The issue of honest and progressive government under Arnall, certain to be continued under Carmichael, as against the corrupt regimes of both Talmadge and Rivers, was submerged. Old prejudices were stirred anew. Carpetbagger days were revived. Talmadge recalled the illustrious Georgians who had won fame in that state and all over the country by their exposure of the cruelties of Reconstruction days. He was drawing tremendous crowds. He put on a real show at every assembly. And then the capsheaf was added. In the early part of June, the Supreme Court of the United States, passing on a case that had come up from the state of Virginia, decided that it was illegal to segregate colored passengers on buses engaged in interstate traffic. The vote in the court was 6 to 1. The event played further into the hands of Talmadge. This new order was to be imposed on Georgia. As always, he had a remedy. He would stop buses at the state line. Passengers could not cross without buying new tickets. These would provide for segregation of the races as long as the holders were in Georgia. He also said he would put inspectors on board all passenger trains coming into the state and have them run the Negroes out of the diners and Pullmans and put them in Jim Crow cars.

The state was thrown into a frenzy. The fates were spinning yet another web. The CIO announced with blare of trumpets that it was descending on the South to organize industry. Corporate interests remembered how Talmadge had dealt with labor troubles in his previous tenure in office. In a strike soon after he was inaugurated governor, he had called out state troops who, at the point of bayonet, herded male and female strikers into concentration camps. In many instances they were evicted from their homes by force. It was about this time that the Talmadge treasury seemed to be growing affluent. Money was being spent for every conceivable political campaign device. Great motor cavalcades were organized to give color and drama to the Talmadge meetings. No one will ever know how large were the sums of money expended in his behalf. Rivers, too, gave evidence of having abundant funds. Both he and Talmadge spent small fortunes on the radio. One or the other, sometimes both, were on the air every day.

Rivers had no chance of election. This he knew perfectly, but certain influences kept him in the race because every vote he received in the counties would help Talmadge to run up a plurality. In 22 counties the Rivers candidacy gave Talmadge the required vote. The antiquated county unit system was established years ago in order to give the small communities a larger influence in the affairs of the state. A majority vote in the county is not necessary. The plurality rule prevails. There are 84 counties south of Macon, representing over half the 159 of the state. These have 220 of the 410 county unit votes. Here is the large colored population. Talmadge carried 65 of these 84 counties. He did not get in any of these a majority vote.

It will no doubt surprise a great many people to know how the county unit system works. Let us illustrate this by showing that in Chattahoochee County a total of 242 votes were cast for governor, in Towns County 242, in Quitman County 598, or a total of 1082 votes. These three counties, having two unit votes each, cast six unit votes in the final act of election. Fulton County, under this system, cast only six unit votes, yet its total popular vote was 92,550.

The wonder now is that Carmichael was able to carry the state by popular vote. He did this by a margin of 16,144.

What of the future? Will the state be troubled with widespread racial conflicts? Under a governor as wild and despotic as Hitler himself, the issue which he has raised and the bitternesses and prejudices which he has engendered will give new life to the Ku Klux Klan. The followers of the hooded order have always been friendly to Talmadge and he to them. Under his reign will they be tempted to overt acts, confident of a tolerant eye on their deeds?

Intolerable conditions are usually corrected by the offensive conduct of those who defy the inhibitions of law and society. Demagoguery destroys itself. The citizenship of Georgia has in it the stuff of genuine patriotism, and on final reflection it will so reveal itself to the nation.

My experience with the *Journal* has been very interesting. In the great empire which it serves nature has been rich in her endowments. With good government, and that is very necessary, it would have an opportunity for unusual agricultural and industrial development. The first speech I made in Georgia was at Athens, the home of the University of Georgia. I emphasized the two major problems as Government and Grass—a restoration of government to a state of efficiency and cleanliness that would inspire pride, and a radical change in the methods of farming. There has been too much emphasis on cotton raising, and Georgia is endowed with all the elements to make it a cattle-producing state. The State Agricultural College, cooperating with the national Department of Agriculture at Washington in extensive experimentation, has found grasses that provide pasturage nine months in the year. Not only can this be profitable, but it solves the problem of soil erosion.

Within the last few months a movement has been set on foot by Cason J. Callaway, a retired, public-spirited textile manufacturer, to establish demonstration farms of one hundred acres each in one hundred localities. Local citizens put up the money for the purchase of the land. After what can be done is demonstrated, the owners agree to sell the farm without profit to anyone who will carry on, preferably the manager. Mr. Callaway promises to become a pioneer of an ingeniously devised project that may take root in many parts of the United States. He himself has a large acreage where he has demonstrated on supposedly poor land the possibility of modern methods. His goal is not only to feed the state, which has been importing too much of its food essentials, but to ship supplies into other sections.

It was a pleasant coincidence that the two Democratic candidates of 1920, Roosevelt and Cox, partially joined their fortunes with the future of Georgia. At the time of the purchase of the *Journal*, I was happy to receive the following message:

The White House, Washington, D. C., December 14, 1939

Hon. James M. Cox,
Care Atlanta *Journal*, Atlanta

Accept my hearty congratulations as you enlarge your activities and broaden the field of your influence. Just short of a score of years ago you and I were together fighting side by side. In the years that have intervened we have been active in widely different fields. Now, happily, I feel that we are brought closer by the bond of union which your entry into my other state—Georgia—symbolizes. All success and happiness to you as an old friend and now as a fellow Georgian.

Franklin Roosevelt

CHAPTER XXXIV

WILSON, ROOSEVELT, BRYAN AND OTHERS

◆

NOTHING SHOWS the tenacious character of Woodrow Wilson more than the decision which he made with respect to his place of burial. This is something I have never seen in print. On an anniversary of Wilson's birth, Newton D. Baker delivered an address at his tomb in Bethlehem Chapel (Cathedral Church of Saints Peter and Paul) at St. Albans, Washington, D. C.

It was not a large group of people that assembled but everyone was a devoted follower of the former President. As I stood beside Dr. Cary Grayson, I inquired why this selection of a burial place had been made. He told me that Wilson had refused to be buried in Arlington, because he was outraged at the government's taking it away from Robert E. Lee after the War Between the States. The question then arose of whether or not he should be placed between his parents at Columbia, South Carolina. The objection was that it would necessitate the removal of the body of one of his sisters, so St. Albans was chosen.

How much do the great men of the world give thought to the final abiding place of the body? On one of my trips to England, I saw a good deal of Wickham Steed, distinguished editor of the London *Times*. We were discussing the late Lord Northcliffe. On one of the London golf courses is a very tricky hole, par 3. North-cliffe had never been able to do well with it. One day as he and Steed were walking away from the green on this hole, Northcliffe, in disgust with himself for playing it poorly, remarked, "I had sooner play that hole in par than be buried in Westminster Abbey."

Wilson was a stickler for good diction. Bad use of English annoyed him. Judge T. T. Ansberry once told me of an experience while in Congress which revealed not only Wilson's meticulous care

404

in the use of words but also a subtle sense of humor. Ansberry had called at the White House on a matter of some importance. Knowing that the Chief Executive was an acknowledged literary figure, the Congressman thought he would indulge in some fancy style himself. After discussing the subject which had brought him there, Ansberry said: "Well, now, Mr. President, the *grav*amen of the case is this . . ."

It was later necessary for Ansberry to renew his talk with the President, who had looked into the matter involved. Cordially, in addressing the Congressman, Wilson said: "Well, now, Mr. Congressman, the grav*amen* of the matter is this . . ." He never cracked a smile, but Ansberry got the point.

The recent death of Senator Jim Reed of Missouri recalls a conversation which I had with President Wilson. Reed was obstreperous in the Senate and his best friends were annoyed by his behavior. I had told the President that Reed, at the time of the notification ceremony in Dayton in 1920, had begged me not to declare in favor of the League. I had told the Senator that I would be happy if I were able to find a plank upon which he could walk back into the councils of the Democratic party. At the same time, however, I would not be mindful of the self-respect of the Democracy and of my own self-respect if I followed his advice. Wilson's comment was: "The man is a complete mystery to me. The nicer I have been to him, the meaner he has been to me."

Two most regrettable and unfortunate incidents in the career of Wilson were the severing of his relations with Colonel House and with Mr. J. P. Tumulty, his secretary. House discussed the matter with me many times. He said that the change came without any awareness on his part of any differences between them. He had searched his mind intensively, trying to remember something which might have brought it about, but he could remember nothing. House was an astute politician, a man of poise who had been of great use to Wilson even before he had been nominated for the presidency. Wilson consulted him about important appointments and matters of policy. Long before the peace meeting at Versailles, House had been assigned to contacts with the chancelleries of Europe. He had become so thoroughly familiar with what was going on both before and behind the curtain of diplomacy that naturally Wilson's first choice for one of the peace commissioners was House.

Wilson was not a compromiser, House was. When Wilson returned to Washington after his first trip to the peace conference, House made a tentative agreement in Paris on certain matters. Wilson not only rejected them on reaching Paris again, but cast them out of the peace treaty in very emphatic terms. Those who have tried to ascertain what caused the rift between the two men are agreed that this incident paved the way for the final break. Before the conference broke up, House was sent to London on some errand and not recalled. That was the last House saw of Wilson. Nor did he ever hear from him by letter or otherwise.

Tumulty's relationship with Wilson was more intimate than House's, and the break between the two was by that fact the more distressing. Tumulty was very companionable. He had been with his chief so long that he knew him thoroughly and got on with him famously. It is doubtful whether any of the great presidential secretaries was ever more slavish in devotion to his chief than was Tumulty. He was not a "yes man" in any sense and, at great risk of provoking the President, often disagreed with him.

Tumulty told me an interesting story about the famous Peck letters. These letters of the President to Mrs. Peck had been made the occasion for scandal rumors aimed at him. In the campaign of 1916, the Republicans revived and revamped the tales. It was even reported that large sums of money had been paid to prevent their being made public. Tumulty was worried. He tried to muster courage to express his fears to Wilson and finally made bold to open the subject. Wilson smiled in complete reassurance. "Don't worry about that, Joe," he said. "There was not a single word in them that even requires an explanation." And that was the truth.

After Wilson's sickness, Tumulty did not see so much of him. Before going to New York to attend a complimentary dinner to me by the National Democratic Club, Tumulty had a prolonged visit with his chief. The President's mind was evidently centered upon the great cause for which he had so valiantly struggled and he was serenely confident that some day it would prevail. Tumulty was much impressed and at the New York meeting, on his initiative, recited what he thought was in the then former President's mind. Wilson deeply resented what Tumulty had done. Wilson felt that it was like a message from himself. The newspapers gave an odd turn to the whole matter, claiming that Wilson had been made by Tumulty to appear as favoring my renomination. His best friends deplored Wilson's treatment of Tumulty, but were tolerant by reason of the state of Wilson's health. Tumulty wrote two or three letters to Wilson, bitterly regretting having given him offense. The letters made no impression upon the distinguished invalid and the two men who had been so close from Wilson's first entrance into political life never saw each other again. The incident never in any way affected the relations between Wilson and me.

On the day of Wilson's funeral, a memorial service was held in Madison Square Garden. In that vast audience sat Colonel House, unnoticed and recognized by few. The report was that the invitation extended by the White House to House had miscarried.

In Washington, Mr. and Mrs. Tumulty were among the last called to enter carriages as the remains left the residence. He had been scantily recognized in the arrangements and it was a sad experience for him.

The severance of relations with both House and Tumulty undoubtedly would never have occurred if the President had been in health. The confidential matters which came to Wilson after his sickness were apparently known only to the circle of the sickroom, Mrs. Wilson, Dr. Grayson and Mrs. Wilson's brother. This forced Tumulty out of the picture.

More recently there has been another historic break in personal presidential relations. What the general impression is as to the cause of the rupture between President Roosevelt and James A. Farley, I do not know. Roosevelt never had much to say about it to me. Farley discussed it with me a number of times.

The rift was deeply regretted by the friends of both men. They had been very helpful to each other. When Roosevelt requested Farley to take charge of his campaign prior to the Democratic National Convention in 1932, Farley was little known outside of New York State and had had little political experience even there. It may be that Roosevelt discerned Farley's undeveloped political genius. The fact is that Farley was about the only man available, since most of the state's politicians were committed to the political aspirations of Al Smith.

Farley went through the country with a good piece of "political goods" to sell. He did it well, largely because of the honest, forthright way in which he met the local political powers. If he made any mistakes from the very beginning of his espousal of the Roosevelt cause until its triumph I have yet to have them pointed out. As Roosevelt and I were discussing his friend one day, I remarked that Farley, unused to public speaking and finally making as many addresses as anyone in public life, had never once lost control of his tongue. He never brought the slightest embarrassment to his chief. Roosevelt responded to this with warm praise of Farley's character and capacity. There was a genuine affection between the two.

Farley felt that Roosevelt should have been more candid with him prior to the 1940 convention. In the preceding days, Roosevelt, so Farley advised me, never gave any indication that he would be a candidate. Farley believed he was entitled to the confidence of the President. The real occasion of the wound, however, was Roosevelt's alleged statement that Farley could not be elected President because of the religious prejudice prevalent in this country, as evidenced in the Al Smith campaign in 1928. This hurt Farley deeply, and then and there the tie was broken. It might have been different had Roosevelt discussed the matter frankly with Farley. The President may have delayed discussing a subject as sensitive as this, hoping that Farley, in his fine political discernment, would see the obvious. The remark imputed to Roosevelt was never made in Farley's presence.

Farley probably knew more people than anyone else in America. Many times in the campaigns of 1940 and 1944, when the political skies were cloudy, Roosevelt must have felt a great need of his old political chieftain. Farley never gave promises of patronage in bad faith. This fact was largely responsible for his holding in all his contests the confidence and support of the local political leaders and the men in the trenches under them.

I have no doubt that the breaking of the friendship between these two men was the unhappiest episode in the lives of both.

It was a great voice that broke on the country in the early 90's. Its force and eloquence commanded widespread attention. It engaged the public interest by expressing what lay heavily on the hearts of millions of our people. There were symptoms of an economic revolt.

A rising tide of protest came from the Middle West and found political expression in the Populist party. William J. Bryan took up the cause of those who had fallen victims to economic adversity and who found existence hard. He drew to himself millions of devoted followers.

The critic cannot eliminate Bryan as a maker of history. Many of the progressive changes which came in the years following him were a result of his powerful crusades. Theodore Roosevelt capitalized the public opinion which Bryan had done much to create. La Follette followed Bryan's lead. Bryan's influence was still great when the Wilson administration began.

The "new freedom" of Wilson was in large measure a product of the doctrine Bryan had preached. Like most young men of the time, I was drawn to him even before his nomination in 1896. In his first term in Congress, he made a tariff speech which was an outstanding utterance on that subject. It is not going too far to say, although there is a paradox in the fact, that it cleared the way for the election of Grover Cleveland in 1892. In my first congressional campaign in 1908, Bryan made two speeches in my district. He stood a fine chance of election that year. He had but to tell the country, "I told you so." The panic of 1907 had taken place under Theodore Roosevelt. Just previous to this, Bryan had made a tour of Europe, and returned to the United States to find his old followers eagerly awaiting his leadership. Had he played his cards shrewdly, and emphasized some of his old progressive doctrines, including a downward revision of the tariff, he might have touched the enthusiasm of the masses.

Unfortunately for Bryan, he chose to turn an entirely new page in his book of reforms. In the speech he delivered at Madison Square Garden on his return, in August, 1906, he advocated the federal ownership of railroads. The country was not ready for such a step. When Bryan ascended the rostrum, his political strength was impressive. Once the country had read his speech, his chance was gone. Many blamed Tom L. Johnson of Cleveland for this mistake. Then, too, the country recovered rapidly from the panic of 1907. Bryan made a gallant campaign in his third attempt, but to no avail.

Senator Borah once said to me of Bryan: "He never grew an inch after 1896. Speaking became his business and he took his nose out of books." Bryan had moved too fast. The reformers could gain wisdom by tilling the soil and catching from Mother Nature a guidance in their endeavors. The farmer breaks the hardpan with a plow. Then it is necessary by the use of the harrow or disc to prepare the ground further for the seed. Once a program of change in governmental policies has been established, history reveals the necessity of pausing to refine and perfect what has been done. The positions taken must be consolidated.

Bryan opposed my nomination for the presidency. As far as I know, he said nothing in the campaign, but in commenting on the result he said that the Republican tidal wave was started by Wilson and completed by me. This could have had but one meaning: Wilson had been too unbending in his relations with the Senate and I had supported Wilson's position throughout. After Bryan left the cabinet, where his pacifist thinking was out of line with the mood of the country after the sinking of the *Lusitania*, he was caustically critical of Wilson in private conversation. From my first campaign in 1908, Bryan and I had been close personal and political friends. In all my campaigns up to 1920 he had given me sincere and enthusiastic help. When he made treaties with foreign countries pledging both them and our country to the arbitration of disputes, he appointed me as one of the American commissioners.

He spent the week end preceding the election in 1912 at Trails-end, our home near Dayton. He confided to me then his ambition to become Secretary of State under Wilson, whose election seemed certain. He asked me what I thought about it. I told him for one thing that it would do him good because he had always been a free-lance critic having no official responsibility. Now the time had come for him to sit on the other side of the desk and get the viewpoint of those on whose shoulders had fallen the conduct of affairs. Some time later, after the election, he requested me to write President-elect Wilson in his behalf. I did so and Mr. Bryan told me afterwards that Wilson's reply to me contained the first intimation that he intended to put Bryan at the head of the Department of State. When I returned to Washington for the December session of Congress in 1912, I was telling a group of prominent Democrats of the conversation that had ensued between Bryan and myself. William Hughes, then a member of the House and later United States Senator from New Jersey, remarked that his reason for favoring Bryan for the position would have been very different from that expressed by me. As he put it, "When you are on a football team, you never kick the shins of one of your own players. On this theory Bryan can do less harm inside the fold than out."

Bryan's expressed reason for not supporting me in 1920 was that politically he did not like those who had helped in my nomination. Too many of them were anti-prohibitionists. He failed to note that the votes that came to me from the beginning of the San Francisco convention were scattered geographically and divided widely over the liquor question. Joseph W. Folk, former governor of Missouri, took Bryan to task at the San Francisco convention for his attitude. Folk's words, repeated to me, were substantially these: "In the summer of 1919, I was passing through Dayton on my way to Washington. You came to the train at Dayton. Governor Cox had brought you to the station. The three of us talked together for quite a while. When the train started you were full of the subject of Governor Cox, remarking about the fine record he had made as chief executive of his state and emphasizing your belief that he was a fine piece of material for the future. Now what has happened to change all this?"

Bryan's only reply was: "I don't like some of the fellows that are for him."

After 1923, the year I entered the newspaper business in Miami, I saw a great deal of Mr. Bryan. He never mentioned the campaign of 1920, nor did I. From his demeanor no one would have known that anything had happened to create a rift between us. I bore no bitterness. It had long been my conviction, carried into practice, that hating another develops an internal poison that does the hater no good. Certainly one does himself more harm with his hating than he does the other fellow. Bryan told me he thought of running for senator in Florida. I endorsed the idea, believing he would, as the Great Commoner, honor the state of his adoption. At one time, whether before our conversation on the senatorship or afterwards, I do not know, Bryan told Justice James G. Johnson, of the Ohio Supreme Court, that he had made a mistake in the campaign of 1920, that in fact it was the greatest blunder of his political career, ungracious to me personally and not justified by the issues.

Bryan had passed the peak of his influence when he left the Wilson cabinet. He did not add to his fame in the Democratic National Convention of 1924. It was time for him to leave the stage of politics.

The fates decreed what Bryan himself would probably have desired—that he should leave the stage of life at the same time.

It is difficult to appraise the career of any public man without the perspective of years. Time must render the final verdict. The part which time plays in clearing up facts and in excluding prejudice and political bitterness is all-important. We can hear many conflicting opinions as to what Franklin D. Roosevelt's place in history will be. That makes discussion of it now interesting, even though not conclusive.

The American statesmen who have broadened the base of democracy and espoused the cause of the oppressed have, without exception, taken the highest rank in the award of time. Outstanding Presidents of the past, Jefferson, Jackson, Lincoln and Wilson, all came under this description. Since this invites comparison, the part that Roosevelt played in this particular respect cannot be denied. Jefferson, Jackson, Lincoln and Wilson were as bitterly hated as Roosevelt. Their contemporaries could not foresee the fame that awaited them. If we are to judge the future by the past, the Roosevelt achievements in behalf of the unprivileged will individualize his regime and place it in the distinguished list. Of the Presidents in this list, Jefferson and Wilson were more alike, and Jackson and Roosevelt. Jefferson and Wilson were of the scholarly, philosophical type. They believed that only by the principles of democratic government could a just and stable social order be maintained. They warned that to sustain democracy, vigilance would be required to prevent encroachments of privilege under government. Both pointed out that what is awarded unfairly to one class is taken from another. The whole basis of the Jeffersonian principle was equality of rights and opportunity. Of this, his legacy to the ages, he never had a more faithful disciple and heir than Wilson.

Jackson and Roosevelt are notable for instrumenting the principles of Jefferson through their leadership in legislative enactment and administrative policy. The bitterness vented upon these four Presidents expressed the resentment of men and groups deprived of privileges which they had been enjoying by grace of government. Naturally, great wealth accumulated through such unfair practices resents the loss of the preferences by which it is amassed.

There is a further interesting parallel between Jefferson and

412

Roosevelt in that both champions of equality came from the privileged leisure class. Their education was acquired under the easy circumstance of comfortable wealth. It is not unusual, strange as it may seem, to find men born and reared in the upper classes assuming leadership in behalf of the common people. The phenomenon is found in the history of the old countries of Europe. Count Leo Nikolaevich Tolstoy, powerful advocate of Russian democracy, was of the nobility. Englishmen of rank have many times cast aside the predilections common to their class and given their strength and genius to establishing a more equal justice for the lower classes. In America, Jefferson and Roosevelt stand out pre-eminent in this respect.

I knew Franklin D. Roosevelt long and well. We were not always of one mind in applying our philosophy of government, but that never disturbed our pleasant relationship.

His educational beginnings were in keeping with his circumstances. He attended aristocratic Groton, and went on to Harvard, which had a strong aristocratic element. What he saw at these institutions could not but have left a deep impression on him. Many young men flaunted their wealth, and the fact that a great deal of it had been accumulated under privileges improperly granted by law could not be ignored. Too many idle, wasteful lives were in the making, the sad product of riches which cut men off from the realities of life. In contrast, Harvard also had many young men who were working their way through school, keen students, athirst for knowledge but poor in worldly goods. Knowing Roosevelt as we do now, it is not difficult to imagine his reaction. When he left college he must have been keenly conscious of the injustices in our social and economic order.

About this time the country began hearing of the "parlor Socialists" of Eastern cities, a term used opprobriously by wealthy people. Young men and women were showing an interest in public matters, which was something new in these circles. Teddy Roosevelt was in the White House and was growing unpopular with the privileged. The powers dominant in the Republican party were beginning to realize that they had made a mistake in moving the "Rough Rider" out of the governorship of New York into the vice-presidency to get rid of him. Here was the beginning of the break which was to wreck the Republican party in 1912. Out of this interest in public matters came young Roosevelt's candidacy for a seat in the state Senate. He was elected and from here on the fates were kind, although his course could not have been approved by the practical politician.

From the outset Franklin Roosevelt was recognized as an independent. He joined the group which prevented the election to the United States Senate of William F. Sheehan, the Democratic caucus nominee. By all the rules of the political game, this should have wrecked his public career. He opposed the New York State Democratic organization in the national convention at Baltimore in 1912 and this put him in good favor with the Wilson administration. Young Roosevelt was an expert navigator and loved the seas and the ships that sailed them. His cousin, Theodore Roosevelt, had started his national career as Assistant Secretary of the Navy, and this might have influenced Franklin Roosevelt to seek this appointment. It was given to him by President Wilson.

The circumstances of his nomination for the vice-presidency have been told. The factors entering into that decision were both geographic and political. The pivotal states of Ohio and New York were represented at the head of the ticket. Consent of the New York Democratic organization to the nomination of young Roosevelt brought both the regular and irregular groups together in support of the ticket. This gave him his introduction to the country at large.

A photograph of Roosevelt and myself taken in Columbus, Ohio, on his way home from the San Francisco convention makes it difficult now to believe that the nominee for second place could have been as young as he looked in those days. It is interesting to recall that those in charge of the Republican campaign called attention to what they termed the immaturity of the vice-presidential nominee. In 1920 he was too young, the critics said; in 1944 he was too old. Politicians seem to have exacting if inconsistent tastes.

Roosevelt, then, was tall and almost gawkish in appearance. He made an excellent impression in the campaign, made friends easily and handled himself well. The crushing defeat of the Democratic ticket came at the election in 1920 and not long afterwards the friends Roosevelt had made in different parts of the country during the campaign were saddened by the news of the illness that befell him. He passed off the political scene completely and, as most men thought, permanently.

For a long time, little was heard of him. He was devoting himself exclusively and intensively to the task of recovering his health. It was a desperate battle and he mustered all his powers to win it.

In the spring of 1923, he spent a few weeks in the sunshine of south Florida, fishing and following the routine prescribed for his treatment. I went to see him, thinking it would be a sad occasion, but it was not. He was the same vibrant, courageous, cheerful person as of old. He almost seemed to be enjoying the contest he was waging.

Of a sudden, in the midst of the Democratic convention in New York in 1924, he appeared unannounced on the stage, presenting the name of Al Smith for the nomination for President, his "Happy Warrior" speech. The great audience, in its moment of surprise, fell at first into deep silence; then a tremendous ovation came. His task in presenting the name of his old friend was inspiring and the reception which he received could not but have been an inspiration and a happiness to him. Doubtless then and there a change came in his plans of life. He had been given assurance of the faith of the friends who were giving him their prayers in his struggle for life and health, and their earnest political support whenever it should be needed. At this time, under date of June 27, 1924, I wired him my greetings and encouragement in a message which read: "I was proud of you when I heard over the radio every word of your speech. It told me that you were on your way back to health, and that made me very happy. It was an able speech, beautifully delivered."

During the first years of his sickness, considerable correspondence passed between us, but never a note of despair came from him. He was always brave and hopeful.

A great decision was to be made in 1928. Governor Smith was insisting on Roosevelt's accepting the Democratic nomination for governor. There could not but be conflicting considerations. Would giving the strength which his candidacy and the governorship would exact militate against his recovery? Or would it be an inspiriting experience to be turned to advantage physically and otherwise? His wife, a niece of former President Theodore Roosevelt, urged acceptance in the fighting spirit of old "Teddy" himself. The result was a triumph. Not many agreed with me at the time that Roosevelt could be elected even if Al Smith, the presidential nominee, failed to carry New York. My theory was that Smith would poll a tremendous vote and that everyone who voted for him would "vote the ticket straight." Thousands of those who left Smith on religious grounds alone would yet support the rest of the Democratic ticket, making Roosevelt run ahead of Smith. This is what happened.

Again Roosevelt appeared before a Democratic National Convention. At Houston, in 1928, the then governor of New York made another notable speech, again presenting Smith, who was this time nominated.

Roosevelt was re-elected governor in 1930. The Democratic tide was running high and the decisive majority which he received brought him into the presidential picture. It was after this and on to 1932 that the friendship between Roosevelt and Smith began to cool. In early 1932, Smith expressed his own feeling to me by asserting that he believed that by all the rules of the political game he was entitled to renomination. That year, Roosevelt, as he stated, had never mentioned his own candidacy to him. As Smith put it, "If he had come to me and given his grounds for believing that I was not available and pressing his own claims for preference, we could have talked it over and might have come to a satisfactory understanding." Roosevelt and his friends believed that Smith could neither be nominated nor elected, that the party had suffered a severe reverse by precipitating a religious fight and that there should be no repetition of 1928.

The economic scene in America when Roosevelt took his oath of office, on March 4, 1933, was sad and discouraging. The like of it had never confronted any President. Jefferson and Jackson would both have attributed it to a misguided democracy which, possessing the power to prevent the disaster, had lost its senses in the fictitious prosperity incident to an orgy of speculation. Roosevelt, whose inaugural address will rank with the great presidential documents, knew that the wreckage before him was the fruitage of errors and injustices in government. He could not but know that assaulting those injustices would mean a titanic struggle with their beneficiaries, the entrenched powers which had for so long controlled the country's politics.

It would be a bitter struggle, with all the mighty power of privileged wealth and class prejudice pitted against him. It would be no fight with gloves. When special privilege battles for its existence it fights with tooth and claw. He would be slandered. His family would be persecuted. He would be the object of the bitterest hate. Even so had Jefferson, Jackson and Wilson been fought before. Roosevelt could not but have known what cruel enmity lay up the road on which he elected to take his course.

I have pondered much the part which his sickness and his battle for recovery may have played in readying Roosevelt for the ordeal which he here took upon himself. In my mind run the lines, the authorship unknown to me, which go like this:

> . . . *Many lucky elf,*
> *Losing fortune has but found himself.*

One of Roosevelt's most delightful qualities was his ebullient sense of humor. Two incidents in our intercourse happily illustrate it. It will be recalled that just after he came into office in 1933, his administration indulged in a brief spasm of economy. When I was in Congress I had been instrumental in getting a station of the Weather Bureau placed in Dayton; now it was abolished. I spoke to Roosevelt about it. "Why, Frank, that is a special pet of mine," was my good-natured protest. He laughed. "Well, Jim, I'll see that your pet station is left alone," he said. "You know that was just the Scotch streak in me!"

On another occasion, when he was about to bring two Republicans into his cabinet to help meet the war crisis, I urged him to drop two quite unfit men whom he was considering—and whom he later did drop. One day prior to the campaign of 1944 I was lunching with the President in the White House and the discussion of a vice-presidential candidate came up. At that time he was thinking mostly of William O. Douglas. Robert H. Jackson's name was mentioned and I responded with the observation that I felt he was a fine piece of material for the future. Roosevelt's reply was: "He is a very able man but he wouldn't do as a candidate on the ticket because he has no sex appeal." This circumstance revealed the unusual, intuitive political sense of Roosevelt.

And now a word about the much-discussed Eleanor Roosevelt, wife of the President. Not a great while ago I chanced to be in a room of a club adjoining one where a group of women were spend-

417

ing their afternoon at bridge. This was at Miami Beach, where we were awakened every morning by the reveille sounded by the buglers of the regiments of our military forces in training there. Everywhere were marching men, symbol of the strength and patriotism of young America. Most people, including the great number of women in Red Cross work, were doing their utmost for the war. Here in this club one would hardly have known that a war was on. About the only thing under discussion was Eleanor Roosevelt. Silly rumors were hashed and rehashed and their silliness and falsehood grew with each recital. It was a buzzing, animated circle, and when the women had talked themselves out, I chanced to be walking by.

"What do you think of Eleanor Roosevelt?" some member of the group inquired. This is what I said: "I have known her for a great many years. She is a woman of inherent refinement and a great lover of humanity. If she were to come into this presence for half an hour, she would disarm every one of you and make you all ashamed of yourselves. She is not the person you have been discussing. We who view our times with smug complacency, believing that our civilization, since we ourselves are comfortable, is without fault, know too little of what is going on in the dark places of life. She has found them and brought there the kindly touch of her hand and heart. Some of her projects may seem and may be impractical. But as long as she lives, she will continue her labors as a good Samaritan. If she were the wife of a mechanic, she would in that sphere be doing just what she is doing now. If she were the Queen of England, with all the inhibitions which royalty imposes, she would in that sphere be doing just what she is doing now. That is what I think about Eleanor Roosevelt."

A great regret is that I did not see more of Wendell L. Willkie. He was a rare product of our public and political life. To be transplanted from a public service corporation lawyer to the presidential nominee of the Republican party in a brief space of years is an event which stands without parallel. Nothing except the man's ability, sincerity and intellectual honesty, which kept him always free from any inconsistency, made this possible. In the presidential campaign of 1920 he introduced me at the public meeting in the Armory at Akron. Not long before he had come to that city and was employed by the Firestone Rubber Company at a salary of

$250 a month. He was a promising young lawyer, but even then a very commanding personality. He told me once that he was confirmed as a liberal in his political thinking through the complete overhauling of our state government during my administration.

When the *Wilson* picture was to be given its premiere in New York in 1944, he invited Mrs. Cox and me to be present as guests of Mrs. Willkie and himself both at the picture and at a buffet dinner preceding the event. In his letter to me he suggested that we breakfast the following morning at the residence of Albert D. Lasker. We were together three hours. The presidential campaign was under way, both party conventions having been held. Our talk was understood to be confidential, Willkie speaking in the frankest possible way of conditions, events and personalities; and it would be improper for me to repeat a single word of it. In the same way, his letters to me must for the time being remain sealed. But I can say that I was impressed by the fact that his very soul was aflame with his desire to see peace secured by international cooperation.

CHAPTER XXXV

ROOSEVELT IN HIS LETTERS

◆

EVERY LINE which I have written about President Roosevelt and appearing ahead of this was finished before his death. By singular coincidence, I completed it on the day of his death at almost the precise minute of his passing into the shadows. It is doubtful whether the death of any man brought such universal sorrow. Bitterness of other days seemed for the moment to have disappeared. The most striking thing about the nation's grief was that those in the humble walks of life all seemed to be moved by the same sad observation, "We have lost our friend." In many ways, this was the most sublime tribute of all.

In all our Sunday papers was published my tribute to Mr. Roosevelt. Parts of it follow:

In this hour of a nation's grief, we cannot but feel that death, that mute autocrat from whose decisions there is no appeal, has been most unkind. But this has happened before. If Lincoln had been spared, the wounds of war would have been more quickly healed and the South would have been spared the horrible experiences of reconstruction. If Woodrow Wilson had not fallen in the midst of his struggle for peace, the world might have been vastly different today. And now, in this needful hour, with so many things to be done—things that the President knew more about than anyone else—we find ourselves constantly confronted by the question, why did this tragic thing have to be? Perhaps the deep meaning of it all as with Lincoln and Wilson is beyond the finite mind. . . .

While he knew of the part I had played in remaking our whole state government in Ohio under a new constitution and that I was often called a radical and socialist at the time, he still recognized that many liberals, including myself, did not entirely agree with him. But the difference was more in administrative method than principle. And yet, not a single unpleasant incident ever marred our friendship. His attitude of mind toward me in 1920 never changed. This generous gesture continued even though the Fates had altered our ranks. This naturally helped bind me to the man in ties of real affection. . . .

It so happened that at one of our luncheon engagements in 1940, he told me of his plans to create more of a non-political cabinet and said that conditions would seem to justify a coalition arrangement. On a writing pad before him was the list of names of those whom he was considering. I strongly objected to two of them, contending with respectful vigor that they would not be accepted by the country as a real intention on the part of the President to create better efficiency within the government. He ran his pencil through both names. Later he appointed Stimson and Knox as the heads of the War and Navy departments, respectively. . . .

In a telephone conversation I had with him just before he left for Warm Springs, he seemed to be quite himself. I remarked that if he was as well as he sounded, he must be in good shape. He said the most bedeviling thing was sinus trouble which persisted in the Washington climate. Nowhere else was he ever conscious of it.

I apologized for taking his time, but he continued the talk, asking why I did not come to see him. I was complimented because I thought I caught a note of homesickness for old friendships in his voice. . . .

Let no one be deceived nor permit himself in prejudice to believe that Roosevelt was not the real leader in our war movements. Every industrial leader and every military commander, whether on land or sea, was kept on the alert by his untiring vigilance. . . .

No one will doubt that Roosevelt's outstanding act of the war was to sweep away the old timeworn seniority rule in the Army and Navy and pick and promote the most capable officers regardless of rank. We shudder to think what might have happened if this had not been done. . . .

One cannot appraise his works without being reminded of Stanton's remark at the death of Lincoln, "He now belongs to the ages."

I was deeply moved by an editorial utterance of the New York *Times* which said:

Men will thank God on their knees, a hundred years from now, that Franklin D. Roosevelt was in the White House, in a position to give leadership to the thought of the American people and direction to the activities of their government, in that dark hour when a powerful and ruthless barbarism threatened to overrun the civilization of the Western world and to destroy the work of centuries of progress.

I think something else will be thought about one hundred years from now and will be taught to youngsters in their classrooms. It is Mr. Roosevelt's remarkable triumph over physical affliction. For years he labored with a sustained industry that was amazing. Mustering every ounce of his strength, he met the final challenge. Victory was his and he passed into the lists of the immortals. His sitting in a wheel chair throughout the long conferences with Churchill and Stalin is a fact that will never be blotted out from human consciousness. I remember a visit I had with him in the White House in 1940. Momentarily, at that time, he seemed to be forming a resolve in his mind to quit public life. Rather pathetically he said to me, "You see I sit here at this desk all day long. Delegations pass by; conferences run into the hours. With you, in your office it is different. You can get up and walk around and thus relieve the pressure of countless tasks. Sometimes it is hard to take."

Some of the letters which passed between us through the years may be of interest and shed some light upon events. They follow:

February 10, 1921

My dear Governor:

You must have had an interesting time in Washington, and I congratulate you on the splendid way in which you handled the situation, for I am certain that our newspaper friends were on the lookout for all sorts of sensational stories.

Fireworks at this particular time must certainly be avoided.

Don't forget that if you and Mrs. Cox come to New York you must let us know beforehand, and if you are to be here for a Saturday and Sunday we count on your coming to us at Hyde Park.

Mrs. Roosevelt joins me in warm regards to you both.

Very sincerely yours,

Franklin D. Roosevelt.

September 20, 1921

My dear Governor Cox:

My husband was so much pleased at your kind telegram. It is a strange thing to have infantile paralysis at his age, but luckily it has been a mild attack and the doctors say he has every chance for complete recovery and at the worst will only be lame, but it is a slow business and very galling therefore to an active man. However, he is very cheerful and now that six weeks are over, I hope we may see more rapid progress and that before long he may leave the hospital.

We feel we have been very fortunate in that no one else in our household caught it, for we had six children with us all summer.

If you and Mrs. Cox are here at any time, won't you let us know for we do so much want to see you?

With many thanks for your kind interest and warm regards from us both to Mrs. Cox,

Very sincerely yours,
Eleanor Roosevelt.

November 10, 1921

Dear Governor Cox:

Franklin is back from the hospital and able to do a good deal of business now. He is up twice a day in a wheel chair and sees a good many people. Now, too, his health is really gaining and before long we hope he may be on crutches.

It is a very, very slow, long fight back to health and strength, but we hope in the end for a complete recovery.

It was so kind of you to write and we both appreciate your thought. We hope you and Mrs. Cox may be in New York sometime soon and that we may have the pleasure of seeing you.

Sincerely yours,
Eleanor Roosevelt.

March 31, 1922

My dear Governor:

I hear you are coming to New York for the dinner of the National Democratic Club on April 8th, and I hope very much that I shall have an opportunity to see you at that time. I wish we could have you to stay with us, but there is literally not a single spare bed in our somewhat limited quarters. Do, however, dine with us on Friday the 7th, or on Sunday the 9th, and

423

if you cannot do that come in and see me whatever afternoon you have free, at 49 East 65th Street.

I am getting on well though the process is, of course, slow. I have been on crutches for about a month, but all of the muscles are in the process of coming back, and it is simply a question of time.

I liked your Ohio speech and it seems to me that things are certainly looking brighter for the Party.

Always sincerely yours,
Franklin D. Roosevelt.

April 3, 1922

My dear Frank:

I can't tell you how much joy I have in receiving your letter. It indicates a contact with business. I have been confident that your marvelous vitality would pull you through. Your letter is a great reassurance.

I shall not leave here until Friday night, but I shall most certainly get in touch with you some time during my stay in New York.

With every good wish for you and yours, I am

Very sincerely yours,
James M. Cox.

November 29, 1922

My dear Frank:

You have been in my thoughts for a long time and now I cannot delay any longer writing you. Tell me how you are. What progress is being made since I saw you and what are you feeling about further improvement? I felt you were pretty badly bunged up, but your spirit was hopeful and courageous and I said to the gentlemen who were with me on that day that you would pull through. I met your nurse at Milan, Italy. We were on our way to Switzerland and had motored from the hotel to the place where the famous picture of The Last Supper is shown. On arriving there, we were advised that the doors would not open until ten o'clock. The custodian very courteously waived the rules and told us to go in. There were two ladies at the doorway and they seemed to recognize me. One of them explained she had served as your nurse for a considerable time. I told her of my visit to you in the spring. She was a very intelligent and interesting person.

On the ship coming back, I met a Mrs. Roosevelt who, if I

424

am not mistaken, is your cousin—a very charming woman—and while I fancy she is a Republican, she has the international viewpoint as has everyone else who has been abroad recently. Not all of them will permit themselves to be truthful in reporting their own impressions.

Write me a note about yourself—that's what I am most interested in.

Very sincerely yours,
James M. Cox.

December 8, 1922

My dear Jim:

It is mighty nice to get your note and soon I hope to see your own cheering self. I am just back to New York after a very successful summer in the country at Hyde Park. The combination of warm weather, fresh air and swimming has done me a world of good; in fact, in some respects I am in far better physical shape than ever before in my life, and I have developed a chest and pair of shoulders on me which would make Jack Dempsey envious. I have resumed going to my office down town two or three times a week.

Politically also I have had an interesting summer and autumn. You may have heard of the "Dear Al," "Dear Frank" correspondence in August which brought forward Al Smith's candidacy and eventually killed off Hearst's nomination and gave us the enormous majority of over 500,000. What pleases me most, however, is that the return wave to Democracy elected governors in New Hampshire, Rhode Island, Kansas, Oregon, etc.; and senators in Delaware, Indiana, Washington, etc. That is a pretty wide sweep of the country.

I particularly want to talk with you and talk with you soon, about many things of importance. What I am basically convinced of, and I know you are, after your trip abroad, is that the country is beginning to recognize that national isolation on our part will not only allow further disintegration in the Near East, Europe, etc., but from our own purely selfish point of view will bring hard times, cut off exports, etc., etc. How far the Democratic party should go just now is a thing which the leaders should talk over in the near future.

I am not wholly convinced that the country is yet quite ready for a definite stand on our part in favor of immediate entry into the League of Nations. That will come in time, but I am convinced we should stand firmly against the isolation

425

policy of Harding's administration. I hear today, on very good authority, that Hughes says that the administration has abandoned all thought of even an Association of Nations.

Do come to New York soon. I will be here until February 1st when I go to Florida for 4 or 5 weeks to get more swimming. I much wish that we could have you and your charming wife to stay with us, but our house is literally overflowing with children. If you can come on soon do let me know beforehand and it might be worth while to get some of the people from Washington to talk things over.

I hope that all goes well with you and yours. I am keen to hear all about the European trip.

Always sincerely yours,
Franklin D. Roosevelt.

January 27, 1940

Dear Jim:

Peace be with you! Let not magazine stories, nor any other one of the printed arts, worry or give you any concern.

I can assure you, also, the newspapers will have a difficult time finding any report, either from the commission or any of its sub-committees, which will give them headline material.

On the whole, radio is doing a good job. You know how I feel about radio and the press. Such opinions as I have could be given to any group of radio experts and, within five minutes' time, I believe we would be entirely in accord. So you see, I am pretty well satisfied with existing conditions in radio management and in radio relationships and responsibilities to government.

It was good to hear from you. If you find yourself coming this way, let me know. It would be good to see you.

As ever,
F. D. R.

March 20, 1940

Dear Jim:

You must have been blessed with great good fortune in order to move through the years of your life up to 1938 before discovering that you had sinuses. Would that I had been equally blessed—even sufficiently blessed to be able, after my sinuses discovered me, to have found a cure.

Perhaps Florida helped you find a cure for sinus. In any

event, I would gladly give you a Washington winter in exchange for a Miami winter.

Please give Anne my best wishes and tell her I wish her much happiness.

Very sincerely yours,
Franklin D. Roosevelt.

September 5, 1940

My dear Frank:

About the destroyers and the bases:

That was the right thing to do, and a brave thing to do. It may elect you and it may defeat you. If the latter, what does it matter? The important thing is what, in the calm judgment of time, history will say. As an illustration, would you or I change places with the round robiners of 1919 and 1920?

All good wishes.

Sincerely,
James M. Cox.

November 19, 1940

Dear Jim:

On my return from a trip of a few days down the river, I found your two letters.

I was interested to get a copy of Harry Wilson's poll and was struck by the accuracy of your estimate of the situation. The fact that Clarke County, which has rarely gone Democratic, went for me is very noteworthy. All in all, I am very much gratified by the results in Ohio.

I have noted very carefully your remarks about my being the ambassador of good will and that I should cast a smile on business. I am sure you know that I shall do all possible to promote a feeling of good will, trust and friendly cooperation between this administration and the business world. But I believe in *"Reciprocity."*

Very sincerely yours,
Franklin D. Roosevelt.

September 4, 1941

My dear Frank:

While your position with respect to the world menace has been consistent and unwavering from the outset, still after your Monday speech it will be written of you in time to come that

427

in the face of appeasers' shortsighted selfishness and cowardice, you refused to enter into an armistice with the devil.

All good wishes.

Sincerely yours,
James M. Cox.

September 7, 1941

My dear Frank: A nation stands in grief and sympathy with you in your great sorrow. The pattern of Motherhood which Mother Roosevelt bequeathed to her native land, and your beautiful devotion to her, are an inspiration that moves every heart in these trying days.

James M. Cox.

February 4, 1942

Dear Jim:

I genuinely appreciate your birthday greeting with its old-time tone. And, believe me, good wishes at this time are most inspiring.

Very sincerely yours,
F. D. R.

After the defeat of the Talmadge dynasty in Georgia in 1942, the following messages passed:

Atlanta, Ga., September 10, 1942

My dear Frank: The atmosphere of Georgia is so much better this morning. Come back soon.

J. M. C.

September 11, 1942

Dear Jim: I am "perfectly delighted" about Georgia. The good old worm has definitely turned. I hope to see you soon.

As ever yours,
Franklin D. Roosevelt.

April 6, 1943

My dear Frank:

Some time ago a man who is about to write a book on presidential campaigns asked if I had any interesting pictures on the affair of 1920. I found a negative in the Dayton office which I do not recall ever seeing before. I don't know whether it is you or your son Jimmie. I can hardly believe now that you looked so young then. Certainly I did not get the idea at the time. I have often wondered whether you got the real quality of the compliment of having been picked sight unseen. I am sending the picture under separate cover. I also have one which shows Joe Robinson, who was chairman of the convention, if you would like it.

All good wishes.

Sincerely,
James M. Cox.

April 10, 1943

Dear Jim:

Considering the years that have passed since the taking of that photograph, I would say that you and I are exceptionally well preserved—a little less hair now, and a little bit grayer—but thank the Lord neither of us has wholly lost the spirit of youth.

I hope to Heaven that you are right that our politics will in brief time get rid of its pettiness. Sometimes I get awfully discouraged.

However, however, however—I still believe in representative democracy! I shall be delighted to see the photo of Joe Robinson.

Take care of yourself and I do hope to see you soon.

As ever yours,
Franklin D. Roosevelt.

November 5, 1943

Dear Jim:

Many thanks for your wire. You are right about the guerrillas. I sometimes think that there must be an awful lot of Americans who are descended from the Greeks and the Yugoslavs. Like their prototype, they have quit fighting the Germans and are fighting each other.

Do let me know if you come to Washington at any time.

As ever yours,
Franklin D. Roosevelt.

March 28, 1944

Dear Jim:

As your birthday draws near I just want you to know that I am thinking of you and hoping the day will bring you much happiness.

As the years pass I cherish with increasing satisfaction my association with you. Out of that association has deepened a friendship which I highly prize and which I know will continue until one or the other of us can enter into no human relationships. Confidentially I may be away from Washington in the not distant future—exactly when I cannot say. But I want to see you. I will not attempt to set a date now, but after my return I shall ask Pa Watson to give you an appointment.

Hearty congratulations and every good wish.

As ever yours,

Franklin D. Roosevelt.

November 15, 1944

Dear Jim:

I have sent Harllee Branch's name to the Senate for reappointment. He has been a grand fellow and, as you know, he was one of my Georgia finds back in the twenties.

By the way, I understand there was an Election a week ago Tuesday. I was mad for two or three weeks before that and I am still mad. That may not be Christian but it is a human fact. It was the dirtiest campaign I have ever experienced, and I may end up by writing an addition to the Books of the Apocrypha, illustrating that dirty campaigns do not pay the throwers.

I do wish you would come via Washington when you next go South. I do want to see you one of these days.

With my warm regards.

As ever yours,

F. D. R.

November 21, 1944

Dear Jim:

I heard the speech you gave over the radio last month—the coast-to-coast one—and this letter comes to you as a belated piece of "fan mail." I thought it was one of the best speeches of the entire campaign. I remember that you ended it with a declaration of your faith in the people of America—who have since spoken their minds. Your hard-hitting exposure of the isolationists seems to have taken effect.

In working for the kind of peace you and I have in mind, the public enlightenment that you have helped to bring about is basic. For that reason, among many others, I feel a sense of gratitude to you which this brief note is meant to convey.

Sincerely yours,

Franklin D. Roosevelt.

430

PART NINE

Things to Be Learned with the Years

Advice to Roosevelt on Decision and Fatigue

The Meaning of Rhythm in Life

Happy Days in the North Woods

On a Mule Behind Good Bird Dogs

Experiences in Golf

What of Tomorrow?

CHAPTER XXXVI

WORK, RECREATION AND HEALTH

◆

It is a mistake, as I see it, for anyone to attempt to lay out a health formula for others. The best anyone can do is discover what gives best results to himself. In that conviction, I will give no advice, but will confine myself to telling how, after passing the allotted three score and ten without radically changing my manner of living, I am still functioning healthfully and, I think, with a fair measure of efficiency.

Gladstone insisted that his best work was done after he reached the age of seventy. Obviously, mind and body cannot be in prime condition at this time of life unless attention has been given to the fundamentals of health. Borrowing words spoken long ago, I would say it is important at the outset to pick ancestors notable for vitality. The best-built machine needs constant attention if it is to work and wear well, though one should not become obsessed with the subject of health. That is the road to hypochondria.

To me, health is a matter of maintaining a rhythmic way of living. Except for rhythm and the balance which rhythm keeps, the world would collapse. It is the same with the human body. Rhythm is the lubricant of life, the very essence of life, perhaps. Clear thought is a rhythmic process. There is a rhythm in the healthful consumption and assimilation of food. If the student receives information in logical order, you have the proper growth of the mind. If physical exercise is rhythmically maintained, not overdone, you gain strength and vitality in every muscle, fiber and nerve. Our great war effort manifested, as never before, the power of rhythm. We have here had the correlated labors of millions of people both on and away from the battle fronts. It may prove to have been worth the cost of the war to discover in this, the most stupendous human effort in all history, the possibility of human cooperation.

433

If we maintain our rhythm in living we conserve our strength with advancing years.

In our youth we should prepare ourselves, if possible, for an occupation that will give us congenial and hence rhythmic labor which will help to keep us at our tasks into our last days. A businessman should never retire. Wiser through experience, he will not need, to be effective, the hours of work he once required.

Sitting in a canoe or rowboat with a guide or trapper, you will find yourself applying in the use of oar or paddle three or four times as much strength as he requires in his rhythmic motion. The practice of timing in golf reveals how power can be expended unnecessarily. So it is in business, where the practiced mind finds short cuts with problems which in other days seemed involved and difficult. Someone asked me why I had undertaken my largest newspaper enterprise at the age of sixty-nine. My response was: "Running water never grows stagnant."

When a man is tired he should rest. No trying task, physical or mental, should be undertaken then. Once, lunching with President Franklin D. Roosevelt, at the White House, I told him he should never make an important decision when he was fatigued. "But I never get tired," he replied. I told him he would in the course of time, and to remember then what I had said to him. Furthermore, there would be days in the unspeakable Washington climate when the morning view of the great monument off in the distance would be obscured by fog and everything in nature was depressing. On these days, I suggested, if a major problem presented itself it should simply be ushered on into another day.

One born on a farm and remaining there during his boyhood is more apt than others to be a lover of nature. Discovering thus early what communion with nature means to health and efficiency, he begins life with a distinct advantage. I still think with refreshment of my pilgrimages into the wild regions of the north. Here a change of scene built up the reservoirs of health. Usually a camp was found on the banks of a lake. Very often we would take a sleeping bag and go into the very depths of the forest for the night. The strange nocturnal noises of the woods and their inhabitants cannot be described, but a brief season spent in these surroundings serves as a poultice to every nerve.

One such trip took me into New Brunswick, following the course of the Miramichi River. A certain area there was allotted to Ben Norad, a man in his seventies. No other guides with hunters were allowed on it. We lived in abandoned lumber camps. Moose were plentiful and there were some deer. We feasted on their meat as well as on ruffed grouse, wild duck and trout. I made the way back to civilization in a dugout following the current of the river. There are no more beautiful forests on earth than those in the province of New Brunswick. To this highly favored section, Joe Jefferson, the actor, and a companion, Sandy Wood, of Boston, went every spring in the salmon season. They did not go so far up the river. Spring lambs were driven to their camp on foot. Ben Norad, the veteran guide, said they lived like kings on leg of lamb, fish and Scotch whiskey. It was here that Governor Russell of Massachusetts, one of the most promising young men of his day, died in camp. When we penetrated the New Brunswick forest, we took along a milk cow, so that in addition to the gifts of the wilds, we added porridge, as only the English and Scotch can cook it, with fresh cream for breakfast.

Through the Gatineau country north of Ottawa, I fished for small-mouthed bass with Col. Butler, long president of the Canadian Car and Foundry Company, and J. O. Shoup, a dear friend of long standing living in Dayton. Another interesting expedition started overland at Murray Bay in Quebec. Francis Burton Harrison, then a member of Congress and afterwards Governor General of the Philippine Islands, United States Senator William Hughes of New Jersey and I composed the party. This took us to wild country, dotted abundantly with lakes. I have never seen such large or beautiful beaver houses, and it was a natural habitat for caribou. We hunted in weather far below zero with French guides who couldn't speak a word of English. In one of the best shots I ever made I dropped a bull caribou at a distance of three hundred yards.

Burton Harrison was a fine woodsman and the finest type of sportsman. Hughes, both wit and philosopher, although unused to such excursions, was a rare companion. It was a rich experience to go into the lake country north of the Seigniory settlement on the Ottawa River in Canada for trout and grouse. During the glacial age, stones of tremendous size had been brought into this section and many of them rest in the lakes. We would catch our trout, build a fire on the rocks and cook our lunch. An hour's quest in the woodlands was sufficient to get three or four grouse. I once asked

435

the editor of an outdoor publication to give me the name of the best bass lake in Canada. He mentioned the Panache country north of Georgian Bay, which we entered by automobile from the Soo by way of Espanola. The large lake derives its name from the antlers of the deer, since its shore lines are irregular. Here both bass and walleyed pike were numerous. This lake is tremendous in size. Deer could usually be seen on its shores and there must be several hundred islands in it. The automobile has long since deprived it of its primeval charm.

Despite the well-known beauties of the Canadian forests and the abundance of fish and wild life, I am yet compelled to say that a small lake, Brevoort, in the upper peninsula of Michigan was, forty years ago, the most romantic spot I ever saw. Ten miles from the little settlement at the lower end of the lake we built a very comfortable cottage. William H. Schaeffer, who in a long life had followed the retreat of the deer to the north country, William Stroop, an Ohio neighbor, and I joined in the venture. The evenings and mornings there were sublime beyond words. There had been very little lumbering and north of the lake was a forest of tremendous trees. On summer trips, fishing furnished our chief food, green pike, trout and bass. The largest small-mouthed green bass I ever saw we caught there. It weighed 6½ pounds. When pike is properly cooked, even a connoisseur cannot tell the difference between it and muskellunge, regarded as the king of the northern waters. It was no trouble in season to kill all the grouse we needed. In the late fall, there were wild duck and deer. But the automobiles and the construction of a highway to the north destroyed this sportsman's paradise. This is now compelling a great many fishermen to fly into remote sections of Canada in small seaplanes.

It delights the soul to be alone in the big game country of the north, and yet you have the same contentment and happiness fishing and living in the keys off southern Florida. A widely traveled sportsman once told me that he thought Shark River beyond Cape Sable was the wildest spot in the world. He reported going upstream one night in a skiff propelled by an outboard motor. He had a fair-sized electric light which caught reflections from the eyes of panther, wild cat, raccoon and deer. It made the place look, as he put it, like Fifth Avenue after dark. Nature is on proud display in these keys in the season of the full moon. The ebb and flow of the tides and the music of night noises make one feel that here is heaven on earth.

Many companionable hours were spent in these regions with Dr. John Oliver La Gorce, one of the editors of *Geographic Magazine*. He is an authority in matters of nature and can handle a rod and reel as well as anyone I know.

South of the Matecumbe area and west of No Name Key a picture unfolds that I have never seen described. Uncounted islands and running streams through that tremendous expanse of flats afford fine fishing grounds. While there are strong currents in these courses, the water is moved entirely by the action of the tides. Another good fisherman with us in this section was Dr. Hugh Young. He once said to me: "If I had my way I would never again drop the rod and reel to take up the knife of the surgeon at Johns Hopkins University." It was he who operated on Diamond Jim Brady. That operation was a pioneer experiment and the Western man of gold, in appreciation of its success, gave the institution a million dollars to build a surgical unit. Dr. Young once told me he had an assignment to operate on an international figure in Rome. Mussolini vetoed the arrangements. He said it would be a reflection on the Italian surgeons.

I never had much of a yen for Florida hunting. On several occasions I had good duck shooting in submerged lands west of Hialeah during the rainy season, but I could never get the fear of moccasin snakes out of my mind. Once, while snipe shooting, I ran across two of these dangerous specimens, killed both of them, found my way back to the automobile and called it the end for all time for that kind of sport. I have happy memories of days spent with Glenn Curtiss near a settlement called Brighton, west of Lake Okeechobee. He and James H. Bright owned 56,000 acres, most of it fine, high land—high for Florida. There was a fine covering of broom sedge, and wild turkeys and quail feasted on the seeds and berries of the palmetto palm. Once we set off on horseback at dawn, always a heavenly hour in the open spaces.

We had a happy experience on the moors of Scotland. With Mrs. Cox I had gone to Glenn Eagles, which has become quite as famous to golfers as St. Andrews. One evening a telephone call came from Bernard M. Baruch at Feteresso Castle, Stonehaven, a hundred miles away, with an invitation to spend the week end. The grouse season was on, and we accepted. One can understand why this annual event means so much to sportsmen in the British Isles. Mr. Baruch had taken the place for the summer season. He was an ideal host. Grouse shooting is quite different from anything in this country. You take your place in the butts, and the beaters drive the birds into the wind towards you. While it is great sport, it isn't comparable to quail shooting on muleback following a good pair of bird dogs.

The man who has never ridden on a mule behind a pair of fine setters or pointer dogs lacks an experience gained in no other way. While game was abundant, I went every fall to Hodgenville, Kentucky, the county seat village near which Lincoln was born. John Burba, our host, was a fine shot and loved to hunt. Many a day we roamed over the lands made sacred as the boyhood home of Lincoln. The cabin in which he was born is enclosed in a classic structure of granite. Taking up a complete side wall of this structure was a fulsome tribute to old Tom Lincoln, Abe's father. Any student of Lincoln knows that the paternal parent made small impress either upon the time or the mind of his distinguished son; Lincoln always said that whatever he was, he owed to his mother. I was so impressed with the incongruity of the reference to Old Tom that I was happy to learn only recently that the carved words have been plastered over. It was a fitting thing to do.

The cabin was built beside an unusual spring, the waters of which run but a short distance in the open and then go underground, coming out about two miles away into Nolen Creek. Every youngster in this country should be taken to the place of Lincoln's birth. The combined lessons of all the classrooms in America do not give such an appreciation of the fact that in our country a humble beginning is not an impossible barrier to success.

Twenty years ago the finest quail-shooting country in America, in my judgment, was in what is known as the Black Belt in Alabama. I went there regularly once a year. Tom Taggart, of Indiana, and Senator Pat Harrison, of Mississippi, once made the trip with me. Our host was Judge Edward Leslie, of Tuskegee. He presided over the local court, ran one of the town banks and was an extensive dealer in cotton. He had hunting rights on a vast area, and twenty-five coveys of quail a day were common here. We made it a point never to shoot up any one of them badly.

It has often been said that a man gets only one good bird dog during his lifetime. It has been my privilege to have had three. Tom, a setter, named for Tom Taggart, Sport, the most beautiful thing on canine legs I ever saw, and Robert E. Lee, who had the master touch of artistry if any dog ever had. They, and other prize dogs, including beagles—and who can forget the music of their voices?—are buried in our dog cemetery at Trailsend.

What one has missed who has never lived with horses and known their qualities well enough to love them! My experience started with breaking colts on the farm in the springtime, then later owning trotters, which I sometimes drove in matinee races, and winding up in the saddle. Below Trailsend, in the Hills and Dales country, are miles of fine bridle paths. It was my custom for many years to be on horseback at six o'clock in the morning. Attending the annual trots at Lexington one autumn, I had a riding engagement with C. K. G. Billings, who owned more trotting kings and queens of the turf, notably Lou Dillon and Uhlan, than any man of his generation. He was mounted on Lady Forest, a beautiful black mare with a white face, having a pole record of 2.02¼. I was on a mahogany bay stallion subsequently given to the government for a remount station in the Philippines. After leisurely rounding the mile track the reverse way, we turned at the head of the stretch and these finely bred animals were off like a shot. We trotted the mile under saddle in 2.15.

Justice Harlan of the United States Supreme Court once said that golf was not a fad, but a disease. He was one of the earliest disciples of the game in this country, and I, too, must here admit my debt to the great game of golf. The two things about it which most appeal to me are that it is a challenge to self-control and coordination and that it develops treasured human companionships. If one follows the inhibitions which common sense suggests, it can be played by old men. Arthur Balfour, the English statesman, often shot eighty after he reached fourscore years. We now have senior champions over eighty years old.

Golf sometimes breaks down the bars of modesty. If a player does an unusual thing, he is apt to bore his friends talking about it. This recalls two episodes to my mind. The fourteenth hole at La Gorce course at Miami Beach, where the first $15,000 tournament was held, is 335 yards long. The crack players of the world have trod fairways of this course and emitted mild profanity on its greens, yet the fourteenth hole has been played but once in two. It happened in a foursome made up of John Golden, the playwright, Dan J.

Mahoney, my son-in-law, Albert Lasker, the advertising magnate, and myself. I had a beautiful tee shot, about 225 yards. I then took a number five iron and the moment the steel met the ball, I had a feeling that I would have at least a birdie; instead, I got an eagle. This was in the early part of 1932, a presidential year. Jim Farley's followers were whooping it up for Roosevelt, and rumors were spread about the alleged physical infirmities of prominent Democrats who might appear in opposition to Farley's man. The story about me was that I had suffered a stroke. It reached Miami about the time of the dramatic golf shot. A newspaper reporter phoned John Golden to inquire about it because he knew that the playwright and I were good friends. John's reply was, "No, he hasn't had a stroke—he had two of them yesterday on the fourteenth hole!"

To be sure of my facts, I wrote to Willie Klein, summer professional at Wheatley Hills course, Garden City, Long Island, and winter professional at La Gorce. He has served there since La Gorce was built. Here's what he says under date of August 15, 1944:

> You are absolutely correct about the fourteenth hole at La Gorce course being played in two but once. You are the golfer who did it.

For this feat, if that's what it can be called, Dr. John La Gorce, after whom the course had been named, presented me with a beautiful silver eagle bearing a plate with these engraved words:

> To James M. Cox for the first eagle ever made on No. 14 hole, La Gorce Course, Miami Beach, March 8, 1932.

The other occasion I like to recall happened at Sunningdale, near London, England. I played there a few weeks after Bobby Jones had established a course record which will probably stand for all time. His score was 66—33 going out and 33 coming in. On the fifteenth hole, which is 229 yards long, Bobby had a twelve-foot putt for a deuce but missed it and took a three. I played it in two, using a spoon and one putt. In the times we have been together, I have often reminded Bobby Jones of one more notable thing to do—beat my two on number fifteen at Sunningdale.

It has been my privilege to play golf with most of the "greats" of the world, from Harry Vardon to Bobby Jones and then with some of the present notables. Vardon would doubtless have died as a young man except for golf. When he won his first English championship, his round was interrupted by two hemorrhages of the lungs occasioned by tuberculosis. He took a year off and, playing temperately at first, restored his health. Discussing Jones one day he said to me that anyone was foolish to try to imitate Jones's swing. As he put it, "He's just a miracle." He admired Ed Dudley's swing, too.

Vardon was a good deal of a legend when he first came to this country, although his golf form was criticized then by some experts. His stance was said to be awkward. On his backswing he folded up his left arm like a jackknife. Incidentally, he said to me the last time I saw him that he was still in disagreement with the American professionals on the question of keeping the left arm straight going back. He said it wasn't necessary because it was fully extended when it came in to the ball. In the Open tournament at Brookline, Massachusetts, in 1913, he and Ted Ray were tied in medal play with a youngster named Francis Ouimet of Boston. In the play-off, Ouimet, nineteen years old, was the winner. He has risen to great triumphs in golf history, and is one of the finest and most attractive characters I ever knew. He is now a prominent businessman in his home city of Boston and associated with William H. Danforth, who, by the way, has done more for young golfers than anyone in the history of the game. In discussing how Vardon and Ray were beaten, the former told me that the trouble all grew out of their paying no attention to the "kid." Vardon was simply trying to beat Ray and Big Ted was watching Harry. When they wound up, the young fellow had scored over both of them.

The referee of this famous match was Alexander Campbell, affectionately known to the game as "Nipper." He won the Scotch championship when he was eighteen years old. Coming to America, he served as professional at Brookline, then at Baltimore and wound up his days in Dayton. His dry wit and quaint observations made him an attractive figure in any group.

The American public knows Bobby Jones only as a golfer and a fine sportsman. He is more than that. He has an excellent mind and is well grounded in history and philosophy. You must know him well, however, to find this out. An index to his character is the fact that he had to conquer himself before he conquered the game. As a youngster, he passed through the period of throwing away and breaking his clubs. It took several years to whip his temper. He has given to golf what Babe Ruth gave to baseball, and yet every now and then a writer will assert that Jones did not have the competition faced by present champions. Well, if Walter Hagen, Gene Sarazen, Tommy Armour, Francis Ouimet, Chick Evans, Macdonald Smith, Jim Barnes, Bobby Cruickshank, Willie MacFarlane, Jock Hutchison, Horton Smith, Leo Diegel and Dick Metz were not competitors, then I do not know the meaning of the word. Invidious comparison will not stand against Jones in the face of his magnificent triumph in 1930 when he won the grand slam. The British Amateur and the British Open were taken and then he came home to win both these American events. He had to drop a forty-foot putt on the last hole to defeat Macdonald Smith in the American Open. He was the winner of thirteen major championships.

I would take nothing away from Byron Nelson, Sam Snead, Benny Hogan and "Jug" McSpaden. They can be classed as the best of the present day. You cannot, however, make comparison between them and the outstanding figures of the past without bearing in mind that conditions have changed. We have better courses and infinitely better putting greens, and the steel shaft has many advantages over the wooden shaft. For instance, if a wooden shaft was broken, it was practically impossible to duplicate it; and the slightest change made trouble for the player. Steel shafts are much more uniform.

Not long ago I asked O. B. Keeler of our Atlanta *Journal* what, in his judgment, was Bobby's greatest shot in golf; Keeler had followed Jones in every big event. The scribe thought it came in the American Open between Bobby Cruickshank and Jones at Inwood, Long Island. In the last three holes of the fourth round in the U. S. Open at Inwood, Bobby Jones, playing an hour ahead of Bobby Cruickshank, the only competitor with a chance remaining to collar him, kicked off 4 strokes to par. Par was 4-4-4 for the three holes and Jones went 5-5-6. It still looked as if he had the show sewed up, as Cruickshank, feeling the strain as he got to the sixteenth, blew up to a 6 there, and was still 4 strokes down to Jones, in spite of the latter's gruesome finish. But Cruickshank settled after the boxcar on the sixteenth, got his par 4 at the dangerous seventeenth, and stood on the eighteenth tee needing a birdie 3 to tie.

The hole was 420 yards long, with a dangerous lagoon guarding the immediate front of the green. Cruickshank banged a big iron second shot six feet from the flag, short and to the right—and holed the putt! He had picked up three strokes on that green, and tied with Bobby Jones at 296, six strokes ahead of the field. Next day, in the play-off, the two men came to the eighteenth tee all even. Cruickshank got into trouble. Jones, with a number two iron, made a magnificent second shot across the lagoon to the green. This will doubtless be recorded as Jones's greatest shot in all his career. It won the match.

If one were to ask me the most important thing to think about in golf, I would have to repeat the old-time maxim—"keep your head still." That's eighty per cent of the game, but it must not be over-done so as to take all flexibility out of the body. Harry Vardon once told me what he was compelled to do to break a pupil of a bad habit. The pupil, on one occasion, got peeved and insisted that his head was not moving. Vardon took him under a tree where the low-est branch was fifteen or twenty feet from the ground. He tied a string to the limb and attached a fish hook, which was hooked into the player's cap. With every swing the pupil made, the cap came off his head. Vardon made his point.

My golf caddy on the early Dayton courses is now assistant to the president of the New York *Times*. There was no better caddy than James B. (Scotty) Reston, and he was a good golfer, having at one time won the amateur state championship. He worked his way through the University of Illinois and then did newspaper work on our Dayton and Springfield papers. Afterwards he went with the Associated Press in New York and was assigned to sports, particu-larly golf, in England. He graduated from this into a more impor-tant role and took high rank as a European correspondent. He is now recognized as one of the most brilliant young journalists in America, having recently won the Pulitzer prize for his distin-guished correspondence on the Dumbarton Oaks Conference. He is also the author of *Prelude to Victory*.

After seventy years of age I was playing as good or better golf than at any time in my life. I had gone through all the stages and experimentations and had come to believe that the more completely you wipe out of your mind any thought of wrists, shoulders, hips, knees and feet, the better off you are. In golf psychology, they have

443

probably passed into the subconscious senses and there is no more need, after one has played golf for several years, to keep thinking of them than of the ABC's. I simply try to keep properly balanced and then swing the golf club, emphasizing in my mind before every shot, "swing it, swing it, swing it."

One must be conscious, of course, that the club is in his hands and the hands must play a great part in the swing, but you can't center your thought on this nor any other one thing, except to swing the club. It has always been my experience, although I have never seen it expressed by any golf authority, that if you center objectively on doing one specific thing, you intensify the mind, and the message going to the nerve centers and the muscles causes you to press. If one addresses himself to the single movement of swinging the club without regard to hands, arms, hips or anything else, he will, if his body is relaxed, find himself using all the muscles that are necessary to complete the stroke.

Gene Sarazen told me not many months ago that he now knows more about golf because he has to. He has gained in technique what he lost in physical endurance. He has discovered what other athletes know, which is that legs forty years old are not what they used to be. At the P. G. A. tournament in Dayton in 1945, he gave Nelson the scare of his life. Little Sarazen started right out taking the first two holes.

As long as the game of golf is discussed in locker-room gossip. one of Sarazen's great feats will be referred to as "the shot that rang round the world." It was at the Masters tournament at Augusta, Georgia, in 1935. Sarazen was playing with Walter Hagen, who will always be a shining figure in the traditions of golf, a great player and a fine sportsman. Hagen told me the story in these words: "Gene and I were walking down the fairway on the fifteenth hole of the last round. Gene remarked that if he could get a birdie on each of the four remaining holes, he would win the tournament by one stroke over Craig Wood, who had finished. I casually replied that there was no law in Georgia, so far as I knew, which prohibited his doing that. The fifteenth hole is 490 yards, a par 5. Immediately in front of the green is a moat, even a lake, thirty yards wide, which makes it hazardous to try to reach the green on the second shot. Gene's drive off the tee was straight, though not unusual in length. He then took a number three wood from the bag and fired away.

The ball went straight for the hole and carried the moat. I yelled to him, 'Well, Gene, you have one birdie.' The ball kept rolling and when it got within putting distance of the hole I said, 'You have two birdies.' Then the ball dropped for a 2. And with the shout of an Indian, I yelled, 'By Golly, you now have three birdies on one hole.' Sarazen played the sixteenth, seventeenth and eighteenth holes in par, which gave him the same score as Wood. There was a thirty-six-hole play-off the next day. Gene won it by three strokes."

O. B. Keeler, the famous authority on golf, tells me that in this play-off Sarazen did what has never been equalled. He had twenty-four consecutive pars.

People will differ with Ernest Jones about his theory of swinging the club head, but his list of followers is increasing each year. Here is a man who lost one foot in the First World War and yet plays in the low seventies. I have enjoyed studying the game of golf and there is not a week that passes the year round that I am not swinging the clubs either indoors or out. The plain truth is that the hardest thing to do in the game is to simplify the stroke. Golf, properly played, is very simple; we don't seem able to convince ourselves of that. There can be no tightening of the muscles, a point I can illustrate by means of another story. I once asked Bobby Jones whether he attempted to keep his eye on the ball until the club had swept through it; Vardon laid great stress on this. Jones's reply was, "No, I don't try to do it, but I visualize it before I make my swing." Now there is the very essence of what I am talking about. Jones manifestly believes that if he gives it objective thought, he will swing under stress and get poor results.

Ernest Jones insists that when one has mastered his golf stroke, it is largely controlled by the subconscious sense. That is another way of saying exactly what Jones said to me. Another notable disciple of the principle of swinging the golf club is Bob Barnett. He and I have spent many happy hours on and off the fairways discussing the sport to which we are both devoted. Barnett is professional at Chevy Chase in Washington in the summer and Indian Creek at Miami Beach in the winter. He plays so easily that Francis Ouimet once said Barnett would be playing good golf when he was in his middle eighties.

I once asked Sam Snead what his first impulse was with his down stroke. His reply was: "I never know. If I am hitting the ball straight and far I know I am doing the right thing." This is another confirmation of the subconscious theory.

Benny Hogan, who weighs only 140 pounds, surprises everyone with the length of his tee shots. Grantland Rice once told me that Benny explained this by saying that he had changed his grip by extending his left thumb as far down on the shaft as he comfortably could. That with most golfers the rules of golf are not static is shown by the fact that at the Columbus Invitational golf tournament in July, 1946, Hogan announced to Byron Nelson that he had gone back to the old grip and shortened his backswing. This must have brought improvement in his game, because he has been a large money winner since coming out of the military service.

The secret of mental and physical health lies in constant though moderate activity. Gladstone's dictum about the possibility of doing one's best work after seventy has quite as much truth as Osler's famous remark that men's best work is done before forty. My recreations have been a valuable relief from the strain of my editorial work and other public activities; they have never been allowed to interfere with that work. It is still my habit to spend a large part of at least five days a week, and sometimes six or at critical times seven, in my office. My belief is that a man should strive to make himself useful to society as long as he lives and that he should continue to the end to regard life as a rich adventure—an adventure in constructive work.

CHAPTER XXXVII

THE FUTURE

◆

THE FUTURE is wrapped up in the question of world peace. Our domestic courses will be controlled by international conditions. If a sane, just and workable international order is not created and maintained by the nations, then we must perforce become a warlike power, armed to the teeth, maintaining trade walls of our own and attacking those of other countries.

The lesson of the frightful slaughter of the First World War was not enough. The Almighty seemed to try by reason to bring us to our senses. It did not work. Now, terrified by the new powers of destruction hanging over us, we may gain through fear the peace that reason did not attain.

Human nature may not change, but human intelligence can and does increase. It is clear now that with the new destructiveness of war, nations must conform to the demands of decency and humanity or perish at each other's throats. This is the supreme question before the human race today. Upon it all other issues hinge.

Despite past and present discouragements, I still have faith in the ultimate good and progress of mankind. Whether that ultimate good comes immediately enough to serve our own times is a question to be determined by prompt and intelligent action now.

AFTERWORD

THE BEGINNING was modest — a single Ohio newspaper purchased in 1898 for $26,000 by a 28-year-old young man. But in the intervening decades, Cox Enterprises, Inc. has grown into one of the nation's leading media companies.

By the time of Governor Cox's death in 1957, he had acquired newspapers, radio and television stations in Dayton, Miami and Atlanta. It is unlikely, however, that even someone as forward thinking as Governor Cox could have envisioned the growth that would follow in the next fifty years, much of it under the leadership of his son, James M. Cox, Jr., his son-in-law, Garner Anthony, and grandson, James Cox Kennedy.

Today, Cox Enterprises, Inc. is divided into six business divisions, each a leader within its industry, and all guided by the values that Governor Cox first infused into his companies:

- **Cox Newspapers, Inc.** — newspapers, local and national direct mail advertising and customized newsletters

- **Cox Radio, Inc.** — [NYSE: CXR] broadcast radio stations and interactive web sites

- **Cox Television** — television, television sales rep firms and research

- **Cox Communications, Inc.** — [NYSE: COX] cable television distribution, telephone, high-speed Internet access and other advanced broadband services

- **Manheim Auctions, Inc.** — vehicle auctions, repair and certification services and web-based technology products

- **AutoTrader.com** — the world's largest and most visited source of used vehicle listings for dealers and consumers

Cox Enterprises, Inc. is a company keenly aware of its heritage but fully committed to the future. We already have begun conquering the challenges of a second century in business and eagerly anticipate continued growth. We are confident that Governor Cox would approve.

INDEX

Cornwall, John J., 229
Cortelyou, George B., 29
Corwin, Franklin, 70
Corwin, Moses Bledsoe, 70
Corwin, Tom, 68-70
Coshocton, Ohio, 138
Couzens, James, 356
Cox, Abel, 5
Cox, Anne (daughter), 374, 427. *See also* Mrs. Louis G. Johnson
Cox, Anne (sister). *See* Mrs. Anne Cox Baker
Cox, Anne Craig, 5-6, 10
Cox, Barbara, 374. *See also* Mrs. Stanley C. Kennedy, Jr.
Cox, Benjamin, 5
Cox, Boss, 303
Cox, Eliza Andrew, 7
Cox, Gilbert (grandfather), 3-6, 10; (father), 7, 11
Cox, Harold R., 321
Cox, Helen, 130
Cox, Rev. Henry Miller, 4
Cox, General James, 5
Cox, Mrs. James M., 240, 356, 373, 374, 375, 376, 378, 379, 419, 422, 423, 437
Cox, James McMahon (James M., Jr.), 58, 75, 291, 393
Cox, Glenn L., 393
Cox, Maryan, 5
Cox, Samuel S., 5
Cox, Thomas, 4
Coxey, General Jacob S., 235
Crandon, Charles H., 319
Crane, Joseph H., 45
Crédit Mobilier, 122
Crisp, Charles R., 30
Crounse, Lorenzo, 104
Crow, Philip, 220
Croxton, Fred, 383
Cruickshank, Bobby, 442, 443
Cummings, Homer S., 228, 230, 238, 239
Cummins, Albert B., 117
Cummins, Gaylord, 175
Cunliffe-Lister, Sir Philip, 360
Curtiss, Glenn, 320, 437
Curtiss Company, 86-90, 92
Cushman, Francis W., 113, 114
Czechoslovakia, 362

Daladier, Edouard, 362

Daltons, the, 7
Danforth, William H., 441
Daniels, Josephus, 230, 233, 235, 285
Darrow, Clarence, 155
Daugherty, Harry M., 182, 301-308
Daugherty, M. A., 226
Daugherty, Mal, 302
Davies, Joseph E., 233
Davis, Cushman K., 33
Davis, David, 77
Davis, Frank Parker, 50
Davis, Frank R., 136
Davis, Jefferson, 30, 31, 107
Davis, John W., 226, 229, 230, 231, 285, 327-330
Dawes, Charles G., 67, 207, 208, 300
Dayton, Ohio, 14, 36, 37, 39, 44-49, 53, 65, 70, 72-75, 79, 83-85, 88, 91-93, 130, 135, 160, 165-170, 174, 176, 182, 185, 191, 194, 196, 205, 231, 232, 248, 309, 347, 393, 417, 441, 443, 444
Dayton & Lebanon Railroad, 42
Dayton State Hospital, 166
Dean, Bobo, 313
Dearborn, Mich., 92
Debs, Eugene, 129
Deeds, Colonel E. A., 50, 93, 174, 176, 177
Delaware, Ohio, 37
Delbrück, Hans, 213
Delco Company, 50
Dempsey, Jack, 215, 216
Denison University, 37
Denver, M. R., 226
Depew, Chauncey M., 106
Detroit, 79, 91, 116
Dewey, Admiral George, 33
Dewey, Orville, 84
Dickens, Charles, 12
Dickey family, 37
Diegel, Leo, 442
Dingley tariff, 62
Ditzler, Frank L., 50
Dixon, Thomas, 216
Doheny, E. L., 230, 232
Doherty, Henry L., 323
Dollfuss, Engelbert, 359
Dolliver, Joseph P., 30, 63
Donaghey, G. W., 149
Donnelly, Thomas, 217, 219
Dore, Frank T., 226
Doren, Charles L., 17

Doren, John G., 37
Douglas, Stephen A., 339
Douglas, William O., 417
Dowling, Joseph H., 226
Dudley, Ed, 441
Duffy, Thomas J., 142, 217, 219, 226
Dumbarton Oaks, 443
Dunn, James Clement, 356
Durbin, W. W., 226
Dwyer, Dennis J., 126, 179

Eaton, Ohio, 3
Eddy, Mary Baker, 382
Eden, Anthony, 372, 373
Eden, Mrs. Anthony, 373
Edward VII, 374
Edwards, Edward I., 230
Eighteenth Amendment, 340
Eighty-ninth Division, 207
Elder, Thomas E., 39, 40
Electrical Workers' Union, 348
Eliot, Charles W., 270
Elkins, Stephen B., 34
Elliot, Walter E., 360, 372
Ellis, Allston, 146
Elyria, Ohio, 126
Employers' Association, 347
Endicott, William C., 28
England, 139, 273, 274, 291, 293-295,
  297, 343, 345, 346, 348, 354, 367, 372,
  375, 377. See also Great Britain;
  United Kingdom
Equity League, 143
Ericsson, John, 51
Evans, Chick, 442
Evans, Harmon, 95
Evans, Hiram Wesley, 398, 399
Evanston, Ill., 59

Fairchild, Dr. David, 318
Fall, Albert B., 279, 305, 324
Farley, James A., 341, 407, 408, 440
Farnsworth, Charles S., 196
Fassett, J. Sloat, 106
Fatio, Maurice, 319
Faulkner, James W., 17, 125, 163, 170,
  186-188, 270, 279, 280
Federal Corrupt Practices Act, 262
Federal Drainage Investigations, 175
Federal Housing Administration Act,
  346
Federal Land Bank System, 252
Federal Reserve Act, 142, 190

Federal Reserve System, 109, 110, 170,
  252, 358
Federal Trade Commission, 252
Feis, Herbert, 356
Felton, Samuel M., 18, 19
FEPC, 346, 349
Ferber, Edna, 380
Fess, Simeon D., 179, 180, 250
Fields, Joseph E., 50
Fillmore, Millard, 70
Finley, William L., 129, 178
Firestone, Harvey E., 140
Firestone Tire and Rubber Company,
  140, 418
Fisher, Carl, 309-313, 316, 318, 319, 323
Fisher, Irving, 279
Fiske, Wilbur, 84
Fitzgerald, John J., 64, 65, 96, 99, 106
Fitzgerald, Lady, 374, 380, 381
Fiume, 273
Flagler, Henry M., 319
Fleming, D. F., 255
Flood Commission of Ohio, 169, 171
Florida, 252, 436, 437
Florida Bar Association, 97
Foch, Marshal Ferdinand, 198, 205,
  299
Folk, Joseph W., 411
Foraker, Joseph B., 79, 80, 159, 160,
  182, 183, 189, 303, 304, 307
Forbes, George William, 374
Force bill, 66, 67
Ford, Edsel, 91
Ford, Henry, 67, 90-92
Fordney-McCumber Act, 353
Forrest, General Nathan Bedford,
  208, 209
Foster, Charles, 189
Foulois, Benjamin D., 91
Fourteen Points, 250
Fourth Ohio Regiment, 197
France, 291, 293, 294, 297, 298, 300,
  354, 357, 362, 367
Francis, David R., 233
Frank, Leo, 99
Franklin, Ohio, 5, 6
Fraser, Leon, 363, 364
Frelinghuysen, Frederick Theodore,
  77, 78, 305
Friebolin, Carl D., 164, 268
Frizell, W. G., 58
Fuel Administration, 197

Joffre, General Joseph J. C., 203
Johnson, Albert Sidney, 112
Johnson, Andrew, 71, 72
Johnson, Ben, 102
Johnson, H. H., 169
Johnson, Hiram, 123, 259, 266, 271
Johnson, James G., 78, 229, 411
Johnson, Mrs. Louis G., 356
Johnson, Tom L., 116, 117, 218, 409
Johnston, Joseph E., 108
Jones, Bobby, 440, 441, 442, 443, 445
Jones, Ernest, 445
Jones, Samuel M., "Golden Rule," 116, 117
Jones, Harrison, 389
Jones, W. Alton, 323
Jones, William Cole, 350, 391, 392
Jones Act, 252
Josephine, Empress, 293
Joyce-Cridland Company, 50
Julian, W. A., 226
Jung, Guido, 362, 363, 378

Karger, Gus J., 279, 280
Kauffman, Admiral James L., 320
Keating-Owen Labor Act, 252
Keeler, O. B., 442, 445
Keifer, J. Warren, 115
Kellogg Company, 39
Kendrick, John B., 227
Kennedy, Mrs. Stanley C., Jr., 356
Kenton, Simon, 70
Kenton, Ohio, 129, 220
Kentucky, 31, 331
Kettering, Charles F., 50, 51, 174, 176
Key, Philip Barton, 31
Keynes, John Maynard, 360, 367
Kidder, Walter S., 175
Kienbock, Victor, 359
Kinney, Charles, 305
Kiser, Earl, 309
Kitchener, Lord, 377
Kitchin, Claude, 108, 285
Kitty Hawk, N.C., 90
Klein, Willie, 440
Knight, Charles S., 53
Knox, Frank, 382, 383, 421
Knox, Philander C., 249, 259, 279, 341
Koo, V. K. Wellington, 360
Kremer, J. Bruce, 239
Krock, Arthur, 104
Krogstad, Arnold M., 322

Ku Klux Klan, 307, 308, 324-326, 330, 399, 402
Kumler, Daniel E., 83, 130
Kumler, Henry, 11
Kumler, Henry P., 13
Kumler, I. G., 40
Kumler, Joseph, 11, 13
Kumler family, 39
Kurtz, Charles J., 304

La Follette, Robert M., 63, 65, 116, 117, 330, 409, 437, 440
La Follette seamen's law, 252
La Gorce, John Oliver, 98
Lamar, Lucius Quintus Cincinnatus, 28, 66, 111
Lamont, Daniel S., 27
Lancaster Home for Boys, 150
Landis, Kenesaw Mountain, 13
Landis, Robert K., 13
Lane, Franklin K., 285
Langley, S. P., 85-90, 92, 94
Lasker, Albert D., 201, 272, 419, 440
Lattimer, G. W., 169
Lausche, Frank, 179
Lawrence, James E., 105
Layton, F. C., 32
League to Enforce Peace, 248
League of Nations, 105, 187, 225, 228, 229, 240, 242-244, 246-264, 266, 268-279, 282, 284, 286, 291, 299, 301, 324, 326, 327, 331, 332, 353, 354, 357, 425
Leavenworth, Kan., 60, 61
Lebanon, Ohio, 42, 52, 70, 74, 80
Lee, Robert E., 31, 108, 112, 404
Leffler, C. D., 320
Lehman, Frederick W., 285
Lehman, Harry S., 311
Leith-Ross, Sir F. W., 360, 374
Lenroot, Irvine L., 64, 65, 202
Leslie, Edward, 438
Levi, John, 311
Lewis, David J., 64
Lewis, J. Hamilton, 233
Lewis, Len, 313
Liberia, 332
Li Hung Chang, 26
Lima, Ohio, 26, 36
Lincoln, Abraham, 31, 34, 77, 102, 108, 115, 208, 214, 234, 251, 254, 295, 299, 339, 349, 360, 412, 420, 421, 438
Lincoln, Isham & Beale, 19